MXAE
7-15 12

Joe, the Slave Who Became an Alamo Legend

Joe, the Slave Who Became an Alamo Legend

Ron J. Jackson, Jr.
and
Lee Spencer White

Foreword by Phil Collins

University of Oklahoma Press : Norman

Library of Congress Cataloging-in-Publication Data

Jackson, Ron, 1966–
Joe, the slave who became an Alamo legend / Ron J. Jackson, Jr.,
and Lee Spencer White ; foreword by Phil Collins.
    pages cm
  Includes bibliographical references and index.
  ISBN 978-0-8061-4703-1 (hardback : alkaline paper)
    1. Joe, 1815–   2. Alamo (San Antonio, Tex.)—Seige, 1836.   3. Texas—
History—Revolution, 1835–1836—Biography.   4. African Americans—Texas—
Biography.   5. Slaves—Texas—Biography.   6. Fugitive slaves—Texas—
Biography.   7. Travis, William Barret, 1809–1836—Friends and associates.
8. Legends—Texas.
I. White, Lee Spencer, 1955–   II. Title.
  F390.J64J33 2015
  976.4'03092—dc23
  [B]

                                                                      2014032061

The paper in this book meets the guidelines for permanence and durability of
the Committee on Production Guidelines for Book Longevity of the Council
on Library Resources, Inc. ∞

1 2 3 4 5 6 7 8 9 10

Loyalty to petrified opinion never yet broke a chain or freed a human soul.

—Mark Twain

CONTENTS

List of Illustrations

Figures

Maps

FOREWORD

PHIL COLLINS

There are many myths surrounding the last days of the Alamo siege. Over the years, people have added their own theories to the already existing foggy folklore that has shrouded the events of February and March 1836. Unfortunately for historians, both qualified and amateur, there were no Texian survivors among those active that final morning assault.

Many historians have preferred to disregard the accounts made by various Mexican officers and soldiers, on the grounds that they may be biased or unreliable due to some conflicting details among the reports given. During the final assault it was still dark, and the intensity of the assault made it impossible to tell friend from foe. No one can agree on how many defenders there were, nor can an agreement be reached on the number of Mexican troops involved.

Various reports have Colonel Travis committing suicide, while others state that he was shot in the head shortly after the assault commenced, and there are also conflicting reports about where he fell. The same goes for Crockett and Bowie. How and where they died will forever be a mystery. It's generally agreed that Bowie lay sick in the Low

Barracks and was killed there in his bed, but even that has its doubters. Crockett's death is best left alone as there are so many theories it would take too much space to discuss them.

However, lest we forget, a few Texians did survive, although they saw nothing until they left their hiding places in the church after the carnage had ended. For these few women and children, the predawn of March 6 was a terrifying ordeal spent in the darkness. And there was one more: despite the many theories, even Alamo skeptics accept that one man, a slave, witnessed the final assault and survived. He was there throughout the siege, and on March 6 he had been awakened by the same shouts of panic as his master, Lt. Col. William Barret Travis.

Rising from a cot in Travis's quarters, Travis's slave Joe followed him out into the garrison's plaza, and took up position beside Travis at his artillery emplacement at the center of the Alamo's north wall. It was dark, but everyone knew the Mexican Army was attacking, possibly going for the final kill. Joe witnessed and was involved in those terrifying moments as the final assault started. No one is sure what he did after Travis was killed. It would be understandable if Joe had turned and run to his freedom, and he likely would have done so had he known that Mexico had abolished slavery.

Despite the bedlam around him, he seems to have had the composure to return to Travis's quarters and gather various items and put them in a bag that bore Travis's initials. History has it that, clutching his bag, he joined Susanna Dickinson and her baby, Angelina, on the road to Gonzales after she had been released by Santa Anna. After that, Joe's life blurs: little is heard from him.

In this book, authors Ron J. Jackson, Jr., and Lee Spencer White, have delved deeply, and in the process discovered the life Joe had lived before his Alamo experience, and the life he lived following those traumatic events. That this book is only appearing now is hard to believe, as Joe was the only Texian survivor to witness so much. The questions he could have answered are innumerable.

Joe's family tree will surprise many people, but I'll let Ron and Lee tell the rest of the story.

PREFACE

A slave named Joe. Lee and I started with little else when we embarked on our quest to discover Joe's story in December 1997. In those days, there were only a few known primary sources related to Joe: a diary kept by William Barret Travis between August 1833 and June 1834; William Fairfax Gray's diary, which documented Joe's most detailed account of the Alamo battle; a ledger kept by John Rice Jones, executor of the Travis estate; and a runaway ad from 1837. At the time we were grateful for what we had to work with, and too naïve to know just how great the odds were against us. We were not the first researchers to hunt for Joe's history. We were simply the first too stubborn to quit.

From the start, we were captivated by a sense of adventure. Joe's survival at the Alamo had been documented since March 6, 1836, but prominent historians in the field had been able to discover little else about this African American who had witnessed one of the most storied events in the history of the American West. Joe had long been a shooting star in the Alamo saga, burning brightly for a moment and then disappearing. No one knew where he had come from before the Alamo siege, or where he went after the Texas Revolution. There were only whispers of speculation. His history was cloaked in mystery, a puzzle we were determined to solve.

Our journey took a dramatic turn March 6, 1998—162 years after the fall of the Alamo. That day we left San Antonio before sunrise, and made the 150-mile journey to the Austin County Courthouse in Bellville, Texas. In the three previous months, we had read and reread every source, hoping to glean clues about Joe's past. Our single most important document at that time was the Travis diary, which offered a tantalizing entry on February 13, 1834: "Wrote bond for J. W. Moore to sheriff indem[n]ifying him to buy one Boy Joe belonging to Mansfield." On March 7, 1834, Travis wrote, "Joe & Isaac Mansfield vs the Sheriff petition to be set at liberty." The next day Travis noted, "Joe Mansfield vs sheff—argued case &c." Joe, we surmised, clearly belonged to a man named Isaac Mansfield, and Travis hoped to add Mansfield's young servant to his own small stable of slaves. We also realized that Joe had been involved in some sort of court case, but it was a notation by historian Robert E. Davis—the diary's editor—on page 146 that especially grabbed our attention: "Mansfield's estate was prepared by Travis on August 20, 1834."[1]

Davis obviously had seen documents related to the Mansfield estate prior to the diary's publication in 1966. Did such documents still exist? Time and a rash of thefts of rare documents throughout Texas during that period left some doubt. A document signed by Travis would have fetched a nice price on the black market. Still, maybe Mansfield's probate remained untouched. And maybe, just maybe, Joe was listed as part of the Mansfield estate if he hadn't already been sold. So we hoped.

Our speculation led us to Bellville, where San Felipe de Austin's legal records are still held today. San Felipe de Austin is where Travis lived when he was faithfully writing in his diary. We had called the Austin County court clerk to inquire whether Mansfield's probate still existed. The woman who answered the telephone graciously walked down to the basement to check the old records. "Yes, we have a probate for an Isaac Mansfield from 1834," she said upon her return. "There are several pages here. Looks like there are some slaves mentioned."

Her words hung in the air. We were frozen by the possibilities. We needed to hear nothing further. We were determined to make the trip to Bellville to read the documents for ourselves, and the days prior to our journey seemed to drag at an agonizing pace. Finally, we were standing in the court clerk's office, waiting for the clerk to bring us the

Mansfield file. The office buzzed with routine business: phones ringing, papers shuffling, and clerks conversing with visitors. Our hearts, meanwhile, beat rapidly. Suddenly, a worn manila folder was laid on the table in front of us. We opened it and began to study its contents. The pages were stained that familiar, deep, antique yellow, and they were brittle around the edges, although clear enough to read. Then a page stopped us cold: "Process verbal of the sale of Joe—Succession of Isaac Mansfield."[2]

Lee and I looked at each other as if we had unearthed King Tut's tomb. We trembled with excitement as we anxiously turned to the next page. Our eyes darted across that document as we read it simultaneously. "Isaac Mansfield deceased . . . in the Town of San Felipe de Austin . . . this the 22nd day of December 1834 proceeded to sell at public auction a negro man slave named Joe about nineteen years of age . . . John Cummings being the highest bidder . . . for the sum of four hundred and ten dollars."[3]

We knew instantly that Cummings was the brother of Rebecca Cummings, Travis's fiancée at the time he entered the Alamo. We quickly deduced that there must have been a bill of sale between Cummings and Travis prior to his fateful arrival at San Antonio de Bexar in February 1836. (Lee later confirmed this transaction on one of her countless excursions across Texas to piece together the Travis estate). The Mansfield probate also listed other names of slaves—an old woman named Elizabeth and her two children, Elizabeth and William.[4] We suspected they might be Joe's relatives, but had no way to confirm this. We were now able to confirm at least two of Joe's previous owners before Travis—a feat that had eluded every Alamo historian before us. More importantly, we proved something of profound significance to ourselves. Joe's past could be traced.

In retrospect, the Travis diary proved to be the key to unlocking Joe's history, but it was the discovery of the Mansfield probate that kept the flames of our hope burning, even in our most discouraging hours. We never forgot that magical moment in Bellville. Little did we know that our journey would span nearly eleven more years and carry us through five states and across the border into Mexico. It would be the adventure of a lifetime as we walked in Joe's footsteps. We stood on the bluff of Joe's childhood home of Marthasville, Missouri, overlooking the picturesque Missouri River Valley. We walked the historic St. Louis riverfront where Joe's family last parted, and we sailed a section of the Mississippi River. We ran our fingers along the iconic façade of the Alamo chapel, stood on the banks of the Brazos River at Washington-on-the-Brazos, retraced Joe's epic journey from Texas to Alabama in 1838, and overturned toppled headstones in the piney woods of the Jay Villa Plantation—Joe's probable final resting spot.

Piecing together Joe's life was a joy, an honor, and an obsession. The search required the instincts of an investigator, callousness to dead ends, stubbornness, endurance, luck, common sense, and old-fashioned hard work. We opened and closed county courthouses, state archives, and university collections, often skipping lunch to read old documents until they were blurry from our exhaustion. We sifted through stacks of bound volumes of legal documents in dusty, courthouse attics and basements. We read countless period newspapers and, hundreds of slave narratives, ship logs, census records, journals, and letters in hopes of finding any scrap of information related to Joe. We often felt like half-crazed miners smitten by gold fever.

Joe became part of our families. We spoke of him as though he still walked among us, and our children were raised to understand he was someone special in our lives. Three of our children—Lee's Samantha, and my Tristan and Missouri—were all born after the search for Joe began. To them, and to Lee's husband, Larry, and my wife, Jeannia— Joe was some sort of long, lost uncle who had famously dodged death at the Alamo.

The seemingly endless search for Joe consumed much of our lives. Vacations turned into research trips. Research trips turned into adventures. And those adventures are now priceless memories.

We have often been asked how a seasoned journalist and an Alamo descendant teamed to chase Joe's ghost. Our journey actually began in April 1994 when I was doing research for my first book, *Alamo Legacy*. My goal was to collect and document any oral and written traditions related to the Alamo battle, and I contacted what was then the Daughters of the Republic of Texas Library in San Antonio to inquire about any comprehensive list of Alamo defender descendants. Much to my surprise no such list existed at the time, but a librarian graciously gave me the name of one Alamo descendant: Lee Spencer.

Lee, I soon learned, had just formed the Alamo Defenders Descendants Association and was diligently working to bring the Alamo bloodline together under one organizational banner. Her quest was a labor of love, if not a calling, as she approached her mission with an unbound enthusiasm I came quickly to admire. Once, in the fall of 1994, she learned that crews were exhuming the remains of legendary Texas Ranger Sam Walker at the Odd Fellows Cemetery in San Antonio. A group planned to rebury Walker's remains in Waco, near the Texas Ranger Hall of Fame and Museum. News of the exhumation might have passed without a thought from Lee, except that she knew Walker had been buried in 1856 atop the ashes of Alamo defenders as part of a San Jacinto Day celebration.

Lee wouldn't allow the remains of the Alamo defenders to be disturbed. She famously grabbed a shotgun and a shovel, and drove to San Antonio where she successfully secured a pro bono attorney and a cease-and-desist order from a local judge. Thanks to Lee, the Walker and Alamo gravesite has since been restored and cleaned, and it is now preserved with a marker befitting Texas heroes.

To me, Lee is a reincarnation of Adina De Zavala, a preservationist and historian who saved the Alamo. Like De Zavala, she is a trailblazer. Twenty years ago Lee shattered barriers that had long existed regarding the Alamo between the Anglo-Saxon and Mexican communities, and she opened her arms to one and all who sought to celebrate the memory of those who died at the Alamo. She routinely invited dignitaries who represented various heritages in San Antonio to her organization's annual ceremony. She also welcomed descendants of Alamo scouts, couriers, and noncombatants, as well as defenders. This is how I first learned of her desire to locate Joe's descendants.

"How grand would it be have Joe's descendants honored at our annual candlelight ceremony?" Lee asked me rhetorically years ago.

"That would be quite a sight," I agreed. "Quite a sight indeed."

Joe had long fascinated me too. Ever since reading Walter Lord's great historical narrative about the Alamo, *A Time to Stand*, I have pondered the significance of Joe's presence at the siege in 1836. For me, Joe was the true "Messenger of the Alamo," as Susanna Dickinson had been dubbed. He gave the clearest and most complete account of the final assault on the Alamo in the crucial days following the battle. The fact that he was a slave, and the manservant of the Alamo's co-commander, William Barret Travis, only intrigued me further.

The reporter in me had so many questions. Where was he born? Did he know the whereabouts of his family? How did he come into the possession of Travis? What did he and Travis talk about when they were alone? What did he think about while penned inside the Alamo? Did Travis draw the line? Did Joe see himself as a defender or noncombatant? As a slave, what did Texas independence mean to him? What did it sound like on the north wall on the morning of March 6, 1836? What went through his mind as a Mexican officer pulled him from his hiding place that day? Did his survival at the Alamo change his life?

If I could have had a wish fulfilled to interview one occupant of the Alamo compound, it would have been Joe. He is a special person in the Alamo story for several reasons, but mostly because he was one of the few inside the walls who lived to tell the tale. Since an interview was pure fantasy, I sought to accomplish the next best thing. I dedicated myself to piecing together Joe's life through historical research. Since I'm a native Californian who was always taught to follow my dreams, I failed to see the seemingly insurmountable odds against such a venture. I first committed to it while writing an article on blacks at the Alamo for *True West* magazine. By then, Lee and I had already forged a tight friendship. We talked nearly every day by telephone about the Alamo and our next historical adventures. One day we talked in depth about tracing Joe's roots. We both possessed a passion for Joe, and in looking back now I see that we had instinctively teamed to research his life for a new book. We never verbally committed to writing a book together. The goal was simply understood.

The quest to find Joe presented the ultimate challenge in historical research for one simple reason. Joe was a slave, someone whose life even while he lived it largely remained in the shadows. We understood that if we had any chance of piecing together his life on even the most rudimentary level, then we had to trace him through the movements of others. Slaves, after all, were property, so we clung to one fundamental philosophy: follow the money.

We plotted strategies for the research trails and historical figures we investigated. These changed constantly, as did our theories about Joe's possible whereabouts at different points in time. We became seasoned historical investigators. Our talents meshed well, and we were both dogged researchers. I brought the skills of an investigative reporter to our team, while Lee brought years of experience as a meticulous histori- cal researcher. Together, we were a formidable tandem. We accomplished far more together than we ever would have alone.

Yet nothing came easy. Groundbreaking history never does. We ran into more dead ends than we can even remember. There were entire research trips that yielded nothing of note. Trial and error marked every step. Tracing Joe's life challenged us physically and mentally, but sometimes there was gold at the end of the long trail. For instance, our search for Isaac Mansfield on the 1830 U.S. Census initially began with more than a dozen Isaac Mansfields nationwide. One by one we elimi- nated each Isaac Mansfield until we finally found the one who owned Joe. He lived on the St. Louis waterfront and owned a tin manufactur- ing plant. We initially matched Mansfield's signature from an 1828 business receipt in Missouri to a character certificate he signed when he entered Texas in 1832.[5]

Then, on December 27, 1999, we made a monumental discovery that would forever alter Joe's history. It was Christmas break and I was sit- ting in a nearly vacant Bizzell Memorial Library at the University of Oklahoma in Norman. Lee and I had just started our search for Isaac Mansfield in St. Louis. At the time, we didn't know whether Mansfield had brought Joe into Texas or purchased him after his arrival in Texas in June 1832. I pulled from the stacks a couple of books on early St. Louis, hoping at best to discover some color on the city at the time Mansfield lived there. I first began to read 'Ain't But a Place': An Anthol- ogy of African American Writings about St. Louis, edited by Gerald Early. As I thumbed through its pages, I instantly took an interest in passages of a slave narrative written by the famed fugitive slave, abolitionist, and author William Wells Brown, who had lived in St. Louis in 1827. Having in mind Mansfield's appearance in the 1830 census, I figured that if Joe was owned by Mansfield in St. Louis, then Brown's account might give us some valuable insight regarding slave life in the city dur- ing that period. My eyes scanned each page for details. Suddenly, on the fifth page, Brown's words struck me like a bolt of lightning: "My mother, my brothers Joseph and Millford, and my sister Elizabeth, be- longed to Mr. Isaac Mansfield, formerly from one of the Free States

(Massachusetts, I believe). He was a tinner by trade, and carried on a large manufacturing establishment."[6] My mind raced. I stood up from my chair, and looked around the empty library in speechless euphoria. I wanted to yell. I sat down and reread the passage once again to make sure my mind wasn't playing tricks on me. Heart pounding, unable to sit, I again sprang to my feet. "Yes!" I cried out in a restrained voice. "Yes!" Suddenly, as if delayed by shock, I realized that I was reading the slave narrative of Joe's brother.

Not only had Lee and I now identified the names of Joe's mother and siblings, we were now holding excerpts from a narrative written by his brother. Within minutes, Lee had downloaded an electronic version of Brown's entire book, *Narrative of William W. Brown, An American Slave*. The narrative opened the window to Joe's childhood home of Marthasville, confirmed that he was born in Kentucky, and told us that the slave who survived the Alamo battle was the grandson of legendary trailblazer, Daniel Boone. What were the odds that Joe would have a relative who left a memoir? A hundred thousand to one? A million to one? All we knew for certain was that within a twenty-four-hour period, our research morphed into a full-fledged biography of Joe.

Our journey started to take on Indiana Jones–like proportions. We felt we were destined to tell Joe's story. But this presented two distinct challenges—tracing his life before and after the Alamo, and the latter part of his life proved far more daunting. Why? Because we simply didn't know with any certainty what last name he adopted as a freedman. Most historians and Alamo enthusiasts understandably assumed that he took the name of his famous owner, Travis. As we learned more about his past, however, that assumption became less certain. The fact is that he was a Young slave at birth, and a lot of slaves considered their true surname to be that of their first owner. Or maybe, for some unknown reason, he decided to take Mansfield's name. Still another possibility—and one we dreaded to ponder—was that he took a surname foreign to our research, such as Joe Washington or Joe Lincoln. The possibilities were mind-numbing.

Tracking his whereabouts after his escape from the Travis estate in 1838 was another monumental challenge. Did he flee into Mexico or Canada? Did he find refuge in Texas near relatives? Did he return to Missouri Territory? Canada seemed like a long shot at best, due to the distance. When we discovered William Wells Brown, we also eliminated Mexico as a likely destination. Thanks to Brown, we knew that Joe was an American-born slave. Joe fled the Mexican Army after the Alamo battle, and it was highly improbable that he would have sought refuge among people who didn't speak his language.

Then there were these stories from Alabama. They consistently spoke of Joe's unexpected appearance before the Travis family in 1838 near Brewton, Alabama, and nearly all of those stories originated from James C. Travis, William Barret's youngest sibling. Only the Travis family knew Joe as "Ben Travis." In 1905, James told a newspaper reporter, "I visited the Alamo in the company of Ben and he went over the incidents of the fight as he had seen them."[7] James knew his brother's former slave, and he gave at least two other interviews, in 1914 and 1915, in which he repeated his story about how the Travis family had learned from "Ben" of how William had died. In the latter, his last known interview, James noted that "Ben" had lived "for many years" with "the Travis family" in Alabama.[8] James would know, right? Even as late as 1929, the *Dallas Morning News* was reporting how "Ben" had carried news of the Alamo defeat to Alabama and how his "descendants are still living near Brewton, Ala."[9]

Mark A. Travis, the son of James, corresponded during the 1930s with historians about Travis family history and kept this oral tradition alive. We found the details of one such correspondence tucked away in the private collection of Alabama historian Fannie McGuire at the Alabama Department of Archives and History in Montgomery. McGuire had asked Mark specifically about Joe. Mark replied with a letter, informing her that Joe had traveled forty days on foot from Texas to Alabama, and that he was buried six miles south of Evergreen, Alabama.[10] Jay Villa—the old Travis homestead—is exactly six miles south of Evergreen.

As for the epic forty-day journey, we conducted our own test out of curiosity. Travelers during the 1830s generally averaged fifteen miles a day. So we took the distance between Bailey's Prairie, Texas, and Brewton, Alabama (594 miles) and divided it by forty. The answer: 14.85 miles per day.

In the end, the totality of the evidence convinced us that the Travis family stories about Joe's journey to Alabama in 1838 were indeed true.

Naturally, where slaves are concerned, there will always be gaps in history. Joe's past is no different. Our hope today is that somewhere out there one of Joe's descendants will come forward to fill in some of those gaps. We often think about an old history book we found in a library in Conecuh County, Alabama. A passage in the book quoted the eighty-five-year-old James C. Travis, "The first we knew of William's having joined in the Texas fighting was when we heard that he had been placed in command of the Alamo. He had a negro slave and body guard, Ben Travis, who was with him and aided in the defense of the Alamo." On that page someone had crossed out the word "negro slave" and written "mulatto."

Now who in Alabama would have known that Joe was a mulatto?

Maybe our grand adventure isn't over.

ACKNOWLEDGMENTS

A book of this scope and magnitude is an epic undertaking. Researching the life of a historical figure is always a challenge under normal circumstances. Yet there is nothing normal when that figure is a slave. In terms of time alone, this project has spanned more than seventeen years, dating back to December 1997. Our journey has carried us far and wide, across five states and into Mexico. Naturally, we encountered thousands of helpful souls along the way in state archives, university collections, county courthouses, town libraries, historic sites, and museums—enough to probably cover the pages of another book and far too many to remember over time. To those folks, we humbly say thank you. This book is a product of your service.

We also want to thank a number of people who kindly shared their family histories—all of which added to the richness of our story. They include Albert A. Gallatin, Clyde Glossen, Ralph Gregory, and Linda Halliburton Tart.

Reading and editing a manuscript is no easy chore, yet a number of people kindly accepted our request to do so. Each offered helpful suggestions. Mike Cox, Darlene Giblet, and Melissa Roberts performed the earliest and toughest edits. Those who followed include Michael Blake, an Academy Award–winning screenwriter and author of *Dances with Wolves;* our agent Eleanor Wood, founder and president of the Spectrum

Literary Agency in New York; Stephan Harrigan, author of *Gates of the Alamo;* Dr. James E. Crisp of North Carolina State University; and Ann Close, a veteran editor at Alfred A. Knopf.

We would also like to extend a special thanks to rock legend Phil Collins—an avid Alamo artifacts collector—for graciously writing this book's foreword. Collins's humility and kindness are as memorable as his music.

Artist and historian Gary Zaboly has long been an icon in Alamo circles, and his stunning illustrations in this book are yet another reason why. Zaboly's talent and attention to detail simply bring history to life.

Over the years we experienced a number of emotional highs and lows, and someone was always there with a kind word of support and encouragement to keep us afloat. This list includes, but is not limited to, legendary actor James Earl Jones; JoNell Neese, Lee's sister; Ed Dubvrasky; Jay Grelen, author and columnist; Lydia Grimes, columnist; JoAnn Lovas; Joan Headley, queen of the annual Alamo party; Ira Lott; Gaylord Shaw, Pulitzer Prize-winning journalist; Bill Chemerka, founder of the Alamo Society; Dr. Bruce Winders, the Alamo's official historian; and the late Alamo historians Tom Lindley and Kevin Young. To all, your kind words were not forgotten.

The folks at the University of Oklahoma Press will forever hold a special place in our hearts for believing in this book. Jay Dew, a former acquisitions editor at the press, who now lives in Texas, was the first to recognize this book's potential and importance. Chuck Rankin, editor-in-chief, then carried the book to the finish line with equal enthusiasm. Thank you so much for your hard work and dedication.

Lastly, there are our families. Our spouses—Jeannia Jackson and Larry White—endured countless hours alone while we read files into the night and wrote, brainstormed endlessly on the phone, and were away on research trips. Our children also shared in the many sacrifices— Ashley, Gabriel, Joseph, Missouri, Tristan, and Sam. Frankly, they are as responsible for this book as we are and they deserve more than words can express. All we can say is we love you all, and you make life worth living.

Our last word of thanks goes to Joe, our Alamo survivor and the subject of this book. By now, you too are family. We hope this book honors the life you lived.

Joe, the Slave Who Became an Alamo Legend

1

MARCH 5, 1836

As for man, his days are as grass: as a flower of the
field, so he flourisheth. For the wind passeth over it, and
it is gone; and the place thereof shall know it no more.
—Psalms 103:15–16

Beads of wax trickled down candles that burned brightly, casting shadows of the two men against the dank stone walls of their room. Their silhouettes betrayed the ethnic and social differences between them—one a southern, American-born, white slaveholder, the other a southern, American-born mulatto slave.

Tonight those differences seemed moot.

Beyond the walls of their old missionary refuge lay anywhere from fifteen hundred to six thousand Mexican Army soldiers, waiting to pounce in the sacred name of country and honor. Neither man knew the exact strength of the enemy—only the desperation of their own situation.[1]

By the folly of fate, they had found themselves standing shoulder to shoulder with roughly two hundred Texian revolutionaries, ready to die in defense of freedom and independence. Joe, the slave, surely comprehended the gravity of the situation as well as anyone in the fortification called the Alamo. He would have seen it with great clarity each time he stared into the intense, blue eyes of his master, William Barret Travis, co-commander of the entrapped rebel force. Or each time he watched his master hand another plea for relief to a brave courier. Or whenever he peered beyond the walls across the river at the San Fernando Church in San Antonio de Bexar. A blood-red flag whipped ominously in the wind above the church.[2] The Mexican Army's flag symbolized what Joe clearly understood: No quarter. No mercy.[3] Survival looked bleak.

Although only in the twenty-first year of his life, Joe understood survival as well as anyone within the Alamo's stout, limestone walls.[4] He came from a long line of survivors—people who had endured chains and whips and the sale of loved ones. He had inherited their legacy of physical and emotional scars. In truth, Joe probably visited death daily, if only by wondering what had become of his siblings. For him, they walked among slavery's living dead—a language all too familiar to those in bondage.

Joe had already earned the stripes of a master survivalist. But every life has a beginning and an end, and like every other soul trapped within the Alamo, Joe soberly embraced the realization that this indeed might be his time. Twelve days of continual bombardment by Mexican artillerymen erased the doubts, if any ever existed. Joe likely smelled grave danger the moment he first saw the enemy stream into Bexar in seemingly endless numbers.[5]

Severe fatigue showed on the faces of every defender. The constant threat of incoming cannonballs and grapeshot tested the nerves of those besieged, depriving them of ample sleep.[6]

Joe sat at the edge of his bed, dirt smeared across his clothes and exposed flesh. His rifle lay close by his side. Earlier in the day the Mexican cannons roared with a brisk fury, only to stop suddenly. The weary yet spirited Texans took advantage of the lull to fortify their walls with mounds of dirt, laboring as nightfall arrived and exhaustion settled into their bones.[7]

Outside, there were occasional yips of a coyote or faint noises from the Mexican encampments encircling the compound, but within the Alamo's walls it was silent, except for the occasional bellow of cattle.[8] Surely Joe had experienced the same quiet while watching the Mississippi River flow quietly past his riverfront home on humid Missouri summer nights.

Those times had not been long ago, but at this moment they must have seemed a lifetime removed.

Less than a decade earlier, Joe and his family had lived and toiled together on an old plantation. There he drew sustenance in the bosom of extended kinship; elders enchanted him with stories and cloaked him in love. There he walked among living legends of his own race, men of color with Herculean strength and mystical powers.[9]

Joe's physical appearance had probably changed since he had last seen some of his family in Missouri. He now filled out a relatively tall frame, standing between five foot ten and five foot eleven, and by one observer's estimation, he appeared older than his age. Joe's looks deceived in more ways than one. His coal-black skin belied his mulatto bloodline.[10] But only slaveholders and slave traders took note of such details. Joe's family members would have looked into his heart. On this cloudy night, he must have yearned for their companionship and love, perhaps missing the way they insisted on calling him by his full name, Joseph. Then there was his beloved mother, a pillar of strength. Surely Joe wondered if he would live to embrace her once again.

Across the room his master tossed restlessly under his blanket, prepared for the worst, his sword and shotgun within reach.[11] Nearby sat the table where Joe had watched his master feverishly scratch out pleas for aid. The quill pen now lay silent in the flickering glow of the candlelight.

Whatever remained to be said, Travis and Joe surely said it that night, but probably not as a master and slave would talk. Given their perilous position, they likely spoke as equals, as two souls standing on the doorstep of eternity.

2

Marthasville

This white man can't whip me himself, and therefore
he has called you to help.
—Randall, Dr. John Young's slave

S laves on Dr. John Young's plantation simply called it the "Negro-whip." Its handle stretched about three feet from a butt-end filled with lead, and the whip itself extended another six or seven feet to the end of a strip of rawhide capped by platted wire. No slave needed a second glance to remember its wicked details, but one could spend a lifetime trying to forget its purpose.

On Young's plantation this whip was carried by a hardened overseer named Grove Cook. He used it whenever his mood dictated. Cook often boasted how he would "flog any nigger" who didn't obey him, and he routinely followed through on his claim. The slaves knew Cook as a drunkard and, when the least bit intoxicated, an extremely dangerous man.[1] Over time Cook earned a reputation on the plantation for unmercifully whipping slaves whenever drunk, which was frequently.

Physically, Cook offered an intimidating presence. He stood tall and large with rough features, red hair, and large, bushy eyebrows similar to those on a spaniel. Yet his most chilling features were his eyes. Cold gray.[2]

Joe spent much of his childhood avoiding the glare of those eyes, as well as the wrath of the "Negro-whip." Warned by his mother and other elder slaves, one of Joe's earliest lessons in life would have been to fear the whip.

Fear came easily. Avoiding Cook didn't. All too often a slave unknowingly encountered Cook's bad side. That's when Joe's senses were branded with the crackle of the whip and the wails of the soul on its receiving end. Cook's whip had an everlasting effect on those who saw it in action. For Joe, it likely launched a life with an emphasis on sheer survival.

As an infant, Joe was one of dozens of slaves brought to the Missouri Territory by Young in 1816 from a farm near Lexington, Kentucky. Joe was most likely born in 1815, probably at Young's Mount Sterling farm, where the enterprising physician meticulously logged the births of his slaves in a book.[3]

Joe's mother was a mulatto slave named Elizabeth, one of Young's most prized field hands. Noted for her strength of body and mind, Elizabeth gave birth to seven children. Aside from Joe, Elizabeth had five other sons—Solomon, Leander, Benjamin, Millford, and William—and one daughter, also named Elizabeth. No two children had the same father.[4]

Despite their varied bloodline, Joe and his siblings forged a loving bond. From infancy, they learned to shield one another from the dangers that surrounded them. They protected each other the best they could under their restricting status as slaves. Their love flourished inside a one-room log cabin, where daily hardships were eased by the comfort of kinship.[5] Marthasville was home. In Marthasville, at least, Joe and his family had each other.

They were also blessed with the necessities of life. Food was bountiful in the fertile valley where they lived, a breathtaking place that produced giant pumpkins, squash, melons, apricots, peaches, and pears by the barrel. Juicy red apples were also grown to perfection, along with a variety of grapes harvested throughout the summer, fall, and even winter months. Potatoes, carrots, and spinach were cultivated in great abundance. No crop in Missouri surpassed that of Indian corn in terms of quality and quantity. Farms generally yielded close to seventy-five bushels an acre, enough to feed a small village.[6]

Slaves were generally allowed to partake in the bounty if they maintained their own gardens—an industrious endeavor many shouldered after laboring for their master from sunrise to sunset. In Missouri, Saturday afternoons were generally designated as a time when slaves could hire themselves out if they desired. Joe may have helped his elders in this way by delivering messages or pulling weeds in the garden, jobs often dolled out to slave children.[7]

Marthasville provided a world of wonderment for a boy eager to explore its frontier treasures. On Sundays or holidays, if Young's slaves were not bound by harvest, Joe and other children from the plantation were allowed the freedom to do as they wished. Adventure beckoned a short distance from their cabins. Countless hours were undoubtedly spent racing through the tall prairie grass that canvassed the undulating terrain and maze of ravines north of Marthasville. Black bear, deer, squirrels, and panthers wandered through the region, and for the experienced youth, that sometimes meant fresh game to proudly present back at the family cabin. Territorial law allowed plantation slaves to keep and use guns with a permit issued by the local justice of the peace, and Young found no objection to the practice. The doctor allowed his slaves the freedom to hunt and fish on Sundays, in addition to tasks such as weaving baskets and making splint brooms.[8]

Joe and his playmates discovered a magical forest beyond the ravines, with towering oak, ash, and walnut trees that guarded the children from gusty winds. Walking through the trees was a peaceful experience: only the rustling of leaves could be heard in even the harshest of storms. (Later, upon returning to their family cabins, they would discover the effects of wood ticks and mosquitoes that laid claim to their bodies in the thick brush of the woods. But such discomforts were considered a small price to pay for children at play.)[9] Every once in a while, Joe and his companions probably passed one of their master's wandering cows or horses grazing in the woods. The horses generally roamed in herds and could easily be located by a bell hanging from the neck of one known to be a leader.[10] Servants and free settlers in the region also frequented the woods, riding on horseback to hunt. When a hunter reached a spot where he wanted to dismount and walk, he simply turned his horse loose to rejoin the farm's herd. The hunters therefore preferred to ride atop a blanket rather than a bulky saddle.[11]

As entertaining as the forest may have been for Joe and his companions, there lurked dangers including, at times, marauding Indians. Women and children were forbidden from wandering too far. Elders routinely implored children to stay close to the farm, and few needed to be told twice. Everyone in the region had heard the harrowing tale of the Ramsay family.

The tight quarters of a slave's cabin invited such storytelling. It is likely that on cold, stormy nights the slaves huddled around the fireplace, clamoring to hear an elder tell the tale. Few words were needed to set the scene in the Ramsay saga, and even fewer were needed to embellish the horrific details.

On the morning of May 20, 1815, a year before Young's arrival in the Missouri Territory, a Sauk war party attacked the cabin of Robert Ramsay's family some seven miles northwest of where Marthasville would eventually be established. News of the attack spread quickly. Several miles away, a messenger interrupted exercises by the fighting men of the Charette settlement. As fate would have it, the famed trailblazer Daniel Boone was there, in charge of a fortified cabin known as Callaway Post, when the news arrived. For Joe and his siblings, the mere mention of Boone probably stirred their blood. Joe had surely heard his mother often refer to Boone as her father. By then the rugged outdoorsman was already a living legend known far and wide for his daring wilderness exploits.[12]

On this day, despite the weight of eighty years, Boone shouldered a rifle and followed the messenger back along the thickly wooded trails to the Ramsay family's remote cabin. In a clearing Boone gazed upon the three Ramsay children lying in pools of blood. Each had been savagely tomahawked, their bodies were mangled and now riddled with flies. Nearby, neighboring women tended to the children's dying, pregnant mother. The Sauk warriors had struck her first, as she milked a cow, before her peg-legged husband could reach his firearm. Now she shrieked uncontrollably as the women assisted her in the premature birth of her child.

According to one storyteller, the bloody scene left Boone's lips compressed as "a fire gleaned from his eyes." Robert Ramsey had suffered a shot in the groin, and Boone calmly extracted the ball and dressed the wound. But there was no saving the life of the mother and infant, and Boone headed off through the deep woods on the trail of the war party.[13]

No matter the dangers lurking within, the woods presented a mystique and an allure few children could resist. So did Marthasville's bluff, where Joe's curiosity was likely stirred. The settlement's few log buildings were perched atop a magnificent bluff with white stone outcroppings wrapped in a thick array of greenery. From this perch Joe could look out over the fertile, black soil of the Missouri Valley below, where the approach of a stagecoach or a visitor on horseback could be seen from miles away. Carving the base of the bluff were the gentle waters of Tuque Creek, where Joe and his friends probably fished for bullhead catfish and crawdads. Farther south flowed the swifter currents of Charette Creek, once part of the route taken by Meriwether Lewis and William Clark on their great exploration. Years earlier, a half mile below Marthasville, French trappers had established a settlement along the creek called La Charette. As late as 1811 it boasted as many as thirty families who primarily raised corn and hunted.[14] But Marthasville would slowly engulf La Charette until that village became a faded memory.

To the east, Joe could see the tree line of the mighty Missouri River a mile away. The magnificent view was surely tantalizing to the imagination. Somewhere beyond the Missouri and below the North Star lay the land the slaves called "Liberty." Joe likely overheard the elders talk about this land in the shadows of their cabins. A few called it the "Land of Freedom." Its true name was Canada.[15]

Of equal interest were the mysteries along the upper Missouri River. Early settlers heard tall tales from vagabond fur trappers and traders who ventured the river, or from second- and third-hand stories published in St. Charles and St. Louis newspapers, which arrived in Marthasville two days after going to press. These tales eventually trickled down to the slave community. In 1822, the year Joe turned seven, news circulated with great enthusiasm to even the most remote settlements outside St. Louis. A fur company was financing a major expedition upriver beyond the Pawnee, Otoe, and Sioux villages. The following advertisement, which appeared March 20, 1822, in a St. Louis newspaper, sparked the excitement:

To enterprising young men. The subscriber wishes to engage one hundred young men to ascend the Missouri river to its source, there to be employed for one, two, or three years. For particulars enquire of Major Andrew Henry, near the lead mines in the county of Washington, who will ascend with, and command, the party; or of the subscriber near St. Louis. [Signed] William H. Ashley.[16]

In less than a month, St. Louis and its surrounding countryside had produced enough gritty volunteers to start the fur-trapping expedition. Among the hardy lot were three adventurers who would become the most legendary mountain men of all: Jim Bridger, Hugh Glass, and Jedediah Smith. Their days as pioneers would be greatly overshadowed by their afterlife as bona fide American folk heroes. Another celebrated volunteer was Mike Fink. People of all colors in every tavern and port between Pittsburgh and New Orleans knew his name. A hard-drinking, hard-fighting, sharp-shooting keelboater who had already earned folk hero status, Fink may have commanded one of the seventy-five-foot keelboats used to carry food and equipment on the ballyhooed Ashley expedition.

All along the river that year, white settlers and slaves alike emerged from remote cabins to watch as the crews of twenty-plus men marched the boats' runways, pushing poles in unison along the river's muddy bottom. The crews maneuvered through countless snags below the murky waters and eventually reached their destination at the mouth of the Yellowstone River.

As for Fink, the adventure would be his last. Word of his death reached St. Louis and was published on July 16, 1823, in the *Missouri Republican*. Readers learned how Fink had engaged in his favorite pastime of shooting a tin cup full of whiskey from another man's head. Only this time Fink had missed, dropping his companion dead with a shot to the forehead. Another man took offense at this and shot Fink dead on the spot.[17]

For free Americans in search of fortunes, these were indeed exciting times. Brighter prospects for success were always thought to be the next valley or territory away, and Dr. John Young fully understood this pursuit of destiny. As one of thirteen children born to Leonard and Mary Young, John had learned what could be gained by being aggressive. In 1805 he married a fellow Virginian, Martha Fuqua, and moved to Fayette County, Kentucky, where he put his Philadelphia Medical College degree to use.[18] Young opened a physician practice in Mount Sterling and provided everything from itch ointments and therapeutic berries to the occasional surgery.[19] Two years later, he won a seat in the Kentucky state legislature.[20]

Young tended to even more important business during the War of 1812, serving as a surgeon for Col. George Trotter's Kentucky Mounted Volunteer Militia in the Thames campaign.[21] Then Young returned home to a new wife, Sarah Scott of Virginia. John and Sarah had wed in 1811 after the death of the doctor's beloved Martha.[22]

By 1815, with his ever-expanding appetite for business, Young had opened a ropewalk and bagging factory in Mount Sterling in addition to his medical practice, but thoughts of his future tugged at his heart.[23] Daring to dream of a new paradise, Kentucky's trailblazing Boone had already led his family and others to fresh settlements in the old Spanish Territory of Missouri, and now a similar wanderlust overwhelmed Young. He sold his factory to David Dodge, a hemp manufacturer in Lexington and Winchester, and followed his heart westward in 1816, moving his family, some forty slaves, and everything else he owned to Missouri Territory.[24] Elizabeth, Joe's mother, made the long journey as one of Young's prized servants. She did so with her infant son Joe and two-year-old son William in tow. The trip undoubtedly added to her family legacy as a woman of strength and endurance. Young, meanwhile, sought a different kind of legacy. There, in Missouri's wilderness interior, Young concluded he would fulfill a lifelong dream. He envisioned a frontier oasis of commerce and trade, a county seat, and a place centrally located to cater to his political constituents and the massive influx of supply-needy settlers. He envisioned a booming city on a hill with himself as lord. Marthasville.

The town, named in honor of his late wife, is where Young would strike the mother lode, he thought. Certainly the fulfillment of Young's dream would depend on his business savvy, as well as the backs of his slaves. In both respects he appeared well prepared. In a bold stroke of ingenuity, Young allied with neighboring entrepreneurs in an effort to ensure Marthasville's instant and permanent success. On December 20, 1817, he and thirty-one others applied to the U.S. Congress to establish a language academy there.

The potential ripple effect of such an institution in Marthasville was obvious to Young. Backed by government funding, students from across the United States and abroad would eventually flock to the academy. A reputation for quality higher education would be established, and a permanent student population would in turn ensure Marthasville's economic success. Not everyone, however, shared Young's vision. Congress denied the petition. Nevertheless, Young did receive clearance to establish the township of Marthasville—a victorious first step for the enterprising doctor.[25] By then, he already had a jump on his plans, having had the town surveyed and platted in June.[26]

Wasting little time in establishing a small village of commerce, he first opened a tavern and then a mercantile, for which he hired relative John B. Scott as clerk, and he established a medical practice with friend and fellow physician John Jones.[27] Construction of a sawmill was next. A reporter from the *Missouri Gazette* noted after a visit to the area: "The subscriber [Young] has opened a general assortment of *Merchandise & Groceries* in Marthasville; the Merchandise he will sell ten to fifteen percent cheaper than they can be bought in St. Louis or St. Charles. This appears somewhat incredible, but when the public are informed, that his firewood costs him nothing, and his provisions fifty per cent less than they are in those places, it will appear reasonable."

Young's enthusiasm had obviously rubbed off on the reporter, who made a prediction that must have left Young flattered. "This town will be very suitably situated for the seat of justice," he wrote, "when St. Charles county is divided, as the county around it for many miles is thickly inhabited by industrious, wealthy persons, together with its being at a very proper distance from St. Charles for a county line to run half way between these two places." The reporter went on to note, "Charette creek, a bold and lasting stream, runs within a mile of the town . . . on which there is a merchant and saw mill now building."[28]

Marthasville's infancy fostered countless dreams for the Young clan. Benjamin Young, the youngest of John's six brothers, shared in the euphoria. He and his wife, Mary Maaro, moved to Marthasville in 1819 and promptly opened a store on the town's quaint public square. Benjamin was followed by another brother, Aaron, and Aaron's wife, Theodosia Winn, of Fayette County, Kentucky. The slave-owning

Aaron and Theodosia arrived in 1819, settling a short distance from Marthasville.[29]

Behind the scenes in Marthasville, Young's stable of slaves labored in the smothering humidity of the Missouri summer to construct the various buildings that would comprise the town. Logs were cut, hand-hewn, and hauled by the slaves from nearby woods and then laid to the specifications of their eager masters. Sweat streamed from the slaves' brows as they built the water-powered sawmill on the steep embankments along Tuque Creek. Young, born with one leg shorter than the other, probably relegated himself to the role of an impatient observer during the construction.[30]

Over the years, Joe and the other adolescent slaves probably grew to appreciate the hard work of the elder slaves. If so, he would have taken pride in their contributions as Marthasville's cofounders, and like numerous slaves in the region, he may have even felt part of his owner's family. A neighboring German settler noted in a letter to his homeland that such feelings were not uncommon:

> Yesterday my neighbor's Negro worked for me. It was a free day, one which the slaves use to earn pocket money. He said to me: "I have heard that you want to go back to Europe. Why? This is such a beautiful country, such a fertile country and such a free country!" I could hardly believe my ears to hear such praise from the mouth of a slave. To explain it, one may not for a moment think that it was merely a thoughtless repetition of the common paean of praise which one hears so often in this country. The Negro is considered to be part of the family not only by his master; what is more important, he thinks of himself as one of them.[31]

At least one Missouri antislavery statesman of the period, Gen. George R. Smith of Sedalia, even recognized the sincerity of relations that sometimes developed between slave and master. Smith noted, "The masters were usually humane and there was often real affection between master and slave—and very often great kindliness. There were merciful services from each to the other."[32]

Still, there is no doubt that Joe, like his brother William, knew deep within his soul there was a difference. Even in the lair of Marthasville's familiar surroundings, there existed a social line a slave could never cross. It was a line drawn by skin color, strict labor demands, economics, and, when necessary, Grove Cook's "Negro-whip." Time after time, Joe witnessed this bitter lesson firsthand in his formative years.

No slave on Young's plantation embodied the true spirit of his fellow bondsmen more than Randall, a brawny, well-proportioned man known for his great strength. Randall stood six feet tall and was generally known as the most valuable and able-bodied slave on the plantation. He was also known for his open defiance of the whip. No other slave on Young's plantation could make this claim.

Privately, slaves admired Randall because he was powerful and fearless enough to stand up to Cook and his whip. To children like Joe, Randall surely towered above all others like some mythic hero spun from the yarns of elders. Yet Randall never flaunted his power. He labored hard in the fields, plowing and hoeing with the understanding he would never allow any man to strike him as long as he breathed.

Cook certainly understood Randall's wishes, even if he had never been told directly. Young himself repeatedly warned Cook not to whip Randall. But that didn't stop Cook from despising Randall's strength and free will. Attitudes like these were dangerous among slaves, in Cook's perspective. They undermined his authority, promoted disobedience, and offended his senses. Cook vowed to make Randall an example for any slave who dared to display free spirit. The opportunity was to present itself before long. The death of Montgomery County representative Jesse B. Boone thrust Young into the political arena, he quickly emerged as the popular choice to become Boone's successor, and he was appointed to Missouri's first House of Representatives in 1821.[33] This meant increased business in St. Louis, and Young soon became weary of the long stagecoach rides and ferry passages to and from Marthasville. Eventually he remained in St. Louis for longer periods, leaving the bulk of the plantation's duties in the hands of his overseer.

Cook became more controlling and tyrannical with the slaves in his care. Before long, Randall's work came under heavy scrutiny. One day Cook ordered Randall to complete a task that Cook knew could not be done. By nightfall, when the task remained unfinished, Cook made a point to tell the slave he would remember him come daybreak. After breakfast the next morning Cook called on Randall and ordered the giant field hand to cross his hands so they might be tied. With his whip dangling in hand, the overseer calmly informed Randall that he intended to whip him because of his unfinished chores the day before.[34]

The task had been impossible, Randall replied, or else it would have been done as requested. Cook said it made no difference and insisted Randall do as he was told. By this time, the other slaves were listening, if not blatantly watching, to see how the confrontation would unfold. A moment of tense silence filled the air before Randall spoke again. "Mr. Cook," Randall said, "I have always tried to please you since you have been on the plantation, and I find you determined not to be satisfied with my work, let me do as well as I may. No man has laid hands on me, to whip me, for the last ten years, and I have long since come to the conclusion not to be whipped by any man living."[35]

Randall's expression grew stern, his body language bold and unyielding. Cook studied Randall for a moment, and then called three other slaves from their work. He commanded them to seize Randall so that he might be tied down. Each slave stood frozen in fear. They knew Randall's power.

"Boys," Randall told the hands, "you all know me; you know I can handle any three of you, and the man that lays hands on me shall die. This white man can't whip me himself, and therefore he has called you to help."[36]

Cook again ordered Randall to be seized, and again the hands stood still. Finally, Cook ordered them all back to work—Randall included.

Over the next week, Joe and his siblings heard the elders cackle at the stupidity of Cook's attempt to challenge Randall. They saw Randall's defiance as a victory. Cook had not even spoken a word to Randall since their showdown. Recollections of Cook's pained expression that day brought instant laughter to the slaves behind closed doors. But all that changed the next week after Cook arrived in the field one morning in the company of three friends. Together they strode to where Randall worked and ordered the slave to join them in the barn. Randall refused, and a melee ensued.[37]

All four men charged Randall. Fists flew in a tornado of violence. Slaves watched nearby in horror, but when calm prevailed, Randall had laid each assailant out on the ground. The slave stood now with his fists clinched, a true portrait of nobility and strength. At that point one of Cook's cronies, a man named Woodbridge, drew his pistol, took aim at the slave in front of him, and fired. Randall dropped to the ground. Instinctively, the three other men rushed Randall and clubbed him until they succeeded in tying his hands. Barely conscious, Randall was dragged to the barn and tied to a beam. His lips were parched, his breathing heavy.

Cook, his adrenaline pumping, unfurled his whip and took aim at Randall's broad, muscular back. The sound of each lash echoed from the barn across the acreage encompassing Young's farm and Marthasville's town square. The crack of the whip reverberated, striking at the nerves of each slave. By the time Randall received his hundredth lash, chunks of red flesh crisscrossed his back. Blood gushed from indistinguishable cuts, streamed down his back, and soaked his pants. Randall was nearly dead. The weary but satiated Cook ordered Randall washed with salt and water and left tied up unattended the rest of the day. Field hands untied Randall the next morning and took him to the blacksmith shop, where at Cook's directions the blacksmith attached a ball and chain to one of his legs. Shortly after, Randall was returned to the field and given the unrealistic command to labor with the same productivity as he had before.

When Young returned from St. Louis, Cook informed the doctor that he had succeeded in breaking Randall of his unruly spirit. The news pleased Young greatly.[38] Slaves on his plantation reacted differently. Randall's beating marked a time of sorrow. Respect for the mighty Randall never wavered, and visions of his brutal whipping scarred them psychologically. For children like Joe, the beating of their hero showed them slavery's harsh realities.

Joe spent his earliest days living in the slave quarters in the back of Young's farm, where some twenty-four other field hands resided. The slave cabins lay clumped toward the back of the property where the "big house" could be seen, as if symbolically, standing alone some distance away.[39] Inside the cabins, slaves used crude, homemade furniture they crafted themselves. Mattresses stuffed with cornhusks, cotton, or even moss gathered from the woods typically rested on bed frames lined with rope or rawhide. A mixture of mud and hog's hair plastered between the layers and cracks of the hand-hewn logs provided protection from the elements. And at night, a cabin's only light came from the fireplace, where the slaves did all their cooking.

Outside, two unpleasant reminders stood ever visible. Each defined the slave's true place in Marthasville, where a coarse blanket and scant clothing were generally all that was allotted a typical field hand. The first reminder was the overseer's quarters. Cook's house sat in the middle of the slaves' various crude dwellings. From this location Cook maintained a close watch over the slaves in his service.[40] The second was a bell.

Each morning the hands rose at four o'clock to the ringing of the bell that hung prominently on a wooden post near the overseer's quarters, serving as a constant reminder of laborious days past and those yet to come.[41] Before long the sound of the blacksmith's hammer chimed with a familiar rhythm. Slaves began the never-ending chores of chopping firewood and feeding the livestock as the town of Marthasville slowly came alive with the sounds of cackling hens, squealing pigs, and the occasional creaking doors of mostly idle merchants. The air carried a heavy aroma of cattle dung, as well as the soulful songs of the laboring field hands.

Only a small village, Marthasville ran like clockwork each day. Those who lived and worked there likely forever shaped Joe's attitudes and personality. Among the residents of its small slave community were men like Uncle Ned, a venerable elder of ninety years who seldom ventured beyond the cracked boards of his cabin door. The ancient bondsman commanded the respect of the other slaves, most of whom listened intently whenever he spoke.[42]

Uncle Ned shared a cabin with Dinkie, a mysterious, one-eyed, full-blood African man who claimed to descend from a king in his native land. Other slaves believed he possessed voodoo powers. Probably in his fifties at the time of Joe's childhood, Dinkie wore a snakeskin around his neck and carried a petrified frog in one pocket and a dried lizard in the other. Although he rarely spoke, the slaves regarded him as the undisputed oracle of Marthasville.[43]

In the fields, Joe also came in contact with an affable hand named Sam. The easygoing Sam had fittingly married the equally laid-back Hannah, a house servant with a chatty and unpretentious demeanor. Hannah often annoyed Mistress Young with her blunt innocence.[44] There also resided among the slaves Dr. Young's trusty body servant, Ike, who had been trained since childhood to wait on whites. Ike spoke with a refinement lacking among the field hands and stood well versed in Scripture, although his fellow servants regarded him the furthest thing from a true Christian. Ike instead used his knowledge of the Bible—and of Dr. Young's favorite prayer—to amuse his fellow servants inside the barn on rainy days.[45]

Joe also grew to know Jim, an old servant; Aunt Nancy, the plantation's "mammy" and proud Maryland native; and Cato, a humorous, self-serving house servant and the resident snitch. Cato had a great number of qualities, none of which had anything to do with humility or thoughtfulness. Still, he always seemed to provide his fellow slaves with a reason to laugh. Whether they laughed at him or with him did not seem to matter much to Cato.[46]

Dr. Young frequently called on Cato to entertain company with a song or joke. Once Young summoned the playful servant to give a toast and handed him a glass of wine. Cato held the glass aloft, flashed his teeth with a wide grin, and mused:

> De big bee flies high,
> De little bees makes de honey,
> De black man raise de cotton,
> An' de white man gets de money.[47]

Young's slaves were a motley band of lifelong survivalists who undoubtedly provided Joe with everything dear to the human appetite beyond bread and water. These people enriched his life with cynicism and humor, selfishness and thoughtfulness, anger and love. Together they shared everything—from soured milk and scraps of butchered meat to laughter and tears and hopes and dreams. Above all they shared the common shelter of extended kinship in a world void of basic freedoms. They ultimately made life bearable.[48]

"There was laughter, song, and happiness in the Negro quarters," recalled Smith, the antislavery statesman on his assessment of slavery in Missouri and Kentucky. "The old negroes had their comfortable quarters, where each family would sit by their own great sparkling log fires. They sang their plantation songs, grew hilarious over their corn shuckings and did the bidding of their gracious master. Their doctor's bills were paid; their clothing bought, or woven by themselves in their cabins, and made by their mistress; their sick nursed; and their dead laid away—all without thought from themselves."[49]

Even under pleasant circumstances that Marthasville sometimes offered, slaves did not have easy lives. Every day began the same for Young's field hands. They had only a half hour to eat their breakfast and reach the field from the time Cook's bell tolled. Once time expired, Cook blew a horn as a signal to commence work. Those who failed to reach the field on time suffered ten lashes from Cook's whip. The overseer allowed no exceptions.

William, Joe's older brother, managed to avoid the fate of his relatives in the field at an early age. Shortly after his ninth birthday, he earned a promotion to the "big house" as a servant. The Youngs had welcomed a new addition to the family—William Moore, the son of Sarah Young's brother. The boy's mother died while he was quite young, prompting his father to ask Sarah if she and John would raise him. Eventually, as the youngster grew, Sarah felt the time had arrived when her nephew needed an older playmate to watch him. She called the young slaves together to select one for that purpose.

Joe, William, and the rest of the boys eagerly gathered to try out for the position, a promotion that meant the shedding of a dreaded body-length shirt for a full linen suit and a bed in the "big house." All slave children delegated to the field had to wear the one-piece garment that buttoned only at the neck. . Mistress Young put the boys through a series of rigorous physical tests to see who would win her favor. To judge their strength and endurance she ordered the boys to run, jump, wrestle, turn somersaults, and walk on their hands.

William would feel great pride if selected. Commonly known as a blood relative to his master, having been told he was the offspring of Dr. Young's uncle, George W. Higgins, William noted years later that "being blood kin to master, I felt that I had more at stake than my companions."[50] His fears of not being selected vanished when Sarah Young told him to step from the ranks as the "lucky boy."

Elizabeth soaked, scrubbed, washed, and dried William later that night in anticipation of his departure to the "big house." The next day a new suit arrived at his family's cabin, where Joseph and the other slave children gathered in awe as William dressed. "I was the star of the plantation," William later recalled. Tears streamed down Elizabeth's face as she tenderly placed her callused hands on William's head. As with each of her other children, Elizabeth had carried William as an infant in the fields as she labored beneath the midday sun.

Elizabeth's motherly bonds ran deep. On many occasions she left the fields to tend to her crying children, even at the risk of being whipped. Now she faced the knowledge that one of her beloved would no longer fall asleep each night within her reach.

"I knowed you was born for good luck, for a fortune-teller told me so when you was a baby lyin' in your little sugar trough," said Elizabeth, fighting back tears. "Go up to de great house where you belong."[51]

With that blessing, William bade his siblings farewell and strode from the dirt floor of his family's cabin toward the hardwood floors of the "big house."[52] A part of Elizabeth went with him. So too, likely, did a part of Joe.

No one who witnessed the tearful scene that day could escape the emotional strain that followed. William's absence had a painful effect on their mother, yet they likely learned how to cope from her inner strength. Every slave on Young's farm had to learn how to harness emotions to survive. Verbal outbreaks could mean severe punishment, if not death. Slaves who hoped to survive the oppression carried the burden of silence even in the whirlwind of personal adversity.

Sometimes the whirlwind became overwhelming.

Joe had already been strapped with a number of emotional scars before entering his teenage years. None cut deeper, however, than the day he saw his dear mother whipped. The dreadful occasion happened shortly after William's removal to the "big house," an event that prompted Dr. Young to change William's name to "Sanford" to avoid confusion with the other William now in his care.[53] Elizabeth, ever the steady field hand, failed to reach her station one morning by the time Cook rang his bell. Roughly ten or fifteen minutes passed before Elizabeth hurriedly took her place in the field. When she arrived an outraged Cook unfurled his whip and began flailing away at Elizabeth on the spot.

"Oh! pray," Elizabeth cried, "Oh! pray—Oh! pray."[54]

The crack of Cook's whip and Elizabeth's piercing pleas for mercy carried to every corner of Young's plantation. A few slaves stopped their work to watch. Others turned away to hide their anger, acting as if nothing were wrong. Nearby, from his bunk in the Youngs' house, William recognized his mother's voice and bolted for the door, but he dared venture no farther out of fear for his life. He remained in the doorway weeping. Cold chills rushed over him as he watched helplessly.[55]

Finally, after ten lashes, the sound of the whip ceased. Tears trickled down Elizabeth's cheeks as she staggered across the dirt with blurry eyes to begin her workday.[56]

William slowly returned to his bed, incapable of further sleep and unable to find consolation in his tears.[57] Somewhere on the farm that day, perhaps even by his mother's side, the nine-year-old Joe endured the same helpless feelings as his brother. The innocence of Joe's youth—if such a thing ever existed—surely eroded with each crack of the whip. The brutal hand of the oppressor undoubtedly seared Joe's heart. Instincts took root, and perhaps he vowed to never forget the barbarity he had witnessed. The cruel days to follow would make any such vow easy to keep.

3

CHATTEL

Such is the uncertainty of a slave's life.
—William, Joe's older brother

Joe likely understood nothing at age eleven as well as he did the daily routine. He arose, ate, and started and finished work at designated times. His white oppressors dictated the food he consumed each morning, the clothes he wore, the labor in which he engaged, and the manner in which he performed his duties. Young, his wife, or Cook ultimately judged how well Joe performed his tasks. If they disapproved, the whip sometimes had the final say.

Surely, Joe viewed Young as the most powerful person in his world. Young wielded authority as Joe's master to control every facet of the young slave's life, including life itself. If mighty Randall could be beaten nearly to death for his open defiance, could not the same be done to any of Young's slaves?

Buried deep underneath this life of servitude lay the glimmer of a personal life, or the hope for one. Slaves in Marthasville, as anywhere, lived two lives: one for their masters and one for themselves.

Joe's older brother, William, kept countless thoughts to himself concerning his oppressors. Only later, in privacy, did he discretely bare his true feelings with those he trusted most. Joe probably revealed his bottled emotions in a similar fashion. If not, he mentally endured a Spartan existence. If one thought ever prevailed to comfort Joe, it might have been the certainty that his master could never take his soul. Everything else appeared fair game. Even his loved ones. One scratch of Young's pen across a sales receipt could send Joe or any of his beloved family away forever. Joe would have realized during his adolescence that he was only one bad financial break away from becoming an instant orphan. The notion surely did not escape his thoughts in the tumultuous year of 1826. That was when Young abandoned perhaps the greatest dream he had ever known: Marthasville.

Young celebrated his forty-seventh birthday in 1826, but little else.[1] Money troubles dogged him throughout the year as the recession plaguing Missouri hit home. The problem was simple. Speculators had gobbled large tracts of land on credit following the War of 1812 as business boomed throughout the land. Merchants, likewise, had purchased immense stocks of pricey goods on credit from the East to keep pace with requests. The whole economic climate proved to be only a mirage. Consequently, when credit on land and goods came due, few had the needed cash. Missouri commerce became paralyzed, and Young became mired in the economic quicksand. His actions left little doubt that he began to question his business decisions, perhaps even the wisdom of building his boomtown so deep in Missouri's interior.[2] Marthasville drained him financially, and the aging physician no longer possessed the money or the youthful vigor to nurse it through the tough times. Besides, Young found himself drawn more and more to St. Louis.

A river town on the rise, St. Louis offered Young far more prospects for economic prosperity in his old age. In St. Louis, where many of his friends and political allies lived, patients might be more abundant. Merchandise shipped by steamboat from all corners of the world could be obtained easier and cheaper. And the city's social scene would be more accessible, no longer requiring two rigorous days of travel by carriage from Marthasville across the Missouri River by ferry and then along bumpy dirt roads. Finally there was the issue of Young's investment in human chattel. The doctor could fetch a better price for them in St. Louis or more clients who might be willing to rent his slaves.

Young thus began to prepare for the relocation of his farm. He ventured first in search of land on the outskirts of St. Louis and found the perfect location four miles northwest of the city on Grand Prairie. The site included two tracts of fertile farmland totaling 125 acres.[3] Shortly thereafter, Young returned to Marthasville to gather his furniture, clothing, farm tools, and slaves by the wagonloads. Once everything had been securely packed and the livestock rounded up, Young's party journeyed east across the prairie toward their new home. Eleven years had elapsed since Young's previous move of that magnitude, when he bade Kentucky farewell with his family and stable of slaves in tow.

Missouri Territory had emerged as the newest land of opportunity with its fertile, untapped valleys, major rivers, and pro-slavery legislation. The new laws clearly stated that slaves would be "held, taken, and adjudged to be personal property." Slaves, whether black or mulatto, were universally regarded throughout the territory in the same manner as cattle, horses, or pigs.[4] Slaveholders, now secure in the knowledge that their human chattel would be protected by law, responded by flooding the new territory.

John Mason Peck, an East Coast Baptist minister, watched from a distance before he joined the migration in 1817, one year after Dr. Young's arrival. Peck later wrote, "Some families came in the spring of 1815, but in the winter, summer, and autumn of 1816, they came like an avalanche. . . . It seemed as though Kentucky and Tennessee were breaking up and moving to the 'Far West.' Caravan after caravan passed over the prairies of Illinois, crossing the 'great river' at St. Louis, all bound to the Boone's Lick."[5]

Dr. Young had followed the same route. Well into middle age, Young probably marveled at how he survived such an arduous journey. Rumbling, rocky trails, the constant threat of land pirates, dangerous river crossings—the thought alone could overwhelm. In 1816, when he stood on the banks of the Mississippi, staring across the river at St. Louis for the first time with his family by his side, Young surely felt a rush of excitement as he stared at the most dangerous river crossing he would ever encounter.

John F. Darby, a fellow Kentuckian, had experienced a similar rush on the banks of the Mississippi two years after Young's arrival in the territory. Darby and his family, like the Youngs, had made the trip by land with a considerable stock of cattle, hogs, sheep, and slaves. A large covered wagon driven by one of the family's male slaves led the procession behind a team of five horses. Although only a lad at the time, Darby later remembered the moment his family reached the east bank of the Mississippi. His recollection, probably not unlike that of Young, was clear: "When we . . . saw for the first time the town of St. Louis, it had even then a striking and imposing appearance when viewed from the opposite shore."[6]

Darby recalled:

> The first thing to be done by the movers was to cross the great river; the current was strong, and the waters seemed boiling up from the bottom, and in places turbid and muddy. The ferry consisted of a small keel-boat, which was managed entirely by Frenchmen . . . [who] with great vivacity and animation talked, cursed, and swore in French so that the enterprise seemed a dangerous and hazardous undertaking. Nevertheless these trusty oarsmen brought us safely to the shore.[7]

Undoubtedly, this is how Joe had encountered the Mississippi for the first time, in 1816—rocking aboard a keelboat with river water splashing his body. Back then he was a mere infant, probably carried in a bundle on his mother's back or by an elder sibling or one of Young's black nursemaids. In 1826, Joe experienced the adventure through the eyes of a boy already intimately acquainted with the stark difference between pleasure and pain. Marthasville gave him both, and he may have had mixed emotions as he departed its humble surroundings. Marthasville, for better or worse, had been home.

Beyond the valley floor, to his rear, rose the silhouette of the tiny town atop a shelf of white rock. If Joe took in the view even for a second, he might have peered into the very window of his soul. Marthasville is where he had taken his first steps, where he had uttered his first words, and where he had grown to see laughter and misery coexist in the oppressive world of slavery. Every experience there had helped define who he had become.

Part of his past would remain there—along with the gravesites of those left behind, plots that would go unattended as months slipped into years. Two other graves lay somewhere in Kentucky, those belonging to Joe's brothers, Solomon and Benjamin. Both died prior to the family's removal to Missouri.[8]

As Marthasville disappeared from the horizon, all who stole one final peek probably felt a sense of loss—slaves included. Not all their memories of Marthasville were bad. Some recollections were, in fact, hilarious. Who would ever forget the suspenseful showdown between Grove
Cook and Dinkie? Cook had just been appointed Dr. Young's new overseer. On his first day in Marthasville, Cook appeared in the field to take
inventory of the slaves now in his charge. He inspected each slave thoroughly, men and women alike, with all the astuteness of a veteran cat-
tleman or horse trader. His reputation as a "hard overseer," a man who
could deliver large quantities of produce, had preceded him, and the
slaves had spoken with dread in the days and weeks prior to his arrival.
On this day, shortly before dismissing the slaves, Cook saw Dinkie exit
his cabin.

"Who is that nigger?" inquired Cook as he gazed at the large-framed
African.

"That is Dinkie," Dr. Young responded.

"What is his place?" Cook asked.

"Oh," Dr. Young said matter-of-factly, "Dinkie is a gentleman at large!"

Cook, perhaps stunned by the doctor's response, pushed the issue further. "Have you any objection to his working?"

"None, whatever."

"Well, sir," Cook said, "I'll put him to work tomorrow morning."

That would be something new. Dinkie enjoyed freedoms on Young's
plantation that no other slave would ever hope to obtain. The mysterious African showed up at the table for every meal and then went about
his business, oblivious to the world around him. He hunted, slept, wandered through the woods, and came and went from the farm as he
pleased without objection or question. No one ever recalled a time when
Dinkie did any work. By all accounts, Dinkie was truly his own master.
Whites in the area tipped their hats whenever the one-eyed African
passed, slave patrollers never questioned him, and his presence struck
fear in other blacks. They knew him as "Uncle Dinkie," a master fortune-
teller, a man whose mystic powers sprung from his voodoo faith. Once
a man had offered to buy Dinkie from Dr. Young, who, as the story goes,
jumped at the opportunity to rid himself of the old conjurer. The man
returned Dinkie the next day and threatened to bring a lawsuit against
the doctor for damages.

Cook, however, knew nothing of this reputation. At roll call the next morning all slaves were present—all except Dinkie. Cook, demanding to know the old conjurer's whereabouts, was informed that he was still asleep. Miffed by Dinkie's blatant insubordination, Cook angrily replied, "I'll bring him out of his bed in a hurry." He then marched straight toward Dinkie's cabin, only to have the old African appear at his door just as the overseer approached.

"Follow me to the barn," Cook ordered. "I make it a point always to whip a nigger the first day that I take charge of a farm, so as to let the hands know who I am. And, now, Mr. Dinkie, they tell me that you have not had your back tanned for many years; and, that being the case, I shall give you a flogging that you will never forget. Follow me to the barn."

As Cook detoured to retrieve his whip from his cabin, Dinkie turned ominously toward the stunned group of slaves and declared, "Ef he lays the weight ob his finger on me, you'll see de top of dat barn come off."

Cook then emerged from his cabin carrying not just a whip in one hand but a club in the other. "Follow me," he ordered, prompting many of the field hands to gasp. The two men entered the barn as the slaves watched the door close behind them. No one spoke. All of Young's slaves—Joe included—knew of Dinkie's voodoo powers. Now they stood outside the barn with hearts pounding.

Dr. Young, anticipating the showdown, had awakened early and the slaves could see him peering out his bedroom window. William later recalled the unforgettable scene: "The news that Dinkie was to be whipped spread far and near over the place, and had called forth men, women, and children. Even Uncle Ned, the old Negro of ninety years, had crawled out of his straw and was at his cabin door. As the doors closed behind the overseer and Dinkie, a death-like silence pervaded the entire group, who, instead of going to their labor, as ordered by the driver, were standing as if paralyzed, gazing intently at the barn, expecting every moment to see the roof lifted."

The roof never moved. Nor did any lips. Only Uncle Ned spoke. Shaking his head and smiling, the elder said, "My word fer it, de oberseer ain't agwine to whip Dinkie."

Fifteen minutes passed, and still no one heard a thing. No whip. No cries. No argument. Nothing but silence. Soon the older slaves began to gather around Uncle Ned, who shared a cabin with Dinkie. They quietly pressed him for information. Uncle Ned told them how Dinkie had stayed up most of the previous night in anticipation of his show-down with Cook. Uncle Ned said that Dinkie, with his snakeskin by his side, had knelt and prayed to Satan.

The sound of the barn door opening shattered the suspense. Cook and Dinkie walked out together, side by side, before parting ways. Cook strode to the field, Dinkie to his cabin. Uncle Ned's hunch proved cor-rect. Cook had not whipped Dinkie, whose victory over the overseer left the slaves shaking their heads in wonderment. How had Dinkie avoided a whipping? No one dared ask the ever-intimidating conjurer. Nor did they expect this man of few words to divulge what had taken place be-hind those closed doors.

In the days that followed, the great mystery took on a life of its own. Day after day, different slaves tried to pry information from Uncle Ned concerning the affair, but Ned remained mum. Then one night Young's cook, Nancy, burst into the kitchen, choked with excitement. She had just returned from Uncle Ned's cabin, where she had fallen into his graces with a freshly baked batch of "crackling bread." Greatly pleased with the treat, the elder had told her what he had learned from Dinkie.

Now the news spread from one cabin to the next. Slaves soon crowded into the kitchen to hear how Dinkie had escaped the flogging. Nancy ordered the door closed, and the usually boisterous cook now spoke in a whisper.

"When dey got in de barn," she said, "de oberseer said to Dinkie, 'Strip yourself; I don't want to tear your clothes with my whip. I'm going to tear your black skin.'

"Den, you see, Dinkie tole de oberseer to look in de east corner ob de barn. He looked, an' he saw hell, wid all de torments, an' de debble, wid his cloven foot, a-struttin' about dar, jes as ef he was cock ob de walk. An' Dinkie tole Cook, dat ef he lay his finger on him, he'd call de debble up to take him away."

Jim, interrupting, anxiously asked, "An' what did Cook say to dat?"

"Let me 'lone," Nancy snapped. "I didn't tell you all. Den you see de oberseer turn pale in de face, an' he say to Dinkie, 'Let me go dis time, and I'll nebber trouble you any more.' "

And, much to everyone's amusement, Cook never did lay so much as a finger on Dinkie during his five years as overseer.[9]

Dinkie also found himself at the center of another memorable Marthasville episode: a coon hunt. The story revolved around a young St. Louis man whom Dr. Young had invited to stay overnight at the farm. The man, an urban dandy, expressed great delight in his country visit and insisted on participating in a real outdoor adventure. He wanted to go on an authentic coon hunt.

Dr. Young, due to his lame leg, sent Ike, Cato, and Sam in his place to oblige his overenthusiastic guest. The young man fell into expert company, for the three servants enjoyed a reputation as Marthasville's best coon hunters. At nightfall the hunt began with a pack of coon dogs leading the way into the woods. The dogs picked up the scent of game thirty minutes into the hunt, further exciting the young visitor, who dashed recklessly through the night armed with a double-barrel pistol and a determination to experience a victorious hunt. Plowing through brush and hurdling logs, the four men pressed forward. They faithfully followed the barking dogs until Ike, Cato, and Sam came to an abrupt stop. Suddenly, the dogs sounded the alarm with short yelps.

The game had been "treed," but Ike, Cato, and Sam instantly sounded another alarm: "Polecat, polecat; get out de way!" The three promptly fled from the tree. Unfazed, the gentleman from the city boldly stepped forward with his pistol, held it aloft, and stared up in search of the "treed" critter. A black-and-white animal appeared a moment later, and the man instantly squeezed the trigger. A shot rang out in the dark, missing its target but revealing to the man the true identity of the animal. He stared up at a skunk—an irritated one—that answered back as only skunks can, raining an odor down on the man like nothing he had ever smelled before in his life.

Now he stood in misery, covered head to toe with the ungodly scent. "Come, let's go home," the unhappy man said quietly. "I've got enough of coon-hunting."

Ike, Cato, and Sam dared not laugh in the face of a white man, but their mirth could only be suppressed for so long. The party's return home prompted hearty laughter across the farm as the city man now found himself the focal point of everyone's amusement. The humiliation continued, much to the delight of the slaves. Cackling servants escorted the man to the barn, where he disrobed and underwent a thorough scrubbing. Still, the foul odor prevailed, and due to the disagreeable smell he had to spend the night in the barn.

At breakfast the next morning, all pondered how they might rid the man of the nasty odor. Finally, they called on Dinkie. The old African studied the man—and his smell—before concluding that it would be a difficult task. The man handed Dinkie a Mexican silver dollar and asked him to do his best. Dinkie smiled and put his plan into motion.

A large pit was dug. Dinkie ordered the man to remove his clothing and step inside the pit, where he was covered up to his neck in fresh dirt. His clothes were buried in another pit. Dinkie sat over the miserable man with an umbrella throughout the day, fanning his protruding head from time to time as needed. Servants removed the man from the pit after eight hours had elapsed. All agreed with Dinkie that the man "smelt sweeter," but a portion of the foul odor still persisted. Dinkie thus ordered the man back into the pit for another five hours the next day. The sight of the submerged city fellow caused great merriment among the slaves. Even Uncle Ned, the superannuated slave who seldom left his cabin, hobbled from his dwelling to see the spectacle.

Each evening, talk inside the slave cabins revolved almost exclusively around the young fellow's misfortune. Hoots and hollers could be heard echoing from the slave quarters throughout the night. Finally, after the additional five hours in the pit, Dinkie rubbed the man down and proclaimed him fit to return to St. Louis. The man eventually departed Marthasville, leaving behind a trail of laughter.[10]

None of Young's slaves knew what awaited them at the new farm. Some may have wondered if they would even make it that far. Slaves realized that they could be sold at any time without warning, perhaps at a roadside tavern to pay a bill or to any of the slave traders canvassing the region for fresh "bucks" and strong black women to send south. "Such is the uncertainty of a slave's life," William solemnly lamented later in life.[11] He spoke from experience.

A slave trader once stopped by Dr. Young's in search of new stock. With Young's blessing, the man thoroughly inspected two field hands, Sam and Sally. He questioned each slave extensively, checked Sam's teeth, and purchased both on the spot for $1,900. Hannah, the slave married to Sam, became an instant widow. William later saw firsthand how hard his fellow house servant received the news.[12]

Whispers of Young's mounting debts and the recession now fueled the slaves' anxiety. Talk of a master's financial troubles almost always led to sales and auctions. One former slave eloquently related: "Intelligent colored people of my circle of acquaintance as a general thing felt *no security whatever for their family ties*. Some, it is true, who belonged to rich families felt some security, but those of us who looked deeper and knew how many were not rich that seemed so, and saw how fast the money slipped away, were always miserable. The trader was all around, the slave pens at hand, and we didn't know what time any of us might be in it."[13]

In Missouri, as with other export states of the upper South, that threat constantly hung overhead like a black cloud. The slave trade was entrenched in St. Louis, a booming port that fed the agricultural South and the Mexican province of Texas with everything from Pennsylvania iron to steamboats laden with slaves. It was a trade that daily turned children into orphans, husbands and wives into widows and widowers, and lovers into lonely, bitter people.

Thousands of slaves left the St. Louis riverfront never to be seen or heard from again by family and friends. They were, as their survivors often put it, victims who were "sold down river" to await certain death on some distant slave plantation. Generally, blacks were shipped to New Orleans, where buyers from Alabama, Arkansas, Mississippi, Louisiana, and Texas scouted slave pens for laborers to plant and harvest their crops. In their wake, these unfortunate souls left behind other unfortunate souls in an extensive web of tragedy.

Amid this madness, Joe forged toward manhood.

On the road between Marthasville and Young's new farm outside St. Louis, Joe had more than enough time to reflect on his own family's vulnerability. Joe already knew the dull ache of total loss, having grieved the deaths of his two older brothers. One loss appeared even greater—one in which a relative disappeared into the slave market, alive, but forever gone.

The early days on Young's new farm perhaps foretold Joe's fate. Each new sunrise seemed to bring more change, including the introduction of a new overseer named Friend Haskell. Young's slaves undoubtedly celebrated the departure of the ruthless Cook, but only briefly.[14] Haskell, a Yankee from New England, proved every bit as mean as his notorious predecessor. William expressed how he felt about Haskell later in life when he remarked, "The Yankees are noted for making the most cruel overseers."[15] Haskell apparently did nothing to change that stereotype.

Young, in turn, did nothing to change Haskell. His inaction spoke volumes. The troubled doctor obviously had other issues on his mind he deemed far more important, namely money matters. Financial woes left Young in search of new business ventures. Before long he turned to his stable of slaves for part of the solution. He decided to engage in the popular practice of leasing slaves, plucking Joe's mother Elizabeth and brother William from among the plantation's ranks. The doctor hired out both to St. Louis residents.[16]

Joe's whereabouts at this time are unknown, but for the first time in his life, his family had been divided by distance. This heart-wrenching state of affairs worsened whenever they received word concerning one another's condition.

William, by now a polished house servant, spared no detail when relating his horrific experiences in the city. Young rented William first to a Major Freeland, who ran a public house. William described the former Virginian as "a horse-racer, cock-fighter, gambler, and withal an inveterate drunkard."[17]

William said ten or twelve servants tended to the major's house, and when Freeland was present, "it was cut and slash—knock down and drag out." William explained how, in his fits of anger, Freeland would take up a chair and throw it at a servant. In his more rational moments, when he wished to chastise one, he would tie one up in the smokehouse and administer a whipping, after which he would make a fire of tobacco stems and then leave the slave behind in the smoky room. Freeland called this "Virginia Play."[18]

When William marched to his master with complaints of Freeland's treatment of him, Young ordered William to return to Freeland at once. "He cared nothing about it," William said of Young, "so long as he received the money for my labor."[19]

Roughly six months later, William reached a breaking point. He determined no longer to endure Freeland's abuse and without much thought, ran into the woods behind St. Louis to make his escape. At nightfall he made his way to Young's farm on Grand Prairie, only to be overtaken by fear. If Haskell discovered him he knew he would be carried back to the brutal hand of Freeland. Minus a plan, William remained hidden in the woods for days.

Then one day he heard the barking and howling of dogs nearby. He knew they were the bloodhounds of Maj. Benjamin O'Fallon, who always kept five or six dogs around to hunt runaway slaves. Escape became futile. William concluded he would take refuge atop a tree and await his punishment. Before an hour had passed, O'Fallon's hounds were barking and clawing at the base of the tree. Two hunters approached. The men ordered William to descend, tied his hands, and escorted him to the St. Louis jail.

Freeland soon appeared and ordered William to follow him home. On their return, Freeland tied William up in the smokehouse and whipped him severely. He then sent his son, Robert, to the smokehouse with instructions to finish the punishment. Robert Freeland gathered tobacco stems. He started a fire, prompting William to cough and sneeze. Once William had been "smoked" sufficiently, Robert untied him and sent him back to work.[20]

William continued to supply Joe and the rest of his family with other accounts of the brutalities he had witnessed or suffered. Much to William's pleasure, Major Freeland's business failed and Young hired William out to the steamboat *Missouri*. William B. Culver commanded the boat, which plied between St. Louis and Galena, Illinois, and as far south as New Orleans.[21] William worked aboard the *Missouri* through the sailing season, calling it "the most pleasant time for me that I had ever experienced."[22]

Young eventually forced William to depart Culver's company for that of a new boss, John Colburn, keeper of the Missouri Hotel. Colburn operated one of the largest hotels in the city, supported by twenty to thirty servants, most of them slaves. "He [Colburn] was from one of the free states," William noted, "but a more inveterate hater of the Negro I do not believe ever walked God's green earth. . . . Mr. Culburn was very abusive."[23]

One incident that always bothered William involved a slave named Aaron, who belonged to the popular St. Louis attorney John F. Darby. Aaron cleaned knives at the hotel. One day Colburn discovered a knife on a table that was not as clean as he desired. Colburn promptly tied Aaron in the woodshed and gave him more than fifty lashes on his bare back with a strap of cowhide. He then ordered William to then wash Aaron down with rum, a treatment William thought "put him into more agony than the whipping."[24]

Aaron returned to his master with complaints of Colburn's abusive behavior. Darby, like Young, paid the slave no heed and sent him back to the hotel. Colburn soon learned of Aaron's complaints to his master. Enraged, Colburn again tied Aaron up and rendered an even more severe beating than the one before. Aaron, his back cut into pieces, could not return to work for nearly two weeks.

In another incident, Colburn tied up a slave girl named Patsey one night and whipped her fiercely until the boarders emerged from their rooms and begged him to stop. Patsey's offense involved Colburn's infatuation with her. As William explained, Patsey was engaged to marry a slave named John, who was owned by Maj. William Christy. Colburn forbade Patsey from seeing John. On this night, Patsey had returned from a meeting with John. Colburn intended to flog John had he taken one step onto his property, but the slave knew the temper of his white rival. He remained outside Colburn's enclosure. Hence Colburn unleashed his anger on poor Patsey.[25]

William told one woeful story after another. His message rang clear: A slave's life was no life. Money dictated with whom a slave lived and where, and the oppressor determined nearly everything else. A change in ownership, overseer, or renter amounted to Russian roulette. Every slave—Joe included—feared being leased or sold. Often they dreaded it as much as death.

Joe surely felt that trauma the day he found out that Young had sold him, his mother, his sister, and his brother Millford to Isaac Mansfield of St. Louis. William, still residing at Colburn's Missouri Hotel at the time, mourned the sale as if they had died.[26] Mansfield owned a tin-manufacturing plant on the riverfront. A native of Connecticut, he had big financial and political ambitions. An avid traveler, he also had an eye on opportunities outside Missouri.[27] Now he was Joe's new master, whether the youngster liked it or not. For his life was not his own.

4

St. Louis

And that servant, which knew his lord's will, and
prepared not himself, neither did according to his will,
shall be beaten with many stripes.
—Luke 12:47

Far in the distance, as if from the bowels of the mighty river's soul, would arise a deep, moaning whistle above the din of noise along the riverfront. The distinct sound was unmistakable to locals but always a curiosity to the naive ears of a newcomer. Again the soulful whistle would moan, and yet again the Mississippi divulged nothing of its secret. The deafening silence of anticipation drowned the riverfront's chaos, if only for a few moments. Then, emerging from the river's dense tree line upstream, would appear the unforgettable sight: a magnificent vessel—a steamboat—gliding into full view with its giant wooden paddles churning river water on both sides. Sooty smoke would belch from crowned, metal stacks while fiery sparks drifted down around the passengers.

Flags flapped in the wind, and music echoed from the decks, competing with the rumblings of the steam engines below. Large crates, barrels, and kegs full of whiskey, fruits, and other cargo crowded the main deck with occasional livestock among the common passengers and, at times, chained slaves en route to a distant southern market.[1]

St. Louis harbored dozens of steamboats weekly in the late 1820s when Joe arrived in the city with his new master, Isaac Mansfield. Probably for the first time in his life, Joe gazed upon these majestic steamboats in awe. Never before had he seen anything like them, certainly not in the rural sanctuary of Marthasville, though he may have heard them from that locale.

Joe found much still foreign to him in the world. Languages of all kinds could be heard along the rough limestone ledge that ran along the riverfront. People both black and white spoke fluent French, words that must have reminded Joe of the La Charette descendants back home at Marthasville. The voices speaking Spanish mixed with those of friendly American Indians, as well as a variety of strange English dialects from merchants, trappers, and travelers passing through St. Louis night and day.

Some voices invoked chills. Joe would have become familiar with the gruff, barking orders of men overseeing large groups of shackled slaves— men he would soon recognize as slave traders, or, as slaves themselves aptly branded them, "soul drivers."[2]

Keelboats, flatboats, steamboats, and private skiffs routinely crowded the water's edge for access along the levee. Sun-bronzed rivermen and brawny slaves combed the riverfront, loading and unloading the region's real bonanza—the array of exotic cargo that flowed along the web of western waterways draining into the Mississippi.

On any given day Joe could watch crews unload spiced oysters from Virginia, sugar from New Orleans, coffee from Havana, flour from Ohio, stationery from Philadelphia, whiskey from Kentucky, or wine from France. The riverfront offered a smorgasbord of merchandise and produce: barrels of salted pork, boxes of beaver and wool hats, bales of cotton, kegs of gunpowder, gin, candlesticks, tea, tools, cutlery, smoked beef, dried fruits, mules, horses, and slaves.[3]

St. Louis defined variety, and that variety seemed endless as the city promised to burst out of its frontier image. Its unsophisticated recent past, however, would make its crude image hard to shake. Only a decade earlier, in 1819, James Haley White (then a lad of fourteen), had seen

St. Louis in a much different light: "The appearance of St. Louis was not calculated to make a favorable impression upon the first visit, with its long dirty and quick-sand beach, numbers of long empty keel boats tied to stakes driven in the sand, squads of idle boatmen passing to and fro, here and there numbers pitching quoits; others running foot races; rough and tumble fights; and shooting at a target."[4]

Those dark days now began to fade with the rapid progress. St. Louis grew quickly, threatening to evolve into a regular river metropolis. One Eastern businessman credited frontier expansion with the boom, noting, "The best business is jobbing to the country merchants, who get most of their supplies from this place, particularly from this state. More merchants from Illinois to N. York for goods. This city is the only market short of New Orleans."[5]

Pierre Laclède Liguest first saw its promise in 1763, when he selected the site for the center of his fur-trading enterprise. The locale offered easy access for boat landings, nearby springs, abundant timber, and relatively level ground atop a small hill or bluff where settlers could reside and still be guarded against floods. Laclède planned to use the exclusive rights he had obtained from the French governor at New Orleans to trade with the Indians west of the Mississippi. He felt certain the site would flourish in time.[6]

By 1829, most likely the year Isaac Mansfield purchased Joe, Laclède's hunch was proving brilliant.[7] Everywhere along the river, people and equipment seemed in motion. Bulky drays, carts, wagons, and "pleasure" carriages came to and fro constantly.[8] Steamboats arrived and departed regularly, sometimes as many as eight or more in a day.[9] Each time a steamboat floated into sight, people flocked to the riverfront in large numbers, eagerly awaiting the arrival of passengers, merchandise, and news. Citizens herded down to the boat landing in droves through a pathway carved from the limestone bluff that paralleled the river. The path began at the foot of Vine and Market—the main east–west streets—and offered the best route for locals who had to haul barrels of drinking water from the river.[10] By day Market Street generally teemed with life on a square where a one-story brick building served as a market house. Brick pillars supported the building, which featured stalls for butchers and stands for farmers and gardeners to sell their fresh produce.[11] Nearly all of the city's inhabitants purchased their produce from these vendors, and Joe likely purchased cuts of wild game, fruits, and vegetables here for Mansfield, or perhaps for his family with money they could earn on their own time.[12]

Joe probably also caught a glimpse of the city's rougher side. Taverns overflowed with traveling gamblers, restless trappers, slave speculators, and a motley assemblage of riverfront hacks. None made a bigger impression on tavern patrons, however, than the bawdy mountain men. They were a rough and vulgar lot, and, fresh from summer campaigns, always the undisputed "life and terror" of St. Louis. One man recalled how these adventurers "told tales of the wilds with graphic and inspiring enthusiasm."[13]

Joe heard and saw a little of everything in St. Louis, where black children might speak fluent French and free black men could by law walk the streets with firearms fastened to their bodies.[14] He might have even been among those younger slaves permitted to attend schools taught by Baptist minister John Mason Peck.[15]

Variety became the city's trademark. People indulged in everything from horse racing to whore houses, and in 1829, a U.S. mail stage between St. Louis and Louisville rolled into service.[16] St. Louis residents enjoyed theater that arrived seasonally with a cast sent via steamboat, and winter meant another favorite pastime: sleighing over the icy countryside beyond the city's limits.[17] Amid this bustle stood Joe. The country slave who had barely reached his teenage years could not help but notice the blur of activity. For now he lived at the heartbeat of it all.

Mansfield opened tin plant and store on March 9, 1829, along North Main Street. The narrow street ran parallel to the levee and had emerged as the city's primary thoroughfare by the time Mansfield arrived.[18] From this location, the Connecticut native and his newly purchased servants had a bird's-eye view of traffic along the waterfront, and they were close enough to smell musky hides and the fishy odor that drifted from the wharf. Mansfield could not have chosen a better spot in the entire city. Nearly all of the city's major business was conducted on Main Street. Sellers, buyers, speculators—all were present and ready to strike a deal at a moment's notice.[19]

Up and down Main Street, Joe surely encountered interesting people, such as Gabriel Helms, a black who ran the city's first barbershop.

Joe would have also seen old Gen. William Clark, who lived on the corner of Main and Vine. Clark housed a large collection of Indian and mineral curiosities at his home. Indians who called him "Great Father" visited often.

Then there was Daniel D. Page, whose home and bakery stood on the east side of Main. Locals seldom found him at that location, though. Page loaded his freshly baked bread into a horse-drawn cart each morning and wandered the dirt and stone streets in search of customers. Locals knew Page was near whenever they heard the ring of a bell the baker carried to announce his arrival.[20]

Main Street, without coincidence, also housed the city's wealthiest families.[21] Col. Auguste Chouteau, the man who had cleared the site for St. Louis, lived in the most luxurious mansion of them all. His house fronted the market square, covering parts of Main, Market, and Walnut Streets, with stone walls two feet thick and ten feet high. The walls featured portholes every ten feet, made to shoot through in case of Indian attack.

Chouteau's mansion resembled a castle. "The floors of the house were made of black walnut, and were polished so finely that they reflected like a mirror," recalled John F. Darby, a friend and frequent visitor to the Chouteau abode. "He had a train of servants, and every morning after breakfast some of these inmates of his household were down on their knees for hours, with brushes and wax, keeping the floors polished."[22]

This is the St. Louis that Joe saw in those early days—the free man's St. Louis, swirling around outside Chouteau's mansion. Several warehouses were being built on the levee, while workers converted numerous private homes on Main Street into stores. Consequently, many of the street's older families began to move to outlying areas, and wealthy estates popped up there overnight. In years past, visitors had remarked on the city's French architecture as being beautiful, then had described it after close inspection as "native meanness." Early settlers had plastered a white coat of lime over the mud or rough stone walls of their dwellings.[23] From a distance this whitewashing gave St. Louis a brilliant allure.[24] Now that characteristic faded with progress.

Brickyards started to emerge to keep pace with the new construction. Brick by brick, Joe witnessed new buildings and homes rising throughout the downtown district in place of the older stone structures. The building spurt also obliterated the early Spanish courtyards that had accompanied numerous early homes. Sometimes entire lots similar to Chouteau's accommodated vegetable gardens, but one by one, those lots disappeared as commercial real estate demands escalated.[25]

The forty-three-year-old Mansfield, meanwhile, cast his lot into the St. Louis boom for better or worse. He did so with unhesitant aggression. With Mansfield having brokered a deal to purchase the stock of copper and tin manufacturer W. Walter & Company, his North Main location boasted all sizes of "Stills, Hatters, Wash, Stew and Tea Kettles" and a wide assortment of iron, copper, and tinware.[26]

Mansfield quickly established himself as a reputable tinner at seemingly the most opportune time in the city's history.[27] He even landed a contract with the U.S. government for tinwork at nearby Jefferson Barracks, where five to six thousand feet of work needed to be done. The steady flow of labor kept Mansfield busier than desired, but he realized it provided a good avenue to spread his name about town. Mansfield privately had other ambitions on his mind, and he mingled with any and all who would lend him a friendly ear in his hope of laying a solid foundation for a political career.[28]

Mansfield appeared to have all the ingredients to make a political up-and-comer, with a popular business, a growing list of friends, ambition, and, above all, money. Relatively few business owners possessed the means of Mansfield to secure prime real estate on North Main Street, where lots sold as high as $120 per storefront foot.[29] That fact alone suggested a status few in the area could claim. Now Mansfield also owned five new black servants to complete the picture of success. Whether the image could hold under the fire of a political campaign would be tested later. For now, he had hands to shake, ears to bend, and dollars to earn.

Meanwhile, Mansfield kept an eye on the prospect of immigration to the Mexican province of Texas. Promising reports seemed to drift upriver daily about this land of opportunity, where more and more people believed they could strike it rich. In Mansfield's tinning circle, one common thought prevailed: a fortune could be made with little effort in Texas.[30]

Ambition, however, is not all that defined Mansfield. By mid-1829, a county judge had appointed Mansfield the legal guardian of Allen C. Turner, described as "a person of unsound mind, and not capable of managing with ordinary prudence his own affairs."[31] Mansfield accepted the responsibility without complaint, adding one more element to his already diverse and busy lifestyle. By 1830, Mansfield housed eleven other people in his home. A U.S. Census worker took the head count while passing through the upper ward of the city, noting that Mansfield lived with six other males. Five of those were between the ages of twenty and thirty, while one was between the ages of fifteen and twenty.[32] The worker also listed two female slaves, one between the ages of twenty-four and thirty-six (Elizabeth) and the other under ten (Elizabeth's infant daughter, also named Elizabeth). The absence of any male slaves on the census report suggests that Joe and Millford were being rented at that time.[33] Another interesting notation is the presence of three free people of color in Mansfield's household. One was a female between the ages of twenty-four and thirty-six, while the other two were listed between the ages of ten and twenty-four.[34]

Life treated Mansfield quite well in St. Louis, where hope and prosperity flirted with him daily. Perched above the wharf, Mansfield could stand in front of his property, look down on the mighty Mississippi, and dream dreams he never would have imagined back home in Connecticut. St. Louis, despite all its frontier trappings, provided that kind of magic. But it was magic reserved solely for the free man. Unquestionably, Joe viewed St. Louis in stark contrast to the view of his new master. Joe identified with St. Louis probably in much the same way as those slaves who polished Chouteau's black walnut floors on their hands and knees each morning. Or perhaps he related to those fellow bondsmen who labored relentlessly on the levee day after day in Missouri's smothering summer heat and humidity. Or those herded into local slave pens like animals to be inspected by prodding speculators and planters. Those slaves were paraded before swarms of prospective buyers, likely destined to die on some distant southern plantation. "One of our neighbors at St. Louis . . . flogged his slaves in public streets, with untiring arm," observed one German visitor of that era. "Sometimes he stopped a moment to rest, and then began anew."[35]

This was the St. Louis that Joe grew to know—a city where local newspapers routinely advertised "CASH FOR NEGROES," or as one chilling notice publicized: "For Sale or Barter, a Negro Woman and Her Child."[36] On any given day Joe could walk down the narrow city streets, pass an auction house, and hear the voice of an auctioneer cry out: "How much is offered for this woman? She is a good cook, good washer, a good, obedient servant. She has got religion!"[37]

Slaves considered it amusing that any buyer would seriously care whether a slave had religion. Yet they did. Missouri slaveholders frequently preached about how their slaves must always be obedient to their masters or else face the lash of the whip. They declared this required behavior biblically founded, and they wielded scripture to support this teaching among their slaves. John Young, Joe's former master, often quoted the Bible to impress this belief among his own slaves, and he cited the gospel of Luke.[38] There it was plainly written: "That servant, which knew his lord's will, and prepared not himself, neither did according to his will, shall be beaten with many stripes."[39] Young stood as a pillar in his church as well as a respected member of St. Louis society. Neither fact was ever lost to Joe and his family.[40]

Travelers visiting St. Louis often remembered the city for its majestic steamboats, bustling riverfront, lucrative fur trade, and picturesque skyline. Slaves knew the city for its whips, chains, handcuffs, bloodhounds, "soul drivers," slave pens, and auction houses. Above all, those who survived slavery remembered the tears.

All routes leading from St. Louis, whether on land or river, presented the potential division of slave families. Slave buyers and sellers came and went from St. Louis in droves, routinely carting off someone's mother, father, daughter, or son. An individual's future could be decided in a matter of moments on an auction stand. One such case took place at the notorious St. Louis auction house of Austin & Savage around the time Joe lived in the city. William, Joe's older brother, witnessed the cruel scene with intense interest and empathy for the helpless couple involved.

A black male slave and his wife were being sold separately. The man was auctioned first, and within minutes he found himself the property of the highest bidder. Auctioneers then ordered his wife to ascend the platform, which she did silently with tear-soaked cheeks.

"Master, if you will only buy Fanny, I know you will get the worth of your money," her husband pleaded to his new owner. "She is a good cook, a good washer, and her last mistress liked her very much. If you will only buy her how happy I shall be."[41]

The new master replied that he was not interested unless she sold cheaply, and the husband watched in anguish as the bidding began. Different people bid on his wife, and finally, the master offered a bid, much to the delight of his nervous slave. Yet the anguish and tears returned as another soon placed a higher bid. This tide of cruelty ended unhappily: the wife was sold to another slaveholder. Once the couple realized that the sale was final, the two burst into tears. Stunned and heartbroken, the man approached his wife as she descended the auction stand. Tenderly he took her hands. "Well, Fanny, we are to part forever, on earth," he said, tears coursing his cheeks. "You have been a good wife to me. I did all that I could to get my new master to buy you; but he did not want you, and all I have to say is, I hope you will try to meet me in heaven. I shall try to meet you there." Tears welled in eyes throughout the crowd, regardless of skin color.[42]

Joe saw St. Louis through similar eyes—eyes seasoned by grief and sharpened by the hope of a free future. Joe did not have to look far for the inspiration that someday he might stand as a free man. All he had to do was glance across the river at the free soil of Illinois a half mile away. Escape now became real for the first time in Joe's young life. Elder bondsmen secretly told stories about fugitive slaves who had passed successfully through St. Louis, leaving a trail of hope for those who dared to follow. Some of the storytellers related wild tales of how runaways hid beneath the city streets in a network of secret caves. The fleeing slaves were then smuggled safely across the river under the cover of darkness, or so the legends held.

The caves were no invention. A series of natural caves, most unknown to St. Louis society in 1829, did indeed lie beneath the city's streets. There, under the very slave pens that corralled human lives, fugitive slaves found temporary refuge in their flight for freedom.[43] Joe probably knew of their existence.[44] If so, he may have found comfort each time he glanced at the ground, perhaps even envisioning his own break for freedom someday. The young slave may have also imagined a daring swim across the Mississippi or even stowing away on a steamboat. On the levee, Joe would have seen a lantern bobbing in the blackness of the night near a shanty at a ghostly place called Illinoistown. The lone structure on the other side of the river—a shack—housed the French ferry workers. A thickly wooden terrain covered the rest of the riverbank.[45] Ferrymen faced fines double the cost of a slave plus any additional expenses incurred if they carried one across the Mississippi without a special permit.[46]

Freedom would not come as simply as reaching the opposite riverbank. Crossing the river merely meant the beginning of a desperate struggle for life. In 1825, Missouri slave codes instituted the practice of slave patrols to keep fugitives to a minimum. These patrollers combed the countryside to monitor the day-to-day movements of slaves.[47] Bounty hunters and their trained bloodhounds tracked runaways over great distances. When the dogs succeeded, the slave's only hope for survival sometimes hinged on the refuge of a large tree. Otherwise, the slave faced the probability of being mauled by the frenzied canines before the bounty hunters even arrived.

Privately, Joe and his family talked extensively of escape.[48] William recounted the many opportunities he had seen while working aboard the steamboat *Missouri*, noting in detail how a slave could easily slip away in the sea of people at certain ports. But his love of family kept him anchored in slavery. Escape meant leaving behind the people he cherished most in the world—perhaps forever.

Further, a successful swim across the Mississippi certainly was not a given. People drowned all the time in Chouteau's pond, where his flour mill stood, let alone in the mighty river, where cold temperatures, swift undertows, and whirlpools often proved unforgiving.[49] Surely Joe found the riptide of slavery just as frightening.

5

THIS SIDE OF THE GRAVE

God be with you!
—Elizabeth, Joe's mother

J oe watched blacks disappear each day "downriver," being shipped, one by one, soul by soul, to the market in New Orleans. So common was the scene in Missouri ports like Hannibal and St. Louis that most passengers hardly noticed large shipments of slaves, despite the noisy stir their clanking chains created.[1]

The St. Louis riverfront served as a stage where slavery's daily dramas unfolded in heart-wrenching fashion. It was a place where children were ripped from the hands of mothers, where those in chains struggled to breathe as they said goodbye to loved ones for the last time on Earth. Alexander Hamilton, a slave who lived in St. Louis at the same time as Joe, later testified to the many sad acts he had seen on the Mississippi's banks. He recounted those scenes years later as a freeman in Canada. Hamilton fled St. Louis at eighteen in 1834, but not before witnessing enough human suffering to last a lifetime. He knew one black man who had chopped off the fingers on his left hand with an ax to prevent his sale downriver. He had seen St. Louis authorities dissect the body of another slave he had known, a man who, upon learning that he had been sold, had shot himself. He told of a female slave, with several children by her master, a woman who had run to the waterfront and jumped into the river, hysterical at the news that she had been sold. Swift currents swallowed, and she drowned. Hamilton had seen the woman's lifeless body after authorities fished it out of the river.[2] Only in death, perhaps, could the grieved woman achieve her freedom. In any case, she chose death over a life of servitude away from her beloved children.

Such incidents caused Joe and his relatives to become more resolute in their conviction that chains should shackle no human. They must have realized that sometimes freedom had to be claimed by whatever means possible—sometimes at any price. Escapes grew more and more common in St. Louis as the slave market increased in productivity. Slaves fled in a variety of ways and for a variety of reasons. Claiborne, a slave in his twenties, escaped one summer morning in 1830 with a white accomplice dressed as a U.S. infantryman. The white man reportedly had enticed Claiborne to run, and the two stowed away aboard a skiff stolen from a keelboat. Claiborne ran despite a crippled foot from a burn on the inside of his right heel, an injury perhaps as telling as the fifty-dollar reward offered for his return.[3]

Eliza, a petite female slave, ran away from St. Louis in the fall of 1830—a dangerous time of year for a fugitive on foot with winter looming. The twenty-four-year-old fled wearing a yellow frock and a thin pair of shoes. Her desperate flight can be reasoned by her wretched circumstances: she had just been sold to the brutal Jesse Colburn.[4]

The trauma of being sold often gave slaves enough courage to flee the chains of bondage. In 1829, two such cases grabbed the attention of residents living in St. Louis. A slaveholder from Saline County, Missouri, brought his bondsman, Harry, to St. Louis to be sold at auction. Harry, a stout man with a speech impediment, sold as his master had desired. Harry wasted little time in expressing his own displeasure over his new situation. He slipped away from his new master, a man who seemingly did not place much hope in securing his wayward slave. The slaveholder offered a meager ten dollars for Harry's return.[5]

Slaveholder Clayton Tiffin was not so pessimistic about the return of his fugitive slave Dulalie, a woman who spoke both English and French. She too had been sold, and she had been missing since February when an advertisement for her apprehension and return appeared in a September 1829 edition of the *St. Louis Beacon*.[6]

Whether any of those men and women successfully secured freedom is unknown, but their bold stories surely fostered hope among their fellow slaves in St. Louis. Most, if not all, slaves dreamed of freedom, Joe and his relatives among them. Although not frequently voiced, even to one another, thoughts of escape consumed their lives.[7] They dreamed of someday owning their own farm, where Joe, William, Millford, and Leander could harvest crops as freemen in the "Land of Liberty." They dreamed of a home where sister Elizabeth could marry whomever she pleased, and where their mother Elizabeth could grow old and enjoy her grandchildren at play.[8] They dreamed in the shadows of their dimly lit quarters, in the drudgery of their workplaces, and in the dark recesses of their souls where they survived.

Now the dream was running out of time. Maybe it was seeing the graphic images of the St. Louis slave market firsthand. Or the betrayal felt from being sold by Dr. Young. Or it could have been hearing Isaac Mansfield's unsettling infatuation with the foreign land of Texas.[9] Whatever the case, the desire to escape intensified. Suddenly, the decision to act seemed urgent.

A bill of sale had divided Joe and his siblings. Would a dash for freedom do the same, and, if so, who would be left behind?[10] No one wanted to answer the question. Each family member knew the potential consequences of making a run for freedom. Speaking of these consequences aloud merely made them real, and with that reality sometimes came an awful moment of reflection and sorrow.

For Joe, the chilling hour probably arrived the evening his brother William appeared at Mansfield's residence on the edge of the Mississippi. William stopped to visit, as he occasionally did whenever his steamboat reached port. His services had been contracted to Otis Reynolds, who captained the steamboat *Enterprise* along the upper reaches of the Mississippi. William worked as a waiter, and, given the kindly nature of Reynolds, felt generally pleased with his situation. But William became struck by the poignancy of his labors. Each day he awoke to cheerful scenes of people traveling up and down the breath-taking Mississippi River, coming and going as they pleased. They were happy, William concluded—happy because they were free, and thoughts of escape became an obsession. Each time his steamboat coasted into a new landing, he envisioned how he might make his break and then safely journey to Canada, where runaway slaves, he'd heard, could find freedom and protection.

The boldness of his visions equaled the despair at the thought of leaving his dear mother in slavery. Nevertheless, William shared his thoughts with his family. Joe, Millford, sister Elizabeth, and their mother listened silently as William unveiled his unrelenting desire to escape to Canada. His words hung in the air, and tears trickled down his sister's cheeks as she took a seat by William and tenderly held his hand. "Brother," Elizabeth said, choking out the words. "You are not going to leave Mother and your dear sister here without a friend, are you?"

William burst into tears. "No," he quickly replied. "I will never desert you and mother!"

Elizabeth realized in that fleeting moment that she had been selfish in her objection. Bravely, she recanted. "Brother, you have often declared that you would not end your days in slavery," she said. "I see no possible way in which you can escape with us; and now, brother, you are on a steamboat where there is some chance for you to escape to a land of liberty. I beseech you not to let us hinder you. If we cannot get our liberty, we do not wish to be the means of keeping you from a land of freedom."

Joe and Millford also encouraged their brother to flee for Canada, as did their mother. No one wished to have William's continued enslavement on his or her conscience. Finally William demanded they stop such talk on this night. "In opposition to their wishes, I pledged myself not to leave them in the hand of the oppressor," William later wrote. "I took leave of them, and returned to the boat, and laid down in my bunk; but 'sleep departed from mine eyes, and slumber from mine eyelids.'"[11]

Any serious thought of escape was put on hold. But each family member realized the subject would be broached again. And an escape attempt appeared as inevitable as life and death.

Joe now belonged to Isaac Mansfield, which meant that his life was connected to Mansfield's in every way imaginable. Mansfield's emotions, health, economics, legal standing, and interests all could affect Joe and his family. A slave's life held no certainty, and Mansfield gave Joe every reason to remember that fact. The tinner's mind fluttered from one interest to the next. By the summer of 1830, his interests varied in enough directions to make even the most hardened slave nervous.

Business at the tinning plant and store had slowed considerably from two years earlier. Mansfield had done virtually no business in 1829, or at least no business that yielded any real money. Most of his work was done on credit as he struggled to pay for his stock, and creditors were knocking at his door. Additionally, he proclaimed himself an official candidate in St. Louis for a seat on the state legislature and spent his days campaigning as a Jacksonian Republican.[12] But Texas remained at the forefront of his thoughts. The more he heard about the foreign land, the more ensnared he became.[13] If Joe were ever privy to Mansfield's financial matters (and he probably was not), he might have viewed change as inevitable.

Mansfield hunted down every penny owed to him. In the summer of 1831, he sued a client for a $37 account that had gone past due. The diligent Yankee won.[14] O. D. Filley, one of Mansfield's hired hands from his home state of Connecticut, speculated in a letter to his brother Marcus, who resided in Hartford, that Mansfield owned as much as $4,000. Filley bemoaned the fact that Mansfield owed him "something like $350 or $375," but for fear of sounding like a gossip, asked his brother to keep that information to himself. Filley further speculated that Mansfield had as much as $2,000 worth of work on hand, but questioned his desire to earnestly pursue it. "Mansfield has not wanted any work for two months," he noted, sarcastically adding, "though I believe he would rather go peddling himself than discharge me for want of work."[15]

Mansfield had clearly focused his attention on his political campaign, which Filley predicted he would win. Mansfield founded his campaign on the promise that, if elected, he would "vote for some tried Jacksonian Republican to represent this State in the Senate of the United States."[16] St. Louis voters did not buy Mansfield's pitch, perhaps suggesting that his debts had finally caught up with him. Regardless of the reason, Mansfield failed to move past the primaries and onto the Jackson Republican ticket he coveted.[17]

His spirits were hardly crushed. Mansfield still had a zest for new challenges, as well as a potential escape route from his financial problems. He still had Texas. The truth is that throughout his campaign he'd had one eye on a seat in the state legislature and another on an application he had already submitted for a Mexican land grant. His intention to secure land in Texas was public knowledge, although it is uncertain what impact if any it played on his failed electoral bid. Such desires were certainly common at the time.

Fellow Missourians talked often of the vast amount of fertile land Texas had for the taking. Texas fever spread with each new bit of intelligence, similar to the kind that appeared in the September 9, 1829, issue of the *St. Louis Beacon*. The report, first published in a Nashville newspaper, offered a detailed manifest of the natural resources in Texas. "The soil is equal to any in the world," the author gushed. "The prairies are carpeted with a great variety of the most luxurious grasses. Some of the prairies are literally cane-brakes. Many, of an inferior quality, have been cultivated, and found to produce astonishingly." The author even made this amazing claim: "There is a number of Indian tribes in this country: most of which, having removed from other parts of America within a few years past, make *no claim to the soil*."[18]

As unreliable as some of these reports were, curiosity gripped settlers. Soon the rush was on. Stories of large migrations into Texas, whether legal or not, sprinkled the pages of American newspapers. In December 1830, the *St. Louis Beacon* reprinted one such account that had appeared in the *Cincinnati American*: "Thirty wagons passed through this city [Cincinnati] last week, in company, bound for Texas. They were, as we understood, from the good State of Connecticut, and were no doubt well supplied with notions."[19] So was Mansfield full of notions. The Yankee slaveholder undoubtedly saw Texas as a place to start anew, as did his close friend and associate Abraham Gallatin. A prominent farmer in an area outlying St. Louis until U.S. authorities seized his land, Gallatin had had the misfortune of backing the security of an Indian agent during Missouri's territorial days. Back then, U.S.-contracted agents sold goods to Indians. But when the system was abolished at the time of statehood, each agent was required to close his accounts and deliver any supplies, furs, and money in his possession. After an agent defaulted on his loans, leaving Gallatin at the mercy of the courts, the government seized his lands and sold the acreage at auction. His property fetched a fraction of its worth thanks to a lone bid, leaving Gallatin still responsible for half the judgment owed to government authorities.[20]

Understandably, then, Gallatin turned his eyes toward Texas. Like Mansfield, he had applied for a land grant and now pursued it with great zeal. Sometime in early 1830, with Mansfield poised to launch his political campaign, Gallatin ventured into Texas hoping to finalize his land grant. He returned to St. Louis that summer, disappointed that the grant remained pending but elated in the confidence that it would be approved. Mexican authorities had informed Gallatin that his land would be secure by winter. He relayed the good news to Mansfield, and the two began to make plans to travel to Texas when winter arrived, or else the following spring.

Gallatin spoke with great joy about his Texas land, which he boasted would exceed five thousand acres. Mansfield bragged about his pending grant with equal enthusiasm. Before long both worked to persuade Filley to join them on their Texas adventure. Gallatin enticed Filley with an offer to crown the young tinner heir to his estate, even proposing his daughter's hand in marriage as part of the deal. Filley believed a diligent tinner could make a financial killing in New Orleans, let alone the growing settlements of Texas. But he was leery about jumping into any venture without careful thought.[21] He eventually decided to stay in St. Louis, where he made a fortune as one of the city's most prominent tin manufacturers. His solid reputation spilled beyond the business district. The people of St. Louis elected him mayor on more than one occasion—a political success that had eluded his former boss.[22]

Much had eluded Mansfield in St. Louis. Especially contentment. Dogged by debt and impatience, Mansfield yearned for something bigger and felt again the same restlessness that had driven him from his native Connecticut years earlier. Now the unstable economic landscape of Missouri had worn him down, and he needed a change. In his mid-forties, Mansfield likely viewed his next move as his last chance to make a fortune. He needed to make his mark in a grand way. He needed Texas.

The decision to move undoubtedly devastated Joe and his family. They needed each other, not Texas. Life in the Mexican province meant a life lived deeper in the belly of the South. Mansfield made it clear to his slaves that they would go where they were told and when they were told, and he had determined that his travel plans would include one less slave than he owned. Someone had to go.

No family member could avoid the trauma and anxiety that now began to sink in. One or more of them appeared destined to be counted among slavery's living dead. William first learned the devastating news on a visit to his mother. Elizabeth looked her son in the eyes and informed him that Mansfield had sold his sister to a man from Natchez. The man intended to return to Mississippi with her in a few days. Until their departure, the younger Elizabeth was to be held at the local jail. William hastened to the jail to see his sister, only to be denied entrance. He returned the next day and was again turned away by the jail keeper. On the third day, he finally received a few moments to say goodbye. Joe, Millford, and their mother had already offered their tearful farewells. William's final bidding promised to be no easier, especially since he and Elizabeth were so closely bonded.

Four other female slaves shared the cell with Elizabeth. They, too now belonged to the Natchez man, a slaveholder who said he had purchased the women "for his own use."[23] Elizabeth sat alone in a corner of the jail cell with her face down as William quietly approached. Suddenly she raised her head, sprang to her feet, and buried her head into his chest. Tears gushed down her puffy face. Struggling to regain her composure, as soon as she could speak she uttered one final request. She pleaded with William to take their mother and run, her fate being already sealed. Escape to Canada, she begged, while time remained.

William glanced down at a ring on his hand. He slipped it off one of his fingers and onto one of hers. Struggling to breathe, William then bade his beloved sister farewell. He briskly exited the jail, never again to see her.[24]

William left behind a piece of himself that day. In the hours that passed, he would take an unprecedented inventory of his life. He might have reflected on the simpler days gone by in Marthasville but ultimately determined that he would indeed escape. Now he had to convince his mother to flee with him, which would not be easy. His mother told William that she refused to leave with her children still in bondage—not with Joe and Millford bound for Texas, Leander laboring as Dr. Young's body servant, and her daughter destined for some distant southern plantation. How, she reasoned, could she escape in good conscience?[25]

William countered with his own sound reasoning. He explained that after they found freedom in Canada, he would find employment and earn enough money to purchase the freedom of all his siblings.[26] He probably also emphasized that his own days were numbered. Dr. Young had informed William that he would be sold to help pay off some debts. William had one week to find a suitable owner in St. Louis or else the doctor would find one for him.[27]

After much debate, Elizabeth finally agreed with William's plan.

The escape would take place the next day, north of the city and under the cover of darkness. In preparation, William purchased some dried beef, crackers, and cheese with the meager money he had earned running errands. He placed the food inside a bag his mother had secured earlier in the day.

A day passed with William dwelling on Dr. Young's betrayal of him and his family. These thoughts made him more resolute in his decision to run, and now at last the hour was at hand. William could hardly contain his excitement, although thoughts of leaving his siblings tempered his joy. Evening came and a clock struck nine as William and his mother departed the city limits. Before long they stood before a small skiff that William had spotted earlier in the day. William pried the skiff loose from an anchored pole with little effort, and moments later they pushed off, William paddling with a board he had scavenged nearby.

The Mississippi's swift current quickly carried them downstream. Water splashed against the skiff as the blackness of night left it engulfed. Before they could reach midstream, the pair found themselves opposite St. Louis and looking back at the city breathlessly. Light from lanterns on shore bobbed on the water. The view was eerily engaging. For the first time, William and his mother sat on the outside of slavery looking in.

The two soon stood on the free soil of the Illinois shoreline. The last they saw of the stolen skiff was its swift disappearance downstream. Now the fugitives traveled the main route to Alton, a well-trodden dirt road carved by wagon wheels and animal herds. They passed through Alton by daybreak and immediately found cover in the woods. There they remained in hiding throughout the day.

William anticipated that Mansfield would begin tracking his mother as soon as he discovered her missing. Mansfield knew William had been in the city looking for a new owner, information that would likely lead him to Dr. Young's farm in search of Elizabeth's whereabouts. By night-fall, the two resumed their trek in the safety of darkness. The North Star served as their lone guide—the same light that elders used to point to back in Marthasville. Night after night they looked to the North Star for direction. It shone in the sky like a beacon of liberty. Joy swept over William and Elizabeth with each passing day as they placed more distance between them and the land of oppression. Still, hardships abounded. A heavy rain drenched the weary fugitives on the eighth day of their journey. Cold, wet, and miserable, they pressed onward, inspired by the vision of freedom. Two days later, their situation worsened when they ran out of provisions. They finally agreed to take their chances by asking for assistance at a rural farmhouse.

Reluctantly, they approached a house, only to be warmly welcomed by its residents. Elizabeth and William received sincere hospitality, and were fed and supplied further provisions for the remainder of their journey. They learned that they had made it 150 miles from St. Louis and could now safely travel by day and rest at night.

Traveling now under the sun's warm rays, the two started to feel for the first time that Canada with its cloak of freedom was something more than an ideal. Steadily they logged mile after mile through a thickly settled region, even at one point passing through a small village without incident. Soon they began to talk with great anticipation about the land of liberty, and they discussed plans, specifically William's quest to unite his entire family north of the Canadian border. William told his mother again how he would labor long and hard to save money. He daydreamed about buying a farm and then purchasing the freedom of each of his beloved siblings. Someday, he boldly promised, they would all live happily together in a beautiful, fertile region far from the chains of oppression.

The thudding sound of hooves on the path behind them shattered their optimism. Three men approached on horseback. William calmly turned to one of the men and asked what he wanted. The man displayed a handbill showing a warrant for their arrest and a $200 reward for their return to St. Louis. John Young and Isaac Mansfield had put a price on their heads. Sick with grief, Elizabeth locked her eyes on William's and burst into tears. Within seconds, a sturdy rope bound William's hands, and then he and his mother were being led back to Missouri. The next morning a blacksmith attached a set of iron handcuffs to William for the long trip back to St. Louis. The escape attempt had ended.

Once across the Mississippi, the captors took William and Elizabeth to the city jail, where William had said farewell to his sister only a short time ago. Inside the jail, the two fugitives learned that young Elizabeth had been carried away to Natchez just four days earlier. The intelligence was nearly unbearable, but it was not the last grim news they would learn that day.

Mansfield finally appeared at the jail, miffed that he'd had to spend hard-earned money for Elizabeth's return. Sternly he told Elizabeth that he did not intend to whip her, but he threatened to sell her to a trader. Maybe, he angrily added, he would even take her to New Orleans himself to sell at auction at one of those filthy slave pens. Mansfield left Elizabeth in the jail to dwell on her fate.[28] Soon she and William discovered that there would be no mercy. Mansfield swiftly laid plans to depart St. Louis at once. He lined up a renter for his North Main Street shop, a local man named John Shade. Mansfield and Shade agreed to a fee of $75 every three months.[29] Mansfield then ordered Joe and Millford to pack luggage at his home as well as some needed supplies from his riverfront shop. Samuel McKinney would act as his business agent in his absence.[30] Lastly, Mansfield booked passage aboard a steamboat bound for New Orleans. Joe, Millford, and Elizabeth were going with him.

When William received word of his family's removal from St. Louis, he frantically searched for them. He had now been sold by Young to a local merchant tailor, Samuel Willi, and had been busy settling his own affairs when he learned the tragic news.[31] Elizabeth, meanwhile, remained in jail. William tried in vain to talk with her, and did obtain the time of her steamboat's scheduled departure. The next morning William boarded the steamboat. The young bondsman desperately scanned the faces of some fifty or sixty slaves, all chained. Finally he spotted his mother, shackled to another woman.

William approached her, threw his arms around her neck, kissed her, and dropped to his knees. He begged her forgiveness for convincing her to run and for building her hopes. Elizabeth, numb with sorrow, stared into her boy's face. "My dear son, you are not to blame for my being here," she said. "You have done nothing more nor less than your duty. Do not, I pray you, weep for me. I cannot last long upon a cotton plantation. I feel that my heavenly Master will soon call me home, and then I shall be out of the hands of the slave-holders!"[32]

Just then Mansfield appeared. As he walked menacingly toward them, Elizabeth leaned over and whispered in her son's ear, "My child, we must soon part to meet no more this side of the grave. You have ever said that you would not die a slave; that you would be a freeman. Now try to get your liberty!"[33]

Mansfield looked at William and barked, "Leave here this instant; you have been the means of my losing one hundred dollars to get this wench back!"[34] He swung his leg toward William, kicking him full force with the weight of one of his heavy boots. William slowly moved away, but his eyes remained fixed on his mother, who unleashed one last shriek as her child walked out of her life forever: "God be with you!"[35]

Staggering ashore, half-dead with grief, William stared at the steamboat through glassy eyes. The agony that now struck him would haunt him the rest of his days. At times the pain would become so great that William would pray that his sister and brothers were dead rather than living as slaves. He could not bear to think of them subjected to the whips and chains of heartless slave drivers.[36] The very thing he had feared most had come to pass. His beloved mother and brothers would be sold like cattle in the slave pens of New Orleans. Or so he thought.[37]

William never learned the truth. Mansfield stole that from him as well. Joe, Millford, and Elizabeth were not bound for the New Orleans slave market. They were headed for the wilds of Texas.[38] Yet for a slave there was little difference. Downriver was downriver. Texas may have offered an enchanting allure to hardy, white settlers, but for slaves anywhere in the South it meant certain death—living or otherwise.[39]

6

GONE TO TEXAS

What is not prohibited is to be understood as permitted.
—Juan Antonio Padilla, Saltillo's secretary
of state, on slavery in Texas

ivine descriptions of her enchanting beauty reverberated across
rivers and valleys, creeks and hollows, even oceans. Her allure
stretched seductively across New York's cobblestone streets
to Baltimore's crowded wharf and beyond. Words about her echoed
like scripture along the remote, backwoods trails that crisscrossed
states like Tennessee, Kentucky, Alabama, and Missouri. Her story
was known across the great oceans and throughout boroughs in Ireland, England, Germany, and elsewhere. Few appeared free from her
spell.

Texas attracted folks in a special way. She seemed to know no social
lines and beckoned like a virgin goddess of Roman mythology, promising native riches. Droves came to embrace her sanctity sight unseen.
They rode horseback, crossing turbulent rivers, with the Bible in one
hand and a black-powder rifle in the other. They journeyed aboard
cramped steamboats and braved mighty seas on crowded ships. Some
arrived atop the buckboard of a wagon loaded with a year's supply of
flour and a lifetime of dreams. Countless walked.

"One's feelings in Texas are unique and original, and very like a dream or youthful vision realized," one female visitor gushed. "Here, as in Eden, man feels alone with the God of Nature, and seems, in a peculiar manner, to enjoy the rich bounties of heaven, in common with all created things."[1] In Texas the "sun and the air seemed brighter and softer, than elsewhere."[2] Everything appeared better—and bigger. The land tickled the imagination with its vastness, offering a seemingly endless wealth of woodlands, prairies, creeks, and rivers. Dense canebrakes, some three times the height of a man, greeted travelers who crossed the Sabine River from the east. Travelers eventually encountered thick patches of woodlands crowned by mammoth oaks and draped with Spanish moss that dipped into rivers from the tallest trees like curtains from the most elegant New York opera houses. Prairie grass swallowed immigrants on horseback, polishing their leather saddles in the process.

Farther into the interior, the land unveiled gently rolling grasslands fed by the tributaries of the Brazos and Colorado Rivers. Every spring this land exploded with vast blankets of bluebonnets and other wildflowers. Here the heartbeat of the Anglo-American settlements pounded most passionately. Here the rich soil yielded corn, sugar, and cotton, fostering prospects of a better life for those industrious enough to guide a plow. Here Texas earned its reputation as heaven on Earth. And the grandeur extended far beyond the Brazos and Colorado.

Immense herds of buffalo, free-ranging mustangs, and wild cattle trampled the unsettled terrain to the northwest along with the nomadic bands of Comanches, known for their horse-raiding and fierce fighting. Wild game of all kinds roamed Texas in great abundance. Deer were so numerous that a settler could easily kill one a day if needed. Or he could stockpile his makeshift smokehouse with a variety of other meats, such as a plump turkey or a black bear fattened from his fill of acorns, wild berries, and fish. Catfish plucked from Texas creeks and rivers easily tipped the scales in excess of forty pounds. Or so the earliest settlers boasted.

Everywhere people turned, they encountered something grand. Observers often told of what they had witnessed in exaggerated terms: Texas offered the richest soil, the fattest cattle, the tastiest oysters, the sweetest honey, and the most colorful sunsets. Over-enthusiasm could be blamed for some descriptions but not for most. A bee hunter, for example, could easily make a living from selling honey and beeswax. Candles were in great demand on the frontier, and Texas provided the material to manufacture them.

As one visitor wrote, "One feels that Omnipotence has here consecrated in the bosom of Nature and under Heaven's wide canopy, a glorious temple in which to receive praise and adoration of the grateful beholder."[3] Isaac Mansfield bought wholeheartedly into such heavenly rapture by the spring of 1832, further inspired by the scent of adventure and another new beginning. The urge had overpowered him by the time he left St. Louis with his slaves by his side. He locked the doors to his waterfront tin shop for the last time and never looked back.

Actions such as this were hardly uncommon among Texas immigrants of his day. Hordes flooded into the Mexican province with lofty plans—some borne of the light of a civilized world, others from a dark underworld. Texas was a magnet for all, and collectively they mirrored the best and the worst the world had to offer. Among them were dreamers and realists, rebels and loyalists, rich and poor, swindlers and opportunists, thieves and fugitives, the conscientious and the industrious. They were blacksmiths, farmers, hatters, carpenters, doctors, hunters, candlemakers, millers, muleskinners, politicians, and lawyers. Texas crawled with young, aspiring attorneys, referred to by many as "cornstalk lawyers," men who besmirched the legal profession with their questionable credentials.[4]

Shadowy figures descended on Texas. Unscrupulous land speculators preyed on the innocent to score their fortunes. Swindlers with no legal title advertised prime Texas real estate in exchange for cash. One scam in 1829 promoted the sale of more than forty-eight million acres of Texas land at the headwaters of the Red River. Those familiar with the region at that time might have viewed the con with universal amusement, if it were not for the tragic consequences that accompanied each purchase. Honest people undoubtedly lost their savings because of the scheme. The land amounted to nothing more than wild prairie, hundreds of miles removed from any settlement.[5]

Texas was not for the faint-hearted. As one frontier preacher noted, "He who goes in search of fools and greenhorns need not come to Texas."[6] Texans developed shrewdness, a characteristic unseen by Mansfield even on the crude and sometimes ruthless streets of burgeoning St. Louis.

This distinctive trait was perhaps a testament to those Anglo newcomers—honest and dishonest alike. These folks rushed into Texas with a common passion burning in their bellies. In their wake, they left a long trail of adventure stories that chronicled their migration. Bold family legacies were written overnight with each new departure from the north and east, and mythology grew. Usually there was a special sense of pride reserved for those who gambled on Texas.

Texas became a refuge for wayward souls, while some ostensibly headed there seemingly vanished with the wind. William Wells, Sr., is said to have disappeared one day from his Georgia home without a word, prompting speculation about a broken heart.[7] Henry Warnell is said to have left his home in Arkansas without a trace and rumored to have taken along a herd of stolen horses.[8] Whatever the description, whatever the scenario, many men left behind their relatives, friends, and creditors with only a mystery to embrace. Creditors began to routinely close accounts by writing three letters in their ledgers: "G.T.T." (Gone to Texas).[9] People read in their local newspapers about Mexico's invitation for settlers. They read about *empresarios* who had been legally blessed by the Mexican government to accept applications from prospective colonists. Eventually friends of friends confirmed the rumors: Mexico was giving away land by the thousands of acres. In places like Missouri, where an economic recession still held sway, such news spread like the Holy Spirit at a frontier revival. Folks called it "Texas fever."

Isaac Mansfield likely did not care what it was called. He saw Texas as a new lease on life. Texas would allow him the opportunity to reinvent himself as a businessman, maybe even as a person. Regardless of what raced through his mind, he proudly threw in his lot with the mass of restless immigrants. On common ground they stood ready to invest their money, hopes, and dreams. They dug in with their passions, and one and all congregated in Texas, as if by destiny.

One set of souls remained numb to the magic of Texas. Joe and his relatives knew nothing of the hopes and dreams it offered. They remained slaves. Joe likely did not view a journey to the Mexican frontier much differently than a journey to any other territory where slavery flourished. In Louisiana, Mississippi, Georgia, Alabama, and elsewhere, whips, chains, and leg irons ruled, and human flesh still sold at market value. In this respect, Texas offered nothing special.

Mansfield had set into motion a cruel chain of events with the sale of Joe's sister. The transaction forever splintered Joe's family, leaving them with only scant information about her intended destination. They only knew she had been sold to a man from Natchez.[10] Mansfield again showed no concern for the familial ties of his slaves when he booked passage on a steamboat bound for New Orleans in 1832, sometime in the budding days of spring. At that time he also reserved space for his small stable of slaves, who likely experienced the journey down the Mississippi chained in pairs and confined to a large room below deck where the steam engine hissed and moaned relentlessly. In this manner, the slaves could be guarded throughout the entire voyage with greater ease.[11]

Elizabeth, the mother, now faced the greatest trial of her painful life. She looked to her sons Joe and Millford for reason to breathe. Also by her side were two children under the age of three, a toddler named William and a baby named Elizabeth. They were two mulatto children her eldest, William, never spoke of, perhaps because Mansfield himself might have been their father.[12] The little band clung to each other for comfort. Endless speculation about their future likely haunted them en route to Texas. What they discovered there shocked them all.

Debate over slavery swirled in Texas in 1832, having gained intensity after years of legal wrangling over its survival in the Mexican state of Coahuila and Texas. At times the debate swept across the Mexican frontier with the ferocity of a blue norther, cutting to the bone on issues of morality and economics. Government officials and colonists commonly argued whether successful colonization could take root without slavery.[13] Old colonists and prospective settlers routinely weighed in on the debate with fervent opinions. "Do you believe that cane and cotton can be grown to advantage by a sparse white population?" one Pennsylvanian asked. "We must either abandon the finest portion of Texas to its original uselessness or submit to the acknowledged, but lesser evil of Slavery."[14]

Stephen F. Austin, the most successful of the Texan *empresarios*, referred to the slave issue in the summer of 1831 as the "dark question."[15] By the time Mansfield's steamboat paddled into New Orleans a year later, that question had grown even darker. Mexican law forbade Mansfield or any other slaveholder at that time from bringing slaves into Texas. The ban stemmed from the decree of April 6, 1830, issued by then-president

Anastacio Bustamante. The decree terminated further emigration from the United States, indefinitely suspending all unfinished applications for colonization. Mexico now also levied new taxes against the colonists, who until then had enjoyed a special exemption from such financial obligations. Additionally, the decree called for a ban on the further introduction of slaves into Texas and a strict enforcement of the law.[16] The decree aimed clearly to stonewall the influx of American colonists into Texas. Mexican officials had long been leery of American settlers, a great number of whom they viewed as a threat to rip Texas away from Mexico. Abolishing slavery would help stem the tide of such independent-minded immigration.

Each carefully crafted element of the decree could be traced to General Manuel de Mier y Terán's tour of the Coahuila and Texas frontier in 1827–28. Mier y Terán, a man of great intellect and respect, received a federal commission in September 1827 with instructions to investigate Mexico's boundary with the United States. Mexico's elite instructed Mier y Terán to report on what would be necessary to save Texas. Part of those instructions came from Manuel Gomez Pedraza, Mexico's minister of relations, in a brief letter: "Further, the government desires that your excellency in passing beyond the frontiers which we actually hold, will report whether or not there is any necessity for fortifying any points along the same for the necessity of the interior, once the exact boundary is established."[17]

Mexico's brass clearly saw the possibility of Texas slipping away. Sensing a mushrooming population of rebellious American settlers and disturbed by the lax enforcement of federal laws in their northernmost province, they now meant to save Texas at all cost and braced for a crisis. First, however, they needed confirmation of what they had long suspected. For that, they turned to Mier y Terán. A hardened and savvy Mexican patriot who could be trusted to file a candid report on the Texas problem, he did not disappoint. Traveling in a splendid carriage, Mier y Terán leisurely weaved through Mexico's frontier, mingling with local and state officials in San Antonio de Bexar, San Felipe de Austin, and Nacogdoches, all the while keeping his true intentions mum. He even spent some time with Stephen F. Austin in Austin's colony, where Mier y Terán seemed to foster a genuine friendship despite his veiled concerns over the political erosion of Texas. By the time Mier y Terán reached Nacogdoches, he had seen all he needed to see.

Mexican President Guadalupe Victoria would be the first to read Mier y Terán's initial conclusions. Mier y Terán reported that the North Americans who had settled on the Mexican frontier were "a mixture of strange and incoherent parts without parallel in our federation." He judged the colonists "more progressive and informed than the Mexican inhabitants," but warned that they were also "more shrewd and unruly." Mier y Terán left nothing open to interpretation. "Among these foreigners are fugitives from justice, honest laborers, vagabonds and criminals," he wrote, emphatically adding, "but honorable and dishonorable alike travel with their political constitution in their pockets, demanding the privileges, authority and officers which said constitution guarantees."[18]

The report of Mier y Terán substantiated the suspicions of Mexico's leaders, and their path instantly became clear. American infiltration had to be severely deterred, or else the secession of Texas would be inevitable. Slavery became Mexico's greatest political hammer. If slavery could be abolished, American immigration would grind to a standstill, as would any Texas movement to break away from Mexico. Mexican politicians wavered somewhere between morality and hypocrisy when it came to slavery, shifting positions whenever it catered to their interests. The fate of Texas slaves changed with each shift of political winds.

Slaveholders absorbed their first major blow on March 11, 1827, with the finalization of the Constitution of the State of Coahuila and Texas. Article 13 read: "From and after the promulgation of the Constitution in the capital of each district, no one shall be born a slave in the state, and after six months the introduction of slaves under any pretext shall not be permitted."[19]

The Congress of Coahuila and Texas issued a decree six months later that put the controversial Article 13 into effect. The text of the decree began appearing in regional newspapers, clearly outlining the various aspects of the new law. *Ayuntamientos* from each municipality were to maintain a register of each child born of slave parents. Deaths of slaves were to be entered in the same book and the recorded data reported to the state government every three months. Slaves whose owners had no lineal heirs were to be freed upon the death of their masters, as long as they had not "poisoned or assassinated" their owners. Slaves were not to be inherited by any of their owner's relatives under any circumstance. The law also required *ayuntamientos* to supervise the education of the free children of slaves, who were to attend public schools and be placed in trade apprenticeships so that they "might become useful to society." *Ayuntamientos* who violated their duties to enforce the law were to be fined $500—money that would be earmarked for the benefit of public schools. One concession was made to slaveholders two months later: an amendment that allowed them to sell slaves from one owner to another.[20]

Word of the new law caused an instant uproar, both in Texas and throughout the South, where prospective colonists weighed the possibility of losing their property if they relocated to the Mexican frontier. *Empresario* Austin realized that the new law threatened to suffocate the development of Texas colonization and moved quickly to save the dream he knew as Texas, traveling to Saltillo in November 1827 to appeal to the Coahuila and Texas government for a repeal of the new restrictions.[21] Battling his own moral demons, Austin had finally concluded that the survival of Texas was at stake. The moment of truth had arrived.

Colonists spoke out decisively, and on March 31, 1828, the *ayuntamiento* of San Felipe formally requested the legal approval of indentured servitude. Slaves would be introduced into Texas as contracted servants, an ingenious plan where slaves were given a small, annual wage and required to pay their masters for their expenses and eventual freedom. Under this guise, slaveholders skirted the new law and strapped their slaves to a perpetual state of indebtedness.[22] Ironically, Texans used the Mexican system of debt peonage to circumvent the new law.

Austin endorsed the proposal, which read in part: "Considering the paralyzed state of immigration to this Jurisdiction from the U.S. arising from the difficulties encountered by Imigrants in bringing hirelings and servants with them, this Body conceive it their duty to propose to the Legislature of this state . . . a Law whereby emigrants and inhabitants of this state may be secured in the Contracts made by them with servants or hirelings in foreign countries."[23]

Coahuila and Texas congressmen blinked. On May 5, 1828, they adopted a new decree effectively unraveling all that the Constitution of 1827 had done to cleanse Texas of the peculiar institution of slavery. The new decree read:

> The Congress of the State of Coahuila and Texas, attending to the deficiency of workingmen to give actively to agriculture and the other arts, and desiring to facilitate their introduction into the State, as well

as the growth and prosperity of the said branches, has thought proper to decree:

All contracts, not in opposition to the laws of the State, that have been entered into in foreign countries, between the inhabitants thereof, and the servants and day laborers or workingmen whom they introduce, are hereby guaranteed to be valid in said State.[24]

The congressional claim that there was a "deficiency of workingmen" in Texas later proved to be laced with hypocrisy. Less than two years later, Louisiana's legislature ordered the removal of all free blacks and mulattoes who had entered the state illegally since 1825. A substantial workforce for Texas suddenly appeared to be standing at Mexico's doorstep. Yet Mexican officials made no attempt to entice Louisiana's evicted blacks and mulattoes to settle on the Texas frontier. Instead, they told Louisiana's free blacks that they were unwanted on Mexican soil.

James W. Breedlove, the Mexican vice-consul at New Orleans, published notices forbidding free blacks from entering Texas. But the notices stated that shipmasters were not strictly barred from landing them on the Texas coast.[25] Mexico's policies toward slavery were contradictory at best and unconscionable at worst. The doubletalk spewing from the mouths of Mexican politicians led to inconsistent laws and law enforcement. No greater example of this unpredictability can be found than in the events that followed Mexican president Vincente Guerrero's decree of September 15, 1829. The decree presented Austin and Texan slaveholders with yet another crisis, as it called for the immediate emancipation of all slaves.[26] Austin found the decree so utterly harmfulthat he warned of how Texans might resort to resistance. Austin's words echoed across the frontier: "I believe the fatal consequences which must result to the colonial establishments of this department by the publication and circulation of the aforementioned decree, will be very apparent to your excellency, whether they arise from the slaves who claim the benefit of it, or whether from the owners who require the contrary, and without the respect of any authority being sufficient to restrain them."[27]

Again Mexican politicians blinked. Three months later, amid a riptide of debate, a new executive decree surfaced that excluded Texas slaves from the benefit of the general emancipation.[28] Slavery lived for another day, but slaveholding colonists and prospective settlers again wondered for how long.

Such was the turbulent history of Texas slavery when President Bustamante issued his infamous decree of April 6, 1830. The decree not only banned the further introduction of slaves into Texas but also demanded strict enforcement of the new law. Customs houses arose along the Texas coast at various locations to ensure that the law was indeed executed.

At the mouth of the Brazos River—the main waterway entrance for newcomers—a large military contingent was stationed at Velasco under Col. Domingo de Ugartechea. The colonel and his soldiers guarded the river's entrance, routinely checking passports and inspecting each vessel's cargo. Enforcement of Bustamante's edicts had become so strict along the coast that captains who sailed from New Orleans to Texas refused to allow black servants on board. Nearly all importation of slaves at this time thus occurred by land. Slaves were commonly smuggled into Texas, mainly by land across various points along the Louisiana border.[29] Americans introducing slaves in this manner had the dubious distinction of breaking Mexican law twice.

Still others brought their slaves into Texas under the guise of indentured servants as permitted by state law (May 5, 1828). Settlers poured through the legal loophole and into Texas without a hitch for nearly fours years. Then, on April 28, 1832, slaveholders everywhere received sobering news. Coahuila and Texas legislators had added one more restriction that again brought slavery's future existence in Texas into question. Article 36 of the new colonization law read: "Servants and day laborers, hereafter introduced by foreign colonists, cannot be obligated by any contract to continue in the service of the latter longer than ten years."[30] If enforced, slavery as Texans knew it would die off.

Against this backdrop, Mansfield sailed down the Mississippi River, likely oblivious to the new decree. His spring departure from St. Louis probably did not allow him time to receive the news and thus an opportunity to reevaluate his situation. If it had, the fate of Joe and his family might have been different. Joe's destiny would now be sealed in New Orleans, where his legal status likely shifted from slave to indentured servant. Whether Joe realized the potentially profound significance is unknown.

Mansfield entered the port of New Orleans a triumphant man, undoubtedly reinvigorated by the prospects of a new life in a new land. The businessman in him celebrated the fact that he had left a recession in his past in exchange for a potential fortune in his future. The sight of New Orleans merely added to the excitement. By 1832 the city had become the undisputed trade center of the South. Chief among this flurry of trade was the business of human flesh. New Orleans marked the seasons by those times when "all the roads, steamboats, and packets were crowded with troops of Negroes on their way to the slave-markets of the South."[31] The slave market mushroomed with each passing season, creeping toward legendary proportions. Once, in 1831, New Orleans received 371 slaves in one week. Most of those unfortunate souls had been shipped all the way from Virginia.

Joe now witnessed the boom firsthand. At his feet he beheld another St. Louis—only bigger. New Orleans was perhaps everything his older brother had described from his numerous trips there as a cabin boy with slave traders. Mansfield, meanwhile, focused on business at hand. He probably wasted little time in securing his passage into Mexico. One of his first orders of business would have been to obtain a passport from the Mexican consulate. This would have led him to the office of Pizarro Martinez, the Mexican consul at New Orleans. Martinez would have supplied Mansfield with the proper paperwork for a passport and briefed him on the current emigration laws. Martinez would have informed Mansfield about the rights of his slaves and the new laws regarding indentured contracts. The news might not have stunned Mansfield, who had surely monitored Mexico's slave laws throughout his application process, which began sometime prior to July 1830.[32] Mansfield also would have been privy to Mexico's lax enforcement of its own laws. Regardless, Mexican law required Mansfield to enter into indentured contracts with Joe, Millford, Elizabeth, and her two youngest children. The contracts could be no longer than ten years and had to be executed before a notary and witnesses.[33] Whether Joe and his relatives were knowing parties to the agreement is unknown. Martinez did file a complaint in 1831 that slaveholders had been making these contracts alone prior to their departures, thus leaving their slaves in total ignorance that such a document even existed. Martinez found the practice appalling.[34]

However questionable his intentions with the indentured contracts, Mansfield now traveled into the teeth of change. Mexican authorities had seriously begun to tighten the net on illegally imported goods, including slaves, and word of Col. Domingo de Ugartechea's military contingent at Velasco likely reached Mansfield at some point on his trip. If so, Mansfield learned that the colonel and his soldiers strictly monitored the passage of vessels up the Brazos River. The troops, he would also discover, stood equally determined to enforce the presidential edict that all captains were forbidden from carrying black servants from New Orleans to Texas aboard their vessels.[35] Mansfield, in all likelihood, carried his slaves into Texas overland.[36]

In New Orleans, Mansfield may have purchased a wagon and enough flour, sugar, and cornmeal to last a year. A few chickens, geese, or sheep might also have been secured for the trip, as well as oxen or mules to pull the wagon and a horse to ride, provided he did not bring one from St. Louis aboard the steamboat. Kettles, ladles, and skillets from Mansfield's tin shop would have rattled from the bed of the wagon as the group traversed the Old San Antonio Road westward across the Louisiana frontier. On the trail they would have reached an important milestone: Fort Jesup, an American military garrison built in 1822. Fort Jesup provided settlers with one last refuge on U.S. soil before they journeyed onward to Mexico. From Fort Jesup, the party would have pressed onward to Gaines Ferry on the banks of the Sabine River—the true boundary between the United States and Mexico. James Gaines, who operated the ferry from 1819 to 1843, probably stood beside Mansfield, Joe, and the others as they crossed into Mexico in June 1832.[37] Mansfield undoubtedly felt a sense of accomplishment the moment his boots touched Mexican soil.

Joe now walked as an indentured servant who, barring Mansfield's death, would be legally free in ten years. But perhaps Joe still viewed himself as a slave, being uninformed of his legal status. Only one thing is certain. Joe's heart did not yet beat as a free man. Until that day, he would survive to live and live to be free.

7

HARRISBURG

The man was a stranger in a strange land, but was
nursed and buried by good people and mourned by all.
—*Dilue Rose, a young Texas settler*

J oe walked amid a primeval pine forest in May 1833, a time when
long shadows fell over the handful of log cabins that constituted his
new home of Harrisburg. The lonely Texas hamlet offered but a few
merchant shops of a handful of settlers then and relied economically
almost solely on a small sawmill built on the southern side of Buffalo
Bayou.

From the sawmill's front piazza one could savor a full view of the
bayou, as well as the magnolia trees that crowded the water's edge on
the north side. The water lay deep there and clear enough for Joe or any
other bystander to see clusters of fish near the bottom.[1] Wildflowers and
berries grew in abundance throughout the piney woods and just beyond
the faint walking trails of the settlement.[2]

The sawmill, which doubled as a gristmill, sat at what most considered the headwaters of Buffalo Bayou. At that juncture the bayou split
into two and headed west; the southern branch was known as Bray's
Bayou. The terrain on the north side of Bray's Bayou rose more than

thirty feet onto a terrace and opened into a vast prairie—the gateway to the heart of the Anglo-American settlements of Austin's Colony.[3] That gateway began on Buffalo Bayou, considered the safest route for saltwater navigation to penetrate the interior of the colony.[4] One man recognized the bayou's importance as early as 1828, when he wrote, "This is the most remarkable stream I have ever seen—as its junction with the San Jacinto [River] is about 150 yds in breadth having about three fathoms water with little variation in depth as high up as Harrisburg—20 miles—the ebbing and flowing of the tide is observable about 12 miles higher the water being of navigable depth close up to each bank giving to this most enchanting little stream the appearance of an artificial canal in the design and course of which Nature has lent her masterly hand."[5]

Bulky steamboats reached Harrisburg through Galveston Bay, where vessels plied up the bayou to intermittently deliver newcomers and desperately needed supplies to isolated settlers. Steamboats, like the region's freshly felled pines, arrived directly at the sawmill's dock. The mammoth pine logs were rafted by water, while the steamboat's route involved much greater vigilance in consideration of ever-present dangers. Overhanging branches and submerged tree trunks always made the bayou's navigation a risky venture. Occasionally a steamboat sank to its watery grave. Schooners bound for Harrisburg often were mired on a sandbar at low tide. The ebbs and flows of the bayou routinely ensnared captains and their passengers in this manner and released them only as high tides permitted. Trapped vessels sometimes sat stranded for several days.[6]

Harrisburg offered the Texas frontier on raw terms. By nightfall, Joe would have heard the chilling screams of panthers and the yip of coyotes or seen the flickering lights of fireflies that danced in the darkness outside his log dwelling. The isolation could be both a blessing and a curse to a Texan—sometimes simultaneously.

Joe experienced this strange, hybrid sensation along with every other inhabitant of Harrisburg in the summer of 1833, when a neighbor died. The deceased had no family to mourn him. Nor did his newfound neighbors appear to have much to offer him in death. No one owned a carriage or hearse. A church had not yet been built, and there was no preacher to direct the funeral. Harrisburg's settlers merely had each other, and that's what they gave. One man—a Mr. Lytle—carried the man's corpse in his oxcart while men, women, and children trailed behind in a procession. Another man—Moses L. Choate—presided over the burial. A feeling of utter loneliness overwhelmed observers as spiritual hymns reverberated in the wind. Standing at the gravesite, at least one young witness observed the haunting beauty of the moment. "I don't remember the man's name," recalled Dilue Rose, then an eight-year-old fresh from the cobblestone streets of St. Louis. "The man was a stranger in a strange land, but was nursed and buried by the good people and mourned by all."[7]

A unique spirit existed on the Texas frontier. Neighbors relied on one another in ways hardly imaginable in eastern cities. Settlers shared freely and unconditionally of their homes, clothes, and food to any and all in need. The isolation tended to thrust people together, oftentimes regardless of color or legal status, slaves and slaveholders sharing equally in the early Texas experience. The rugged, often merciless frontier left settlers with no other choice. Social lines blurred at times between master and slave for the sake of survival. Since a majority of Texas colonists owned one or two slaves, and lived in close contact with them, it was not uncommon to see a slaveholder laboring side by side with his slaves to ensure the basic necessities for all.[8]

Slaveholders even sometimes shared their humble dwellings with their chattel in those early days, as was probably the case with Isaac Mansfield and his five slaves in Harrisburg. All six people likely crammed into a one-room log home, quarters that might have equaled slave cabins on any large southern plantation. Mansfield's cabin probably featured nothing more than a rustic, plank floor—if one existed at all.[9]

With housing scarce in Harrisburg, it is highly probable that Joe and Millford helped Mansfield cut and haul logs to build their cabin. Elizabeth might have mixed mud to fill in the cracks between logs while tending to her two youngest children.[10] If so, that might explain why it took Mansfield three months after his arrival in Texas to sign his character certificate, a document that Mexican authorities required from all prospective colonists. Regardless of the circumstances, Mansfield appeared at the San Felipe de Austin land office on September 15 and wrote the following testimonial to his adopted country:

To Mr. S. F. Austin Empresario

I have emigrated to this country for the purpose of seteling myself. And am desirous to be admitted under your contracts as a settler. I agree to your terms of settlement and am ready to comply with the provisions of the laws.

Isaac Mansfield 46 years of age, single, native of Connecticut and arrived in this Colony in June 1832

Austin 15th Septem 1832

Mansfield firmly pressed one hand on the coarse paper and then neatly signed his name, a signature lacking the hurriedness characterized in his previous business transactions. Perhaps Mansfield attached some historical significance to the event. Or maybe he simply felt more relaxed now that he was far removed from the daily strains of his manufacturing business.

Mansfield embraced Texas wholeheartedly, just as he had St. Louis years earlier. The people of Harrisburg certainly made his transition easier. In Harrisburg, newcomers were treated as if they were among old friends. When the Rose family arrived from St. Louis in April 1833, the entire town turned out to welcome them. Pleasant W. Rose—undoubtedly an acquaintance of Mansfield in St. Louis—was carried ashore from his boat by some of the town's men. Rose had become severely ill during the voyage from New Orleans. A widow offered her home to the sick Missourian and helped nurse him until his family could find a suitable shelter. No homes were vacant at that time, but as luck would have it, a new frame house—one of the few in the vicinity—became available that afternoon a half-mile outside town. The Rose family gratefully agreed to move in, and upon their arrival discovered another kind surprise. Town women had already tidied the house, prepared a hot meal, and left a supply of cornmeal, butter, eggs, milk, and honey as a house-warming gift.

Pleasant Rose later recovered from his illness and became a doctor. Neither Rose nor his family ever forgot the kindness they had received in Harrisburg.[11] The town was a magnet for a unique collection of people whose stories would someday be told under the Texas sky. These people of destiny included, among others, John W. Moore and William Barret Travis. Moore had left Tennessee for the Texas frontier in 1830, landing in Harrisburg. In December 1831, the *ayuntamiento* of San Felipe de Austin announced Moore's election as commissary of police for the precinct of the San Jacinto, an area that incorporated Harrisburg.[12] Travis, an ambitious, young attorney from Alabama, shuffled between Harrisburg, San Felipe de Austin, and Anahuac during this period. He had first entered Texas in May 1831 after an abrupt split from his pregnant wife. He left behind a son, and his cloudy departure would eventually give rise to numerous rumors and legends. Travis too embraced Texas and immediately began to study Spanish to enhance his legal versatility. He fielded a wide range of legal chores from both his clients and jurisdiction, such as compiling a quarterly statement of all births, deaths, and marriages for the government. The data also included a meticulous register of all slave births and deaths, as required by the Coahuila and Texas state constitution of 1827.[13] Loud and often harshspoken, Travis made his mark early in frontier courtrooms despite the wave of lawyers who flooded into Texas.[14] Yet, like his close friend Moore, Travis's fame would come later.

One life whose legacy had already been etched by 1833 was that of Harrisburg founder John Richardson Harris. A native New Yorker, Harris became enamored with Texas while living in Missouri. There, in the town of St. Genevieve, Harris first encountered Moses Austin and learned of his dream for Texas colonization. The two became fast friends, and in 1824 Harris traveled on his own schooner to Texas. He received a title of 4,428 acres at the junction of Bray's and Buffalo Bayous, where he built a store, a warehouse, and a home on the peninsula. The store provided settlers with the most varied choice of goods in the region, including medicines, crockery, hardware, saddlery, candles, slate pencils, lead pencils, Murray's *English Grammar*, dictionaries, lace, silk vests, flour, sugar, and salt.[15] He later established a second trading post with his brother David at Bell's Landing on the Brazos River. Settlers throughout the region relied on those two trading posts.

In 1826, Harris employed Francis W. Johnson to lay out the town of Harrisburg. Within two years, a small fleet of sloops and schooners owned by Harris plied between New Orleans and Texas with goods. One such vessel, *The Rights of Man*, carried eighty-four bales of cotton to New

Orleans in 1828. A year later, Harris contracted with Jared E. Groce for the purchase of between ninety and one hundred bales of cotton, marking perhaps the first large cotton contract in Texas.

By late 1829, a sawmill and gristmill were nearly complete. Harris merely lacked a belt for final operation, and he departed for New Orleans to purchase his missing component.[16] He never returned. The *Texas Gazette*, published in San Felipe de Austin, told of his fate in its October 3 issue, summing up the general feelings of colonists in a glowing memorial: "The fatality of yellow fever this season in New Orleans has deprived this colony of one of its citizens, who for the enterprise which characterized him, was not only a very useful and important member of this young community, but one to whom it is indebted for the undertaking of a very valuable and considerable branch of mechanical industry."[17]

Harris and his vision lived on in the spirit of Harrisburg's hardy residents—men like Moses L. Choate, who sprinkled joy throughout town with his musical talent. Choate often serenaded his neighbors with the sweet sound of his violin. In many respects, the people of Harrisburg were dreamers in the image of Harris, folks who had journeyed to Texas to taste the Promised Land. Isaac Mansfield certainly fit into that category. Yet Harrisburg had an element beyond neighborly kindness and the happy sound of a violin, a darker side where human souls cried for freedom. They were the same cries heard in St. Louis, New Orleans, Mobile, and throughout the South.

For Joe, oppression probably stunk in Texas as it had in Missouri. By law, Joe was either a free man who had been illegally smuggled into Mexico or an indentured servant under a ten-year contract. Whether Joe knew the law at this time is unknown, but likely it would not have mattered. Government officials in Mexico fostered slavery on the Texas frontier through both action and inaction. That was a reality Joe could not escape. Texans dealt openly in slaves. Contracts were drawn, signed, witnessed, and legally filed. Newspapers routinely ran advertisements for slave rentals and runaway slaves. Public auctions were also freely advertised in print and then overseen by local *alcaldes*. One such auction in Brazoria offered a husband and wife and six other slaves "at a credit of six months." Scheduled to oversee the auction was *alcalde* John Austin.[18] Buyers were encouraged to use their imaginations in some advertisements, as was the case with one headline: "A LIKELY YOUNG NEGRO

Girl for Sale." The girl was described as between the ages of fourteen and fifteen, a good house girl, and a tolerably active hand in the field.[19]

These public auctions mocked the 1827 Constitution of the State of Coahuila and Texas. And the death of a slaveholder rarely, if ever, meant the immediate emancipation of his slaves, as mandated by the constitution.[20] Mansfield contributed to the institution of slavery in his own small way. Roughly one month after arriving in Texas, he was already trying to make money, and that revolved around slave labor. As always, Mansfield wasted little time before diving headlong into a new business venture. On September 1, he and John Gates put a notice in the Brazoria newspaper seeking five male slaves "who could be well recommended." Slaveholders would be paid twenty dollars a month for the service of their bondsmen, who would labor at the steam sawmill in Harrisburg.[21] The advertisement gives no other hint as to the plans of Mansfield and Gates, but Mansfield probably used his own slaves, seventeen-year-old Joe and his brother Millford, to generate additional income.

The relationship between Mansfield and Gates is as murky as Joe's labors at this time. It is unknown whether they knew each other previously or if they were simply thrown together by their work at the sawmill. Gates may have originally been from Massachusetts, having come to Texas in 1829 from Tennessee. He was married with one child by the time he signed his character certificate three years later.[22] Apparently Gates was in no hurry to secure his place in Texas.

Mansfield obviously did not share the patience of his new business associate, but they could find common ground in their choice of settlement. Harrisburg provided a friendly, supportive environment for newcomers. Mansfield never was among total strangers there. He knew the Rose family from St. Louis, as well as his old pal Abraham Gallatin and his son Albert. The Gallatins also hailed from St. Louis, where they had bred horses on a farm outside the city and engaged in business at the local racetrack. The seventy-year-old Abraham Gallatin and Mansfield also shared a common love for tinning. Gallatin once owned a copper and tin store in Lexington, Kentucky, where he likely knew Joe's old master, Dr. John Young. Gallatin was definitely an acquaintance of Young and his wife, Sarah, in St. Louis. He sold Sarah a tract of St. Louis County land in April 1828. Mansfield witnessed the signing of the contract.[23]

Mansfield and Gallatin's close relationship is evidenced by their shared plans to relocate to Texas.[24] Gallatin and son may have even made the long trek to Texas in the company of Mansfield and his slaves in 1832. Family tradition holds that the Gallatins drove a herd of horses to Texas that year hoping for a profitable return on their investment. The story survived more than 170 years, but not because of any success on the part of Abraham and his son. Their plan went bust. They found that Texas had no shortage of horses. As the years rolled on, the Gallatins learned to laugh at their financial misstep.[25]

Mansfield certainly faced his own struggles while trying to establish himself on the Texas frontier. One nagging problem lingered in St. Louis, where Mansfield rented his Main Street store to John Shade. The contract between the two was simple. Shade was to pay Mansfield $75 for three months' rent, beginning the last day of December 1832 and ending the last day of March 1833. Yet when the rent became due, Shade did not pay. Mansfield displayed no tolerance for Shade's inability to uphold his contractual obligations. He directed his St. Louis agent, Sam McKinney, to file a civil lawsuit on his behalf in order to recover his rent. On April 23, 1833, less than one month after Shade's rental due date, a jury of six men awarded Mansfield a winning verdict. Jurors ordered Shade to pay Mansfield the full $75 judgment, plus whatever court costs had been incurred.[26] But Mansfield was soon to encounter far greater problems in Texas.

On June 15, the Brazos and Colorado Rivers overflowed, causing severe flooding throughout the region, including the Buffalo Bayou area. Water gushed out of the banks of the two rivers with alarming fury. Farmers watched helplessly as their crops of corn and cotton—both regional staples—were destroyed. Settlers depended heavily on the farmers along the Brazos for their main food supply. Now only sporadic corn crops survived at Buffalo Bayou and Galveston Bay, and a crisis ensued for the residents of Harrisburg. Hunters faced the prospect of tracking game in swampy conditions; the distant prairie was soaked with standing water. Also, no boats arrived with shipments of supplies. Occasionally, a few bags of flour surfaced but only enough to tease the needy. Slaves were last on the food chain, and many in the area reportedly went hungry.

Mansfield felt the impact. Production at his steam sawmill was cut back to one day a week to grind corn, a task that hardly required a large workforce. A number of men were let go. The timing couldn't have been worse for Joe and his family. On April 30, 1833, St. Louis probate clerk Henry Chouteau officially recorded the last will and testament of

Dr. John Young, who had died months earlier in Lawrence County, Alabama.[27] The death of Joe's former master, probably unbeknownst to him, would have a direct impact on the future of his brother Leander.

Young had written his will on December 1, 1832, in Alabama while seemingly on his deathbed with his wife sitting nearby. The dying doctor opened the will with a request that his "Negro man Leander be sold if he wishes" to "Isaac Mansfield of the Province of Texas" with the proceeds of such a sale to go toward his debts.[28] "Should the said slave not wish to be sold to any other person," the will further stated, "then & in that case it is my will that he & as many as can be spared from the family be hired out."[29] Two days later, Young amended the will with an additional notation that if Leander chose to remain with the family, he would be hired out to pay any remaining debts. In that case, he would remain the property of Young's wife until her death, and then his title would be transferred to his nephew, William M. L. Young.[30]

Leander's decision on the matter is not recorded, although he may not have wanted to leave St. Louis if he had in fact started a family of his own. The wording in Young's will certainly leaves that possibility open for conjecture. If Leander had wanted to be in Texas with his mother and siblings, it likely would not have mattered. Mansfield did not have much money of his own. Once again he had fallen into the trap of relying on credit, and the flood had made his economic situation even worse.[31]

The hardships caused by the Harrisburg flood may have played a crucial factor in Leander's failure to appear in Texas. In the end, the flood of 1833 affected many lives. It eventually drove several families from Harrisburg. Dr. Rose moved his family to nearby Stafford's Point that Christmas in search of brighter prospects.[32] At some point Mansfield may have entertained the notion of joining the exodus, despite his friendly ties to Harrisburg. Perhaps he thought of moving to the more central location of San Felipe de Austin, the center of the Anglo-American colony. Or perhaps he thought about the prospects of finding work on the coast at Anahuac.

Behind closed doors, Joe and his family prepared for yet another change. By now, the routine of moving had become as familiar as Grove Cook's whip but still as uncertain as the direction of the wind. As always, they prayed for the best and braced for the worst. Mansfield delivered both.

8

North Star

Saturday—Joe Mansfield vs sheff—argued case.
—William Barret Travis journal entry,
March 8, 1834

A bove the Texas prairie, suspended somewhere between heaven and hell, hung the North Star. Slaves who desperately desired to escape to Canada's free soil looked to it as a beacon of hope. They spoke of it often in whispers or rejoiced in coded song about how to plot a course northward. Joe surely heard those whispers and songs around the cabin fireplace of his childhood home. Slaves learned that there were many ways to find the passage north. One way was to follow the moss, which usually grows on the north side of trees. Another was to follow the northward migration of birds. Slaves also looked to the group of stars known as "the Big Dipper" for its ladle-like shape, calling this "the Drinking Gourd." The heavenly marker always pointed to Polaris, the North Star. Unlike other stars, the North Star never changed position, and it served as an unmistakable beacon for fugitive slaves as they traveled by night.

Joe may have looked to the North Star in February 1834. On the thirteenth day of that month, Alabama attorney William Barret Travis wrote a bond to San Felipe de Austin sheriff John W. Moore "indemnifying

him to buy one Boy Joe" from Mansfield. The proposed deal marked
the second time in his life that Joe had been targeted for sale, the first
being when his original master, Dr. Young, had sold him to Mansfield
in St. Louis.[1] Young's decision to sell Joe had probably created feelings
of betrayal for the young slave, but this new transaction promised to be
much more traumatic. This time Joe would be separated from his mother.
Evidence gleaned from a journal Travis kept suggests that Joe reacted
to news of the sale the same way countless other slaves reacted in similar circumstances: he ran.

Joe's probable flight meant he would have had to elude San Felipe
de Austin's newly formed group of patrollers. Regular patrols were
conducted under the leadership of Capt. Thomas Gay.[2] Whatever
the circumstances beforehand, Sheriff John W. Moore held Joe in
San Felipe by March 7, about three weeks after Travis secured his
bond.

Naturally, Travis handled the legalities of the matter on behalf of
Mansfield. He recorded the case just as he did hundreds of others in
his journal. In a short, abbreviated sentence, Travis wrote: "Joe & Isaac
Mansfield vs the Sheriff petition to be set at liberty."[3] The following
day, Travis noted: "Joe Mansfield vs sheff—argued case &c."[4] Travis
never spelled out the nature of the case, probably because such matters
as runaway slaves were mundane. Recaptured slaves routinely sat behind prison bars until their owners reimbursed the sheriff for the costs
to bring them back. Joe's mother and brother had suffered a similar fate
in St. Louis. Now, by all appearances, it was Joe's turn to feel the anguish
that only a captured runaway slave could understand.[5] Yet San Felipe
did not have a jail at this time.[6] Joe's days in incarceration were probably
spent in much greater indignation. Authorities may have simply chained
Joe to a tree. Such a fate befell at least one other man—a white man who
clashed with the law in the San Felipe jurisdiction. Other whites were
appalled at the sight of seeing one of their own chained to a tree like a
wild dog. A chained slave, however, raised few eyebrows, especially in
San Felipe.

Far from the center of government, San Felipe was a rough-and-tumble
place. Shady drifters filtered through its dirt streets with alarming regularity. The village's unsavory reputation even reached lyrical form, as
one old-timer recorded in a verse from a popular song of the period:

The United States, as we understand,
Took sick and did vomit the dregs of the land.
Her murderers, bankrupts and rogues you may see,
All congregated in San Felipe.[7]

One man who undoubtedly took note of Joe's circumstance was Mansfield, who probably felt his own indignation thanks to his slave's attempted escape. Those feelings would have been exacerbated by the judge's ruling that ordered Mansfield to pay Sheriff Moore $300 for Joe's release.[8] Travis probably became involved because Mansfield contested the fine associated with his slave's release or, more probable, did not have the money to pay the cost. Joe's incarceration definitely came at a bad time, given the financial hardships Mansfield had experienced along with every other Harrisburg settler. Hoping for assistance, Mansfield turned to Travis and other associates.

Two men stepped forward as security for Mansfield in Joe's release: Virginia physician George Moffit Patrick and Louisiana farmer James Routh. Both gave the court their word that they would pay any fees should Mansfield default on his financial obligation.[9] With the court satisfied, Moore finally released Joe from his custody on March 10, 1834.[10] Two days after his release, Joe felt Mansfield's wrath in a painful way. The irate owner sold Joe's brother Millford to Routh, a major slaveholder who had obtained a quarter-league of land (1,107 acres) two years earlier near Harrisburg.[11] Routh owned fifteen slaves when he migrated to Texas.[12] As for Millford, his worth was placed at $500.[13]

Mansfield probably used the money from the sale to recoup his losses from Joe's escape, an event neither he nor his young slave would likely ever forget. Slavery had again mercilessly ripped Joe's family apart, and there appeared no way to stop the emotional upheaval. Joe had already endured the heart-wrenching farewells of his sister, Elizabeth, and brothers William and Leander in St. Louis. He now had to deal with separation from Millford, whose life would soon revolve around Routh's plantation.

Elizabeth, their mother, had learned how to hide her emotional scars from white folks, while standing firmly on the belief that her family would live to see a better day. She taught them to find hope for that day in the alignment of the stars. When she and William were fugitives some 150 miles from St. Louis, they trusted no one then, only the North Star.[14] Elizabeth clung to the dream of freedom for herself and her children. Though time would eventually unveil her true feelings once and for all, for the longest time she silently dreamed for that better day to arrive for her family.[15]

Such a dream came with a price. Mansfield rendered that price in the form of a rental contract with Travis for Joe's services. The contract, probably a six- or twelve-month agreement, meant that Joe would again be physically removed from family members.[16] No removal would kill the dream, though. Elizabeth had instilled that dream in all her children, and at least one of them pursued its fulfillment at the risk of life and limb. More than a thousand miles away from the Texas prairie, Joe's brother William once again made his escape from the land of oppression. Traveling by foot, he carried nothing more than the worn suit of clothes on his body, a batch of meager supplies, and perhaps visions of his mother, sister, and brothers. He trusted no one, only the North Star.[17]

Nothing seemed to matter much to William after his mother's departure from St. Louis—nothing except freedom. By December 1833, William legally belonged to Enoch Price, a riverboat captain who mainly plied the waters of the Mississippi. Price had purchased William two months earlier for $650 from a St. Louis tailor named Samuel Willi.[18] Dr. Young had sold William to Willi in the days that followed his failed escape with his mother. Since that time, William lived for the moment he could escape the house of bondage.[19] And he did so smartly. He disguised his desire masterfully. Price never sensed William's unhappiness.[20]

William's opportunity finally arrived on New Year's Eve aboard Price's steamboat, *Chester*. By morning, the boat was expected to land at the Cincinnati wharf—or, by William's way of thinking, in the free state of Ohio. This is where William concluded he would make his break. The night did not pass without anxiety and sadness for him. William wrestled with his emotions as he imagined his mother laboring in a cotton field in the shadow of a hardened overseer, or his sister being forced to submit to a slave-driver's cruel edicts. He realized that a successful flight to freedom likely meant, despite all their hopeful talk to the contrary, that he would never again see them or his brother Leander, who remained Dr. Young's private servant in St. Louis.

William wished that his family members were all dead. At least then he could live in peace with the knowledge that his beloved family members suffered no more as slaves. The year 1834 began, and William was sorrowful, sleepless, and restless. He waited impatiently for the moment when the passengers and crew would to go ashore with their baggage and other cargo. When it came time, he grabbed a trunk, disembarked, melted into a crowd on the wharf, and soon disappeared into nearby woods. There, camouflaged by trees and brush, he remained hidden until nightfall, aware that he could still be legally captured and returned to Price despite standing on free soil.

William waited for the appearance of the North Star. But Mother Nature tested his resolve that night. William had to wait several hours until cloud cover dispersed. Then he finally saw his salvation shining in the midnight sky. He followed the star until daybreak, estimating his distance traveled at around twenty to twenty-five miles.[21] He repeated this mode of travel throughout his journey, traveling by night and hiding by day. He sometimes stowed away for a few hours in a farmer's barn if one could be found. Otherwise, he slept outside. Occasionally, he rummaged through barns for a corncrib, swiping a small supply of kernels. By daylight, he roasted the kernels over a small fire while finding refuge in the density of the forest. He drank from streams.[22]

One day he discovered a mound of dirt that he figured for a farmer's potato cache. For more than an hour, the weary slave dug into the mound with a sharp stick until he unearthed his treasure—turnips. He grabbed a half-dozen turnips, and then gratefully feasted on the uncooked treats as he traveled.[23]

The journey grew tougher with each passing day. William spent several days sleeping in the elements and traveling by night in sleet and rain. He refused to ask anyone for refuge for fear of being betrayed by bounty-hungry northerners or southern sympathizers.[24] On the fifth or sixth day of his journey, sleet and rain blanketed his scant clothing and face with ice, raising the stakes of his escape to the ultimate price. Numbed, William took shelter in a barn where he paced the floor to keep from freezing. The next morning he awoke, thankful to God for being alive despite a severe cold that had dropped into his lungs. Now he coughed uncontrollably, battled a fever, and walked gingerly on feet that had suffered frostbite. He bravely traveled in this wretched condition for the next two days.

Finally William resolved to seek shelter or die. He secured himself behind a pile of logs and brush near a road and watched as people passed. Apprehensively, he waited to approach someone he thought he might be able to trust. He let a few men go by before he stirred enough courage to stumble into the road. At that very moment he stared at an elderly white man who approached with a broad-brimmed hat and a trench coat. The man appeared to be walking for exercise as he led a white horse.[25]

A thought flashed through William's mind: "You are the man that I have been looking for!"[26] And the hunch proved correct.

The man took one glance at William's woeful condition and asked if he was a slave. William hesitated to answer, instead shifting the subject to his sickly condition. Again, the man asked if William was a slave. William finally told him the truth. The man informed William that he was standing in a pro-slavery neighborhood, and that he would have to go home to fetch a horse-drawn covered wagon to secretly carry him to his home. Weary and pained, William agreed to wait for the man to return, but his apprehension heightened as time passed. He had been taught from the earliest age to trust no white man, and now, with freedom so near, could he place his destiny in the hands of one?[27]

After nearly two hours, the elderly man appeared with a horse-drawn covered wagon just as he had promised. The wagon looked similar to those William had seen parked beneath the shed of a Quaker meeting-house on Sundays and Thursdays. He would later learn that his estimation had been right. The man was a Quaker and a staunch friend to slaves. Initially, however, William could not be induced inside the man's house. Only after the man's wife appeared outside did he feel safe to enter. Once inside, William sat spellbound by the couple's generous hospitality. They kindly treated him as an equal. The bounty of food placed before him presented him with an odd feeling. Years of servitude taught him to find comfort by eating in the kitchen, separate from white folks. Now he sat across the table from two white people encouraging him to help himself as he desired. Before long, William began to feel at home with the Quaker couple. He told them of his trials in slavery, of his family, and of his desperate flight for freedom.[28]

For the next fifteen days, the couple nursed the fugitive slave back to health. During that time they also made him clothes, and neighbors sympathetic to William's plight donated extra clothes for his journey.[29] Wells Brown—the man whom William would never forget—even purchased him a pair of boots and gave him whatever change he could spare for William's trip to Canada.[30]

Prior to their parting, Brown asked William if he had any other name. William shook his head no. "Well," Brown replied, "thee must have another name. Since thee has got out of slavery, thee has become a man, and men always have two names."William looked his new friend in the eyes and explained that Brown had been the first man to extend him friendship. He said that Brown must thus have the privilege of bestowing him with a new name. "If I name thee," Brown responded, "I shall call thee Wells Brown, after myself."[31]

William paused momentarily. Dr. Young had once renamed him Sanford to make room for Young's nephew named William in the big house. William told Brown that he would not lose his first name twice in one lifetime. "Then," Brown concluded, "I will name thee William Wells Brown." "So be it," said William, satisfied with his honorable new name.[32] The two men embraced one final time, and the freeman William Wells Brown was born.

In time, William would honor his freedom and his earthly savior with a legacy unparalleled in the annals of African American history. Thirteen years after the fateful encounter with his Quaker friend, William published a hugely successful narrative of his life, embarking on a celebrated career as an author, abolitionist, and lecturer. Among his most memorable works is his 1853 book *Clotel*, a fictional saga of the mulatto daughter of a U.S. president and the first known novel ever published by an African American.

At every turn William sought to further the cause of his enslaved kin. For a time he helped fugitive slaves reach Canada while he worked aboard a Lake Erie steamboat. By his own record, he assisted sixty-nine slaves in reaching Canadian soil between May and December of 1842.[33]

William's legacy is even interwoven in the greatest of all American struggles for emancipation, the Civil War. He helped recruit black soldiers for the Fifty-fourth Massachusetts Regiment, the first black regiment recruited by the North and one that earned eternal fame by leading a courageous and costly assault on Fort Wagner (South Carolina) on

July 18, 1864.[34] Yet William's life would be forever scarred over what became of Joe, Millford, Leander, his sister, and his mother. The mystery
haunted him the rest of his days.[35]

Joe's destiny, meanwhile, continued to play out a world away in the
wilds of the Texas frontier. There he would face a series of daunting challenges for survival, undoubtedly plagued by his own questions over the
fate of his family's living dead.

9

ANOTHER SOUL GONE

*I James Cochran appointed by the judge & sworn for
the purpose have appraised a Negro man slave named
Joe . . . at the sum of five hundred dollars in cash.*
—*James Cochran*

The winds of fate blew with profound strength in the summer of
1834 for Isaac Mansfield and Joe. The season brought the master
and his slave to a crossroad that would determine their destiny.
By then, Mansfield's visions of fortune had started to fade, as if wilted
by the scorching heat of the Texas frontier. The economic recession that
prompted Mansfield's flight from Missouri two years earlier had seemingly trailed him to Texas. Financial misfortune shadowed his every step,
a story not uncommon in Texas.

Mansfield worked off credit for years in St. Louis, where business
flowed steadily through the doors of his riverfront tin shop. He simply
handled very little hard cash in that time. Deals were frequently made
on credit until the system—one built on promissory bank notes—
collapsed.[1] Texas had offered Mansfield new hope, but now that hope
was fleeting as debts mounted quickly in his adopted homeland. He
owed Robert Wilson and William P. Harris, co-owners of Harrisburg's
sawmill, $1,400 in loans, Sheriff Moore $300, and Kentuckian Thomas

Barnett $222. Then there were James Routh and George Moffit Patrick, to whom he was indebted another $300 for Joe's release following his trial in San Felipe.[2] Mansfield's friends and associates had extended themselves a total of $2,222 on his behalf.

These substantial debts had become a major preoccupation for Mansfield by the spring of 1834 when he planted a cotton crop. He plowed his hopes into farmland located on the east side of the San Jacinto River in partnership with David Levi Kokernot, a Dutchman who had migrated to Texas in 1830. Kokernot owned the land where Mansfield's cotton grew.[3] But even that enterprise soured for Mansfield, who now crept into his late forties. His money ran low, and he soon realized he would not have enough to harvest his crop. In addition, he no longer had Joe and Millford at his disposal to assist him with the task. Millford had been sold and Joe rented.

Once again Mansfield sought a lender, and once again he found a friend in Routh, who loaned him $250 to obtain the "necessary supplies" to harvest his crop. The two men agreed that Routh would be repaid with the revenue generated by Mansfield's harvest.[4] Mansfield signed the loan agreement before Judge David G. Burnet on July 31, 1834, possibly the last legal document to bear his name. He died nine days later, presumably at home with Elizabeth and her two youngest children in Harrisburg. The cause of death is unknown, although the impact of his departure is clear where Joe and his family were concerned. Mansfield's passing triggered a chain of events that would forever alter the lives of his now-homeless slaves. By Mexican law, Joe, Elizabeth, and her two youngsters were supposed to receive immediate emancipation upon their owner's death. But they would soon learn that the law was only as good as those sworn to enforce it in Texas.

Creditors quickly swooped in to claim the scraps of Mansfield's meager estate. Less than a week after his burial, attorney William Barret Travis petitioned the court on behalf of his clients John W. Moore, William Harris, and Robert Wilson, each one claiming debts against the estate. Travis requested that Moore be named executor. Acting judge Robert Peebles subsequently granted the request.[5]

On September 22, 1834, an inventory and appraisal of Mansfield's belongings were compiled at Harrisburg. The list of Mansfield's property covered less than half a page, including such items as two axes, eighteen coffee pots, one chest, four oak jugs, three picks, coffee cups, and the like. Nearly all of Mansfield's money was tied to his slaves. Elizabeth, her five-year-old daughter Elizabeth, and her three-year-old son William were estimated at a combined value of $550. The appraisers valued Mansfield's entire estate at $634.77, rendering his net worth at $84.77 without his slaves. The total estimate did not include Mansfield's unharvested cotton crop or Joe, who remained with Travis. But by November 11, Moore deemed it necessary to sell Joe to pay another of Mansfield's debtors, Thomas Barnett. Mansfield still owed him $222 at the time of his death. Moore asked the court to approve the sale of Joe at a public auction. The document was written and signed by Travis, who acted on behalf of his close friend and client. The motion was approved and an auction date set for December 22 at San Felipe.

By now, Joe knew the brutal process all too well. A price was first placed on the slave, who was then left to be prodded by prospective buyers in the days prior to the public auction. Teeth would be tugged, hairs plucked, skin pinched, private parts studied. Sometimes the slave was forced to strip for a closer inspection of his or her body, or made to dance to display nimbleness. Slaves generally remembered the smallest details of a public sale after witnessing one, and Joe would have been no different. He had experienced them in St. Louis and witnessed them time and again after arriving in Texas. He undoubtedly remembered William's chilling tales of the slave pens and auctions in New Orleans. Now Joe would be forced to experience the hellish indignity of a public sale again.

Slave sales always created angst for the slave. Would one be a house servant or a field hand? Where would one live? And, most importantly, would one's master be kind or cruel?[6] If Joe had learned anything from his older brother, it was how to survive in the slave market. William had worked many months as an assistant to a slave trader in St. Louis, where he likely shared his invaluable knowledge with friends and relatives.[7]

Perhaps now Joe looked back on those conversations with renewed urgency, the kind inspired by a man's will to live.[8]

Joe's auction day arrived amid the spirit of Christmas. Sheriff Moore probably escorted him to the site of the public auction, which likely amounted to nothing more than the simple wooden structure that served as San Felipe's makeshift courthouse. James Cochran, a local merchant and a slaveholder, had been appointed by the court to appraise Joe's value, and he would have studied the teenage slave to his satisfaction. Shortly after his inspection, Cochran hastily documented his conclusion at a table in the presence of Judge Burnet. He wrote, "I James Cochran appointed by the judge & sworn for the purpose have appraised a Negro man slave named Joe belonging to the estate of Isaac Mansfield at the sum of five hundred dollars in cash."[9]

As the auction drew closer, prospective buyers stared at Joe as if they were inspecting a racehorse. A few may have poked and prodded. Serious bidders likely asked him about his skills, history, and pedigree. If the questions were answered honestly, Joe's mulatto blood would have certainly placed him in a higher class than the average field hand in the minds of most slaveholders. Such a bloodline often qualified a bondsman to work as a house servant or carriage driver or personal body servant. Joe certainly saw that in the cases of his two brothers, William and Leander.[10]

Handbills advertising Joe's sale circulated throughout the crowd. In the month prior to the auction, the flyers served as a public notice, dangling from the walls at public houses. Spectators now strolled around with them in their hands, some crumpled and folded, others rolled tightly in a fist.[11] Joe likely stood in a cloud of uncertainty, perhaps the same uncertainty that dogged his people when they first moved away from Marthasville seven years earlier. But this time was different. This time Joe stood alone.

Aside from Cochran, the crowd included the usual officials associated with San Felipe. Judge Burnet, himself vehemently opposed to the African slave trade, stood nearby to oversee the proceedings and sign off on a final sale. Sheriff Moore also stood close by, possibly telling Joe to stand atop a crate or wagon so he might be viewed more easily. At some point Moore took the opportunity to handle another aspect of Mansfield's estate: Joe's mother and two youngest siblings. Moore formally requested that the judge approve the sale of the three mulatto slaves and Mansfield's remaining property to satisfy the $300 debt to Routh and Patrick.[12] Terms of sale called for the buyer to pay $300 in cash to close Routh and Patrick's claim, with the balance of the purchase price to be applied to a credit line of six months. The terms were typical for early

Texas. Burnet again approved Moore's request, setting an auction date of January 31, 1835, in Mansfield's adopted hometown of Harrisburg.[13]

Whether Joe knew the specifics of his mother's upcoming auction is unknown. That did not matter much at the present time. His future now fluttered in the balance of an unpredictable bidding process. In a matter of moments, the blur of the auction concluded with the clarity of one heart-stopping word—"Sold!"—and Joe instantly recognized the "highest & best bidder," John Cummings. He was a friend of Travis's, as well as the proprietor of a public house at the Mill Creek crossing near San Felipe. Cummings had opened his establishment in February 1832 as a supplemental business to his lumber and gristmill operation, which he had created with his brother William eight years earlier.[14] Rebecca Cummings, John's sister, contributed greatly to the family business as a hostess at the public house, and she also helped with the day-to-day chores of the family plantation.[15]

Travis had frequently visited Mill Creek aboard his trusty mule during his continuous travels. He undoubtedly made at least a few of those visits, if not all, in the company of Joe, who served as his personal body servant. Cummings probably knew Joe quite well before purchasing him. For Travis, his friend's public house offered home-cooked meals, lodging, and the greatest love interest since his arrival in Texas. He and Rebecca had grown close over the past year. A romance first sparked in September 1833, when Travis stopped at Mill Creek on his way home from a business trip. He ate a meal that day at the public house and met Rebecca, who served him.[16]

Travis made sure his mule carried him in Rebecca's direction regularly from that day forward.[17] On a visit in March 1834, Travis gave Rebecca a breast pin and left with a lock of her hair. Their relationship became more serious the following month when Travis stayed overnight and spent a day in Rebecca's company at Mill Creek. The blooming love affair certainly meant nothing to Joe, who for a winning bid of $410 now became someone else's possession.[18] Soon his mother's fate would soon be revealed. On January 31, 1835, she and her two youngest children were sold as advertised in Harrisburg. Sheriff Moore collected a combined $610 for the three slaves, in addition to a meager $56.79 for the remainder of Mansfield's personal items. Moore documented the sale for the court but never mentioned the highest bidders by name.[19]

Refusing to passively accept the outcome of the auction, Joe's mother deemed it illegal at best. Two months later, she boldly sued for the freedom of her two youngest children and herself. She obviously knew Mexican law, or at least Article 13 of the 1827 Constitution of the State of Coahuila and Texas, which held that slaves were to receive immediate emancipation upon the death of their masters.[20] Then there was Mexican president Bustamante's thunderous decree of April 6, 1830, which had flatly banned the further introduction of slaves into Texas.[21]

Texans, of course, had blatantly ignored those laws. Yet the political winds were shifting like the sandy banks of the Rio Grande. Mexican federal officials were beginning to ask questions about the rights of Texas slaves. Col. Juan N. Almonte spent most of 1834 asking those questions on a tour through Texas. Almonte's visit amounted to nothing more than a politically motivated inspection of the troubled Mexican province. Mexico's secretary of foreign relations clearly spelled out Almonte's mission in January 1834, noting that he was to report on everything from prospective sites for future military posts to the "number of fighting men . . . the colonists might be able to count on in the event of necessity."[22]

Almonte's instructions also specifically addressed slavery. On that front, Almonte was expected "by all possible and prudent means" to inform slaves who had been brought to Texas illegally "that the fact of having put foot on the territory of the republic gives them freedom, and that the supreme government and the authorities will declare them free the moment that they invoke the protection of the law of April 6, 1830."[23]

Elizabeth may also have been living as a concubine with Mansfield, who might have been the father of her two youngest children. They certainly would not have been the first Texans to live in such a manner.[24] Mansfield may have promised Elizabeth her freedom upon his death and never put it in writing. Then again, Elizabeth may have simply known her rights under Mexican law. Regardless, she obviously thought she had a chance to win. Unfortunately, the outcome of Elizabeth's groundbreaking lawsuit is unknown. No court records of her trial are known to exist, lending credence to the possibility that the case never made it into a Texas courtroom.

The fate of Joe's mother and two youngest siblings is lost to the pages of time. But Gen. Manuel de Mier y Terán, the hardened Mexican patriot, had predicted the emergence of her brave kind seven years earlier when he noted that most of the Texan colonists owned slaves, "and these slaves are beginning to learn the favorable intent of the Mexican law toward their unfortunate condition and are becoming restless under their yoke, and their masters, in the effort to retain them, are making that yoke even heavier."[25] Unquestionably, Elizabeth died knowing full well the weight of that yoke.

Joe's life, meanwhile, forged toward a rendezvous with destiny after the materialization of yet another bill of sale. This time, Cummings turned around and sold Joe to Travis, who may have asked his friend to act on his behalf at the auction.[26] Travis possibly viewed the auction as a conflict of interest given his legal involvement with Mansfield's probate, but he probably would not have been above an insider's deal.[27] Speculating in slaves was a profitable business in Texas, as Travis and Cummings both knew well. Travis boasted in his journal about a sale involving his slave Matilda. He proudly noted that he had sold her for a whopping $700 in Brazoria. Travis purchased Joe sometime between the December 22, 1834, auction and February 3, 1835, when he wrote to Judge Burnet, "I have had Joe for the year."[28]

Ever the businessman, Travis weighed his options with Joe and shared his thoughts openly with his close friend Burnet. Regarding his teenage slave, Travis wrote to Burnet, "I cannot now say, whether I will sell him or not."[29]

His decision would have epic ramifications on Joe's life.

10

WILLIAM BARRET TRAVIS

*Sunday—Started to Mill Creek waters all swimming
& prairie so boggy—could not go—The first time
I ever turned back in my life.*
—William Barret Travis journal entry,
March 9, 1834

"Joe Travis." Wanted or unwanted, it became Joe's new name. "Joe Mansfield" died the moment the auctioneer yelled "Sold!" The transition happened as fast as it took John Cummings to write a bill of sale to his friend and Joe's new master, William Barret Travis. From that moment forward, Texans would know Joe as a Travis, the body servant of an industrious and often outspoken attorney from Alabama. "Travis" was Joe's third surname in less than a decade. Inheritance of a master's surname was customary, but it also served as a reminder for both slaveholder and slave of who held the power.

In Joe's world, surnames were fleeting. The only constant was the person in the mirror. By February 1835, Joe's persona may have belied his life filled with trauma. He spoke well and presented a good countenance in front of strangers, which suggested that he had long been plucked from the fields and groomed as a personal servant like his brothers, Leander and William.[1] Joe's partial white ancestry may have been the reason for his relatively privileged station. His grandfather, after all, was said to be the famed white frontiersman Daniel Boone. Yet Joe's physical appearance betrayed at least part of his family bloodline.[2] His skin was coal black.[3]

Only one description of Joe is known to exist, a runaway slave advertisement in which he is said to stand relatively tall, between five ten and five eleven, and looked older than his age.[4] Joe had at least two close relatives whose images have been preserved—his brother William and the legendary Boone. The earliest known sketch of William appears in his 1848 autobiography *Narrative of William W. Brown: An American Slave.* William was thirty-five at the time the sketch first appeared. Reportedly drawn by William himself, the sketch shows a stately young black man with chiseled cheekbones, well-rounded lips, and a strong jaw line accentuated by a cleft chin. His high forehead borders a neatly styled Afro, tightly cropped, with a slight flair at the ears. His nose is long and slender but flared at the nostrils. The defining feature is his eyes, which appear attentive and full of energy.[5]

Some of Boone's facial features are strikingly similar. He too carried a high forehead with pronounced cheekbones and a long nose. His eyes were a blue-gray and, by most accounts, steely and penetrating. In addition, Boone stood about five eight, with broad shoulders and chest, muscular arms, and thick legs. One observer described him as "a sort of pony-built man," suggesting that his slightly undersized body was structured like a thoroughbred.[6]

Joe probably shared some of these familial features. Most important, he shared his brother's and Boone's resolve. Despite the trauma and uncertainty he had known, he remained respectable in the eyes of white people. He had a privileged role among slaves as a body servant, whether by design or upbringing—or both.[7] Socially, he ranked above the common field hand. The Travis name added another layer to his refined persona. Joe surely knew that the name carried much more clout in Texas than that of Mansfield. One man floundered in debt, while the other increased his land holdings and grew his law practice. One man stumbled into the midnight of his life in Texas, while the other awoke to the optimistic morning light.

Texas gave Travis a second chance at life, and he was determined to capitalize on his opportunity. He aggressively walked amid the movers and shakers of Texas, counting some of its most prominent citizens among his friends, including David Burnet, William H. Jack, Franklin J. Starr, and Robert M. Williamson, whom friends called "Three-Legged Willie" for a wooden prosthesis that was attached to his permanently bent right leg. All were attorneys and land speculators. To them, Travis exemplified the spirit of Texas with his enterprising law practice and unbound enthusiasm.

Travis lived as if he were racing against the hourglass, engaging in social events and business ventures and soaking up political news. He devoured books with a relentless passion, reading Herodotus and the likes of *Rob Roy, Roderick Random, Westward Ho, Guy Mannering, Life of Josephine,* and *Court and Camp of Bonaparte.*[8] Perhaps he read a newly published work floating around Texas at the time: *The Life and Adventures of Col. David Crockett of West Tennessee.* A Brazoria newspaper published anecdotes from the book with much fanfare.[9]

Just as literature tickled his interest, so did writing. Once Travis sold an article to the Planters' and Farmers' Jockey Club of Mill Creek. He received two dollars for the effort but probably would have done the project for nothing more than the mental stimulation.[10] His intellect demanded constant learning, new knowledge. He also liked to have fun, once hiring a fiddler to play at an 1833 Christmas party hosted by Maj. Ira R. Lewis. He also bought a fair share of the liquor consumed that night. His generosity seems to have paid off, for it was probably on that night that he met Rebecca Cummings. Travis also engaged routinely in games of chance, such as three-card monte and brag, the stud poker of its day. He especially loved to test his luck at faro, once winning $17.75 on a Wednesday afternoon just hours before he preached from the Bible.[11]

To Joe, Travis would have been a slaveholder first and foremost. Travis subscribed to definite views of slavery and the southern social order of his youth, as evidenced by his words and actions. His sentiments toward the expansion of the slave market were evident in a letter to his friend David Burnet: "Many emigrants are coming into the country. A few Negroes also, I understand have been landed on the coast." Travis, respecting Burnet's distaste for the importation of slaves, politely added, "But we disagree on this subject."[12]

Work alone kept Travis tied to the slave market. His legal duties in San Felipe called for him to dispense of slaves from time to time to settle a client's estate. He also occasionally acted as an agent in private sales, drawing contracts for slaveholders and sometimes serving as a legal witness.[13] Such work probably even prompted Travis to dabble in his own speculation on slaves, which he appears to have done more than once.[14]

Joe encountered his share of slaves passing in and out of the Travis household, where the atmosphere did not resemble that of the plantation community of his childhood. By the time he joined Travis in the spring of 1834, Travis owned a five-year-old boy named Jared and rented a slave named Peter.[15] In all likelihood, Travis also owned Matilda at this time. Matilda may have been whom Travis referred to on January 15, 1834, when he noted in his diary, "Had sale of negro girl indefinitely postponed."[16] He may have also owned a slave couple—John and his wife (her name may have been Kiz), although he likely purchased them at a later date. Travis makes no reference to them in his diary, which ends with an entry in June 1834. John and his wife were sold to John Rice Jones on May 29, 1835, for a combined price of $805.[17]

Boarding was never a great concern for the slaveholding Travis. He moved from Jones's tavern in October 1833 to a simple house that doubled as his law office in San Felipe de Austin. In the months to follow, Travis attempted to make the residence more livable. He purchased a case to organize his papers, a table, a clock, an inkstand, blankets, counterpanes and sheets, a mosquito bar, a dust brush, two tumblers, and a washbowl. Fellow attorney Luke Lassasier gave him a "looking glass" as a gift and Major Lewis loaned him a chamber pot, perhaps the most appreciated item in the Travis house on bone-chilling nights.[18] Outside the residence sat a small garden, where Travis grew peppers, cabbage, and potatoes.[19] He did not appear to rely solely on his servants to work his garden. A year earlier, in the spring of 1834, he hired Pierre Blanchet at $1.25 a day to prepare his soil and plant his seeds. Travis even arranged for Blanchet to stay at Connell's boardinghouse, but the Frenchman left after only six and a half days. Three days later, Travis purchased some supplies and planted potatoes himself in the rain.[20]

All in all, his living quarters were simple and small. Travis avoided any boarding problem by using his slaves as an investment to generate some lease income. He routinely bought or hired slaves, and then farmed them out to friends and neighbors. Travis first hired Peter on January 17, 1834, from Elizabeth Miller for six months at a price of twenty-five dollars. He sent Jared to stay at a Mrs. Hammer's for eight days later while he went to Brazoria on business.[21] In March, about the time of Joe's arrival, Travis appears to have made room for his new body servant by shipping Peter to Thomas Gay's for boarding.

Travis continued his flurry of slave activity a month later by purchasing three more slaves for $1,000 from the Eli Holley estate: Jack (age fifty), Simon (twenty-five), and Eliza (eleven). He promptly resold Eliza to his friend John Rice Jones for $300 but opted to keep Jack and Simon. Travis posted $75 as a down payment for his two newest bondsmen, with a promise to pay the remaining $625 in twenty-five days.[22] Jack, whom Travis had been leasing to Lewis for the year on behalf of the Holley estate, ended up at Connell's boardinghouse a couple of weeks later. Connell charged Travis six dollars a month for Jack's room and board, meaning that the thriving attorney now had three slaves living at three different locations simultaneously.[23]

Simon, meanwhile, appears to have remained with Travis and Joe at the rental property in San Felipe. Travis makes no mention as to the sleeping arrangements, although Joe and Simon may have each slept on a cot or even a pallet on the floor. Clearly, neither servant lived lavishly. Nor did Travis, despite his growing prosperity, though he did make every effort to dress the part of success. He sported the best clothes money could buy, always wearing new boots and pantaloons. He loved a variety of colors of pantaloons and routinely donned a vest, a frock coat, a black cashmere shawl, and a sparkling white hat. Rarely, if ever, did anyone see him without a silk or linen handkerchief draped from a vest or shirt pocket. During the winter he always had clean stockings, undershirts, flannel drawers, and gloves available. The Travis wardrobe even featured dancing pumps.[24]

Beyond the dandified surface, Travis offered something much more complex and compelling: the passion and righteousness of the Romantic era to which he belonged, as well as the impulsive behavior of his youth. The result was a fiery, energetic young man who rarely left onlookers standing on middle ground. "Though generally recognized as both able and honest, Travis was not a very popular man," recalled Jonathan H. Kuykendall, who worked as an apprentice under Travis. "His brusque manner often gave offense and some times provoked insults upon which he turned his back." Kuykendall also described Travis's voice as "loud and somewhat harsh"—in other words, that of a trained trial attorney.[25]

This is the Travis whom Joe came to know intimately, arguably as well as anyone in Texas. The survivor in Joe would have known when to speak and when to remain silent, when to work and when to rest. Likewise, Joe would have been able to tell when others had crossed that line with Travis. Attorney Ephraim Roddy provided just such an occasion one day while arguing a case in Washington, a village thirty miles up the Brazos River from San Felipe. Roddy, as the story goes, incurred the wrath of Travis for using sarcasm against him in the courtroom. Enraged, Travis pulled a Bowie knife in his possession, leaving no one unclear as to his intentions. Roddy, unmoved by the overdramatic action of his counterpart, instead drew on his quick wit. He thrust his hand into his pocket and pulled out a little knife he used to carve quill pens.

"Your honor," Roddy declared in his Irish accent, "owing to the discrepancy of our weapons I cannot do opposing counsel much bodily harm, but if he insists upon it I will try."[26] Laughter erupted in the courtroom. Instantly the tension had been defused and Travis sobered to the foolishness of his outburst. The judge quickly adjourned the courtroom, and Travis took the opportunity to buy a round of drinks. Travis and Roddy became fast friends, although an undercurrent of rivalry seems to have always existed. On November 14, 1833, Travis noted in his diary with much glee: "I whipped old Roddy."[27] Those words defined his competitive nature, but Travis was much more an intellect than a brute. "He certainly was not a man of impulsive physical courage," his young friend Kuykendall later recalled. "It required a strong moral stimulus to rouse his combativeness."

All told, Travis was a maturing young man simply trying to find his way in life. Joe certainly would have understood the struggles associated with a young man caught between both worlds. In this sense, Joe and Travis shared much more in common than even Texas society allowed them to admit. Onlookers began to routinely refer to Joe as Travis's "boy." Travis, meanwhile, referred to his body servant by name: "Joe."[28] Perhaps it symbolized a small degree of respect or gratitude for Joe's services and loyalty, both of which were attested to by white Texans. Whatever the reason, Travis clearly displayed kindness to those in his charge. He generously tipped slaves for running various errands, even shelling out a dollar to a girl one Christmas Eve for delivering a letter.[29]

Where slaves were concerned, though, he demanded obedience in return. Jack, whom Travis had purchased from the Holley estate in April 1834, crossed that line with his new master while living at Connell's boardinghouse when he got drunk. Travis found Jack's indulgence embarrassing and an offense to his moral standards. Aside from an occasional glass of wine at a festive event or holiday party, Travis detested the overconsumption of alcohol and took measures to ensure that his eldest slave understood his expectations. He whipped the fifty-year-old Jack.[30]

Despite his youth, Travis displayed a strong sense of right and wrong that often danced dangerously close to self-righteous behavior. At best he was intensely passionate about life; at worst he was cocky and overconfident. Travis never stood on neutral ground. Respected women of his day routinely commanded his attention, which was always laced with chivalrous manners. To the downtrodden, he was generous. To the local Mexican population, he was friendly and courteous. A Mexican man named Alejandro once needed a pair of shoes. Travis sent him to Dinsmore and Cochrane's with a three-month credit order, but Alejandro did not understand and returned the credit slip to Travis. The next day Travis sent Alejandro back to Dinsmore and Cochrane's with instructions to charge the order to his account.[31]

Travis believed strongly in giving. He also believed strongly in justice—regardless of race. By the time Joe joined Travis in early 1834, Travis had already developed a reputation among black Texans for being fair. This was apparent on May 14, 1834, when a black woman named Belinda asked Travis to examine papers that related to her freedom.[32] Travis agreed, and not merely for show.

Blacks were well aware of Travis's legal battle five months earlier to secure the freedom of Celia, a free woman of color. Celia served as a slave for John M. Allen, who emancipated her on March 22, 1832, for her long and faithful service. Yet William H. Jack, a friend of Travis, claimed Celia as his own in a case that ended up in court. Travis elected to defend Celia on December 6, 1833, and the case was dismissed five days later.[33] Celia retained her freedom.[34]

Helping Celia in her inspiring struggle to remain free did not change the way Travis felt about slavery itself. In that regard he still subscribed to the social order of the southern United States of his childhood. As a child, Travis had watched his father, Mark, prosper on the gulf plains of Alabama with a pioneering spirit—and a stable of slaves. At the time of his death in 1836 the elder Travis owned a home, several hundred acres, several hundred head of cattle, and a dozen slaves.[35]

William Travis inherited his father's attitude toward slavery—even in Texas. He held fast to his views on the peculiar institution despite contradicting laws on the subject. Certainly he left no doubt about where he stood on the issue when he received updated news regarding the law of April 6, 1830, which among other things banned the further introduction of slaves into Texas. When Travis heard that the infamous law had been repealed, he noted in his diary on January 13, 1834, that he had just received "joyous intelligence!"[36]

Slaves came in and out of Travis's life in ever-increasing numbers as his law practice prospered. The situation had a great impact on Joe, who was probably questioned by incoming slaves as to what they could and could not do under the watchful eye of their new master. Happenstance placed Joe squarely between two worlds: that of trusted servant and that of trusted friend to fellow slaves. He surely developed relationships on some level with the slaves he encountered during this period, whether with the five-year-old Jared or the fifty-year-old Jack. The extended kinship he had enjoyed in his youth now served him well as he journeyed into the twentieth year of his life in 1835.

Joe had become increasingly reliable. He juggled a number of tasks as Travis's personal body servant, probably laying out his clothes each morning, saddling his mule, and driving his carriage about the countryside. Joe's mere presence also spoke well of his master's prestige and newfound prosperity, neither of which Travis had enjoyed just four years earlier in Claiborne, Alabama. His last years in Alabama had been a complete bust, and he had left behind a wife who was pregnant, an infant son, and, like many other Texas immigrants, a trail of debt. He also left behind some pride.

Success had first seemed to court Travis as a young adult in Alabama. He had taught school in Claiborne and later dove headlong into the study of law under the respected guidance of attorney James Dellet. While teaching, Travis became smitten with one of his pupils, Rosanna E. Cato, the youngest daughter of William Cato, a Monroe County farmer. A love affair quickly blossomed, and the two youngsters were married the evening October 26, 1828. The following year, on August 8, Travis and his newlywed celebrated the birth of a son, Charles Edward.[37] Twenty-one months later, the honeymoon had mysteriously ended. By then, the twenty-one-year-old Travis stood in San Felipe filing for land as an aspiring Mexican citizen. He stood alone, having left Alabama and everything he knew and loved behind in a cloud of red-orange dust.

Legend from one former slave family holds that Travis traveled overland to Texas with a small company of other emigrants. Dr. William Scull and his half-blood concubine Elsie were among those who journeyed with Travis from Alabama. Dr. Scull and Travis were friends who shared a craving for the newness that Texas had to offer. Their trail had been marked by hours of hopeful conversations about what awaited them, as well as the strong tobacco aroma that arose from Elsie's corncob pipe.[38]

Whether Rosanna was ever a topic of conversation is unknown. Travis rarely spoke of his failed marriage. One explanation of his split with Rosanna appears in an unpublished autobiographical sketch in which Travis wrote, "My wife and I had a feud which resulted in our separation." Other than that, Travis appears to have remained mum on the subject, probably because of the intense emotional pain involved.[39]

Rosanna gave her own account of their breakup in a letter to Dellet, whom she hoped would secure her divorce from William. In the letter dated September 6, 1834, Rosanna wrote how Travis had continually reassured her that he "would return to his family or send for them as soon as he could obtain the means to make them comfortable." Clearly, Rosanna felt torn between her love for William and the disgrace he had bestowed upon their family with his abrupt departure. "My friends advised me long since to seek a divorce," Rosanna told Dellet, "but as I had not lost confidence in his integrity to me, however deficient he may have been to others I confided in his assurances to me."[40]

William Cato, Rosanna's older brother, became suspicious of Travis's repeated promises and surmised that his only intention was abandonment. He confronted Travis with his suspicions in a letter written in "plain language," demanding an "explicit explanation" of his conduct and "future intentions" toward his sister. Only then did Travis confess to his desire for a "final separation." By then Rosanna had given birth to a second child, Susan Isabella—a girl Travis had never seen. "For so far as I was able to do so or knew how," Rosanna confided in Dellet, "I endeavored to perform my duty as a wife with the most undeviating integrity and faithfulness, and if any thing occurred to dissatisfy him with me it was the result of my ignorance [of] his entire satisfaction."[41]

William and Rosanna's breakup seems to have revolved around something that plagues many young marriages—debt. Mounting debts smothered the struggling young attorney by the spring of 1831. Overdue bills were being transformed into suits filed by frustrated creditors. Dellet alone held outstanding notes from Travis that totaled $834, and in all likelihood other attorneys were prepared to make claims on behalf of their clients. Humiliation choked the prideful Travis with each passing day. Trips into Claiborne for supplies became increasingly harder to stomach as the spring docket approached. Hearings for those suits were scheduled to begin in March, and Travis knew his outstanding bills would be publicly called into question.

The embarrassing circumstances did little for his fledgling law practice, let alone his marriage. As an attorney, Travis found himself constantly in the public eye. He had nowhere to go to avoid the uncomfortable scrutiny. Dellet, meanwhile, showed no empathy. The seasoned Dellet pressed forward with a suit against Travis in which his one-time protégé entered the plea of "infancy," meaning he was too young to know better. Dellet took great exception to Travis's plea. He summoned Travis to his side and placed a hand upon his broad shoulder. Jurors glanced over at the manly figure now standing beside Dellet. Travis stood stout and erect—"fully six feet in height," Porter recalled—with brilliant auburn hair and clear blue eyes. He appeared puzzled by Dellet's request.

"Gentlemen," Dellet said in a playful and sarcastic tone, "behold the infant who interposes this plea!" Booming above the cackling in the courtroom, Dellet concluded: "If, in view of his lofty stature and the maturity of his manhood, you can find the issue in favor of his minority, do so!"[42]

Dellet's public ridicule cut deeply. Travis departed Claiborne for the last time soon after this humiliating event, leaving his pregnant wife to search for answers. Before leaving, Travis promised Rosanna he would return for her and little Charles, but it was a promise he did not keep. By May in Texas he was passing himself off as a single man when he filed application No. 588 in San Felipe for the standard quarter-league of land for single men. Married men were entitled to more land, but Travis did not care. He had every intention of starting fresh as a bachelor. But if Travis felt no remnants of love for Rosanna, the opposite was true about his feelings for his children. Travis corresponded regularly with Rosanna and the Cato family from September 1833 through June 1834, and it is reasonable to conclude that his children were foremost in his thoughts. He left no doubt about his loyalty and affections toward his children when he penned his last will and testament on May 25, 1835. He made Charles and Susan his sole heirs, with all his property to be divided equally between the two. Travis also made sure he had a say in their care, designating his brother-in-law William M. Cato and Alabama minister James A. Butler as Susan's and Charles's guardians, respectively.[43]

Close by, Joe surely began to see his master grow in maturity, as his permanent separation from Rosanna became inevitable. Travis expressed an increasing desire to foster a closer relationship with his children, especially with young Charles, whom he became convinced needed the influence of a father. Rosanna painfully agreed. Legal documents in Alabama would reveal that there was much more to the story than in the rumors floating around Texas. Rosanna signed papers that gave legal guardianship of both children to Travis.[44]

Following through on that agreement, Rosanna landed at Brazoria on April 16, 1835, with Charles and Susan, along with her forty-two-year-old fiancé, Samuel G. Cloud. Rosanna, now twenty-two, and Cloud had booked passage in New Orleans and traveled aboard the ship *Elizabeth Jane*.[45] The trip marked the first time William had ever seen little Susan, now four months shy of her fourth birthday. William and Rosanna had originally agreed to have William P. Huff escort Charles to Texas from New Orleans in the spring of 1834, but for reasons unknown, that plan had fallen through.

Now the estranged couple began ironing out the details for their divorce. Their visit was said to have been "friendly," albeit difficult in light of the guardianship issue they had already resolved in the courts. Neither one wanted to say goodbye to their children. But such were the excruciating circumstances that now ensnared them both. Perhaps for the first time since their breakup William and Rosanna realized the true pain of their past decisions.

Joe, meanwhile, may have found more sorrow in the family split than even his white master. As a slave, Joe had no choices where his own family was concerned. William and Rosanna at least had choices. Travis, however, was determined to make the most of his situation and build a fortune for both of his children. His journey began in earnest that April day in Brazoria. He hoisted his five-year-old son—a "lively, prattling little fellow"—onto his horse and rode off toward San Felipe.[46] He would soon enroll Charles in a private boarding school, while Susan would remain with her mother until she grew older. No one knew at the time that Travis would never live to see his daughter again. Few would likely understand the tragedy as poignantly as Joe did.

11

SHADOWING LEGENDS

*Jim Bowie was like Barnum's show, wherever he
went, everybody wanted to see him.*
—*Capt. William Y. Lacey*

J oe quickly learned that life would never be dull. Travis always had
social events to attend, deals to make, court cases to handle, trips to
take, opinions to express, and causes to defend—at all costs. Travis
would have it no other way.

Politics monopolized much of the conversation of the colonists. Joe
often found Travis engaged in heated debate over the political affairs of
the Texans, such as those times when he accompanied his master to the
home of Judge Alexander Hodge on Oyster Creek.[1] Hodge, one of Stephen F. Austin's original colonists, was a tall, upright man who possessed
great moral integrity and respect. By 1835 he had reached his early sev-
enties and never seemed to tire of talking about the social and political
climate around him. He often hosted neighboring men who could burn
candles late into the night to chatter about politics.[2] Joe likely listened
to Travis and Hodge exchange verbal jabs on those evenings.

Travis despised the Mexican government for its threats to crack down
on immigration and suggested that the colonists take a more aggressive
stance. Hodge disagreed with his young friend, contending that Texans

should exhibit more patience. He trusted that Austin's diplomatic ways would eventually win the day.[3] Still, political tension increased across Texas, and even Hodge felt the strains. A year earlier he had hosted a large barbecue for which neighbors traveled great distances to attend. Among the guests were friends like Travis, who likely made the trip with Joe to tend to his needs. Travis also brought a childhood friend from South Carolina, James Butler Bonham. Women swooned at the sight of the handsome Bonham, who probably had journeyed to Texas to scout the prospects for settlement like countless others. The social event was memorable. Guests mingled about the Hodge homestead, admiring the judge's stable of horses as well as the sweet strains of a violin. But no one dared discuss politics because of one guest: Mexican colonel Juan N. Almonte.[4] Many Texans were convinced that Almonte was watching them closely, and they were right.

Almonte was touring Texas with government orders to report on the mood of the colonists and the security of the villages, towns, and ports. He also had been asked to investigate the potential evasion of the country's immigration laws, which had forbade the further introduction of slaves since the creation of the decree of April 6, 1830.[5] Almonte specifically focused on the "contract labor" that many Texans entered into with their black servants.[6] Joe fell squarely into that category, and Almonte may have told him so personally. Chances are that Joe already knew about the laws, as most likely did his mother, but realized that Texas slaveholders did not accept them, especially men like Travis. Texans lobbied increasingly against their enforcement, which only promised to choke immigration from the United States. Colonists opposing the laws reached a new level of unity when they convened the Convention of 1833 in San Felipe de Austin on April 1. Weary of an increasing presence by the central government, Texan leaders adopted a bold list of demands to present to the new Mexican president Antonio López de Santa Anna. Colonists wanted to repeal the law of April 6, 1830, to extend the tariff break that they had enjoyed since 1824, and to separate from Coahuila. The message was clear: Texans wanted to establish a new state government in Texas.

Austin, renowned for his measured actions, found favor from even his critics on this occasion. They overwhelmingly selected him to deliver their petition to the central government in Mexico City, and Austin reluctantly agreed. He left Texas that April and arrived in Mexico City three months later in the hopes of obtaining a one-on-one meeting with Santa Anna, but the Mexican president proved to be an elusive figure. Austin eventually grew weary from months of finagling and waiting for an audience. In frustration, he fired off a letter to the San Antonio de Bexar *ayuntamiento*, recommending that Texas begin to take steps toward self-governance by breaking away from Coahuila. The language was uncharacteristically rebellious for the trailblazing *empresario* who had become the voice of the Peace Party.

As soon as he posted his letter, the plates of Texas history begin to shift. Santa Anna suddenly agreed to a meeting, and Austin tried to make the most of his opportunity, though the president refused to budge on the issue of a separate Texan state. Within weeks, however, the government approved a repeal to the anti-immigration law of 1830 and revised the tariff law. Satisfied that he had done all he could, Austin packed his saddlebags in December and bade farewell to his political acquaintances. He then rode north with a renewed sense of hope for the future of Texas—a hope that proved to be a mirage. Mexican authorities had intercepted Austin's letter to Bexar and arrested him in January on the dusty streets of Saltillo under suspicion of trying to incite insurrection in Texas. No formal charges were filed but none needed to be as far as the Mexican government was concerned. Austin then moved from one jail to the next while all of Texas anxiously awaited word of his fate.

By the dawn of 1835, Travis clearly saw no cause greater than a Texas free from the yoke of such Mexican tyranny. The theme was a familiar one to Joe, who had seen such patriotic fervor before from politicians stumping on the cobblestone streets of St. Louis. Those men also spoke of freedom in evoking the spirit of patriotism, not to mention enough support to gain elected office. But Travis's motives were far simpler at their core. He wanted freedom or war, victory or death. Travis was not merely a talker. He was a man of purpose, passion, and action. Even those who may have viewed Travis as a self-righteous hothead had to respect his unwavering loyalty to his beliefs. Stories of Travis's loyalties abounded, such as the one about Alabaman Eli Holley's last hours on earth. On September 6, 1833, John McQueen and Travis remained by their friend's bedside throughout the night until Holley finally died. Travis and McQueen did not want their friend to die alone.[7]

Travis's friends affectionately referred to him as "Buck" and saw him as a man who could be counted on in times of need. Travis had not always possessed this quality. After all, he had left behind a trail of debt in Alabama and questions about his character. In Texas, though, he learned about making the most of second chances.[8] In fact, he began to take the first steps toward restoring his name in Alabama in September 1833. He made arrangements to begin repaying some of his outstanding debts.[9]

Travis cultivated an aura of respectability in Texas. He developed a reputation as both a solid trial lawyer and friend. Neighbors often boasted of his thoughtfulness. Spirited people attracted the energetic Travis, and it showed in his friendships and travels. He knew some of the most influential and interesting people in Texas, and Joe knew them all by association. Joe also became familiar with Texas trails aboard the back of a mule or horse as he often accompanied Travis on his travels. They always traveled lightly, each usually carrying only a knife, gun, tin cup, bottle gourd, and blanket.[10] On business trips Travis carried his legal papers and sometimes even a few of his law books. He also carried his thirst for conversation, which may have initially prompted him to select Joe as his manservant. Joe spoke with a refinement that set him apart from the average black field hand, a gift he likely acquired in part from his older brother, William. Together, they experienced Texas and the unique people who called it home. No one caused as much stir publicly among these as James Bowie, whose legend had already gripped the Southwest by the time Joe arrived in Texas. Joe saw Bowie in occasional dealings with Travis.[11]

"Jim Bowie was like Barnum's show," recalled Capt. William Y. Lacey, an early settler of Palestine, Texas. "Wherever he went, everybody wanted to see him."[12] In person, Bowie had a powerful physique. He stood slightly taller than six feet with a muscular, raw-boned structure that tipped the scales at around 180 pounds. He featured high cheekbones, a long, pointed nose, and broad, cleft chin. His complexion was light, his hair auburn, and his eyes a penetrating bluish-gray.[13] People who met Bowie generally admired his intellect, energy, and gentlemanly manners. Lacey remembered him as "always a gentleman from top to bottom" and one "not in the habit of using profane language." In eight months of land speculating in the Texas wilderness in 1834, Lacey claims he never recalled Bowie uttering "an indecent or vulgar word."[14]

John J. Bowie left perhaps the most vivid portrait of his famous younger brother, noting that he "was social with all men, fond of music and amusements, and would take a glass in merry mood."[15] Juana Navarro Alsbury, Bowie's sister-in-law, called him a "gentleman" of "a very serious countenance" and "few words." She remembered him as above all "a warm friend." "In his family he was affectionate," kind, and so acted as to secure the love and confidence of all," Alsbury once stated.[16]

Bowie the person belied Bowie the legend, however, and his fierce reputation as a duelist often preceded him wherever he traveled. Capt. William G. Hunt found Bowie's renown quite perplexing after meeting the famed knife-fighter and his wife, Maria Ursula Veramendi, at a Christmas party in 1831 on the Colorado River. "Mrs. Bowie was a beautiful Castilian lady, and won the hearts by her sweet manners," Hunt recalled. "Bowie was supremely happy with her, very devoted and more like a kind and tender lover than the terrible duelist he has since been represented to be."[17] Yet Bowie's fierce reputation as a knife-fighter was hardly without basis. Beneath his gentlemanly exterior lurked a primal rage. "His anger was terrible," John Bowie recalled, "and frequently terminated in some tragic scene."[18]

Such a tragic scene sprang up around Bowie in September 1827 in what became widely known as "the sandbar fight"—the signature event of the Bowie legend. A series of petty arguments and threats provided the backdrop to violence, which began with the first shots of an on-again, off-again duel between Dr. Thomas Maddox and Samuel Wells, Bowie's friend. Maddox and Wells had chosen a partially wooded sandbar a few hundred yards upstream from Natchez on the Mississippi side of the river to defend their honor. On the scheduled day of the duel, Bowie disembarked a skiff to serve as second for Wells. Supporters of both factions peered through the brush to witness the showdown, adding to the tension already filling the morning air. Even so, Dr. Robert Crain and Dr. James Denny—both of them Maddox backers—offered one last plea for the antagonists to call it a truce, but neither would agree.

Maddox and Wells each fired a round from their pistols, only to miss. Bowie watched as the two rivals lined up again and discharged their firearms a second time. Again both shots missed the mark. Satisfied that their honor had been preserved, the two men shook hands and began to trudge through the sand to return home. Mercifully, the duel had ended. But then someone opened his mouth. Crain exchanged harsh words with Gen. Samuel Cuny, whom he threatened to shoot on sight. Cuny, a supporter of Wells, then wheeled to face his adversary. Bowie, finding himself in the middle of a deadly situation, drew his pistol, fired, and clipped Crain in the cravat. Crain fired simultaneously, hitting Cuny in the thigh and severing an artery. Crain ran as Bowie fired at him and missed. Bowie then pulled his long knife and began pursuit. Crain turned and chucked his empty pistol at Bowie, catching his target square in the side of the head. The force of the blow dropped Bowie to his knees.

Maddox then rushed Bowie, who threw him off. Denny then grabbed Bowie by the coat lapel and urged him to stop at once. At that moment Norris Wright—Bowie's most bitter enemy—fired his pistol at Bowie, striking him in the breast. Denny's middle finger was shot off in the process. Now a wounded Bowie clenched his hunting knife tightly as he chased Wright. Two brothers, Alfred and Carey Blanchard, intercepted Bowie by opening fire on him. They struck Bowie in the thigh, again dropping him to the ground. At this, Wright turned and went for the kill. He charged Bowie and, in concert with Alfred Blanchard, drew his sword. Together, they thrust their swords at Bowie, who flailed about, wielding his knife. Bowie inflicted some minor cuts on each of his assailants as he desperately fought for his life. Finally Wright pierced Bowie in the left hand, ripping away flesh as Bowie turned to parry another blow. One of the swords sank so deeply into the flesh that it bent the blade as it hit Bowie's breastbone and then slid along one of his ribs.

Bowie, numb with fury, made one last lunge at Wright and grabbed him by the collar. Wright struggled to rise, pulling Bowie to his feet in the process. "Now, Major, you die!" said Bowie, his eyes fixed on Wright's. He then thrust his knife into Wright's chest, boasting later that he "twisted it to cut his heart strings." Wright died on the spot.[19]

The melee had ended after little more than ninety seconds. Yet for Bowie it would last a lifetime. The legend of the sandbar brawl shadowed him the rest of his days. So would his legend as a savage duelist. By the time young Joe set eyes upon Bowie in Texas, he was already a living legend shrouded in mythology.

Stephen F. Austin lived a short distance from Travis and Joe in San Felipe. His dogtrot log cabin, located half a mile from the Brazos River, doubled as both home and office, the whole of which was tended to by an old black cook named Mary. Austin was slender, wiry, and graceful, with curly black hair and brown eyes, behind which existed the mind of a thinker. He was also a peaceful man, and out of his element on the frontier.

Travis admired Austin's intellect and his political views, despite the fact that the latter often clashed with his own. Austin lobbied tirelessly for peace; Travis argued increasingly for war. Yet the two men found common ground where it counted: Texas. Now Austin languished in jail somewhere in Mexico, and for all anyone knew in Texas he faced execution. The matter weighed heavily among the colonists.

Joe, meanwhile, watched Travis move closer to the forefront of political affairs during Austin's absence. In February 1834, Travis gained appointment as secretary to the San Felipe *ayuntamiento*, a position he owed to his friendship with the town's newly elected *alcalde*, Robert M. Williamson. Finding the work tedious, Travis had to read and translate documents that circulated through the colony's office. He also copied letters and resolutions, filed reports for the department political chief in Bexar, and attended all official meetings of the *ayuntamiento*. In addition, he documented all of the community's vital statistics, including the births and deaths of slaves.

Despite the mundane nature of the work, the position allowed Travis to stay close to the political fires. Soon Joe would see those fires raging uncontrollably. From the shadows of bondage, he watched intently as an epic for freedom unfolded.

William Wells Brown escaped to Canada after his younger brother, Joe, was taken to Texas by Isaac Mansfield. Brown became a celebrated abolitionist and author—likely unbeknownst to Joe in his lifetime.

William W. Brown. From William Wells Brown, *Narrative of William W. Brown, an American Slave Written by Himself.* (Boston: The Anti-Slavery Office, 1848), frontis. Image courtesy The University of Oklahoma Libraries, Western History Collections.

The author caught by the bloodhounds. (See p. 21.)

William W. Brown, Joe's older brother, is shown in this engraving
as a fugitive slave, treed by a pack of bloodhounds.

"The author caught by the bloodhounds." From William Wells Brown, *Narrative of
William W. Brown, an American Slave Written by Himself,* 2nd ed. (Boston: The Anti-
Slavery Office, 1848), 2. In the authors' collection.

The author and his mother arrested and carried back into slavery.

Slave catchers apprehended William and his mother, Elizabeth, during an attempted escape. Shortly afterward, Elizabeth, her two youngest children, and two sons—Joe and Millford—are carried into Texas by their master Isaac Mansfield.

"The author and his mother arrested and carried back into slavery." From William Wells Brown, *Narrative of William W. Brown, an American Slave Written by Himself,* 2nd ed. (Boston: The Anti-Slavery Office, 1848), 72. In the authors' collection.

The Issac Mansfield probate verifies that Joe had at least two previous owners before William Barret Travis and is critical to revealing Joe's past. One document from the probate reads in part, "Isaac Mansfield deceased . . . in the Town of San Felipe de Austin . . . this the 22nd day of December 1834 proceeded to sell at public auction a negro man slave named Joe about nineteen years of age . . . John Cummings being the highest bidder . . . for the sum of four hundred and ten dollars."

Isaac Mansfield's probate from 1834. From the authors' collection.

Artist Gary Zaboly created this sketch of William Barret
Travis from various descriptions of the Alamo co-
commander and Joe's owner from period accounts. Travis
brought Joe into the Alamo as his manservant.

William Barret Travis, by Gary Zaboly. Used by permission of
the artist.

This estate inventory was found among the papers of the Travis probate.
The document is dated March 30, 1840, and reads, "A Bill of Sale from
John Cummings to W. B. Travis for Negro man named Joe." No sale price
is listed. The document is proof that Cummings sold Joe to Travis after
purchasing the slave from the Mansfield estate in 1834.

William Barett Travis's probate inventory from 1840. From the
authors' collection.

When asked to describe Mexican dictator Antonio López de Santa Anna, Joe said he looked like a "Methodist preacher." Santa Anna spared Joe's life because he was a slave.

El E.mo S.or G.1 de Division d. A.o López de Santa-Anna: Presidente de la Republica Mexicana, Julio Michaud y Tomas, color lithograph. Courtesy Daughters of the Republic of Texas Library at the Alamo, San Antonio, Texas, SC11144.

A wounded Joe is forced at the point of bayonet to identity key members of
the Alamo garrison after the final attack of March 6, 1836.

Joe Identifies Alamo Bodies, by Gary Zaboly. Used by permission
of the artist.

Joe accompanied fellow Alamo survivor Susanna Dickinson
and her infant daughter, Angelina, on the road to Gonzales
after escaping the Mexican guard.

Susanna Dickinson, copyprint. Courtesy Daughters of the Republic of Texas Library at
the Alamo, San Antonio, Texas, SC95.342.

At Washington-on-the-Brazos, William Fairfax Gray recorded in his diary Joe's account of the fall of the Alamo. Gray noted with surprise at how Joe "related the affair with such modesty, apparent candor, and remarkably distinctly for one of his class" From William Fairfax Gray, *From Virginia to Texas, 1835: Diary of Col. Wm. F. Gray* (Houston: Gray, Dillaye, 1909).

William Fairfax Gray, courtesy of the San Jacinto Museum of History.

After his survival at the Alamo, Joe was hired out to various people to earn money for the Travis estate. In this Gary Zaboly sketch, he is shown working for Bernard Holtzclaw at Washington-on-the Brazos. Holtzclaw was a former overseer for President Andrew Jackson.

Bernard Holtzclaw's Tavern, by Gary Zaboly. Used by permission of the artist.

John Rice Jones, the executor of William Barret Travis' estate, placed this ad in the newspaper after Joe ran away on the night of April 21, 1837—the one-year anniversary of the Texan Army's victory at San Jacinto.

Newspaper ad for runaway slave, Bailey's Prairie, May 21, 1837. From the authors' collection.

In this sketch by artist Gary Zaboly, Joe is depicted as a fugitive slave. In 1838, he traveled from Texas to the Travis family in Alabama. Travis family oral tradition states Joe's epic journey spanned forty days.

Joe Runs Away, 1838, by Gary Zaboly. Used by permission of the artist.

This 1849 daguerreotype is the oldest known photograph of the Alamo.

The Alamo, 1849. Courtesy of The University of Texas Dolph Briscoe Center for American History.

"Uncle" Ben Riley often regaled neighborhood children with stories
of his survival at the Alamo and his epic journey from Texas
to Alabama "along the railroad." Riley, who died in 1956
at age 107, probably heard Joe tell his story of survival
as a child or might have even been a relative.

Ben Riley of Brewton, Alabama. From the authors' collection.

12

DOGS OF WAR

God knows what we are to do! I am determined, for one,
to go with my countrymen, "right or wrong, sink or
swim, live or die, survive or perish," I am with them.
—William Barret Travis to James Bowie
in a letter dated July 30, 1835

Memories of Missouri probably drifted into Joe's conscious-
ness without warning on the Texas frontier. Hardly a day
would have passed without encountering a reminder of his
past. A traveling merchant peddling his tin wares, a fellow slave lug-
ging a bag of flour, or the passing words of a transplanted Missourian
might trigger reflection. Moments such as those could easily transport
Joe back to his roots on the bluff above Tuque Creek, where he once gazed
across the Missouri Valley.

Texas, from that viewpoint, was not so strange for the young servant.
His bondage did not negate the fact that he shared a common heritage
with many of its inhabitants. Joe was a Missourian in heart and equally
an American by birth, and Texas was crawling with both. Stephen Austin himself proudly carried those labels of distinction, even as Mexican
authorities shifted him from one dank prison to the next. Nothing would
erase his American heritage, not even now as he fought for a free land

in a foreign country. For the very essence of the struggle was American at its core, and Austin sensed it in his gut.

Now, perhaps fittingly, the lives of these two Missourians became interwoven as the threat of revolution loomed. Austin's fate promised to alter the destiny of every Texan, including that of Joe. This was hardly a first where Joe was concerned. The actions of other men had directly or indirectly affected his life more than once. Slavery had taught Joe many things, including the reality that life-altering decisions were rarely, if ever, his own. Such lessons had repeatedly been thrust upon him by slaveholders John Young, Isaac Mansfield, and William Barret Travis. Dr. Young's poor business decisions had led him to divide Joe's family with a slave sale. Mansfield's floundering tin shop and wanderlust had prompted him to carry Joe into the wilds of Texas, where Austin's enchanting words promised land and prosperity. Everyone was connected.

Texas was surely not the first place Joe had heard Austin's name. Nor was it likely the first place he saw him. Austin had traveled frequently to St. Louis on recruiting trips and for visits with old friends. His ties ran deep in the region. The *St. Louis Beacon* wrote often of Austin's work as an *empresario* in Texas, enticing the dreamers who ran the gamut of St. Louis society. Merchants, sailors, travelers, and prominent citizens talked regularly about the ever-evolving settlement opportunities in the Mexican province. Taverns and market houses echoed with chatter about the latest news downriver. Missourians who talked about Texas spoke of Austin's vision.

Joe, in all likelihood, never realized how Austin's work would forever change the course of his own life. As Austin's life teetered on the scales of Mexican justice, Texans watched guardedly. Finally, in May 1835, his fate promised to be a trigger for war. At home in San Felipe, Joe watched Travis follow Austin's circumstances closely. Travis gleaned details wherever he could, tapping into the scuttlebutt of local political leaders, friends, and legal associates. Finally in May news filtered back to Texas concerning Austin's fate. The statesman had been released from prison in December. But this glorious news was tempered by learning that Austin would not be permitted to leave Mexico City until the end of July.[1] Until then, Travis and others hoped to maintain a low profile with Mexican authorities for fear of jeopardizing Austin's life. Such restraint proved harder to sustain as time passed. Disturbing events began to unfold, slowly changing the undercurrents of resistance.

Entrepreneur Robert Wilson, owner of the Harrisburg mill, found himself at the center of this stormy period without a choice or warning. Joe knew of Wilson, having spent most of his time at the riverside hamlet of Harrisburg since entering Texas. So he may have listened with added interest as Travis bemoaned Wilson's encounter with Mexican officials. Customs authorities had seized Wilson's ship *Montezuma*, laden with much-needed goods from New Orleans. The seizure underlined the seriousness of the Mexican government's determination to enforce the regulations of April 6, 1830. The seizure left Wilson's mill paralyzed with empty shelves.

"I am vexed and contrite," Wilson complained to Travis in a letter. He may have also been speaking for a growing number of Texans when he warned that "if something is not done Texas is gone."[2] Travis, as might have been expected, did not hesitate to unfurl the banner of war. "All are for energetic resistance to the oppressions of a govt. that seems determined to destroy, to smash & to ruin us," he vented to David Burnet on May 21.[3] "I have as much to lose by revolution as most men in the country," Travis continued. "Yet, I wish to know, for whom I labor—whether for myself or a plundering robbing, autocratical, aristocratical jumbled up govt. which is in fact no govt. at all—one day a republic—one day a fanatical heptarchy, the next a military despotism—then a mixture of the evil qualities of all."[4]

Wilson summed up what Travis was already thinking when he said, "Santa Anna is not our friend."[5] The businessman would soon find out how true those words were when his partner, DeWitt Clinton Harris, traveled to Anahuac on June 10 to buy goods from merchant Andrew Briscoe. Anahuac, the location of a Mexican customshouse, also had a company of soldiers under the command of Capt. Antonio Tenorio, who ordered Briscoe not to move the goods. An argument broke out, and a Texan got shot. Harris and Briscoe were both arrested. Authorities released Harris the next day, prompting him to rush back to Harrisburg with the news. He immediately scratched out a letter to Travis.

Joe watched Travis leap to action. Travis rounded up a small company of volunteers around Harrisburg. They mounted a small, six-pound cannon atop a cart normally used for hauling logs to the mill and loaded it aboard the chartered sloop *Ohio*. Within a short time, the rebels were sailing across Galveston Bay toward Anahuac and revolution. Travis and his company of war dogs intended to take the garrison by force. A gathering of curious onlookers greeted them on their arrival. One in the group handed Travis a note from Tenorio, who demanded to know his intentions. Travis sent the messenger back with a demand of surrender. Tenorio then requested that he be given until the next day before giving his final response. Travis, leery of treachery, said he would give Tenorio a one-hour grace period before ordering an attack on the garrison. Yet with the fast-approaching darkness Travis became uneasy and ordered an advance before the expiration of the full hour.

Torches bobbed in the twilight as Travis and his men moved toward the garrison, which, much to their surprise, lay empty. Tenorio had cleverly removed his troops into the nearby woods to avoid bloodshed and perhaps to buy time. Angrily, Travis ordered the cannon fired again, this time into the stillness of the woods.

Silence ensued. Finally, two messengers emerged from the forest with a request from Tenorio to parley with Travis at the river. Travis agreed, but distrustful of Tenorio's true intentions, he selected three volunteers to trail him to the river and secret themselves nearby should Tenorio resort to any treachery. Tenorio, held an equal distrust for Travis. As Travis stepped ashore, he heard only a voice call from the woods. He cautiously moved toward the voice amid a clump of trees. There he found Tenorio, who again asked for a delay until morning before giving his answer. Travis steadfastly refused and gave Tenorio fifteen minutes to surrender, or else "every man" would be "put to the sword."

Travis' bold words would come eventually back to haunt him, but on this occasion they worked. No idiot, Tenorio knew he was deep in the heart of a colony dominated by Anglo-American settlers. Also knowing that his garrison stood ill-equipped for a full-scale battle, he and his officers wisely agreed to surrender. The Mexican captain formally agreed to terms the next day, and his soldiers were allowed to keep only twelve muskets for defense against marauding Indians during their overland evacuation from Texas. Travis escorted them aboard the *Ohio*, which carried the soldiers to Harrisburg along with the celebratory rebel band.

Word of Anahuac's fall reached Harrisburg long before the *Ohio*'s arrival. Townspeople who had been preparing for a large Fourth of July celebration now took additional security measures. They sent word to neighboring settlements, urging Texans to attend en masse. No one knew quite what to expect. For Travis, who had been jailed for a short time following a disturbance at Anahuac in 1832, this was a sweet moment of revenge. But he would soon realize that not everyone stood ready for the path of war. Older citizens in Harrisburg voiced their disapproval over the disarmament of the Anahuac garrison. They measured the cost of war against the homes they had built, the land they had worked, and the families in their care. For a good number of them, the cost of war was still greater than the price of paying the Mexicans' new tariffs.

Mexican soldiers, meanwhile, mocked the rebels by smoking cigars and playing cards at Harrisburg's celebration. Tenorio himself walked among the people, shaking hands as if he were the real hero of the day. By the time Travis returned to San Felipe on July 5, Joe probably began to see a slightly contrite master. Travis fired off a quick letter to his friend Henry Smith, giving an account of the events at Anahuac and adding somewhat apologetically that "this act has been done with the most patriotic motives, and I hope you and my fellow citizens will approve it, or excuse it."[6] Travis even published a notice in the Brazoria *Texas Republican* a few weeks later in defense of his public image. He humbly asked for "a suspension of public opinion in regard to the Capture of the Fort at Anahuac" until he could publish his own version of events.[7]

Inside, however, Travis felt little remorse. His true feelings are clearly evident in a letter he wrote to fellow war dog James Bowie a mere twelve days later. "God knows what we are to do!" Travis wrote. "I am determined, for one, to go with my countrymen, 'right or wrong, sink or swim, live or die, survive or perish,' I am with them."[8] Travis laced his words with the same patriotic trappings as those already circulating throughout Texas. On the eve of the Anahuac affair, Robert M. "Three-Legged Willie" Williamson boldly delivered his sentiments in a public speech at San Felipe. Williamson, a close friend of Travis, told an audience, "Let us no longer sleep at our posts; let us resolve to prepare for War—and resolve to defend our country against the danger that threatens it. . . . Liberty or Death should be our determination."[9]

Now Travis realized something the peace advocates could not grasp. He knew that time was precious if he and his fellow Texans were to take a firm stand. The colonists could ill-afford Santa Anna time to march troops into Texas. "Let the towns be at once garrisoned," Travis warned, "and we are slaves."[10] Those words had more than a tinge of irony, as the slaveholding Travis understood the severity of his foreboding message as well as anyone. Only Joe, who might have heard Travis utter those words aloud, would have understood better. Regardless, both Travis and Joe now found themselves in the line of fire should a full-fledged revolution erupt. All that stood between them and war was a popular leader who could unite Texas under one banner. Austin, for better or worse, was that leader.

His imprisonment educated Austin in the ways of Mexican justice, and by the time he again stepped on American soil in August at New Orleans he had become a different man. He no longer preached patience and compromise but swift action and complete independence. The politician in him seemed to have died somewhere in the bowels of a Mexican prison cell. Austin now left no doubt about where he stood on the issue of a free and independent Texas. He had not even departed New Orleans before committing those feelings to paper in an August 21 letter to his cousin, Mary Austin Holley. "I am, as you will see by my date, once more in the land of my birth, and of *Freedom*—a word I can well appreciate," he wrote. "I shall leave here in a day or two for Texas. . . . The situation in Texas is daily becoming more and more interesting, so much so that I doubt whether the Government of the United States or that of Mexico can much longer look on with indifference, or inaction." Austin cut to the meat of his sentiments, writing, "It is very evident that Texas should be effectually, and fully, *Americanized,* that is—settled by a population that will harmonize with their neighbors on the East, in language, political principles, common origin, sympathy, and even interest. *Texas must be a slave country. It is no longer a matter of doubt."* Austin then outlined his plan of action with philosophical prose. "A gentle breeze shakes off a ripe peach," he continued. "Can it be supposed that the violent political convulsions of Mexico will not shake off Texas as soon as it is ripe enough to fall? All that is now wanting is a great migration of good and efficient families this fall and winter. Should we get such an immigration, especially from the Western States—all is done; the peach will be ripe." Then Austin made it plain what type of emigrant stock he desired. He wanted hardy Kentuckians and Tennesseans, noting that "each man with his rifle or musket, would be of great use to us—very great indeed." And he wanted them immediately: "If they go by sea, they must take passports from the Mexican consul, comply with all the requirements of the law, and get *legally* into the country, so long as the door is legally open," he added. "Should it be closed it will then be time enough to force it open." Austin closed his letter with a few prophetic words: "This fall and winter will fix our fate—a great immigration will settle the question."[11]

Austin stressed the importance of unity in a public speech September 8 at Brazoria. "Let all personalities, or divisions, or excitements, or passions, or violence be banished from among us," Austin stated. "Let a general Consultation of the people of Texas be convened as speedily as possible, to be composed of the best, the most calm, and intelligent, and firm men in the country, and let them decide what representations out [sic] to be made to the general government, and what out [sic] to be done in the future."[12] Measures adopted by such a meeting would give Texas one "voice," Austin felt, "instead of the opinion of a few."[13]

The peace process died before it started. Within two weeks, Austin had received intelligence that Mexican general Martín Perfecto de Cos stood ready to march into the colonies from his garrison at San Antonio de Bexar to settle the matter once and for all. Austin suddenly saw only one path to travel. "There must now be no half way measure—War in full," he wrote on September 21. "The sword is drawn and the scabbard must be put on one side until the military are all driven out of Texas."[14] A day later, every man in Texas was being asked to seize his weapon and defend his country.[15]

Travis felt emboldened by the strength of Austin despite their past political differences. "All eyes are turned toward you," he wrote to Austin on September 22. "Texas can be wielded by you and you alone; and her destiny is now completely in your hands. I have every confidence that you will guide us safely through all our perils."[16] Providence, however, seemed to beat Austin to the punch. Shots rang out less than two weeks later, on October 2 at Gonzales, a settlement situated between San Felipe de Austin and San Antonio de Bexar. The shots signaled the beginning of war. A small detachment of Mexican dragoons rode to Gonzales with the intention of confiscating a single cannon that had been loaned to the townspeople for protection against marauding Indians. The cannon, which had been buried in a farmer's peach orchard, was later unearthed, mounted on an ox wagon, and loaded with grapeshot forged from pieces of cut chains. The Gonzales men discharged the cannon in the face of the Mexican soldiers, and its distinct sound reverberated across valleys and into the hearts of Texans everywhere. The Mexicans retreated with one casualty.[17] The revolution had begun.

On October 28, in a prelude to a major battle at San Antonio de Bexar, Bowie led a Texan patrol into a gunfight with a Mexican contingent near Mission Concepción. Texan riflemen occupied a wooded bend in the San Antonio River that was protected by a natural embankment. In a thirty-minute battle, the riflemen squelched three Mexican charges with blistering accuracy, killing or wounding fifty-three infantrymen and cavalrymen. Mexican soldiers retreated, only to be chased by the emboldened Texans, including the overzealous Travis on horseback. He rode enthusiastically onto the battlefield after hearing the crackling of gunfire, only to see the backs of the retreating enemy. Austin ordered his troops to hold their position. There would be no all-out assault on Bexar at this time.

In a few days, a frustrated Travis returned to his home in San Felipe. The next major news he received about the war shocked him. The Texan army had stormed Bexar, prompting the Mexican commander, General Cos, to seek terms for surrender. Travis marveled at the thought: the Texans now held Bexar. The revolution was progressing as Travis had hoped.

13

INTO THE UNKNOWN

I have strained every nerve—I have used my
personal credit & have neither slept day or night
since I was ordered to march—and with all this
exertion I have barely been able to get horses
& equipment for the few men I have.
—William Barret Travis to Governor Henry Smith
in a letter dated January 28, 1836

Stress and uncertainty shadowed Joe wherever he traveled. They trailed him in good times and bad, like the vicious bloodhounds of some relentless slave hunter. Circumstances had forced him to cope with the splintering of his family, the move to Texas, the death of his master, and the sale of his very flesh. Texas now threw him yet another trial of the soul—a revolution.

On December 20, the Texan General Council "unanimously elected" Travis as lieutenant colonel to command the newly created "Legion of Cavalry." Governor Henry Smith confirmed the appointment four days later, and by December 25 the council had ordered Travis "to the frontier or the seat of war, with all the troops he can bring into the field at this time, under his command." Joe, in turn, took his orders from Travis to follow him into the field.

Stories of war and bloody skirmishes with Indians were surely nothing new to Joe. He would have grown up on such stories, spun from the heroics of hardened frontiersmen like Daniel Boone. As a child he may have even overheard Dr. Young recount some of his military experiences from the War of 1812, or listened to elder slaves talk with captivating detail about the days of his grandfathers and the American Revolution. The storytellers in all likelihood witnessed the horrors of those war stories firsthand, lending gravity and clarity to their words. Yet there remained a mythical quality to such accounts. Travis's orders to advance to the "seat of war" meant something entirely different. This time Joe would be part of the story as his master's body servant, and what awaited both men was entirely unknown.

Travis felt stressed by the situation. The recruitment of supplies, horses, and men had gone poorly, and Travis did not hide his emotions as he now rode with his unit's quartermaster, Thomas R. Jackson, and its lone company commander, John H. Forysth. Jackson and Forysth shared the duties to prepare the legion for war. In nearly a month, their combined success had been minimal at best. Eight men had deserted, including six volunteers on the road from Washington-on-the-Brazos to their present location at Burnam's Crossing on the Colorado River. Horses, saddles, blankets, food, and other supplies trickled in as the provisional government's strained finances allowed.

By the time the legion set up headquarters January 28 on the banks of the Colorado, Travis found himself entirely vexed by the whirlwind of war that he had helped to create. He had hoped to have a hundred soldiers enlisted under his command by now. Instead he had thirty. Travis committed his frustrations to paper by candlelight in a letter to Governor Smith. Nearby, Joe and the legion's soldiers huddled next to campfires, stoking the burning embers as needed with only the sound of the rushing river to soothe their souls. With stiff joints, wearing mud-caked clothes, and tired after just a few hours of sleep, the men wearily savored the few pleasures at their disposal in camp—a sip of hot coffee, a small tin plate of cornbread, a dry blanket.

"In obedience of my orders," Travis wrote, "I have done every thing in my power to get ready to march to the relief of Bexar, but owing to the difficulty of getting horses & provisions, and owing to desertions, I shall march to-day with only about thirty men, all regulars except four. I shall however, go on & of my duty, if I am sacrificed, unless I receive new orders to countermarch." Travis pessimistically spared no thoughts. "Our affairs are gloomy indeed," he continued. "The people are cold & indifferent. They are worn down & and exhausted with the war, & in consequence of dissentions between contending and rival chieftains, they have lost all confidence in their own govt. & officers[.] You have no idea of [the] exhausted state of the country—volunteers can no longer be had or relied upon—A speedy organization, classification & draft of the Militia is all that can save us now."

Turning to the most powerful weapon of war, he stressed, "Money must be raised or Texas is gone to *ruin*—Without it war cannot be again carried on in Texas. The patriotism of a few has done much; but that is becoming worn down—I have strained every nerve—I have used my personal credit & have neither slept day or night since I was ordered to march—and with all this exertion I have barely been able to get horses & equipment for the few men I have."[1]

The life of a military man began to discourage Travis, a fact that might have amused Joe under different circumstances. One thing is certain: the lofty station of a servant must have seemed far less appealing to Joe on the muddy banks of the Colorado River. Joe likely did more than his share of work around camp, where he may have chipped in with cooking, hauling firewood, watering horses, and relaying messages. He also may have tended to equipment or driven a supply wagon. His reward would have been a night's rest beside Travis in one of the legion's few tents. Joe earned his keep.

Travis, meanwhile, stewed over the army's predicament a full day before firing off another letter to Smith. In this letter, dated January 29, Travis wrote, "I leave here with the troops under Capt. Forsyth, but shall await your orders at Gonzales or some other point on the road. I shall however keep the 30 men of Forsyth's Company in motion towards Bexar, so they may arrive as soon as possible." He again emphasized his struggle to recruit enough men, concluding, "I must beg that your Excellency will recall the order for me to go on to Bexar in command of so few men. I am willing, nay anxious to go to the defense of Bexar, And I have done many things in my power to equip the Enlisted men & get them off. But, Sir, I am unwilling to risk my reputation (which is ever dear to a soldier) by going off into enemie's [*sic*] country with such little means, so few men, & them too badly equipped."

The unselfish attitude Travis had so often donned in the name of a free Texas seemed to vanish. A man of ambition and ego instead emerged: "Therefore I hope your excellency will take my situation into consideration, & relieve me from the orders which I have heretofore received, so far as they compel me to command in person the men who are now on their way to Bexar—otherwise I shall feel it due to myself to resign my commission." Travis ended with one last plea for new orders, even suggesting that he would be more "useful at present, in Superintending the recruiting service."[2]

On the eve of the legion's departure, while Travis penned his final pleas to Governor Smith, Joe was likely ordered to help prepare for the long journey ahead. The unit packed clothes, checked saddlebags, filled water gourds, greased wagon wheels, and meticulously inspected and cleaned rifles and shotguns. Travis did not expect to encounter the Mexican Army so soon after the storming of Bexar, but his cavalrymen could not let their guard down. A brush with an Indian war party was also a possibility en route to Bexar.[3]

By dawn on February 1, the legion departed Burnam's Crossing donned in spurs and leggings, but not until after the quartermaster had purchased another $385.85 worth of supplies from Jesse Burnam's trading post. Travis, meanwhile, secured a $200 loan from William Brookfield.[4] And he made one other pressing trip before venturing to Gonzales. He rode twenty-five miles north to Montville to visit little Charles, who would attend a new boarding school, created by Travis's friend David Ayers. Travis, possibly with Joe by his side, read to the children for a while before Charles approached and whispered in his father's ear. He wanted fifty cents.

"My son," Travis playfully asked, "what do you want with four bits?"

"To buy a bottle of molasses from Mrs. Scott to make some candy," the six-year-old replied.

Smiling, Travis handed his son a coin, but it fell on the floor and rolled away. The lad ran after the coin until he had it securely in his grasp. Travis departed that night, comforted by the thought of his son and his classmates indulging in a fresh batch of candy.[5]

Travis and his men soon traveled toward Gonzales along a little-used road running southwest from Burnam's. The road eventually connected with a main route that cut westward from Columbus to Gonzales. Later that day, near the junction of those two roads, Joe found rest when Travis ordered his men to dismount at Thomas Chadoin's homestead. Chadoin sold Jackson a bay horse and one "beef" for forty dollars. That night the men feasted on freshly butchered beef, which Joe may have helped prepare over an open fire. Joe and the troops then bedded down for the night in the vicinity of Chadoin's home.[6]

The legion resumed its march the next morning, probably arriving in Gonzales by midafternoon. When the men entered the town they passed George W. Davis's peach orchard, where the cannon had been hidden from Mexican soldiers the previous fall. The townsmen buried the cannon and then camouflaged their work by plowing over the soil.[7] On February 4, still some seventy miles from Bexar, Joe followed Travis and the others as they departed Gonzales. The group looked for the best spot to ford the Guadalupe River and crossed without serious incident. Beneath them now lay rich, red soil, which stained everything it touched. Tall grass dominated the region. Across the skyline Joe may have occasionally spotted groups of peering Comanche warriors, who would have kept a safe distance from the armed men of the legion. Marauding Comanches preferred better odds.

At sundown, Travis ordered Joe and his men to stop for the night, probably choosing Forty-Mile-Hole as the site of the legion's encampment. Weary travelers camped at that location often, indulging in the site's spring and large water basin. A tree with the number forty carved into its trunk marked the spot of the spring, and signified the distance to Bexar.

Sunrise brought the beginning of the final leg of the journey into Bexar, a day's ride away. A bounding buck or jackrabbit may have broken the monotony of the trail as the steady trot of the horses supplied the drumbeat of progress across the mesquite-infested terrain. The supply wagon dipped and lurched over the old road, jerking at each encounter with a large stone or depression in the dirt. Finally, at the crest of a hill, Joe and his companions gazed on Bexar. For Joe, the view was likely his first. The rustic, frontier town sat pristinely in the valley below, as if on the stage of a giant amphitheater. Eyes instantly fixed on the bright, whitewashed buildings below, a scene one traveler described as "a city of white marble."[8] The scene probably reminded Joe of St. Louis and its alluring whitewash seen from a distance on the river. Early St. Louis settlers plastered their mud and stone buildings with a lime mortar, just as he now beheld below in Bexar.

The road led them down a large avenue of cottonwood trees located a short distance to the southeast of the Alamo—an old Spanish mission and now the coveted prize for those hoping to seize Bexar. Texan riders likely greeted the party and escorted them into the Alamo compound, past several mounted cannons. Inside, Joe would have seen a large rectangular courtyard of intermittent single-story adobe houses framed by an outer limestone wall. Thatched roofs of long, wooden branches covered each house. Earthen ramps rose to the top of the wall at various points to sturdy parapets with mounted cannons, such as the eighteen-pounder that sat ominously in the northwest corner of the compound. Maj. Green B. Jameson, the garrison's chief engineer, thought it the best spot to position the massive cannon to guard against both the open country to the north and the town to the west. Another earthen ramp and mounted cannons were on the north wall, as well as a pile of stones from a section of damaged wall. The breach presented an obvious weak spot.

The eastern boundary of the courtyard was as stout as any in the compound, with a long row of single- and two-story stone buildings. This section, known as the *covento*, or long barracks, comprised narrow, dank rooms where a number of the soldiers slept at night. The long barracks stretched nearly the length of the rectangular courtyard but ended abruptly before it connected with the south wall. A chest-high wall of crumbling mud and stone finished the framing of the courtyard at that point by connecting with the south wall.

Beyond the low wall, and breaking off to the east, the long barracks ran into the northern wall of the Alamo church. From this vantage point, Joe would have seen the striking façade of the church for the first time. Four life-sized, hand-carved statues stood in its rounded entrance. Carved from solid stone, they depicted religious figures.

Above the doorway observers could see the carved date "1758," perhaps the only sign of the church's true age. The Spanish originally established the Alamo in 1719 as Mission San Antonio de Valero to convert "uncivilized" Indians to Christianity. A series of setbacks and relocations plagued the mission before it was finally situated along the banks of the San Antonio River. By the time Joe arrived in 1836, locals simply called the old mission *El Alamo*, the Spanish word for "cottonwood."

Though it was far from a military garrison, the Texans did their best to secure the Alamo by reinforcing what the Mexican Army had left behind. The mission's Indian workforce had begun construction of a rounded, stone ceiling inside the church, but they had never finished the job. Visitors thus found only sky above and a mammoth earthen ramp that extended nearly the length of the church to an east wall. On each side of the church's entryway were also located a couple of ten-foot-square rooms with four-foot-thick walls.

Perhaps the greatest example of the compound's military inadequacy was the gap from the church façade to the south wall. A picket palisade now enclosed the gap with a ditch running parallel along its crude, outer wall of small tree trunks. Beyond the ditch lay a thick row of felled trees and sharpened wooden stakes buried into the ground to greet attackers.

To the east of the long barracks and north from the church sat the Alamo's horse pen, where Travis ordered the placement of the legion's extra horses. Beyond the stone corral to the north was a picket-lined pen full of cattle purchased from local ranchers. East of those areas, in the direction of Gonzales and the open prairie, lay two small ponds. Irrigation canals that fed the cornfields of Native farmers extended from the ponds on both the north and south sides, partially circling the Alamo compound. One branch of the aqueduct ran under the Alamo's walls to provide water within.

By now, Alamo co-commanders Col. James Neill and Col. James Bowie had briefed Travis on the garrison's latest intelligence. The newcomers found the news stunning, if not unbelievable. Informants passed through Bexar daily with word that forces of the Mexican Army were gathering on the Rio Grande. Lending gravity to the information was the fact that trusted friends and associates had gathered much of the intelligence.

Nearly two weeks earlier, a courier who had ridden twenty days from San Luis Potosi with a dispatch from Eugene Navarro to his brother in Bexar had alerted Neill of developments in the interior. Navarro reported that President Santa Anna himself had arrived in Saltillo with three thousand troops and intended to raise more soldiers to ride against the Texan insurrectionists.[9] A local Catholic priest also informed Bowie that he had heard that Santa Anna intended to launch attacks against Copono, Goliad, and Bexar simultaneously.[10]

Neill and Bowie told Travis that the presence on the border of some 1,400 Mexican soldiers had been confirmed four days later and that those troops were preparing to attack Bexar. In fact, every courier from the west had reported similar information.[11] No one in Bexar doubted that an attack loomed, although speculation varied as to where the Mexican Army would strike first. New seeds of paranoia sprouted daily in Bexar thanks to the unsettling news. Texan patrollers roamed nightly on the lookout for enemy spies.[12] "I have no doubt but the enemy have spies in town every twenty-four hours," Jameson wrote to Sam Houston on January 18. Even at that early date, Jameson declared he was certain that "there are 1,500 of the enemy at the town of Rio Grande, and as many more at Loredo [sic]." Jameson even quipped wryly, "And I believe they know our situation as well as we do ourselves."[13]

Bowie knew an attack was imminent and had told Governor Smith as much in a letter only days before the arrival of Travis. "Our force is very small, the returns this day to the Comdt. Is only one hundred and twenty officers and & men," he wrote. "It would be a waste of men to put our brave little band against thousands." Even so, Bowie stated, "Colonel Neill and myself have come to the solemn resolution that we will rather die in these ditches than give up this post to the enemy."[14]

Joe might have sensed the severity of the situation as Travis toured the Alamo compound. Neill and Bowie escorted Travis to the garrison's hospital, which, according to Dr. Amos Pollard, was "nearly destitute of medicine."[15] The sight was pitiful. Dozens of men lay on anything they could, shuffling restlessly to find a moment of comfort in their dingy surroundings. Many had fought gallantly to take the Alamo by storm two months earlier. Now the stench of blood and sickness hung in the dusty air of their makeshift hospital.[16] Men groaned, with nothing more than wine to kill their pain. Some lay in the filth of blood-soaked wraps. If Joe had witnessed the grim scene, it would have been his first encounter with the face of war.

Outside the Alamo, Travis surveyed the scenery along Bexar's irregular, dirt streets at some point. He might have found Bexar's architecture crude and simplistic for all the claims of it as a frontier oasis. The homes across the river amounted to nothing more than huts, which locals called *jacales*. They were constructed of logs daubed with clay and topped clumsily with straw or rushes. Inside most dwellings, inhabitants lay on cowhides or other animal skins covering dirt floors. Fires smoldered in the center of the homes, reminiscent of Indian te-pees or wigwams.

Further into the town Travis would have also noticed other strange structures, some featuring quaint garden lots fed by Bexar's irrigation canal. A number of one-story stone houses encircled a large public square of some two acres. A rough coat of lime mortar covered both the inside and outside of walls, generally four to five feet thick. Iron bars blocked windows, giving numerous dwellings the ambiance of a prison. Again, the homes offered little in the way of comfort. A few featured brick or stone floors but were lacking in amenities aside from a lone chair or table.

Towering over all the town's other structures was an ancient-looking stone church. Two kettle-shaped bells dangled from the bell tower, where a cannon ball could be seen embedded in its wall—an ominous calling card left by the latest bloody battle.[17]

The scene in Bexar would have been alien to Travis, as well as Joe. The young slave had grown up with the infant frontier burgs of Mar-thasville and St. Louis. In Texas, his arrival coincided with the early years of Harrisburg and San Felipe. But Bexar belonged in a different class in that respect. The town preceded Joe by more than a century. Still, Joe likely saw a few similarities between Bexar and St. Louis, besides the whitewash, most notably the various languages. Old World Spanish min-gled with the Native tongues and the English of the Texans. French im-migrants, black freedmen, and Indian traders were all part of Bexar's daily society, also reminiscent of the St. Louis riverfront.

Inside the Alamo, Joe would have followed Travis with their few be-longings to their new quarters and an uncertain future. The room was dark, dank, and musty like every other room in the garrison. Joe was clearly a lifetime removed from Marthasville.

14

A Passing Comet

*Since you have chosen to elect a man with a timber
toe to succeed me, you may all go to hell and
I will go to Texas.*
—*Tennessean David Crockett after losing
his 1835 attempt for reelection to the
U.S. House of Representatives*

A light drizzle fell upon Bexar as a small band of men approached the old graveyard west of town on horseback. The men eased through the dreary mist at a steady trot until their faces could be seen clearly. The sight of friendly faces brought hope to those on the banks of the San Antonio River, especially in light of repeated reports from the Rio Grande that a large force of Mexican soldiers were encamped there. Texan soldiers needed numbers to defend the precious ground they had won two months earlier.

Little did anyone know that one of those approaching men was about to bring something unique to the Texan cause. The man with a large frame sat tall in the saddle, wrapped in a wool overcoat, black hair tucked beneath a crude fur hat. He was noticeably thin and his long, pointed nose was surpassed in distinction only by his queer smile, which belied a deep sense of honor and purpose.[1] The man was David Crockett, the "half-horse, half-alligator" of American frontier fame.[2] Crockett's reputation on the frontier had carried him all the way to the halls of Congress and preceded him now wherever he traveled. By the time he arrived in Bexar on February 10, 1836, he had already become a living caricature of the real buckskin-clad hunter and folksy humorist who emerged from the Tennessee backwoods.

Tall tales of Crockett's exploits were so numerous that it had become hard to distinguish fact from fiction. Crockett himself played freely to his national image, stoking the American public's fascination with the 1834 publication of his autobiography, *A Narrative of the Life of David Crockett of the State of Tennessee*. Yet even Crockett's attempt to capitalize on his own meteoric popularity was belated. A year earlier a New York publishing company distributed the wildly successful *Sketches and Eccentricities of Col. David Crockett, of West Tennessee*. The book spawned countless homespun tales about Crockett, many of which were printed in newspapers and eagerly published in eastern journals such as *The Spirit of the Times*. He enjoyed the rare celebrity of a living legend.

Even his journey to Texas was already front-page copy in distant, eastern papers. The *Albany (N.Y.) Journal* indulged in Crockett's latest adventure with the following report: "Colonel Crockett who has recently gone to Texas is probably one of the best shots in the world. One hundred men like Crockett would be of immense service to the Texans at this time—if you could only make them believe that their enemies were *bears*, instead of men. Crockett has been known to send a rifle ball through the same hole nine times in successive fire."[3]

Relatively few Americans were unfamiliar with Crockett. Joe himself had likely heard of the eccentric Tennessean while living among the taverns and markets that hugged the St. Louis waterfront. Everyone loved a good story, especially in a spirited boomtown like St. Louis, where the legends of men like Mike Fink grew larger over each new jug of whiskey. Crockett may have been born to attain a similar status, but he reached it thanks to his dogged will to survive and his uncanny wit. Crockett once posed for a portrait by painter John G. Chapman. Decades later, Chapman remembered the man: "Say what he might[,] his meaning could never be misinterpreted. He expressed opinions, and told his stories, with unhesitating clearness of diction, often embellished with graphic touches of original wit and humor, sparkling and even startling, yet never out of place." Of Crockett's folksy speech, Chapman noted that "it was to him truly a mother-tongue, in which his ideas flowed most naturally and found most emphatic and unrestrained utterance."[4] As a public speaker "his voice was loud, and well suited to stump oratory," a New York newspaper proclaimed. "If his vocabulary was scanty, he was master of the slang of his vernacular, and was happy in his co[a]rse figures. He spurned his idle rules of grammaries, and had a rhetorick of his own."[5] Once Crockett shared his trademark humor with a crowd in Columbia, Pennsylvania. "God bless you," Crockett said with a slight pause, "for I can't."[6] The one-liner was classic Crockett.

"There are some men whom you cannot report," one reporter wrote of Crockett in 1834. "The colonel is one. His leer you cannot put upon paper—his curious drawl—the odd cant of his body and his self-congratulations. He is an original in every thing, in the tone and structure of his sentences, in the force and novelty of metophores [sic], and his range of ideas."[7]

Joe had probably never seen Crockett in person, a circumstance that would soon change on this wet, February morning. First Crockett requested the presence of James Bowie upon his arrival. He hoped Bowie would escort him on a tour of Bexar and its fortifications and apprise him of their military situation. A messenger promptly left to retrieve Bowie, who returned in the company of his friend and volunteer Antonio Menchaca. Alamo commander Col. James Neill and Travis soon joined the men to discuss Bexar's defenses. Joe may have watched as the almost mythical Crockett came to life before his eyes, and the commanding presence of Bowie would not have been lost on the young slave, either. Now those who stood nearby witnessed an astonishing, encounter: the legendary American hunter chatting with the famed American knife-fighter. Anyone present would have deduced that the quick-witted Crockett had not come to Texas to simply spin yarns. He had come to fight.

The previous fall Crockett had lost his bid for reelection to the House of Representatives by 252 votes to Adam Huntsman, a peg-legged lawyer backed by President Andrew Jackson. Then he had dealt with the defeat as one might have predicted, seeking a new adventure. On November 1, 1835, Crockett saddled his horse and left to explore the wilds of "Texes," as he spelled it. William Patton, Abner Burgin, and Lindsey K. Tinkle accompanied Crockett on the journey, perhaps not knowing what they might ultimately encounter as the drumbeat of war grew louder from Texas.[8]

After their first day of travel, the four found refuge—and a few fare-well drinks—at the Union Hotel in Memphis. Crockett, as expected, made a speech where he summed up his feelings: "Since you have cho-sen to elect a man with a timber toe to succeed me," he said, "you may all go to hell and I will go to Texas."[9] The room erupted in laughter. Crockett would repeat the line at various dinners and gatherings along his journey. The closer he got to Texas, the more his remarks strongly suggested that he intended to join the fight for Texas independence. In Little Rock, Arkansas, Crockett boasted that he would "have Santa An-na's head, and wear it for a watch seal."[10] By the time Crockett crossed into Texas, he was firing war-themed wisecracks at a rapid pace, obvi-ously playing to the anti–Santa Anna crowds. At a Nacogdoches din-ner given in his honor, Crockett said his "go to hell" line with renewed enthusiasm and promised to "lick up the Mexicans like fine salt" and to personally "grin all the Mexicans out of Texas." Each time, his com-ments brought roars of laughter.[11]

Beneath Crockett's wit dwelled something much more profound. Yes, he had come to Texas to explore the land, hunt with his buddies, and lay the political foundation as the champion of the common man in a founding republic. But Crockett also entered Texas with his rifle firmly in hand, ready to do what he saw as his duty in a fight for freedom. As a former militia scout during the Creek War, he understood the grim reality of such a commitment. Yet he embraced his path with the same spirit in which his famous motto prescribed: "Be always sure you are right, then go ahead."

Traveling between Tennessee and Texas, Crockett clearly made up his mind to go ahead. He first explored the upper reaches of Texas, where he discovered a land of milk and honey. In a letter he began to write on January 9, 1836, to his daughter and son-in-law, Crockett proclaimed: "I expect in all probability to settle on the Bodark or Choctaw Bayou of the Red River, that I have no doubt is the richest country in the world, good land, plenty of timber, and the best springs, and good mill streams, good range, clear water & every appearance of health—game a plenty. It is in the pass where the buffalo passes from the north to south and back twice a year and bees and honey a plenty." Crockett found the coun-try mesmerizing, defining it as "the garden spot of the world."[12]

On January 12, three days after starting his letter, he and Patton took the oath of allegiance to the provisional government of Texas. At first, Crockett balked at the oath and pledging allegiance to any "future other government that may be thereafter declared." The oath left too much room for a interpretation as far as Crockett was concerned. He insisted that the word "republican" be inserted before "government." Judge John Forbes happily obliged his celebrity volunteer.[13]

Crockett signed to serve a six-month stint as a volunteer in the Texan army. He again picked up his pen to finish his letter, noting that he thought his prospects of being elected to a Texan constitutional convention were as sound as his abilities to secure a fortune for his family. "I am rejoiced at my fate," Crockett wrote. "I had rather be in my present situation than to be elected to a seat in Congress for Life."[14] Soon after, Crockett took command of a small "Mounted Spy Company," consisting of himself plus five other men.[15] Their role would be to act more as scouts than "spies."

Crockett still found time for playful conversation as he rode deeper into Texas and closer to war. His journey took him to the Gay Hill home of James Swisher near Montville and also to John Berry's home at Bastrop. Berry assisted Crockett by repairing the broken stock on his rifle with a "large silver band." Swisher indulged Crockett by lending him an ear. "Few could eclipse him in conversation," Swisher later remembered. "He was fond of talking, and had an ease and grace about him which, added to his strong natural sense and the fund of anecdotes he had gathered, rendered him irresistible." Swisher noted that he found many of Crockett's stories "were common place and amounted to nothing in themselves, but his irresistible way of telling them would convulse one with laughter."[16]

Still, a deep sense of purpose lay underneath. A fellow Tennessean noticed a distinct determination that was not easily recognized behind Crockett's avalanche of homespun tales. "Crockett[,] who cannot blow his nose without a queer remark or observation, was regarded as a passing comet, not to be seen again, and every hand extended either in courtesy or regard," Calvin Jones wrote several days after Crockett's visit to his home in Bolivar, Tennessee. "This occasion proved him to be more of a Lion than I had supposed."[17]

Rumors seemingly flooded into Bexar on an hourly basis. The town's defenses remained the most pressing topic of conversation with Crockett and the others. Neill, Bowie, and Travis defined Bexar's weaknesses and strengths, as well as their prospects for reinforcements.[18] Morale had generally remained high, and Crockett's appearance heightened everyone's enthusiasm. Crockett brought more than a handful of fresh bodies to Bexar's defenses: he brought a winning attitude to the mix. A festive mood quickly spread throughout town as the announcement of a ball in Crockett's honor circulated. All the principal women of Bexar were invited.[19] The ball afforded Texans the opportunity to cut loose for an evening and to become acquainted with the living legend himself, and Crockett did not disappoint. He drew his bow across his fiddle and energetically played, matching his mammoth reputation. Perhaps Crockett's fiddle playing reminded Joe of those raucous shindigs of his youth around the slave quarters at Marthasville, or his time at Harrisburg, where Moses L. Choate joyfully entertained the townspeople with his violin.

Travis, as expected, hopped along the dance floor, gleefully bouncing from one pretty *señorita* to another. Laughter flowed as freely as the whiskey until Crockett climbed atop a crate in Bexar's main plaza to the hoots and hollers of the men who gathered around. Crockett began with his now favorite one-liner. He spoke of his recent defeat for a seat in Congress, noting that he had told his constituents in Tennessee that "if they did not elect him, they might all go to hell, and he would go to Texas." A roar of laughter went up from the crowd encircling Crockett, who grinned and held his hands aloft until he regained the silence of his listeners. "And fellow citizens," Crockett bellowed, "I am among you. I have come to your country, though not, I hope, through any selfish motive whatever. I have come to aid you all that I can in your noble cause. I shall identify myself with your interests, and all the honor that I desire is that of defending as a high private, in common with my fellow citizens, the liberties of our common country." Men who did not even know Crockett now called him friend.[20]

The fandango stretched into the early morning hours, and at one o'clock Travis twirled with yet another beautiful señorita. Around that time a courier arrived at the ballroom door and asked for Juan Seguín, who was not present. The man then asked to speak to Antonio Menchaca, saying he had a letter of great importance to share. Menchaca greeted the man and received a letter written by Placido Benavides, who had been scouting near Camargo, some two hundred miles south of the Rio

Grande. Menchaca began to read aloud: "At this moment I have received a very certain notice, that the commander in chief, Antonio López de Santa Anna, marches for the city of San Antonio to take possession thereof, with 13,000 men."[21]

Bowie approached as Menchaca was reading. Hearing the letter's contents, he turned to Travis and called him to read the letter himself. Playfully, Travis told Bowie he was too busy dancing with the most beautiful lady in Bexar. Bowie's tone of voice changed when he asked Travis a second time, suggesting he leave his partner and pay heed to the "grave importance" of the message. Travis, finally realizing that Bowie was serious, excused himself from his dance partner and approached with Crockett. Together, the three men read the letter and pondered the approximate distance of the Mexican troops. After further consideration of their plight, Travis smiled and said, "Let us dance tonight and tomorrow we will make provisions for our defense."[22]

By the time the ball ended that morning, the pleasurable residue of the fandango had dissipated with blurry-eyed exhaustion. Texan soldiers grudgingly returned to work, while Travis and the other officers grew more consumed with the whereabouts of Santa Anna's army. And the day brought yet another bit of sobering news. Colonel Neill was about to leave Bexar after having received an express informing him of his family's ill health. A popular commander who had gained the respect of his men, Neill's absence, however temporary, promised to be felt by all.[23] Before leaving, Neill left command of the post to Travis until his return.[24]

By now Travis talked openly with his fellow officers about the dire need for reinforcements. He felt certain that the first point of attack would be Bexar, for it was the "door for the invaders to enter the sacred Territory of the colonies." Yet how, Travis asked, could they keep that door shut with no more than 150 men who were growing more discouraged every day?[25]

"We hope our countrymen will open their eyes to the present danger," Travis wrote to Governor Smith. The realization of what was at stake began to toy with his darkest fears. If Bexar fell, Santa Anna's army would have an open path into the colonies, where he envisioned the "pollution" of "wives and daughters," the cries of "Famished Children," and the rising smoke of "burning dwellings."[26]

In his twenty-plus years, Joe had seen horrific atrocities inflicted against his fellow humans, not the least of which were the bloodlettings produced by an overseer's whip. The kind of destruction that Travis predicted would have brought a whole new layer of fear for someone like Joe. Travis, meanwhile, had other problems. The volunteers did not appear willing to take orders from him. Perhaps they viewed him as too young or brash, or maybe they simply wanted to complain. Travis allowed the volunteers to vote for their own representative, someone who could speak on their behalf. His peace offering was misinterpreted by many of the volunteers, who selected Bowie as their leader.[27]

Bowie, in turn, viewed the vote as an opportunity to take control of the entire garrison. He took it upon himself to inspect the carts of families leaving for the countryside. He also released one man convicted of theft from Bexar's prison, as well as others under military court-martial, placing them on work detail at the Alamo. His domineering actions were worsened by his constant drunkenness.[28]

Travis, calling his situation "awkward & delicate," appealed to Governor Smith for guidance and reinforcements in a letter he sent with scout Erastus "Deaf" Smith on February 13. Bowie aside, Travis still recognized the bigger picture and the danger that lurked just beyond the Rio Grande. Joe surely heard the whispers of the messengers who reported to his master. Texan spies judged Santa Anna's army at "one thousand strong" on the Rio Grande and preparing to invade. Travis projected that the invasion would take place by March 15—only thirty-one days away. Time was slipping away quickly. "I hope you will immediately order some regular troops to this place—as it is more important to occupy this Post than I imagined when I last saw you," Travis wrote. "It is the key to Texas."[29]

The severity of the situation begged for cooler heads to prevail, and that, perhaps as much as anything, prompted Bowie and Travis to reach a compromise about the post's command. Bowie, after all, was no fool when it came to combat. Nor was he willing to jeopardize any semblance of solidarity in the face of an onrushing enemy. The fighter who dwelled in Bowie's soul would not allow such an edge to any adversary. Bowie and Travis reached an agreement one day after Travis's seething letter to Smith, in which he declared that he would not tolerate any man's "drunken irregularities." This time, Bowie and Travis jointly signed a letter to Smith, saying they agreed on a split command. Bowie would command the garrison's volunteers, while Travis would oversee its regular troops and volunteer cavalry. Both men would sign all future orders and correspondence until Neill's return.[30]

The enemy's position on the Rio Grande hardly came as a surprise to the Alamo's defenders or Bexar's occupants. A number of local Mexicans readily discussed all they had heard from relatives or travelers passing through from the south. The stories generally agreed: large Mexican forces were gathering on the Rio Grande, some 180 miles from Bexar. Texan spies provided similar intelligence. Many formed their own opinions as to when the hostile Mexican forces would attack. Soldiers like David Cummings, a rifleman from Pennsylvania, either repeated Travis's mid-March theory or independently agreed with it when he wrote his father during a lull in the long hours of work shoring up the Alamo. Cummings told his father he did not expect the Mexican Army to "make any movement this way until the weather becomes warm or until the grass is sufficiently up to support their horses." The hard winter certainly did not bode well for any animal—including human—during a forced march. Regardless, Cummings said he and his comrades fully expected "a heavy attack" from Santa Anna himself, noting that "the despot will use every possible means and strain every nerve to conquer and exterminate us from the land." Of this, Cummings concluded, "we have no fear."[31]

Travis and Joe heard more than their share of ominous forebodings from Bexar's residents. Each day Travis walked to town from his Alamo headquarters to visit with the locals, cultivating relationships and staying abreast of the scuttlebutt. Joe may have shadowed Travis on these daily excursions as his body servant, stopping frequently at the Rodriguez home just across the San Antonio River. The family had become quite fond of Travis, whom they viewed as "a very popular man" among their neighbors.[32] One day Rodriquez summoned Travis to his home. He informed the co-commander that "a reliable source" had told the family that Santa Anna had already started his march toward Bexar with seven thousand troops in tow. Travis doubted the accuracy of the report, primarily given the fact that the storming of Bexar had occurred less than three months earlier. Could Santa Anna have mobilized his army in such a short time? The family urged Travis to abandon the Alamo and retreat toward the Texas interior, but Travis calmly and politely shrugged off any such thoughts. He told them the same thing he told

Governor Smith. "Well," Travis replied, "we have made up our minds to die at the Alamo fighting for Texas."[33]

Dying, of course, was the last thing Travis or any other Texan soldier wanted to do. Talk of death surely would not have sat well with Joe, who had limited options as a slave. Both found small comfort in the officers' never-ending appeals for supplies, money, and most of all, reinforcements, and Joe watched couriers leave the Alamo daily with pleas for help. Would anyone answer the call? Any chance of rallying reinforcements rested in the success of couriers like David Harmon, a scrawny youngster dispatched by Bowie and Crockett at some point in February. Harmon had orders to ride with a plea for volunteers to hurry to Bexar. Before leaving, Harmon stood on an embankment where he and his companions had staked their horses. Four other soldiers and Crockett accompanied him. Two of the soldiers asked Crockett "if he thought there was any chance for a fight, [for] if not they were going home." Crockett said that there "had been plenty of men there to take the town, but that the men were going away as fast as they came, and remarked that if he was in command he would have given them 'Sheet' long ago, meaning that he would whip them [reinforcements] out [of the colonies]—& [he] said that they needed someone to carry orders back to hurry up the drafted men & all soldiers at home."[34]

Crockett would eventually volunteer to place that responsibility on his own shoulders. But until that time arrived, he continued to bolster morale with his unique wit. His presence alone gave the garrison periodic diversion from the long, laborious days spent strengthening the Alamo's defenses. Every able man contributed to the daily grind. Work crews shoveled mounds of dirt to reinforce the Alamo's gun ramparts, as well as other strategic locations throughout the sprawling compound. Horses had to be fed and shod, firewood cut and collected, clothes cleaned, cattle butchered, meals cooked, and the sick tended to as much as possible. Mostly, the Texans prepared for combat. For part of this task, they turned to a blacksmith who owned a shop near the Alamo, pressing blacksmith Antonio Saez to repair many of their firearms.[35] Capt. Almeron Dickinson, an artillery officer and blacksmith by trade, may have assisted Saez.

Nightfall brought well-deserved rest for the Alamo's soldiers, who splintered into smaller groups if they had not already been assigned to guard detail. Campfires flickered throughout the compound as men huddled to stay warm against the sting of the north wind. A few men sought respite in a game of cards, others in a few swigs of whiskey or sips of hot coffee. Talk often drifted toward the subject of families and homesteads, neither of which rested far from the common soldier's heart. Many spoke often of their children. Naturally, the talk nearly turned to their present revolution and the whereabouts of Santa Anna and his army. Crockett entertained as only he could. He spun one yarn after another, and when moved to do so, played one of his favorite tunes on his trusty fiddle.

Not everyone spent their nights inside the Alamo, though. Dickinson and his wife, Susanna, stayed in town at the Ramon Musquiz home near the main plaza. The Musquiz home offered a little more privacy for the young couple and their fifteen-month-old daughter, Angelina.[36] Joe, meanwhile, spent his evenings either with Travis or among the other slaves inside the garrison.[37]

Few—if any—Texans passed on the chance to celebrate. They always had enough energy for a good time, and George Washington's birthday presented an excuse to stage another fandango. February 22 meant something in those days. The townspeople of Bexar planned a large ball for that evening with all the prominent *señoritas* again invited to attend. The dance—done Texas style—picked up where the Crockett ball had left off eleven days earlier. Bowie's volunteers cut loose as always, the wildest of whom sold their rifles to purchase some alcohol.[38] Crockett, of course, brought his fiddle and his endless bag of tall tales.

Likewise, Travis came well prepared. He brought his favorite pair of dancing shoes, and he spun and twirled into the night—a sight familiar to Joe in the three and a half years they had known each other. Travis had no shyness around women, and on this night he whirled his partners around the dance floor as if there were no tomorrow.

A sudden rainstorm pelted Bexar's dirt streets as the Texans partied into the night, seemingly oblivious to the weather. Those in attendance shared a feeling of comfort and camaraderie amid the sound of music, laughter, and conversation. They were, in that moment, carefree, but it would be their final hours of peace. Advance elements of Santa Anna's centralist army were camped eight miles away on the overflowing banks of the Medina River.[39]

15

THE WOLF

The people now begin to think the wolf has actually
come at last, and are preparing for a march.
—William Fairfax Gray, diary entry at
San Felipe de Austin

A ringing bell meant trouble to Joe. As a child it struck fear in his heart and soul. Even now, worlds away from Marthasville, how could he forget Grove Cook's bell hanging on the post outside his house? The overseer rang the bell precisely at four each morning there, signaling another day of hard labor and oppression for every slave. Toil and pain became the bell's legacy.[1]

Now, as the late-afternoon sun beat down on the plastered adobe houses and *jacales* of Bexar, Joe heard that sound from his childhood. The clanging emanated from the San Fernando Church bell tower, where a sentinel frantically tugged on the bell rope. "The enemy is in view!" the sentinel cried.[2] All motion stopped briefly and silence momentarily befell the town. Then the gravity of the words sank in, sparking a powder keg of reaction.

The signs had been clear that something was about to happen. Local Mexicans had streamed steadily into the countryside all morning with loaded ox carts of household supplies, furnishings, and baskets of food.

Each cart moved on giant wheels hewn from mammoth oak or cotton-wood trees, creaking along at a slow pace, jolted with each stone and rut. Those stopped and questioned offered nothing in the way of new information, saying only that they were destined for their ranches to prepare for the coming crop. Once released, they lurched down the dirt road and out of sight.[3] Travis, though, deduced that they were lying. He worked the local populace with his usual charm, assuming someone would eventually talk. Finally, someone told Travis that Mexican cavalry had reached Leon Creek and that an informant had warned locals the previous evening to leave town at sunrise because there would be an attack on the Texan rebels. Based on that, Travis had summoned a sentinel to the bell tower. He had also sent both Capt. Phillip Dimmit and Lt. Benjamin Noble to reconnoiter the enemy but had yet to hear back from them.[4]

As soon as the alarm sounded, Travis and a number of other men ran quickly to the church, bounding up the narrow stairway leading to its bell tower. The excited sentinel awaited them, but the Mexican soldiers were nowhere to be seen. Each man strained to spot the enemy on the horizon. "It's a false alarm!" one man finally shouted. But the sentinel insisted he had seen lancers riding through clouds of dust in the distance.[5] Unbeknown to the Texans, the Mexican cavalry had filed off the road and behind a grove of mesquite.

Meanwhile, a commotion took root in Bexar. Men began to speculate on what the sentinel had seen, creating a stir. Travis needed to know the enemy's location with certainty. Dr. John Sutherland, a fellow Alabaman, volunteered to ride out and scout. Travis agreed and called on John W. Smith to accompany Sutherland on the mission. Smith, known to friends as "El Colorado," made a solid choice. A highly respected merchant and carpenter in Bexar, he knew the terrain well. Together, Smith and Sutherland heeled their horses westward, uncertain of what they might encounter. Their mystery ended less than two miles out, when they crested a hill and suddenly saw an advance unit of Mexican cavalry. Hundreds of lances and sabers glistened in the sun, presenting a brilliant, albeit sobering, sight.

Wheeling their horses, the Texans dashed back to report the news. But Sutherland's horse began to slide in the mud, finally toppling on its side only three hundred yards from the enemy. A grove of mesquite trees shielded his spill. Instantly dismounting, Smith pulled a grimacing Sutherland to his feet and hurriedly hoisted him back into the saddle of the horse that had struggled back to its feet. The two men then galloped back to Bexar, where Travis and a number of other men had already made their way across the river and into the Alamo.[6]

"Here come the Mexicans!" Smith shouted to his friend Juan Seguín, a local resident who helped raised a volunteer company from the ranches along the San Antonio River. Seguín, whose loyalties clearly lay with Texas, rounded up his men and quickly made his way toward the Alamo.

Confirmation of the Mexican Army's proximity created panic and confusion in town. Regular Texan troops and volunteers alike scurried toward the Alamo, scooping their guns and what necessities they could carry as they hustled for refuge. Several men clamored to buy back the rifles they had sold the evening before for a few swigs of whiskey.[7]

Men with families suddenly faced their worst fears. Capt. Almeron Dickinson did not hesitate. The Gonzales blacksmith galloped in front of the Musquiz house, where he and his twenty-two-year-old wife had been staying. Susanna refused to leave her husband's side. Now Almeron found himself leaning over and hoisting his wife with his powerful right arm. Susanna sat bareback behind her husband's saddle with the couple's infant daughter, Angelina, pressed against her breast. The little family then dashed toward the Alamo.[8]

Gregorio Esparza, one of Seguín's enlisted men from Bexar, had planned to move his family far from the danger of any future military encounter to the Texas interior. Rumors in previous days of Santa Anna's arrival made him increasingly nervous about his family's welfare. Esparza finally decided to send his family to safety in San Felipe. Smith, a family friend, promised to loan him a wagon for the move, but those plans shattered the moment he delivered his stunning news.[9]

The missed opportunity now weighed heavily on Esparza's mind. He concluded that his family's best chance for survival would be to remain in town, out of sight from the enemy in the shadows of their small adobe house along the irrigation canal. Esparza told his wife, Ana, "Well, I'm going to the fort." Ana responded, "Well, if you go, I'm going along, and the whole family too."[10] They had no time to argue. Ana's decision would stand. Gregorio and Ana quickly began gathering their belongings, then made several trips across the river to the Alamo. Sweat poured from their brows as they hoisted one bundle after another over their shoulders. Yet the uncertainty was the greatest burden—uncertainty all too familiar to slaves like Joe.

Bowie, as was his nature, sprang to action. He led a detachment of men and broke into several deserted houses to confiscate corn. Another squad drove a herd of cattle into the pens east of the Alamo's long barracks.[11]

With Joe perhaps by his side, Travis hurriedly scribbled a plea for help to Judge Andrew Ponton in nearby Gonzales: "The enemy in large force are in sight. We want men and provisions. Send them to us. We have 150 men and are determined to defend the Alamo to the last. Give us assistance. P.S. Send an express to San Felipe with news night and day."[12] Travis handed the letter to a courier and ordered him to ride urgently. Soon after, Travis and Bowie jointly addressed a letter to Col. James Fannin at Goliad. "We have removed all the men to the Alamo where we make such resistance as is due our honor, and that of our country, until we can get assistance from you, which we expect you to forward immediately," the letter stated. "In this extremity, we hope you will send us all the men you can spare promptly. We have one hundred and forty six men, who are determined never to retreat. We have but little provisions, but enough to serve us until you and your men arrive." Playing to Fannin's conscience, Travis and Bowie added, "We deem it unnecessary to repeat to a brave officer, who knows his duty, that we call on him for assistance."[13] Another courier left with the letter in all haste.

Meanwhile, in Bexar, local merchant Nat Lewis decided to abandon his store. He stuffed what goods he could into his saddlebags and scrambled into the Alamo for refuge. He would later go to Gonzales, but what he saw in the Alamo never escaped his memory. Confusion ruled. A maze of men, women, children, and animals crisscrossed the Alamo compound franticly, anguish on every woman's face. Officers shouted orders in the din. Babies cried. Dogs barked. Clouds of dirt drifted in the wake of pounding horse hooves. Yet no one thought of flight.

Lewis, still clinging to his bulky saddlebags, gazed across the compound. Amid the madness he noticed something out of the ordinary. One man, an Irish sergeant named William B. Ward, stood resolutely at his artillery post high above the walls of the main gate, ready to do his duty for Texas. Ward had a reputation as a drunkard, but in the flicker of a moment, Lewis saw someone quite different. He saw a hero.[14]

Outside the walls, soldiers continued to frantically gather supplies as they hurried to take refuge in the Alamo. Juan Seguín rode his horse through the gates with a number of *Tejano* volunteers, only to realize he had not locked the doors to his villa. Candelario Villanueva, a loyal Seguín volunteer, rode back to town to secure Seguín's villa, but Villanueva would not return to his comrades—he was cut off by Santa Anna's troops. This would prove both a blessing and a curse to Villanueva.

Others escaped narrowly. Enrique Esparza, then a diminutive twelve-year-old, recalled how he was playing with other children in Bexar's Main Plaza when Santa Anna first appeared astride a brilliant horse. Santa Anna dismounted and handed his reins to a lackey, prompting the children to flee to their respective homes. That's when Esparza's family began their frantic flight into the Alamo. One by one they stuffed bundles of goods through a window, scurrying back and forth across the river until they could take no more chances. Finally, as the family crossed the footbridge one last time, they heard the beating drums of the Mexican Army behind them in the town's square.

A neighboring Mexican boy named Juan Diaz watched the procession from the church bell tower. "I will never forget how that army looked as it swept into town," Diaz recalled more than sixty years later. "At the head of the soldiers came the regimental band, playing the liveliest airs, and with the band came a squad of men bearing the flags and banners of Mexico and an immense image that looked like an alligator's head."[15]

Moments later, a gun roared as the Esparza family scurried across the ditch just outside the Alamo's walls.[16] Gregorio Esparza, Enrique's father, lifted his wife and children through one of the Alamo's windows. He climbed in behind them, closing and barring the window. A siege had begun.

16

BESIEGED

The enemy has demanded a surrender at discretion,
otherwise, the garrison are to be put to the sword, if
the fort is taken—I have answered the demand with a
cannon shot, & our flag still waves proudly from the
walls—I shall never surrender or retreat.
—William Barret Travis, February 24, 1836

At some point Joe gripped the cold iron barrel of the gun Travis had given him should the Mexican forces attack. Firearms would have been nothing new to Joe. Slaves had been permitted to use flintlock rifles with regularity around Marthasville and St. Louis to hunt squirrels, rabbits, and other small game. Whether Joe had ever held a gun before, he was likely struck now by the profound weight of its intended purpose. Squirrels and rabbits were one thing, but this gun might be used to shoot another man—a stranger. Joe, like every member of the garrison, would probably fire without hesitation. The stakes were life and death.

By now, Joe possessed a clear idea of the character of the Mexican soldier, compliments of Travis and his comrades. He had surely heard their warnings of Mexican treachery and their predictions about what would

transpire if Texas fell to Santa Anna and his minions. The yoke of oppression, they echoed, would be strapped to every man, woman, and
child under their domain. Oppression was all too familiar to Joe, who
could now see the hundreds of Mexican troops streaming into Bexar.
Those soldiers had traveled great distances to squash a rebellion, and a
full-scale assault would likely bring death to those in the Alamo. Santa
Anna had ordered a blood-red flag hoisted high above the San Fernando
bell tower for all to see.[1] Texans who did not understand its meaning at
first learned it in blunt language quickly: it meant no quarter, no mercy.

There were additional signs of pending doom, some subtler than others. Travis, as Joe might have expected, heightened tensions by brazenly
answering the red flag with a theatrical move of his own. Travis ordered
a lone cannon shot to be fired.[2] The blast said more than Travis could
have in a thousand letters.

Bowie, far more seasoned in matters of life and death, found the actions of the young lieutenant colonel appalling. For his taste, Bowie subscribed to a different philosophy: live to fight another day. He did not
have to be a military genius to understand the odds. At best, the Texans
had 150 men with another "50 or 60" who were recovering from wounds
suffered in the fight to capture Bexar more than two months earlier.
Meanwhile, hundreds of Mexican soldiers continued to file into Bexar
each hour. Now the Mexicans began to lob cannonballs into the garrison from a five-inch howitzer. The firing ceased when a lone rider
emerged from the Alamo compound carrying a dirty white flag. Bowie
delegated Green B. Jameson, the garrison's engineer, to carry a letter to
whoever was in charge of the Mexican forces.[3] In the letter, Bowie inquired whether the Mexican Army had requested a parley. Bowie's inquiry was a stretch but a worthwhile charade if it bought time and therefore lives.

Mexican colonel Juan N. Almonte, Santa Anna's courtly bilingual
aide-de-camp, met Jameson and forwarded the letter back to the Mexican camp. Joe would have recognized Almonte from his journey
through the colonies two years before at the time of Mansfield's death.
He may have also remembered how popular Almonte had been with
the ladies—and how the men distrusted him. Jameson, meanwhile,
chatted with Almonte as he waited for an answer. The talkative engineer,

probably nervous, informed the Mexican colonel of the Alamo's poor condition and is said to have divulged Bowie's desire for an honorable surrender.[4]

Soon Jameson received a reply in a letter written by Mexican colonel Jose Batres. The letter read: "I reply to you, according to the order of His Excellency, that the Mexican army cannot come to terms under any condition with rebellious foreigners to whom there is no other recourse left, if they wish to save their lives, than to place themselves immediately at the disposal of the Supreme Government from whom alone they may expect clemency after some considerations. God and liberty!"[5]

Bowie knew better than to trust Santa Anna with an unconditional surrender. Travis, meanwhile, strongly disapproved of the term "rebellious foreigners" as well as Bowie's unilateral decision to request a parley without his permission. Travis fumed as he sent his own messenger to meet Almonte. That duty fell to Albert Martin, a twenty-eight-year-old merchant from New Orleans who resided now in Gonzales. Martin expressed Travis's desire to visit with Almonte.

"I answered," Almonte later wrote in his journal, "that it did not become the Mexican Government to make any propositions through me, and that I had only permission to hear such as might be made on the part of the rebels."[6] Almonte's response clearly meant that there would be no parley, and from that moment Travis resumed his commitment to defend the Alamo to the last—with or without reinforcements. Joe, in all likelihood, did not have to be told of his master's determination. He probably saw it in his eyes. Slaves instilled resolve into their children from their earliest days, and Elizabeth had been no exception. She would have taught her children to be tough, to improvise as circumstances dictated, and to endure when all appeared futile. Did her words rush back to Joe now?

The sun set for the first time on the besieged garrison. No one knew what the coming hours would bring, but that situation was nothing new for Joe. Uncertainty had shadowed his life.

The next day, after having endured continual bombardment all morning, Travis holed up in his dank room to craft another plea for help. Joe may have quietly sat nearby, perhaps at his master's hand as it briskly guided a quill pen across a piece of paper. In broad, firm strokes, Travis penned a letter that defined the peril of their situation:

To the People of Texas & all Americans in the world—

Fellow citizens & compatriots—

I am besieged, by a thousand or more of the Mexicans under Santa Anna—I have sustained a continual Bombardment & cannonade for 24 hours & have not lost a man—the enemy has demanded a surrender at discretion, otherwise, the garrison are to be put to the sword, if the fort is taken—I have answered the demand with a cannon shot, & our flag still waves proudly from the walls—*I shall never surrender or retreat.* Then, I call on you in the name of Liberty, of patriotism & every thing dear to the American character, to come to our aid, with all dispatch—The enemy is receiving reinforcements daily & will no doubt increase to three or four thousand in four or five days. If this call is neglected, I am determined to sustain myself as long as possible & die like a soldier who never forgets what is due to his own honor & that of his country—

VICTORY OR DEATH

William Barret Travis
Lt. Col. Comdt

P.S. The Lord is on our side—When the enemy appeared in sight we had not three bushels of corn—We have since found in deserted houses 80 or 90 bushels & got into the walls 20 or 30 heads of Beeves—

Travis[7]

Again Travis turned to Martin to deliver his message. This time Travis ordered Martin to carry his plea seventy miles east to Gonzales, where he believed Martin could rally fledgling Gonzales rangers. Martin waited for sunset before riding out of the Alamo and disappearing into the darkness of the prairie. By daybreak, Martin would have heard the thunder of cannons emanating from Bexar. The cannons roared throughout the day as he galloped toward Gonzales, and he thought of the garrison's sparse supply of ammunition. He feared the worst.[8]

Still he pressed on with his own measure of resolve, determined to return to aid his brave comrades, with or without reinforcements. In this hour of peril, it was the kind of fortitude that men of all skin colors understood and respected.

Meanwhile, the shadows of time closed in on the tiny Alamo garrison. Mexican troops had advanced on the old mission, crossing the river around 10:00 A.M. and taking cover among the crude, thatched-roofed houses some hundred yards beyond its walls. Travis estimated their strength at "two or three hundred" soldiers, the force of which opened fire on the Texans with random volleys. From a greater distance Mexican gunners maintained a constant bombardment of cannon balls, canister, and grapeshot.

The Alamo defenders answered with a fierce rainstorm of their own artillery. Captains Dickinson, fellow Tennessean Samuel Blair, and Virginian William Carey worked feverishly to help maintain the fire of the Alamo's undermanned artillery units. Each earned Travis's praise, as did Crockett. The quick-witted backwoodsman proved to be as steady under fire as he was on a crate spinning a yarn. Crockett rushed into the heart of the firestorm, "animating the men to do their duty."[9]

Mexican artillery fire crashed into the Alamo's walls, spraying pieces of rock, but no Texan was injured during the exchange. Joe, meanwhile, likely remained within earshot of Travis. The young slave may have fired his gun at the enemy or loaded the firearms of others, or he may have watched in paralyzed awe. Regardless, Joe saw the intimacy of battle for the first time in his life. The fight raged for two hours before the Mexican forces finally withdrew, dragging their dead and wounded with them. Almonte noted four Mexican wounded and two dead—a small yet costly price to pay to test the garrison's resolve.[10]

Santa Anna later ordered a tighter stranglehold on his enemy. As nightfall arrived, he directed new batteries to be erected across the river and cavalry units to be posted in the hills east of the Alamo and on the road to Gonzales.[11] Having their own agenda, the Texans responded under the cover of darkness. Charles Despallier and Robert Brown sallied from the fort and dodged enemy gunshot to set fire to the thatch-roofed houses providing shelter for Mexican riflemen. Both men returned safely to the cheers of their comrades.[12]

Meanwhile, unbeknown to the Alamo defenders, at Goliad's Fort Defiance some ninety miles southeast of Bexar, Col. James Fannin prepared to march 320 soldiers to their aid by daybreak on February 26. Word of the Alamo's perilous situation had reached Fannin earlier in the day via a courier sent by Travis—more than likely John Johnson. The young Johnson, who rode an "elegant Bay horse," told Fannin of the thunderous cannon fire he had heard en route to Goliad.[13] Johnson, like Martin, feared for the garrison.

"I am well aware that my present movement toward Bexar is anything but a military one," Fannin wrote. "The appeal of cols Travis & Bowie cannot however pass unnoticed—particularly by troops now on the field—Sanguine, chivalrous Volunteers—Much must be risked to relieve the besieger."[14] Fannin did not speak of such a price carelessly. Of the 420 men under his command, most wore tattered clothes and few possessed shoes. "We are almost naked and without provisions and very little ammunition," John Sowers Brooks, a twenty-two-year-old Virginian and Fannin's aide de camp, wrote to his father.[15]

Fannin's men lived off fresh beef and little else. Yet their physical pains and discomforts failed to diminish their desire to assist their brothers in arms. "We have suffered much and may reasonably anticipate much greater suffering," Brooks wrote. "But if we succeed in reaching Bexar, before the Garrison is compelled to surrender and are successful in taking the place and its gallant defenders, we shall deem ourselves amply repaid for our trials and hardships." Brooks measured the odds and confessed to his father, "We are undisciplined in a great measure; they are regulars, the elite of Santa Anna's army, well fed, well clothed, and well appointed and accompanied by a formidable battery of heavy field and battering pieces. We have a few pieces but no experienced artillerists and but a few rounds of fixed ammunition, and perhaps less of loose powder and balls. We can not therefore calculate very sanguinely upon victory. However, we will do our best, and if we perish, Texas and our friends will remember that we have done our duty."[16]

Sleep called to Brooks shortly thereafter as the coming day gnawed at his nerves. He was not alone. Inside the Alamo, a black man he had never met surely wrestled with the same anxieties. Joe, like those around him, may have envisioned the potential dark hours to come and perhaps even fretted about a life not fully lived. He too fell asleep uncertain of his fate but perhaps more certain of his own will to live than at any point in his life. A battle was now inevitable, and Joe would be forced to fight. His intentions were not marked by bravado or documented in letters sent out by couriers but rather symbolized by the loaded gun that sat at his bedside. The gun lay ready to discharge death. So did a scared kid from Missouri.

17

FATE

*I think we had better march out and die in the open
air. I don't like being hemmed up.*
—*David Crockett, sometime during the siege*

An icy norther whipped into Bexar as daylight pushed through the clouds on the fourth day of the siege. The temperatures dipped to thirty-nine degrees Fahrenheit, delivering a chill that numbed the body and cut to the bone.[1] Joe and the garrison's defenders huddled near fires throughout the Alamo compound. Some passed the time by chatting about loved ones back home, or enjoying the precious, last stores of coffee and tea they had been rationing.[2]

Wood had become another precious commodity. To retrieve wood from outside, men sallied from the Alamo throughout the day under the fire of Mexican sharpshooters. The Texans also retrieved water.[3] No one was killed.

The dawn ushered in another constant bombardment by Mexican artillerymen. Round after round whistled into the Alamo with little physical effect, but the bombings began to take an emotional toll. No one inside the garrison felt completely free to roam the compound as long as the Mexican gunners remained busy. Ducking, dodging, flinching, crouching—all strained the nerves of the besieged. Deprived of any real rest, the defenders knew that the fateful hour would arrive when their souls would be tried by battle.

Between Mexican cannonades, time stood still. Hours passed in watchful waiting, menial tasks, conversation, and more waiting. Jacob Walker, an artilleryman under Capt. William Carey's command, talked often of his children.[4] Words tumbled out in rapid succession as James Rose, a private from Arkansas, told of how he had narrowly escaped from a Mexican officer during the last attack.[5] Crockett, losing his taste for idle chat, spoke his mind bluntly. In a defining moment of contemplation, he deadpanned, "I think we had better march out and die in the open air. I don't like being hemmed up."[6] He was not joking.

By nightfall, the moon and stars shined brilliantly through spotty clouds in a sky as vast as the promise of Texas. The moonlight carried Micajah Autry back home to Jackson, Tennessee, and his wife, Martha, and their children, Mary and James. Two months earlier on guard duty, Autry could not help but think of his beloved Martha as he stood on the Alamo's walls and gazed at the moon. "With what pleasure did I contemplate that lovely orb chiefly because I recollected how often you and I have taken pleasure in standing in the door and contemplating her together," Autry wrote his wife. "Indeed I imagined that you might be looking at her at the same time. Farewell Dear Martha."[7]

Romantic as he was, Autry had been a failure in nearly everything he had tried. He had farmed for a period before trying his hand at teaching. He later entered the law field, only to realize the ever-shifting tides of the legal profession were not for him. His most recent stab at success had been as a merchant, which also failed. Never lacking enthusiasm for a fresh start, Autry followed the lure of promise to Texas. From the beginning he believed his prosperity lay rooted in his military service and the coming revolution. On January 14, 1836, he enlisted in the Volunteer Auxiliary Corps, known popularly as "the Tennessee Mounted Volunteers," and rode for Bexar. If only the boys back in Jackson could have seen Autry as he rode alongside the legendary Crockett. By then, Autry had committed to his path, having boldly written his wife, "I am determined to provide you a home or perish."[8] Now, trapped by enemy forces and fate, Autry possibly began to take inventory of his life, realizing perhaps for the first time that his real wealth all along had been his family. So it may have been for may of the men inside the Alamo.

The winds of chance had swept others into Bexar with equal cruelty. Crockett, for one, found himself inside the besieged Alamo because he had lost his reelection bid to Congress by 252 votes, which spurred him to start anew in Texas. Had Crockett won, he may have been lounging by a fire in a comfortable Washington, D.C., home rather than on the Texas frontier in the middle of a revolution.

Eighteen-year-old William Malone's story offered another twist. Malone had grown up in Alabama under the strict guidance of his father Thomas, a Methodist preacher who had no patience for disobedience of God's laws. William, on the contrary, did not mind a little fun. He was a handsome lad with a dark complexion and black hair, and among those his age he was regarded as bigger and stronger than most. He was noted equally for his fearlessness and socializing, especially when it came to gambling and drinking.

One night William had stumbled home drunk. The elder Malone became enraged and sternly warned his son never to make that mistake again or else he would pay severely for his foolishness. William never doubted the seriousness of his father's threat. Yet it was not enough to prevent another such encounter with alcohol. Instead of facing the wrath of his father, a drunken William clumsily climbed aboard a horse and rode west. Thomas followed his son as far as New Orleans, only to learn he had departed for Texas. Disheartened, the preacher returned to Alabama to his weeping wife, Elizabeth. Months would pass before they learned of their son's whereabouts. William disclosed the circumstances of his new life in a letter, which his mother would carry in her pocket at all times. She cried whenever someone mentioned her son's name.[9]

Daniel Cloud's path to Bexar had been much smoother. A twenty-seven-year-old attorney from Logan County, Kentucky, Cloud had traveled westward in the company of Peter J. Bailey, William Fauntleroy, Joseph G. Washington, and B. Archer Thomas. Cloud sought opportunity, the kind that would allow him to reap the rewards of a busy trial schedule. The group leisurely journeyed through Illinois, Missouri, Arkansas, and Louisiana before finally entering Texas. Along the way, Cloud's mind drifted often to his grandmother, whom he had left extremely ill and in the care of relatives. His journey almost ended in Illinois, where he reported that the soil "was the best I ever saw." But the land could not keep him anchored. He reasoned: "First our curiosity was unsatisfied, second, Law Dockets were not large, fees low, and yankee lawyers numerous." Texas, he discovered, provided attorneys with greater prospects—Yankee lawyers be damned. But Cloud and his companions encountered something they had not anticipated. "Ever since Texas has unfurled the banner of freedom, and commenced a warfare for liberty or death, our hearts have been enlisted in her behalf," Cloud wrote. "The progress of her cause has increased the ardor of our feelings until we have resolved to embark in the vessel which contains the flag of Liberty and sink or swim in its defense."[10]

Smitten by this fight for freedom, Cloud continued as if trying the case of his life. "The cause of Philanthropy, of Humanity, of Liberty and human happiness throughout the world, called loudly on every man who can to aid Texas," he wrote. "If we succeed, the Country is ours. It is immense in extent, and fertile in its soil, and will amply reward all our toil. If we fail, death in the cause of liberty and humanity is not cause for shuddering."[11]

Tapley Holland understood such fervor as well as anyone. Holland represented old Texas, having entered the Mexican province in 1822 with his family at age twelve among Stephen F. Austin's original three hundred settlers. Now twenty-six, he lived in Grimes County along with his brothers, James and Frank. Raised on the wilds of the frontier and bred to defend freedom, they had rushed to the aid of their Texan kin as war approached, and each took part in the Battle of Concepción. James fell ill with measles shortly thereafter, and a cold settled into his lungs. His brothers decided to return James back to their home in Grimes County in hopes he would recover. They determined that Frank would escort his brother on the trip, leaving Tapley to carry on with his military duties and uphold the family honor. Tapley did not flinch. He possessed all the qualities of a true rugged frontiersman, whose concept of survival of the fittest was founded on firsthand experience. Although not widely known like Bowie or Crockett, Tapley Holland's prowess on the frontier had become legendary among those who lived in his region.

Once, while hunting on the prairie, Holland had spotted magnificent bucks. Too far to level an accurate shot, he knelt and quietly crawled through the tall grass to conceal himself from the unsuspecting animals as they grazed. Wavering grass ahead instantly put Holland on the defense. Indians lurked nearby, and Holland quickly deduced that they were located between him and the herd. Certain of a trap, Holland sprang to his feet. Eight Indians—three carrying rifles—suddenly appeared from tall grass, and they saw Holland clutching his Yager rifle. At first they waved Holland forward, but sensing his uneasiness they let out piercing screams and sprinted toward him. Holland turned and ran back toward his camp, hearing gunfire behind him. Suddenly, he wheeled and took careful aim. Coolly squeezing the trigger, he sent a ball into the chest of one of his pursuers. The Indian dropped dead.

Realizing Holland's rifle was empty, the emboldened warriors continued their pursuit with a vigorous charge and cries. Holland retreated again, loading his rifle as he ran. He again wheeled and fired at the onrushing Indians, and at roughly seventy yards again hit his mark. Another Indian fell dead. The remaining Indians now closed rapidly. By this time, Holland's traveling companion, Robert Moffett, had heard the commotion and rushed forward with his gun. Holland took Moffett's gun from his hand and picked off yet another warrior at roughly ten yards. Hand-to-hand combat now appeared inevitable. Fortunately for Holland and his friend, the remaining Indians figured they had seen enough blood and retreated. Holland reloaded his rifle and again fired, this time wounding a fourth warrior as the group's shaken survivors scampered away. It was the kind of story that would be retold time and again in the hollows that surrounded Holland's homestead, and one that probably followed him into the gates of the Alamo. Tapley Holland—the Indian fighter—was just the kind of man Texan defenders wanted by their side at this trying hour. But Holland seemed more concerned with rest and clean clothes. He had been wearing the same two tattered suits since he joined the Texan army the previous autumn, and he griped regularly to his cousin, John Peterson, about how much he desired clean clothes.[12]

By now, Holland had probably come to think that his brothers were better off at home than by his side. Joe Travis could have easily come to the same conclusion, although he did not enjoy the comfort of knowing how or where most of his siblings were living. Aside from Millford, who resided in Texas, the whereabouts of Leander, William, and his sister, Elizabeth, were unknown to him. Joe may have never realized how different his life might have been had his old master, Dr. Young, sold William instead of him to Isaac Mansfield. Riverboat captain Enoch Price convinced the doctor in 1833 to sell William, who escaped to the north on January 1, 1834. Word of William's escape may have reached Joe in Harrisburg or San Felipe, although his whereabouts would have remained a mystery.

By the winter of 1834, as Joe settled in with Travis, his brother William had arrived in Cleveland, Ohio, where he found work aboard a steamboat that plied the waters of Lake Erie. He was a free man newly christened William Wells Brown. But William discovered that freedom did not shield him entirely from struggle and injustice. William labored diligently aboard the steamboat through the summer of 1835, only to watch the captain run off with his seasonal wages. Penniless, William journeyed elsewhere to find employment. A world away, his brother reluctantly embarked for the Texas warfront.

William's search ended in the town of Monroe, Michigan. Joe's journey ended in Bexar. By February 1836, as Joe counted his lot among the Alamo's besieged, William finally enjoyed the fruits of his newfound freedom. He had ventured into business as a barber, or, as the sign declared above his shop: "Fashionable Hair-Dresser from New York—Emperor of the West." William figured it did not matter that he had never been to New York. Customers poured into his shop anyway, much to the displeasure of a rival "shop over the way."[13] Unknown to William, his younger brother's life hung in peril at frontier military outpost called the Alamo.

18

DEFINING HOUR

This time we may see blood.
—Andrew Kent, en route to the Alamo

Prudence Kimble knelt awkwardly by the creek, dipping a piece of clothing into the icy water and then pressing it firmly against her worn washboard. Kimble, eight months pregnant, moved slowly—her lower back was hurting. She found the talk of war disturbing. By now, news of the besieged Alamo had spread throughout the colonies. The talk intensified, especially in Gonzales, where Kimble and her husband, George, lived and ran a moderately successful hat store in partnership with Almeron Dickinson—one of the Alamo's besieged. Some of the men inside the Alamo were neighbors. They were common yet brave men who had, in some cases, already shed blood in the siege and storming of Bexar. Now they were in desperate trouble, a mere seventy miles away—a two-day horseback ride.

George Kimble had willingly attached himself to the cause. The native Pennsylvanian signed up as a lieutenant with the Gonzales Ranging Company on February 23, and the men chose him to serve as company commander. Little had he known that the Alamo garrison would encounter the enemy that day.

While Prudence scrubbed her clothes diligently, as if trying to wash the inevitable out her mind, her toddler, Charles, played on the bank. The two-year-old shared his father's eyes and offered Prudence fleeting refuge from the madness that now affected her life. Suddenly she heard crush of footfall and looked up to see her husband approaching. He stood well over six feet tall, dwarfing his wife of three years, and carried a lean, muscular frame. His eyes now revealed dark news, showing sorrow that preempted words. Looking into Prudence's eyes, George said that he and his company intended to ride to the aid of the men trapped inside the Alamo. "Prudence," he concluded, "I probably won't return."[1]

Similar farewells repeated throughout the countryside. Farther east, at the headwaters of the Lavaca River, Isaac Millsaps bade a tearful goodbye to his wife, Mary, and their seven children as he joined neighbor and fellow Tennessean William E. Summers en route to Bexar. The forty-one-year-old Millsaps knew the hardships of battle, having served with the East Tennessee Militia in the War of 1812. He had then been seventeen, a mere boy. The thought of war did not bother Millsaps as much as the thought of leaving behind his children and wife. Mary was strong but she was blind. The couple embraced a final time, not knowing whether they would ever again feel the other's touch. Isaac climbed onto his horse, encouraging his children to take care of their mother. Summers and Millsaps then rode out, following the Lavaca River, and eventually came to the homestead of Andrew Jackson Kent. He agreed to join the company, although no one doubted where the Kent family stood in this revolution.

Andrew and his eighteen-year-old son, David, had participated in the taking of the cannon at Gonzales and later fought in the siege and battle of Bexar, where the younger Kent received a slight wound. Andrew brought his son home in December after the Alamo had been secured, but David again returned to Bexar to rejoin the Texan army. The family feared David numbered among those trapped inside the Alamo. Despite reports of large Mexican forces in Bexar, Andrew Kent had determined to join his son and compatriots in this defining hour. Kent sensed grave danger, something he had never felt in previous engagements, and the Kent children felt their father's tension. Mary Ann Kent, then nine years old, never forgot her father's words as he departed that day. Flanked by

Millsaps and Summers, Andrew Kent wheeled his horse and remarked, "This time we may see blood."[2]

The three men reached Gonzales by late afternoon the next day. To Kent's surprise and relief, he found his son waiting among the other volunteers. David Kent had been sent from the Alamo to round up cattle at a ranch south of Bexar. When he returned he found the town occupied by vast numbers of Mexican soldiers and the Alamo encircled by enemy forces. Mexican scouts spotted Kent, who later recounted how he had made a dash for safety. He found refuge in some nearby foothills, and after a daylong wait figured he should return to Gonzales for help. He was all too happy to find his father in the process. The reunion, however, turned into an argument. David insisted on riding back to the Alamo with the Gonzales contingent. The elder Kent would not hear of such nonsense, contending that the family needed the teenager at home, where his mother and siblings needed protection from marauding Indians or foraging Mexican soldiers. Andrew Kent's word was final. Years later, David Kent would become emotional at the thought of his father's deed.

John G. King swelled with a similar pride in the years that followed whenever he thought of the actions of his son, William, in the spring of 1836. King boasted often of the day that members of the Gonzales Ranging Company had reached his homestead fifteen miles north of Gonzales. The thunder of their horses' hooves created a stir as family members gathered around the Texan patriots. Firm handshakes were given all around, as were the hasty glances of men on a mission. Everyone realized that this was not a social visit. The time had arrived to go to the aid of the men inside the Alamo. John King grabbed his rifle and a small bag and hoisted himself aboard his horse. He lovingly gazed down at his wife, Parmelia. Then he glanced at his children, nine in all, and with sorrowful eyes told them goodbye. At that moment King's oldest son, William, grabbed his reins. "Please don't go," the sixteen-year-old begged his father. "You are needed at home. Let me go in your place." Overcome with emotion, the elder King hesitated at his son's request before finally yielding to his logic. It was a decision John King would forever regret.[3]

This is how the men of Gonzales answered the call of their besieged countrymen. Joe would not encounter them for a few more days. By February 28, the garrison's defenders might have been peeking over the

Alamo's low, wooden palisade or standing atop a parapet in search of relief forces on the distant prairie. They longed for news from the outside. Any news. To date—the sixth day of the siege—none had arrived. No couriers, no relief forces, nothing in which to invest hope. Travis and his men began to wonder if help would come. The question grew heavier with each passing hour as the Mexican artillerymen dug closer entrenchments.

A council of war prompted Travis to dispatch one more courier. He selected Capt. Seguín, the rancher who now served as the commander of a local cavalry unit. Travis ordered Seguín to rally reinforcements at Gonzales. After a brief protest, Seguín consented and made preparations for nighttime departure. Seguín left with Antonio Cruz y Arocha around 8:00 P.M.[4]

To the west, one could see the gigantic, twisting cottonwood trees looming over the San Antonio River. The view to the north and northeast offered mostly a sea of prairie grass, where members of the garrison held their greatest hope for spotting reinforcements. But the prairie held its secrets, rustling quietly with the shifting winds. Was a relief force on the way? Part of the answer rested with Fannin, who, unknown to the Alamo's defenders, had departed Goliad for Bexar with three hundred tattered troops on the morning of February 26. He apologetically called his decision "anything but a military one" but nonetheless vowed to relieve the Alamo's gallant souls.[5]

Fannin's resolve faded in the face of his pathetic circumstances. "Within two hundred yards of town, one of the wagons broke down, and it was necessary to double teams in order to draw Artillery across the river, each piece having but one yoke of oxen," he later explained. Then there was the issue of rations: "not a particle of breadstuff, with the exception of half a tierce of rice, with us—no beef, with the exception of a small portion which had been dried—and not a head of cattle, except those used to draw the Artillery, the ammunition, &c."[6]

Fannin called a meeting. The officers unanimously decided to turn back in light of their scant provisions, inability to pull the artillery, and fear that the Goliad outpost "might fall into the hands of the enemy" if they marched to Bexar.[7] Realizing that another enemy force operated in his region, Fannin recommended that the Alamo look instead to the townships of Victoria and Gonzales for assistance.

Meanwhile, the hourglass continued to empty for the Alamo's besieged. Their fortunes stalled elsewhere too. At Washington-on-the-Brazos, east of Gonzales, convention delegates began to trickle into the makeshift town with the sole intention of crafting a declaration of independence. Samuel A. Maverick and Jesse B. Badgett, the Alamo's elected delegates, were among those en route to the convention when word of the Mexican Army's presence in Bexar reached the banks of the Brazos River. William Fairfax Gray, the Virginia land speculator, noted the arrival of the news in his diary: "Another express is received from Travis, dated the 24th, stating Santa Anna, with his army, were in Bexar, and bombarded the Alamo for twenty four hours. An unconditional surrender had been demanded, which he answered by a cannon shot. He was determined to defend the place to the last, and called earnestly for assistance." Appalled at the local reaction, Gray added in disgust, "Some are going, but the vile rabble here cannot be moved."[8]

Such would have been unfathomable to the Alamo's defenders—men defiantly holding their ground under great anguish and overwhelming numbers. They were men born in the mold of Asa Walker, a twenty-three-year-old Tennessean who could not wait to aid his fellow Texans on the war front. The unarmed Walker's urgency to fight was so great that he entered the vacant home of friend John Grant and helped himself to some needed supplies. He left behind a hastily written, apologetic letter. "I take responsibility of taking your overcoat and gun," he wrote. "Your gun they would have anyhow, and I might as well have it as anyone else. If I live to return, I will satisfy you for all. If I die, I leave you my clothes to do the best you can with. You can sell them for something. If you overtake me, you can take your rifle and I will trust to chance. The hurry of the moment and my want of means to do better are all the excuses I have to plead for fitting out at your expense. Forgive the presumption and remember your friend at heart."[9]

Walker clung to his friend's rifle now as Mexican cannons roared intermittently throughout the day and night, depriving the Texan rebels of sleep. Enrique Esparza, then a boy inside the Alamo, remembered how Mexican gunners lobbed "a shot into the fort" every fifteen minutes.[10] Nights were the worst for the defenders. Sleep was almost unimaginable. Mexican soldiers would sometimes discharge a volley of rifles under the cover of darkness to simulate a night assault. The enemy's tactics were meant to create mental and physical strain among the Alamo's defenders.

The Texans engaged in their own mental warfare. Gregorio Esparza, Enrique's father, did his part by forcing a Mexican prisoner to interpret the enemy's bugle calls throughout the siege. In this way, the Texans tried to stay abreast of the enemy's movements.[11] For men like Esparza, the struggle meant something far greater than his own survival. The sight of his wife and four children sustained his defiance, as all shared his perilous moment inside the Alamo. Even a stranger could see the fierceness in Esparza's eyes.

Dickinson also fretted constantly about the presence of his wife, Susanna, and his infant daughter, Angelina, inside the Alamo. Susanna played the role of the brave military wife, but she too could not deny the burden of being her daughter's protector. Anthony Wolfe, a fifty-four-year-old who was rumored to have once served alongside the pirate Jean Lafitte in Louisiana and Texas, shared in the angst. Wolfe's greatest concern wasn't the thousands of Mexican soldiers beyond the garrison's walls but rather his eleven- and twelve-year-old boys who stood now by his side.[12]

Nevertheless, the Texans stood tall. "From the windows and parapets of the low buildings, when taunted by Mexican troops, they shouted back their defiance in the liveliest terms," recalled retired Mexican captain Rafael Soldana decades later. One Texan rebel who stood out was "a tall man, with flowing hair," seen firing from the same location atop a parapet throughout the siege. He was an iconic American hunter-warrior. "He wore a buckskin suit and a cap of the pattern entirely different from those worn by his comrades," Soldana remembered. "This man would kneel or lie down behind the low parapet, rest his long gun and fire, and we learned to keep at a distance when he was seen to make ready to shoot. He rarely missed his mark and when he fired he always rose to his feet and calmly reloaded his gun seemingly indifferent to the shots fired at him by our men. He had a strong resonant voice and often railed at us, but as we did not understand English we could not comprehend the import of his words further than that they were defiant."[13]

Was this the renowned Crockett who Soldana describes? Crockett could indeed be classified as a sharpshooter, but his contributions clearly extended beyond marksmanship. Crockett lifted the spirits of those besieged. During lulls in the fighting, he reached into his luggage and dusted off his fiddle. With his foot tapping, he bowed his favorite tunes. Scotsman John McGregor routinely joined in with his bagpipes, adding his "strange, dreadful sound" to the amusement of all.[14] These were brief moments of pleasure but they said something about the spirit of the Texans and their drive for freedom. The Alamo garrison knew something that Joe Travis had likely comprehended years earlier: dreaming of freedom and living freely are entirely different. And freedom comes at a price.

The early morning hours of March 1 brought rain and near-gale-force wind. Shortly after 3 A.M., the defenders were awakened by a commotion in the compound and the ensuing cheers of the Texan rebels. Thirty-two men from Gonzales had entered the Alamo, slipping past Mexican patrols in the cover of darkness and rain. Originally, the group had included at least thirty-six volunteers, but four men had been cut off in their effort to relieve their compatriots. Sam Bastian was one of those men. He later recalled: "When near the fort we were discovered and fired on by the Mexican troops. Most of the party got through; but I and three others had to take to the chaparral to save our lives."[15]

John W. Smith, Albert Martin, big George Kimble, Andrew Kent, and Isaac Millsaps were five who galloped into the Alamo that morning. For Smith and Martin, it was their second time inside the Alamo gates since the opening volleys of the siege. Each already knew what was at stake: victory or death, as Travis would write time and again.

Joe watched as strangers embraced in the muddy grounds of the compound. They embraced as brothers in arms, united by a cause to shake free from an oppressor. A norther whipped against their rain-drenched faces but the bleak circumstances failed to deter them in their mission. These men had ridden for victory—for freedom—and they would settle for nothing less or otherwise die. Joe would have understood such a mentality more than anyone would ever know.

19

The Hourglass

For God's sake, sustain yourselves until
we can assist you.
—Maj. Robert M. Williamson in a letter to his
friend Lt. Col. William Barret Travis

Astillness veiled James Butler Bonham as he pulled the reins on his dove-colored horse. By midday on March 3 he overlooked Bexar from atop Powderhouse Hill.[1] The sky was clear. There was no breeze. Bonham's heart pounded as he patted his lathered steed's muscular neck. Its mouth was foamy as it had been raced from Gonzales to Bexar, where Bonham now intended to deliver an urgent message to his besieged comrades. Bonham surveyed the scene in silence. In the valley below, three hundred yards away, the desperate state of his compatriots was evident. Scores of Mexican soldiers encircled the Alamo. Artillery entrenchments choked the garrison like a noose, and cavalry patrols could be seen crisscrossing the open prairie. Bonham could clearly recognize a number of his entrapped comrades silhouetted along the Alamo's battered walls, presenting a foreboding portrait for the South Carolina–bred courier.[2]

John W. Smith sat mounted by Bonham's side. Two days earlier, Smith and thirty-two volunteers from Gonzales had slashed their way into the

Alamo under the cover of darkness. Afterward, carrying a bundle of letters from Alamo defenders, Smith had returned to Gonzales, hoping to
retrieve more reinforcements. Now he feared he was too late. Staring
into the valley, Smith urged Bonham to reevaluate the danger of riding
into the Alamo. Bonham turned to tie a large white scarf to a nearby
tree—a prearranged signal for his return. The scarf hung limply in the
crisp, still air.[3]

Bonham had arrived in Texas four months earlier. After opening a
legal practice in Brazoria, he quickly staked his honor on the future of
his new country when danger arose. "Permit me through you to volunteer my services in the present struggle of Texas without conditions,"
Bonham wrote Texan general Sam Houston in December. "I shall receive
nothing, either in the form of service pay, or lands or rations."[4]

Words such as those may have now rushed back to Bonham, a twenty-
nine-year-old reared on southern chivalry. Bonham possessed a sinewy,
rugged appearance, standing six foot two and weighing 175 pounds.
Women were said to swoon over his good looks wherever he traveled.[5]
Yet beneath his handsome features existed a man of soulful substance.
Bonham believed foremost in honor.

"It is useless, Bonham, to attempt to enter," Smith said in resignation.
"The Alamo is surrounded." Bonham looked down at his weary comrades, then stared at Smith and paused. "I must," he finally replied.[6]

"You are a braver man than I," said Smith. "I cannot."[7]

Bonham pulled his cloak tight and spurred his horse toward the Alamo's main gate. Within seconds, the horse was racing down the hill in
full gallop. Bonham leaned into its neck as if he were a Comanche warrior in battle.

Perched atop the Alamo's walls, the Texan soldiers scurried to gain
a view of Bonham's ride. Fists punched the air as men cheered wildly.
A hail of rifle shots whizzed by Bonham as he miraculously dashed un-
scathed past the Mexican lines. A gate swung open, and Bonham's horse
lunged into the Alamo unmolested.[8]

Within minutes, Travis was breaking the wax seal on the letter the
breathless Bonham had pulled from his saddlebag. The letter had been
written by one of Travis's closest friends, Robert Williamson. "You cannot know my anxiety, sir," Williamson wrote. "Today makes four full
days that we have not received the slightest report regarding your

dangerous situation, and therefore we have indulged in a thousand conjectures."[9]

Travis's eyes darted over the letter.

"Sixty men have set out from this municipality and in all human probability they are with you at this date," the letter continued. "Colonel Fannin, with three hundred men and four pieces of artillery, has been on the march toward Bejar for three days. Tonight we expect some three hundred reinforcements from Washington, Bastrop, Brazoria, and San Felipe, and no time will be wasted in seeking their help for you." Williamson added a postscript: "For God's sake, sustain yourselves until we can assist you."[10]

A handful of fresh volunteers could mean another day of life for the besieged, but their hourglass appeared almost empty. Travis suspected that other volunteers had reached the frontier, based on information provided by his Gonzales contingent. Williamson's mention of "sixty men" en route to Bexar confirmed earlier reports.[11] Where were those men? And who would be bold enough to escort them in under the present circumstances? Crockett answered the latter question for Travis when he volunteered for the risky assignment. With two companions, Crockett planned to slip past the Mexican guards at nightfall, locate the reinforcements, and return as quickly as possible. Bonham likely shared what information he had learned about the Mexican positions, although Crockett had almost assuredly deduced their precarious situation days earlier.[12] Yet where there was life, there was hope.

Travis wasted no time returning to his quarters to apprise those on the outside of his garrison's present circumstances. He would write two letters—one to Texas convention president Richard Ellis and the other to convention delegate Jesse Grimes. In his letter to Ellis, Travis enthusiastically reported that the "spirits of my men are still high, although they have had much to depress them. We have contended for ten days against an enemy whose numbers are variously estimated at from fifteen hundred to six thousand. I will, however, do the best I can under the circumstances, and I feel confident that the determined valour and desperate courage, heretofore evidenced by my men, will not fail them in the last struggle; and although they may be sacrificed to the vengeance of a Gothic enemy, the victory will cost the enemy so dear, that it will

be worse for him than a defeat." With reinforcements, Travis then predicted, "this neighborhood will be the great and decisive battle ground."
Travis signed the letter with his usual gusto: "God and Texas!—Victory
or Death!" In a postscript, he added matter-of-factly, "The enemy's troops
are still arriving, and the reinforcements will probably amount to two or
three thousand."[13]

Shuffling a small stack of papers, Travis then began to write his second letter. This time he addressed delegate Grimes, a Georgian whose
eighteen-year-old son, Albert, numbered among the Alamo's besieged.
Joe might have sensed his master's strain as he searched for the right
words. "Let the Convention go on and make a declaration of independence, and we will then understand, and the world will understand,
what we are fighting for," Travis wrote. "If independence is not declared,
I shall lay down my arms, and so will the men under my command. But
under the flag of independence, we are ready to peril our lives a hundred times a day, and to drive away the monster who is fighting us under a blood-red flag, threatening to murder all prisoners and make Texas
a waste desert."[14]

Hastily Travis sealed his two missives with wax. A call for outgoing
mail was announced, and several defenders, men wearing tattered
clothes from months in the field, came forward. Some had letters that
were written days ago while others had scurried at the last moment to
scratch down a few words to friends or loved ones.[15]

Dusk arrived quickly. The Mexican cannons had ceased firing,
and Travis sensed an opportunity that might never arrive again. He
ordered the men to assemble in the courtyard, and officers quickly
relayed his order. The Texan defenders—unshaven and dirt-smeared—
began to gather within moments. Their eyes restless with anxiety and
dark-lidded from lack of sleep, they had their firearms in hand. Travis
scanned the ranks. Among them stood eighteen-year-old William
Malone, who had run away from his Alabama home rather than face
his Bible-thumping father after a drunken binge; the widowed Anthony Wolfe and his two young boys; big George Kimble, who had left
behind his pregnant wife to defend his country; and Tapley Holland,
whose prowess with a rifle once allowed him to escape death at the
hands of marauding Indians.

Somewhere in the courtyard also stood Joe. The mulatto servant might never have seen the Texas frontier had Dr. Young's finances been more stable or had Mansfield won his campaign for public office. In either case, Joe might instead have been serving tea in a St. Louis parlor rather than staring at death at the end of a Mexican bayonet. Or he might have been experiencing freedom alongside his brother William in Canada—a thought Joe was spared due to a lack of information from Missouri.

By now, a few men had carried Bowie into the courtyard on his cot. Bowie had fallen ill from typhoid fever and had since relinquished full command to Travis. Bowie's health worsened each passing hour.[16] Finally Travis removed his sword from his sheath and strode the length of his ranks. Sticking the tip of his sword in the dirt, he scratched a line the entire length of his men, and then began to speak. "My soldiers," Travis stated, "I am going to meet the fate that becomes me. Those who will stand by me, let them remain, but those who desire to go, let them go. . . ."[17]

Only one man stepped from the ranks: Louis Moses Rose of Nacogdoches, Texas. The fifty-year-old Frenchman had once fought under Napoleon Bonaparte during the Russian campaign, and he had been present when the Texans took Bexar in December. Rose had already seen enough blood to last a lifetime. On this day he concluded he would avoid death if at all possible. He gathered his bundle of clothes, scaled the top of a wall, and took one final glance at his determined comrades below. Suddenly he jumped from the wall and was never to be seen again.[18]

Inside the Alamo, each defender searched his soul. Wolfe probably stayed close to his boys. Almeron Dickinson may have taken a moment to embrace his wife and infant daughter. Millsaps might have mentally retraced the features of his wife's face. Gregorio Esparza huddled his family together, proclaiming, "I will stay and die fighting." Ana Esparza, Gregorio's wife, stared back at her husband and firmly replied, "I will stay by your side and with our children die too. They will soon kill us. We will not linger in pain."[19]

After the last call for outgoing letters, perhaps as Crockett and his two companions stuffed the mail into their saddlebags, Travis grabbed a scrap of yellowed wrapping paper and scratched out a hastily written note to his son's caretaker in San Felipe, David Ayers:

Dear Sir,

Take care of my little boy. If the country should be saved I may make him a splendid fortune. But if the country should be lost, and I should perish, he will have nothing but the proud recollection that he is the son of a man who died for his country.

Yours, &c.,
Wm. B. Travis[20]

The weary Travis shoved the note into the hands of one of the outgoing riders, who tucked it into his saddlebag. Quietly, Crockett and his companions guided their horses to a gate and passed through, as if into another world. Then the men disappeared, carrying the prayers and hopes of their comrades with them into the darkness.

The runaway slave in Joe probably watched restlessly.

20

Between Two Worlds

*My heart quaked when the shot tore
through the timbers.*
*—Enrique Esparza, remembering when he was
a child inside the Alamo*

Faint images could be seen through dense fog at sunrise on March
5 atop the Alamo's north wall. Texan sentinels reported hearing
noises in the darkness several hours earlier, lending to speculation about the enemy's movements. Travis, alerted by the reports, stood
atop the north wall as the fog began to lift.

Only hours earlier, the tiny garrison had found reason to celebrate. Crockett had somehow slashed his way back into the Alamo
with some fifty men he had found twenty miles away at the Cibolo
ford on the Gonzales road. Crockett and his companions inspired
their comrades with "sanguine hopes of speedy relief, and thus animated the men to contend to the last."[1] The Texans responded by
unleashing grateful and defiant cheers. A different mood had surfaced in the fort.

Outside, the garrison's situation clearly came into focus. Mexican
soldiers and engineers had moved their north battery several hundred yards closer along a course of water. The enemy's freshly erected

parapet could be seen less than two hundred yards away.[2] The day before, that same battery had stood some eight hundred yards away. The close proximity of the battery meant imminent danger. For the first time since the siege began, a Mexican cannon sat close enough to inflict major damage on the Alamo's stout walls.

The bold move had not come without risks for Mexican gunners. The battery now lay within reach of Texan riflemen. Santa Anna and his officers, however, had chosen to open a breach in the Alamo's walls before ordering a final assault, and soon the Mexican north battery roared with brisk fire. "My heart quaked when the shot tore through the timbers," Enrique Esparza later recalled.[3]

The enemy cannons battered the Alamo's north wall, sending rocks flying or cascading down a fresh pile of rubble. Cannonballs had previously fallen harmlessly inside the compound, but now they exploded through the walls. Texans located near the north wall hunkered down, holding firm to their firearms and prayers. They may have wondered if the cannons would ever quit. By noon, they had their answer.[4] The Mexican cannons fell silent and the Texans emerged from their battered refuge to see prairie through a breach that now existed in the north wall. Alarmed, Travis immediately ordered his men to reinforce the breach under the guidance and command of chief engineer Green B. Jameson. Joe labored alongside the garrison's slaves and defenders, hoisting rocks and dirt up to the wall.[5]

The Texans noticed an eerie silence from the Mexican gunners. Travis sensed something ominous and called for a volunteer courier to ride to Goliad with one final plea for help. Several men volunteered. Travis reviewed his prospects and selected young James L. Allen, who rode a fleet mare. Like Joe, Allen was twenty-one-year-old who was born in Kentucky. Allen listened to Travis's final instructions, hugged his horse's neck, and spurred the horse toward the Mexican lines, disappearing into the darkness.[6]

Part of Joe may have gone with Allen that night. Was Joe resigned to his fate and the notion that he might have to settle for a life unfulfilled. Freedom probably never seemed more elusive. Reuniting with his brothers, William, Leander, and Millford, and sister, Elizabeth, was now inconceivable, as was a reunion with his mother. She had endured a hard life, sacrificing herself at every turn for her children. Joe might have recalled all the times she had shielded him from danger, such as a master's tongue-lashing or an overseer's whip. We can only guess what raced through Joe's mind in this defining hour. Now he stood in the company of men entrapped within the Alamo's walls—men resolved to meet their fate. Many of them huddled alone, scratching out their wills on used envelopes, a blank page in a book, on the inside of their haversacks.[7]

Almeron Dickinson handled the situation the only way he knew—by living. Beneath an umbrella of stars that night, Dickinson invited Bonham to join him and his wife, Susanna, for tea at their cramped quarters within the Alamo chapel. Bonham politely accepted the couple's invitation.[8] The three migrant Americans sipped hot tea on a couch and reminisced about bygone days. For a moment, perhaps, war was put aside and dreams engaged.

Travis soon appeared in the stone doorway of the tiny room. The flicker of a fire flashed behind him in the chapel's main, open-aired room as he begged intrusion. Travis asked if he might give the baby Angelina a gift once imparted him by his fiancée, Rebecca. Removing a black, bull's-eye ring from one of his fingers, Travis slipped the beloved keepsake onto a string and tenderly tied it around Angelina's neck. He believed the ring possessed the power to protect one in battle. Travis bade the family goodnight and returned to his quarters.[9]

Beyond the Alamo walls, in the solitude of the Yturri house, Santa Anna conversed with Almonte into the night.[10] Ben Harris, Almonte's black body servant, stood armed with a hot pot of coffee nearby just as Santa Anna had ordered. The servant had worked aboard numerous American vessels before he had agreed to serve as Almonte's personal body servant in New York. Destiny carried Harris to Veracruz and then to Bexar with the Mexican Army.

As the hours passed, Ben watched Santa Anna and Almonte converse. He sensed their serious mood. The two officers eventually departed the house around midnight and returned three hours later. Agitated, Santa Anna ordered Ben to immediately bring a hot cup of coffee or else the servant would be run through with a sword. Ben instantly responded.

"It will cost us much," Ben heard Almonte tell Santa Anna at that moment. The dictator paused before coldly replying that cost was of no importance.[11]

Candlelight danced on the mud-plastered walls that framed Travis and Joe's tiny room. Words may have been exchanged between the two as they lay in their cots, weary from a hard day of labor. The work had stretched late into the night in an effort to reinforce the battered north wall, but there was no shoring up the anxiety of their perilous situation. A final battle appeared inevitable. Now Joe lay exhausted, hungry, restless, and scared until he finally dozed off somewhere between this world and the next.

21

MARCH 6, 1836

It was but a small affair.
—*Mexican dictator Antonio López de Santa Anna*

D eath struck swiftly.
A Mexican bugler signaled the commencement of bloodshed around five in the morning beneath moonlight filtered by patchy clouds. Some eleven hundred Mexican soldiers, most of whom had lain prostrate outside the Alamo walls for more than two and a half hours, arose in unison. "A bugle call to attention was the agreed signal and we soon heard that terrible bugle call of death, which stirred our hearts, altered our expressions, and aroused us all suddenly from our painful meditations," recalled Jose Enrique de la Peña, a Mexican soldier. "Worn out by fatigue and lack of sleep, I had just closed my eyes to nap when my ears were pierced by this fatal note."[1]

Santa Anna's buglers then blew "El Degüello," a cavalry call that would have meant nothing to his common soldiers, much less the roughly two hundred Alamo defenders but was meaningful for Santa Anna. "Degüello" means "cutthroat" or "behead": no mercy.[2] The song was a fitting prelude to the hell that followed. Hearts pounded and adrenaline flowed as the Mexican soldiers hurled themselves against the compound's walls carrying axes, crowbars, picks, planks, and rickety ladders. Defiant shouts and cursing accompanied their mad dash. "Viva México!" many shouted, prematurely arousing the defenders. "Viva Santa Anna!"[3]

Rockets soon burst in the air, illuminating the sky and raining a brilliant momentary light on the hordes of soldiers now converging on the Alamo. The attack came in four columns: one led by Col. Juan Morales that struck the wooden palisade defended by Crockett and his men on the south, one led by Col. José Romero near the cattle pens on the east, one led by Gen. Martín Perfecto de Cos from the northwest, and one led by Col. Francisco Duque against the battered north wall. None would prove an easy mark.

From a window in Bexar some five hundred yards away, Almonte's servant Ben watched numbly as blazing rockets shot through the air. In the flashes of light he recognized large bodies of soldiers pressing against the Alamo walls. Ben became overwhelmed with patriotic sentiment, and in that moment harkened back to "Master George Washington and old Virginia, and prayed to God that the Americans might whip."[4] The outmanned Texan defenders did their best.

"Their own artillery was ready and alert so that when the fatal trumpet sounded, there was no doubt that the ultimate scene was at hand—conquer or die," Mexican general Vicente Filisola wrote. "And if there had been any doubt, they were promptly disillusioned by the reckless shouting and *vivas* by the attacking columns as soon as they were seen. They were hit by a hail of shrapnel and bullets that the besieged men let loose on them. The attackers at the first sound of the trumpet were all on their feet at their respective posts with their arms at the ready."[5]

Each Texan had three or four loaded rifles by his side and leveled a rapid and deadly fire at the first wave of attackers. As one Mexican officer recalled, the enemy's first rounds of gunfire left "a wide trail of blood, of wounded, and of dead."[6]

Inside the Alamo, in a pitch-black room along the west wall, Joe was lying asleep when Capt. John J. Baugh burst through the doorway. The Virginian aroused Travis and Joe, bellowing, "The Mexicans are coming!" Travis sprang from his bed, instinctively seizing his double-barreled shotgun and sword. He called for Joe to follow. Joe grabbed his rifle, squeezing it tightly as he bolted out the door behind Baugh and his master. The three men sprinted up the earthen ramp at the north wall. Heavy gunfire was underway. "Come on boys!" Travis shouted from the parapet. "The Mexicans are upon us, and we'll give them Hell!"[7]

Joe saw the Mexican horde for the first time through the flashes of bursting rockets, discharging Texan cannons, and the frightful crackle of gunfire. Below, in a din of maddening screams and shouted words in Spanish, Mexican soldiers struggled for a foothold up the wall, trampling one another in a race to overtake the enemy position. Scaling-ladders, hastily made for the attack, now snapped from the weight of too many bodies. The first Mexicans to reach the tops of walls were bayoneted or clubbed by equally desperate Texan defenders, who sent bodies hurdling back into the masses below.[8]

Bullets whistled through the air. Repulsed by the unexpected marksmanship of the Texan defenders, the Mexican columns on the east, west, and north all hesitated momentarily in indecision and chaos. Inspired by a few bold officers who led by example, the soldiers redoubled their efforts to storm the garrison. In doing so, the columns to the east and west "both swung to the North so that the three columns almost merged into a single mass."[9]

Watching from Bexar, Santa Anna ordered four hundred reserves to join the attack. Enraged Texans, meanwhile, continued to rain gunfire and shrapnel down on their foes. Mexican colonel Duque, leading the north wall attack, received a fatal wound in the charge. Despite being trampled by his subordinates, Duque continued to encourage his troops as they pressed forward with panther-like screams. Other Mexican soldiers, less enthusiastic, had to be prodded along by their commanders at the point of a bayonet.[10]

Travis discharged his shotgun into the wild throng. Joe followed his master's example. He aimed his gun at the jammed masses below and firmly squeezed the trigger, igniting a flash of fire and a discharge that jerked his shoulder. The Mexicans answered with shots of their own, one of which struck Travis in the temple. Travis tumbled down an earthen slope. There the young colonel sat, unable to rise.[11]

Joe watched his master fall in shock. Glancing back, he could see Mexicans successfully mounting the wall in increasing numbers. A few brave Texans defiantly clubbed away at their attackers with the butts of their long rifles, while others fell back to a second line of defense among the rooms and houses that encircled the compound. Joe retreated hurriedly into a nearby house and peered through a loophole. He trembled in fright. From this vantage point the servant fired his gun at the onrushing Mexican soldiers now storming the garrison in the darkness. From this room, Joe also witnessed the death of his master as he sat wounded and cheering on his men. A Mexican officer whom Joe later identified as "General Mora" (Col. Esteban Mora) raised his sword at Travis, intending to deal a fatal blow to the Alamo commander. Travis, summoning what little strength he had left, beat Mora to the punch, piercing the officer's body with his own sword until a bloodied blade penetrated his back. Mora died on the spot along with Travis.[12]

The death of Travis underscored that Joe was truly alone to live or die. The slave lifted his gun, aimed through a loophole, and continued to fire at Mexican assailants. Joe would make his own last stand.

Once inside the compound, Mexican officers and soldiers alike frantically surveyed the scene. Heavily armed Texans could still be seen on rooftops, discharging deadly gunfire while barricaded behind mounds of sandbags. Everywhere the Mexicans turned, they encountered windows and doors barricaded by iron bars, piles of sandbags, and pockets of resistance. The Texans had thoroughly planned their fallback positions, realizing they could only defend the main walls for a short time at best.[13] The Mexicans also encountered valor beyond description. Among their own, a young officer named José María Torres covered himself in glory on this morning when he scaled a roof amid deadly gunfire. Torres proudly planted the Mexican flag atop the mount just before he was shot dead by a Texan sniper.[14]

One American equally caught the attention of his enemy. This man stood tall with a dark complexion. He wore a long buckskin coat and a fox-skin hat with a long tail, and he possessed a deadly shot. "This man apparently had a charmed life," one Mexican soldier noted. "Of the many soldiers who took deliberate aim at him and fired, not one ever hit him. On the contrary he never missed a shot. He killed at least eight of our men, besides wounding several others. This fact being observed by a lieutenant who had come in over the wall[,] he sprung at him and dealt him a deadly blow with his sword, just above the right eye, which felled him to the ground and in an instant he was pierced by not less than twenty bayonets."[15]

Bravery seemed infectious. One or two Texan could be seen at various moments stubbornly holding their ground against entire squads of Mexican soldiers as they attempted to advance. They fought muzzle-to-muzzle, bayonet-to-Bowie knife, and hand-to-hand. The clash of arms and the crazed screams made an infernal imprint on the psyche of the eyewitness.

The greatest fury occurred in the old long barracks. In this building, where the Texans burrowed themselves in entrenchments, men groped in the dark for life. Blackened hands latched onto throats, bodies slammed against stone walls, sharpened knives plunged into flesh, and piercing screams echoed in strange unison with the hellish musket fire. Sweat mixed with pools of blood deep enough to soak a man's shoes.

"The Texians fought like devils," a Mexican officer recounted. "The Texians defended desperately every inch of the fort—overpowered by numbers, they would be forced to abandon a room; they would rally in the next and defend it until further resistance became impossible."[16]

Trickery became another Texan ploy. A few Texan rebels waved a white cloth or sock from the point of a bayonet they had stuck through a window or door. Trusting this as a sign of surrender, Mexican soldiers confidently entered the darkened rooms, only to be savagely shot or butchered by Texans lying in wait. Amazingly, the trick worked more than once. "Thus betrayed," Peña later recalled, "our men rekindled their anger and at every moment fresh skirmishes broke out with renewed fury."[17]

The Texans matched fury with fury. Mexican captain Don Rafael Soldana recalled decades later the unforgettable deeds of one brave Texan. "He stood on the inside to the left of the door and plunged his long knife into the bosom of every soldier that tried to enter," Soldana stated. "They were powerless to fire upon him because of the fact that he was backed up against the wall and, the doorway being narrow, they could not bring their guns to bear upon him. And, moreover, the pressure from the rear was so great that many near the doorway were forced into the room only to receive a deadly thrust from that lone knife." Finally a shot broke the Texan's right arm, and his hand dangled uselessly by his side. "He then seized his long rifle with his left hand and leaped toward the center of the room where he could wield the weapon without obstruction, felling every man that came through the doorway," Soldana recalled. An officer finally ordered the doorway cleared. A volley of fire from point-blank range instantly killed the defiant Texan.[18]

In another ground-level room—"a hospital," as described by one Mexican eyewitness—Mexican troops discovered a number of sick and wounded defenders firing their guns gallantly from their beds and pallets. Mexicans placed a small artillery piece loaded with grapeshot and canister in the doorway and fired it twice. Subsequent examination of the room uncovered the corpses of fifteen Texans.[19]

A nearby room revealed yet another sickly man lying in a bed. Sgt. Francisco Becerra later claimed he saw the man and, disregarding Santa Anna's orders to give no quarter, opted to leave the Texan mercifully where he lay. But before exiting the room, another Mexican sergeant entered and leveled his gun at the prostrate man. The Texan raised his hand and shot the sergeant through the head with a pistol. A Mexican soldier then tried to shoot the Texan and was likewise killed with another pistol shot. "I then fired and killed the Texian," Becerra claimed. "I took his two empty pistols, and found his rifle standing by his bed. It seemed he was too weak to use it."[20]

Deadly nests of defenders held out throughout the compound, causing the Mexican soldiers to approach every room with caution. Noncombatant Juana Alsbury, her infant son Alejo, and her sister Gertrudis Navarro Cantu learned of this danger the hard way. Alsbury naively asked her sister to go to the door of their room and announce their presence as only women and children. Gertrudis opened the door, only to be cursed by a passing Mexican soldier. The soldier ripped her shawl from her shoulders as she backpedaled into the room. Another soldier glared at Gertrudis and demanded, "Your money or your husband." Frightened, Gertrudis replied, "I have neither money nor husband." Just then a sick defender—either Edwin T. Mitchell or Napoleon B. Mitchell—rushed to the aid of the women. The Mexican soldiers promptly bayoneted the man where he stood.[21] Moments later, native Texan defender Toribio Losoya ran into the room ahead of pursuing Mexicans. The cowering Losoya grabbed Alsbury by the arms as she still clung to her baby. Losoya proceeded to shield himself from his assailants with her body, jerking the woman about as the Mexican soldiers parried with their bayonets. Losoya finally lost his grip and died riddled with bullets and bayonets. The soldiers then broke into

Alsbury's trunk. They stole her money and clothes, and the jewelry of Travis and other Texan officers.[22]

Inside the chapel, Susanna Dickinson pressed her baby tightly against her breast while standing on a couch in her private room. She peeked out a window. Dickinson saw little in the darkness beyond but heard enough cries of the dying to haunt her a lifetime. On this day, her eyes would behold much horror.[23] "Great God, Sue, the Mexicans are inside our walls!" Almeron Dickinson yelled to his wife as he burst into their room. "All is lost! If they spare you, save my child." Dickinson kissed his wife goodbye, drew his sword, and hastily departed the room to "help the boys." Susanna never saw her husband again—dead or alive.[24]

Moments later, the teenage Galba Fuqua of Gonzales appeared in the doorway, his jaw shattered by a lead ball. Blood dripped from Fuqua's hands as he tried to hold the pieces of his jaw in place. He gurgled a few unrecognizable words to Susanna, trying to relay some sort of a message. He tried again to no avail. Finally, the frustrated boy disappeared forever into the haze of battle. Then gunner Anthony Wolfe and his two boys suddenly appeared in Susanna's room, followed closely by several Mexican soldiers. Wolfe pleaded for mercy for his children but was shot and bayoneted along with his eleven- and twelve-year-old boys.[25] A terror-stricken Susanna watched in shock as the Mexicans butchered Wolfe and his sons.

Jacob Walker, another artilleryman, ran into the room seconds later in a frantic search for somewhere to escape. Earlier during the siege, Walker had often conversed with Susanna about his children. Now he stood wounded and trapped as wide-eyed Mexican soldiers cautiously encircled him. Shots rang out. Walker's body convulsed backward. The soldiers pounced upon him in a frenzy, stabbing their bayonets into his body and lifting him overhead "like a farmer does a bundle of fodder with his pitchfork when he loads his wagon." Walker's blood streamed down on his killers, who screamed wildly during their barbaric deed. As with the Wolfes, Walker pleaded for instantaneous death to terminate his anguish, until he was too weak to speak and died in convulsions.[26]

Room by room, Mexican soldiers hunted for the last of the Texan defenders. In one room, near the wooden palisade, they found the celebrated Bowie slumped behind a mattress. He was alone, and unbeknownst to those who now stalked him, sick and dying. Bowie feebly sat propped to make his last stand, loaded pistols in each hand and his famed knife within reach. The end came swiftly. Bowie greeted his assailants with deadly gunfire before being viciously put out of his misery.[27] A frenzy of bayonets pierced his body until a lead ball struck him in the head, splattering his blood and brains against the wall. Ironically, Bowie had been mistaken for a coward. One Mexican soldier later wrote home in disgust about how the "perverse braggart Santiago Bowie died like a woman, almost hidden beneath a mattress."[28] So ended the life of one of the most feared men of his era.

Bowie's comrades, meanwhile, carved out their own legends in death. A Mexican officer saw one desperate and gallant Texan leap from a high wall with a child in his arms. The Texan and child were killed before they hit the ground.[29]

Maj. Robert Evans, master of ordnance, was seen within the chapel, rushing toward the garrison's magazine room with a torch clenched in his fist. The Irishman planned to blow up the powder—and himself—in order to keep it out of enemy hands. Mexican riflemen shot Evans dead before he completed his mission.[30]

At some point during the melee, Arkansan Henry Warnell jumped on a horse in an attempt to ride past the Mexican ranks with a message for Texan general Sam Houston. If anyone stood a chance of outrunning the Mexican lancers, it was probably the red-headed, twenty-four-year-old, 118-pound jockey. Despite being severely wounded, Warnell escaped with the missive. He reportedly died less than three months later at Port Lavaca due to his wounds.[31]

Little Enrique Esparza, whose father Gregorio manned one of the Alamo cannons, recounted numerous acts of courage from his family's dank refuge within the chapel. None were as unforgettable as that of a large American boy who stood by the eight-year-old Enrique's side as the battle raged outside their room. As soldiers stormed the room, the unarmed boy "stood calmly and across his shoulders drew his blanket on which he had slept." They killed the boy unmercifully, his bloody corpse falling across Enrique's lap.[32] Jittery Mexican soldiers fired into the room for the next fifteen minutes, miraculously killing no one else. The crackle of sporadic gunfire could now be heard echoing throughout the compound. The mop-up had begun. Enrique later stated with a touch of resignation, "If I had been given a weapon I would have fought likewise."[33] Sensing the end, children no older than Enrique scooped up the weapons of their elders and plunged into the fight. All died.[34]

Survival proved elusive. Native Texan defender Brigido Guerrero spun the yarn of his life in order to live another day. The quick-thinking Guerrero pleaded with his Mexican captors, claiming to be a Texan prisoner. Guerrero's lying grew as the seconds passed, as he added for good measure that he had been trying to escape to join Santa Anna's forces. The tale worked so well that an officer escorted Guerrero from the compound and set him free. He would receive a pension from the state of Texas decades later for his service at the battles of Bexar and Concepcion.[35]

A brawny slave named Charlie would also live to tell of his miraculous survival. Mexican soldiers discovered Charlie in a cooking area along with Bowie's slave, Bettie. The soldiers jerked Charlie from his hiding place, and when they began to carry him away he panicked. In a desperate rage, he grabbed the diminutive Mexican officer in front of him and used him as shield as the soldiers lunged with their bayonets. Charlie parried each thrust with the officer's body until the *soldados* broke down laughing. The officer promised to give the slave his freedom if he released him safely. Charlie obliged and was set free as promised. Charlie and Bettie survived.[36]

Susanna Dickinson, mortified by the butchery, huddled in her smoke-filled room with her baby. She had already been shot in the calf by stray gunfire and now expected to die. Suddenly, an English-speaking Mexican officer appeared through the smoke. "Are you Mrs. Dickinson?" the officer asked briskly. "Yes," she tearfully replied. "If you wish to save your life," he gruffly said, "follow me."[37]

Seventy miles away in the town of Gonzales, settlers distinctly heard the thunderous rumble of cannon fire. James Tumlinson, Jr., the father of twenty-two-year-old Texan defender George Tumlinson, listened until there was silence. He turned to his family and sadly stated, "Our boy is gone."[38]

Ghostly images darted through the thick blue haze of smoke beyond the loophole from which Joe peered. He stared wildly into the interior of the compound, his eyes darting about at the report of every gunshot or wail or scream. Sweat soaked his dirt-caked shirt and pantaloons.

Muscles strained from the tense grip on his loaded gun. Survival looked bleak. Sounds beyond the door—cursing men, steel clashing with steel, cannons roaring—drew closer. Joe concealed himself the best he could within the shadows of the room. Nearby, a weak Texan named Warner was in similar despair. He hid himself under a pile of bodies.[39]

Finally, the door violently flew open and Joe heard a Mexican voice cry, "Are there any Negroes here?" Joe hesitantly emerged from the shadows. "Yes," he replied, "here's one."[40] Two frenzied Mexican soldiers instantly tried to kill him. One fired into his side, while the other lunged at him with a bayonet, nicking the other side of the young servant as he tried to defend himself.[41] Just then Mexican officer Miguel Barragan intervened, beating back the soldiers with his sword and saving Joe's life.[42]

Barragan, a rough-and-tumble captain, had experience in dealing with insubordinates. He disarmed Joe and placed him under arrest. Almost instantaneously, Barragan discovered Warner as they dug through the pile of bodies.[43] Barragan offered to spare Warner's life if he could identify the bodies of Travis and Bowie. Warner agreed, and the officer ordered both captors to exit the room at the point of a bayonet.[44]

Joe and Warner emerged from their darkened room into the morning sunlight.[45] Smoke hung in the air, as did the stench of death. Mangled and mutilated bodies littered the Alamo courtyard. Clumps of dead Mexican soldiers here, bloodied and lifeless Texans there. Blackened faces of the dead stared up at Joe as he struggled to step over and around them. Blood soaked the dirt. A few of the gravely wounded moaned for help. Some, as if from the grave, tugged at his feet. In the distance, Mexican soldiers poked and prodded at the bodies of the Texans, searching for survivors. Those found alive were executed on the spot.[46] Joe noticed a black woman "lying between two guns." He deduced she must have rushed into the melee out of fright.[47]

Chillingly, Joe again beheld the lifeless Travis, whose bloody corpse was heaped with Mora's. Joe probably wondered if he soon would join his master in death. Warner and Joe both identified Travis for Barragan. Poking them with his bayonet, the Mexican officer ordered the two men to show him Bowie's body. They walked across the compound amid the sporadic sound of stray gunfire and into a tiny room on the west side, next to the wooden palisade. Inside the room they found the legendary knife-fighter, his mutilated body nearly unrecognizable.[48]

Once the grisly identification task had been accomplished, Joe and Warner were ordered back into the main courtyard. There, for the first time, Joe gazed upon a tall, slender man with animated features and plain dress similar to that of "a Methodist preacher." The man stood about five foot ten and had black hair atop a moderately high forehead, his face covered with short, black whiskers.[49] The man's eyes were coal black.[50]

Joe soon discovered he was staring at the Mexican dictator, Antonio López de Santa Anna. Within moments, the slave understood exactly what that meant. "What's that fellow doing here?" snapped Santa Anna, casting his eyes on Warner. Barragan explained how the man's life had been spared in exchange for the identities of Travis and Bowie. Santa Anna bristled, "We have no use for any such men!"[51] He ordered Warner shot.[52] A group of Mexican soldiers executed the order instantly. If Santa Anna would order the execution of a free, white man, what would he do to a slave? Joe surely shuddered at the thought.

Moments passed before Susanna Dickinson emerged from a side door of the chapel, still with her baby pressed tightly against her chest. Blood trickled down her right calf. Only seconds earlier the officer who escorted her had given her a choice: climb over the bodies of the Texans at the chapel entrance or wade through the blood leading to a side door. Susanna walked through pools of blood that reached the tops of her shoes. Once beyond the chapel walls the dazed widow saw Mexican soldiers plunging their bayonets into dying Texans, and then she distinctly "recognized Col. Crockett lying dead and mutilated between the church and the two-story barrack building" with his "peculiar cap lying by his side."[53] Crockett's face, like many images that Sabbath morning, would haunt her for the rest of her days.

The scene affected Santa Anna far differently. In silence, the dictator surveyed the carnage. Then he scoffed, "It was but a small affair."[54]

22

FROM THE ASHES

*This is a bald prairie, and if it is the enemy we must
meet them face to face.*
— *Susanna Dickinson, Alamo survivor*

Vultures circled in the sky by the hundreds. They soared around
plumes of black smoke, which billowed from two pyres of Texan
dead. Massive flames jumped skyward, in symphony with the
crackling of branches and kindling. Tallow had been splattered in heaps
around the piles to help fuel the fires.

Each funeral pyre presented a hellish portrait. Blackened and bloodied hands, arms, and legs dangled from the layers of wood. Ghostly faces
of the dead peered from the flames as the putrid odor of burning flesh
and hair permeated the air.[1]

Joe undoubtedly witnessed the ghastly scene in horror. "Grease that
had exuded from the bodies saturated the earth for several feet beyond
the ashes and smoldering mesquite fagots," one native Texan eyewitness
recalled. "I placed my head aside and left the place in shame."[2]

Torches ignited the pyres hours after the survivors had been whisked
away to town under Mexican guard. The women and children were escorted from the Alamo past Mexican soldiers who had not participated
in the battle. The refugees were taken to the home of Ramon Musquiz

on the Main Plaza.[3] Joe remained behind, as ordered. Soon officers ordered the soldiers to assemble before their commander-in-chief in the Alamo square, still littered with corpses. Joe watched in awe as thousands of soldiers, many bloodied, bandaged, and scarred by the battle, stood before the general. Six thousand soldiers, Joe guessed. No, maybe eight thousand. There was no way to digest the numbers.[4]

Santa Anna stood erectly in front of his troops, his mere presence prompting raucous cheers and repeated cries of *"Viva Santa Anna! Viva México!"* Santa Anna responded by delivering an animated victory speech, praising his battle-weary troops for their brave service to God and country. The soldiers cheered wildly.[5]

Afterward Joe stood before Santa Anna, "who took much notice" of the young slave and his association with the Alamo commander. Leering at Joe, Santa Anna began to question him about Texas and the state of its rebel army. Santa Anna wanted to know if there were any U.S. soldiers among the Texans and if more were expected to arrive. Joe, blood now seeping from his side onto his shirt, nervously answered in the affirmative. Santa Anna sneered, saying he had enough men to march all the way to Washington, D.C., if he chose.[6] Satisfied that Joe was of no more use to him, Santa Anna abruptly dismissed the slave from his presence and ordered him taken away by guards.

Joe passed a number of young local women on the road back to town. Arms filled with linens and rags, they had been pressed into service by Mexican officers to care for their dead and dying. One such woman was Eulalia Yorba, a young Mexican who had watched the battle in fright from the windows of the priest's home in town. "Such a dreadful sight," she later recalled. "The roadway was thronged with Mexican soldiers with smoke and dirt begrimed faces[,] haggard eyes and wild, insane expression. There were twelve or fifteen bodies of Mexicans lying dead and bleeding here and there, and others were being carried to an adobe house across the way. The stones of the church wall were spotted with blood, and the doors were splintered and battered in."[7]

Yorba then entered the church, which was filled with hot, heavy air still thick with smoke. Blood covered the ground. In the rear of the church, she spotted the sacred altar "cut and slashed by cannon balls and bullets." Dead Texans lay "singly and in heaps of three or four or in irregular rows . . . just as they had fallen." So thick were the bodies that she could scarcely avoid stepping over the dead to reach others who were still drawing their last breaths. "Close to my feet was a young man who had been shot through the forehead and who had dropped dead with his eyes staring wildly open, as he seemingly gazed up into my face," Yorba remembered. "A yard away was a grizzled old Texan whose beard and long unkept hair were clotted with blood that trickled from his mouth and ears. Over there was a handsome young man whose determined resolution was shown in his corpse, for he died grappling tight to a musket in one hand while he held a ramrod in the other. He was in the act of loading when shot down."[8]

Yorba moved from one corpse to the next. Finally, to her great surprise, two young Texan defenders were discovered alive in the rumble, although clearly dying. One had been shot in the throat; the other had been shot in the chest. The two men—whom Yorba remembered being named "Lyon and Randall"—said they hailed from Louisiana. They were carefully carried from the scene of death by the citizens and placed beneath a nearby tree where everything possible was done to comfort them in their final hours. There, Randall revealed an amazing story of courage—one Yorba would never forget. Randall described how Travis had "coolly and calmly" told the men he would remain in the Alamo "as long as he could move" and that he was determined to "sell his life as dearly as possible." Travis told those who wanted to surrender to Santa Anna that they were free to go. He had then drawn his sword and scratched it across the ground, asking if anyone wished cross the line and stand by his side. Randall then proudly related how the Texan band "moved by a common impulse" across the line.[9] Yorba was overwhelmed with emotion.

Back on the Main Plaza, inside the Musquiz house, the other Alamo survivors waited to be interrogated by Santa Anna. As the morning grew longer so did the hunger of the children. Anna Esparza, with four restless children in tow, boldly brushed past the Mexican guards to search the home for food. Nervous and jittery, Ramon Musquiz explained how dangerous it was for her to move about the house and pleaded with her to stay in the room where she was under guard. Esparza bristled at Musquiz's advice, blurting how she would find food for her children, her companions, and herself whether Santa Anna intended to or not.

Musquiz admonished her to remain silent and disappeared. He returned momentarily with his domestic servants, who served the prisoners meat, bread, and coffee.[10]

Santa Anna finally returned to his headquarters at the Yturri house around 3:00 P.M., and one by one the women survivors were ordered to appear before him to pledge an oath of loyalty to the Republic of Mexico. A pile of blankets and silver pesos sat in front of him on a table. He would give each woman two pesos and one blanket for their troubles. Guards carried the wounded Susanna into the room. The interview dragged on for some time. Susanna begged to join the honorable fate of her husband. "I am not warring against women," Santa Anna coolly replied before dismissing her abruptly.[11]

Anna Esparza appeared next before Santa Anna. Her children clung to her skirt. Enrique peered around his mother at the Mexican dictator, listening to every word. "Where is your husband?" Santa Anna asked. Sobbing, Esparza replied, "He's dead in the Alamo."[12]

Back at the Musquiz house, Dickinson asked to return to the Alamo to view her husband's body. The guards told her that would not be permitted because Santa Anna had ordered the bodies of the Texans burned. Susanna shook her head in disbelief, only to be escorted to a window. Aghast, she saw a pillar of smoke rising skyward in the distance near the Alamo.[13] Tears rolled down her cheeks.

Anna Esparza received the news similarly. Upon being set free by Santa Anna, a determined Anna immediately returned to the Alamo to retrieve her husband's body. She arrived to find two pyres with the Texan dead stacked like animals on layers of wood. Frantically, Anna tried to get close enough to the pyres to identify Gregorio, whose lifeless body had been found near a cannon in the chapel. The soldiers, however, kept her at a distance before tossing more torches on the two piles. Anna covered her face with her mantilla and ran screaming from the scene, dragging Enrique behind her by the hand.[14]

A pall fell over the town as the burning embers of the mammoth funeral pyres glowed at night. Joe probably searched in vain for reassurances that his life would be spared. He had seen no action by the Mexican soldiers—or more importantly Santa Anna—that would lead him to believe he was safe. At some point during his confinement, Joe likely heard about Santa Anna's orders to send Susanna and her baby under escort toward Gonzales, perhaps hearing this from the widow herself. Almonte had convinced Santa Anna to release Susanna back to the rebel colonists, a decision he likely concluded would wreak havoc on the psyche of the Texans. Susanna would, in exchange, carry a proclamation to the rebels, offering a pardon for anyone who would lay down arms and submit to the Mexican government.[15]

Joe sensed an opportunity. The survivalist in him had previously followed his instincts, just as he had two years earlier in the wake of Mansfield's death. Fear had driven him to run then rather than face the terror of an estate auction. A similar fear called to him now, urging him to take flight or perhaps be forced into service for the Mexican Army. Or worse. By the next day, perhaps before sunrise, Joe had successfully escaped the Mexican guard. He quietly slipped out of town and ventured into the open prairie in the direction of Gonzales, ever wary of Mexican patrols. Joe walked or ran through thick grass and a rough landscape scattered with briar thickets and scrub brush. Five miles into his journey, he arrived at the perfect shelter for an escaping prisoner—Salado Creek.[16] Cottonwood, oak, and pecan trees as well as thick layers of canebrakes loomed all along the steep embankment of the creek. The heavy vegetation created an abundance of cover for the fleeing slave. He slipped into the brush and waited for his next opportunity. Whether anyone noticed or cared about Joe's disappearance is unknown.

Later that evening, after dinner, Susanna departed Bexar under the escort of a small cavalry unit and Almonte's servant, Ben. Susanna cradled her baby aboard a mule as the small party followed the worn dirt path southeast toward Gonzales. They rode past the battered walls of the Alamo and the smoldering piles of Alamo dead. Vultures could still be seen circling overhead.[17] Not far from town, the Mexican cavalrymen wheeled their horses and left Susanna and Ben to travel alone. Another cowardly act by a band of cowards, Susanna thought in disgust. She did not care.[18]

A short distance away, Joe lurked in the brush of Salado Creek. As Susanna and Ben passed, Joe emerged from the brush and fell in behind them. He followed in this manner for a short while before finally popping from the tall grass and making his presence known.[19] A startled Susanna stoically welcomed the familiar face. Joe trudged along from that point on, ducking into the brush each time he heard a noise.

Joe had a lot to fear: Mexican patrols, roadside bandits, and marauding Indians. He trusted no stranger.

Some sixty miles away, in the town of Gonzales, Texan soldiers gathered daily on the banks of the Guadalupe River. Their number included a stout, fifteen-year-old lad named John Holland Jenkins who epitomized the spirit of most of the soldiers in camp. Jenkins had grown up to be a crack shot with the rifle and, like most young recruits, had eagerly joined the Texan army with little regard to the consequences of war. At night, Jenkins had anxiously sat in camp and listened to the low rumblings of cannon emanating across the prairie in Bexar. His blood had stirred with excitement. Now the boy heard only silence.

On March 10, Gen. Sam Houston arrived in Gonzales to the raucous cheers of hundreds of troops. He found an undisciplined yet spirited band of men eager for a fight. "I yet consider him about the finest looking man I ever saw, as he stood over six feet tall, in the very prime of mature manhood," Jenkins later recalled.[20] Houston instantly took command. He gathered the men at DeWitt's tavern, where the commander-in-chief read the nine-day-old Declaration of Independence. Texan delegates had unanimously signed the document in a crude, plank structure at Washington-on-the-Brazos on March 2—Houston's forty-third birthday.

The document summed up the frustrations of most colonists, reading in part:

> The Mexican Government, by its colonization laws, invited and induced the Anglo American population of Texas to colonize its wilderness under the pledged faith of a written constitution, that they should continue to enjoy that constitutional liberty and republican government to which they had been habituated in the land of their birth, the United States of America.
>
> In this expectation they have been cruelly disappointed, inasmuch as the Mexican nation has acquiesced in the late changes made in the government by General Antonio Lopez Santa Ana, who having overturned the constitution of his country, now offers, as the cruel alternative, either to abandon our homes acquired by so many privations, or submit to the most intolerable of all tyranny, the combined despotism of the sword and the priesthood.[21]

At DeWitt's, Houston delivered a short, inspiring speech that touched off another round of wild cheers. But moods changed the next day. Two Mexican *vaqueros*, both claiming to be friendly to the Texan cause, arrived in Gonzales with news that the Alamo had been overtaken. Houston listened to their stories and then ordered the two men jailed as spies. Now Houston wished to quell the panic that was spreading through town. People were already frantically packing food and supplies for an exodus to the east. Reports of a wholesale slaughter at the Alamo were the last thing anyone wanted or needed to hear. Houston demanded calm. At the same time, however, he sent an urgent dispatch to Colonel Fannin at Goliad. The letter revealed Houston's true feelings about the reports.

> Head Quarters
> Gonzales 11 March 1836
>
> Col. J. W. Fannin
> Commanding at Goliad
>
> Sir
>
> Upon my arrival here this afternoon, the following intelligence was received through a Mexican supposed to be friendly, which however has been contradicted in some parts by another who arrived with him—it is therefore only given as rumor, though I fear a melancholy portion of it will be found true.—Anselmo Borgara states that he left the Alamo on Sunday 6th inst. and is three days from Arroches Rancho.—That the Alamo was attacked on Sunday morning at the dawn of day, by about 2300 men—and carried a short time before sunrise, with the loss of 521 Mexicans killed and as many wounded. Colonel Travis had but 150 effective men out of his whole force of 187.—After the fort was carried, *seven* Men surrendered, and called for Genl St Anna and for quarter.—They were *murdered by his order.* Col. Bowie was sick in bed and also murdered.—The enemy expect reinforcements of 1500 men under General Condelle, and 1500 reserve to follow the.—he also informs that Ugartecha had arrived with two millions of dollars for the pay of the troops.—The bodies of the Americans were burned after the massacre, an alternate layer of wood and bodies were laid and set on fire. Lieut. Dickinson who had a wife and child in the fort

having fought with desperate courage tied his child to his back and leaped from the top of a two story building—both were killed by the fall. I have little doubt but that the Alamo has fallen—whether above *particulars* are all true may be questionable. You are therefore referred to the enclosed order.

I am, sir, &cc., Sam Houston

The wife of Lt. Dickinson is now in the possession of one of the officers of S Anna. The men as you will perceive fought gal-lantly—In corroboration of the truth of the *fall* of the Alamo, I have ascertained that Col. Travis intended firing signal guns at three different periods each day until succor should arrive—No signal guns have been heard since Sunday and a scouting party have just returned who approached within 12 miles of it & remained there 48 hours.[22]

Houston had ordered scouts Erastus "Deaf" Smith, Henry Karnes, and Robert E. Handy to ride toward Bexar with all haste to ascertain the truth. The trusty threesome crossed the Guadalupe River ferry and spurred their horses into the vastness of the prairie. They would return two days later with news that would shake Texas.

Fifteen-year-old Sarah Nash and her stepmother, Prudence Kimble, lived among a cluster of oak trees not far from the trail that meandered be-tween Gonzales and Bexar. The trail had been well traveled in recent months by families, soldiers, and couriers, but nothing prepared them for what they encountered on the night of March 12. A knock at the door aroused Kimble and Nash from sleep. Darkness had already converged on the tiny rock home, and travelers were rare after nightfall. Nash glanced at a pocketwatch by candlelight, noticing that it was 9:00 P.M. Prudence—the pregnant wife of Alamo defender George Kimble—and Sarah opened the front door. Holding a candle aloft, they were startled to see a woman and a baby. They recognized them immediately.

Susanna Dickinson wept as she recounted for the first time the de-feat of the Alamo's small band of men. This is how Prudence learned the dreadful news of her husband's death. Susanna was eventually moved near the fire and asked if she had been traveling alone. She pointed out toward the woods, saying that she was also in the company of a Mexican officer's servant and the slave of the late Alamo co-commander. Joe had refused to go near the house. He instead slept outside, insisting he felt more protected in the woods.[23]

By sunrise, Susanna again led the motley band as they continued toward Gonzales. Shortly after they reached the trail, the silhouette of three riders could be seen ahead. Joe instinctively ducked into thick brush. Weary from heartache and perhaps still in shock, Susanna never flinched as the riders drew closer. "This is a bald prairie," Susanna said coldly, "and if it is the enemy we must meet them face to face."[24]

After Joe crouched out of view, his eyes darted behind the brush for any indication of danger. He soon realized that the riders were Texan scouts. Smith, Karnes, and Handy dismounted to assist Susanna and her child. Joe bounded from his hiding place, overjoyed to be in the presence of friendly Texan escorts. Within hours, the scouts and an old Mexican named Bogardo helped the Alamo refugees board a ferry at the Guadalupe River. A white flag signaled their arrival as Texan troops gathered on the opposite bank to watch their approach.[25] The scouts immediately led Susanna, Joe, and Ben to General Houston's private tent. There Houston tenderly held Susanna's hand as she retold the tale of the horrific slaughter she had witnessed at the Alamo. Houston reportedly "wept like a child."[26]

Santa Anna's proclamation sent a strong message to the Texan forces, but the written words could not overpower the image of the widowed Susanna and her baby. News of the Alamo massacre struck hard, especially for dozens of Gonzales families. Gonzales had sent many men to aid the Alamo—good men like Andrew Kent, Isaac Millsap, Almeron Dickinson, William King, and George Kimble. Now all were dead.

Officers and soldiers alike gathered around Joe to hear the haunting details he provided. Bowie? Dead. Travis? Shot in the head on the north wall. Crockett? Also died heroically. James Perry, one of Houston's officers, claimed years later to have heard Joe recount the details of Crockett's death. Joe told how the garrison had been reduced to seven defiant men, Crockett among them. Ordered to surrender, Crockett had bravely "shouted forth defiance, leaped into the crowd below, and rushed toward the city." Crockett had died moments later when a cavalryman thrust him through the breast with a lance.[27] So the story was reported.

All present that night in Gonzales were profoundly affected. Young Jenkins recalled: "Many of the citizens of Gonzales perished in this wholesale slaughter of Texans, and I remembered most distinctly the shrieks of despair with which the soldiers' wives received news of the death of their husbands. The piercing wails of woe reached our camps from these bereaved women thrilled me and filled me with feelings I cannot express, or ever forget."[28] Capt. John Sharpe later recalled: "For hours after the receipt of the intelligence, not a sound was heard, save the wild shrieks of the women, and heartrending screams of the fatherless children."[29]

Houston left an everlasting image with the Texans that night—one that would bolster their resolve. He abruptly ordered his troops to retreat to the Colorado River, where he planned to unite forces with Fannin's men from Goliad, and then ordered Gonzales torched. Creed Taylor and a handful of other men pulled reconnaissance duty on the outskirts of Gonzales that night. Taylor vividly remembered the scene:

> That night was very dark, and as we groped our way toward camp our attention was suddenly attracted by a flare of lights in the direction of Gonzales, tall spires of flame shooting up now and then far above the horizon and illuminating the landscape in every direction. Hastening forward we soon arrived upon the scene and learned the cause of the phenomenon.
>
> Imagine, if you can, our utter bewilderment at finding the town in flames and our army camp deserted, with not a soldier in sight, save a few scouts who, like us, had not been called in from their posts of duty. The terrible story of the Alamo fight told by Mrs. Dickerson [Dickinson] had caused great excitement and the army and the citizens had literally stampeded.[30]

Now Joe trudged along with the procession of livestock, soldiers, women, children, and slaves as they briskly moved eastward away from Gonzales. Looking back, Joe saw only an inferno of flames shooting skyward. The world appeared to be on fire.

23

"Travis's Negro"

He related the affair with much modesty, apparent
candor, and remarkably distinctly for one of his class.
—William Fairfax Gray, regarding Joe's Alamo
battle account

Panic blew into Washington-on-the-Brazos with gale force. A
steady drizzle fell as frantic colonists with wagons, ox carts,
horses, and mules sloshed continuously along the muddy main
street that cut through the infant township. The colonists headed eastward, having decided to try to outrun the storm of war.[1] Santa Anna
and his Mexican Army were rumored to be close behind, and word of
the slaughter of the Alamo's brave defenders now fell from every tongue.
General Houston and his army had camped on the Colorado River, awaiting reinforcements. Texas hung in the balance.

Fear spread unabated as the colonists pressed eastward. Many of them
slogged past a simple, two-story framed structure unaware of its significance—it was the place the Texas Declaration of Independence had
been recently been signed. Ordinary in appearance, weather-proofed
with clapboards and wooden shutters, the building faced east, offering
a view of tree stumps. Steadily the colonists passed a gun shop, a tavern, a carpenter's shop, and a mercantile that belonged to Travis's old

friend David Ayers, all fronting woods that pressed up from behind. And now the street descended a steep embankment to the crowded ferry at the Brazos River. Ferry owner Andrew Robinson had constructed a breastwork of earth-filled cotton bags on the west bank in case of enemy attack.[2]

On March 20, two weeks after the storming of the Alamo, Joe experienced the madness of the mass exodus firsthand in Washington-on-the-Brazos. The last time Joe had seen the riverside town he had watched an emotional Travis bid farewell to little Charles. Then Joe stood quietly by his master's side as a faithful servant. Now Joe entered Washington-on-the-Brazos as a celebrity. Strangers identified him as "Travis's Negro," the servant of the heroic commander, and the only known male to cheat death at the Alamo. Important men took notice of his arrival. "The servant of the late lamented Travis, Joe, a black boy of about twenty-one or twenty-two years of age, is now here," noted Virginia land agent William Fairfax Gray in his diary. "He was in the Alamo when the fatal attack was made. He is the only male, of all who were in the fort, who escaped death, and he, according to his own account, escaped narrowly."[3]

Joe's presence commanded the attention of more than a few observers. "I heard him interrogated in the presence of the cabinet and others," Gray continued. The Virginian was intrigued by Joe's skills with English, noting, "He related the affair with much modesty, apparent candor, and remarkably distinctly for one of his class."[4] Gray clearly had expected an uneducated field hand. Instead he encountered a mulatto servant who had been taught since childhood to survive in a white-dominated world.

Emboldened perhaps by his brush with death, Joe spoke with ease and grace about the Alamo's final hours. The most powerful politicians in Texas hung on his every word as he described how the Mexican soldiers "commenced pouring over the walls like sheep."[5] Joe frequently quoted Travis as yelling, "Come on, boys, the Mexicans are upon us, and we'll give them Hell!"[6] Joe would recount many details over and over in the days and years to come. He told how Travis had died while running a sword through a Mexican officer, how Bowie had gallantly fired through a door from his sick bed, and how every man had fought to the bitter end, wielding "butts of guns, pistols, knives, etc." Of

Crockett, Joe said that he and a few friends were found with twenty-four enemy dead piled around them. The claim may or may not have matched the account he was said to have given to James Perry in Gonzales regarding Crockett's death. Only Joe knew for sure, and no versions other than the one recounted by Gray are known to have been recorded.[7]

Joe made special mention of several blacks inside the Alamo at the time of the final attack, including a woman who had apparently been shot and killed accidentally while running into the open.[8] The more Joe talked, the more he must have realized how fortunate he had been to escape, but the furious pace of events gave him little time for such introspection. The flight from Gonzales had been almost instantaneous. "Uncle" Jeff Parson, a fellow slave, later remembered, "People and things were all mixed, and in confusion. The children were crying, the women praying and the men cursing. I tell you it was a serious time."[9]

Blind Mary Millsaps, whose husband, Isaac, had died in the Alamo, was accidentally left behind in the confusion with her seven children. When Houston realized the blunder, he sent a soldier back to retrieve the frightened and grief-stricken family. The soldier found Mary and her children hidden in the brush along the river.[10]

Joe had found the route from Gonzales to Washington-on-the-Brazos fraught with similar confusion for civilians and soldiers alike. Homesteads along the route had been deserted, and rumors flew from every direction. Houston, for one, firmly grasped the situation facing his army. By March 15, the general and his troops had camped on the Navidad River amid a large contingent of Gonzales residents that included Joe. "I am fearful Goliad is besieged by the enemy," Houston accurately speculated in a letter that day to James Collinsworth. "Our forces must not be shut up in forts, where they can neither be supplied with men nor provisions," he added in frustration.[11]

Houston turned his thoughts to a decisive plan of action, taking comfort in the "uninhibited waste" that lay in his wake. "When the approach of the enemy was known [at Gonzales], there were but two public wagons and two yoke of oxen in camp, and the few horses we had were very poor," Houston wrote. "I hope to reach the Colorado [River] on tomorrow, and collect an army in a short time." He declared: "Let the men of Texas rally to the Colorado!"[12]

Joe had left the Texan soldiers after they had reached the Colorado River the next day, March 16. He had then continued another sixty-five miles on sheer adrenaline, sometimes in torrential downpour, to Washington-on-the Brazos. He had likely hoped to find little Charles Travis, who had been left in the care of David Ayers at his Montville home near Washington-on-the-Brazos. By now, Travis's final note to his son from inside the doomed Alamo had likely reached Ayers, as well as news of his death. Travelers had continued to solicit Joe for tidbits of information regarding the Alamo battle. One couple asked who among the Texans had killed the most Mexican soldiers. Joe is said to have replied, "Colonel Crockett had the biggest pile."[13]

The editor of the *Telegraph and Texas Register* gathered further information from Joe after his arrival at Washington-on-the-Brazos. Joe again spoke of the valor he had witnessed in the face of an overwhelming Mexican onslaught, uttering perhaps for the first time the description of the enemy pouring over the walls "like sheep." Travis, he noted once more, had remained defiant to his last breath. Quoting the enemy, Joe confessed that his life had been spared because "his master had behaved like a brave man." The patriotic editor would run with the Alamo story, dubbing the heroic last stand the "Thermopylae of Texas."[14] But independence would prove more daunting.

On March 23, three days after Joe's arrival at Washington-on-the-Brazos, Houston received more dreadful news. A large Mexican force had defeated and captured Colonel Fannin and his men outside of Goliad. "You know I am not easily depressed," Houston wrote Texan secretary of war Thomas J. Rusk, "but before my God, since we parted, I have found the darkest hours of my past life!" Houston cursed the report. "If what I have learned from Fannin be true, I deplore it, and can only attribute the ill luck to his attempt to retreat in daylight in the face of a superior force," he wrote. "He is an ill-fated man."[15]

Fannin and his men suffered greatly. At sunrise on March 27, 1836—Palm Sunday—the Mexican soldiers marched the Texan prisoners from the Goliad presidio in three groups. The soldiers offered various stories about their destination: they would drive cattle or gather wood or be paroled in New Orleans. The prisoners sang as they marched. Suddenly, the ranking officer ordered them to halt. Without warning, the Mexican guard opened fire on the Texans at point-blank range. The soldiers hunted down those who initially survived and killed them with bayonets and lances. The Mexicans also executed the remaining Texan prisoners at the presidio—some 342 in all.[16]

Fannin died bravely. Informed that he would be executed, he requested only that he not be shot in the face, that his watch be returned to his family, and that he be given a Christian burial. Fannin then coolly slipped a blindfold over his eyes and faced the firing squad while seated in a chair. The squad promptly shot Fannin in the face and callously tossed his body into a funeral pyre with the rest of the dead. A commanding officer concluded the indignation by pocketing Fannin's watch.[17]

Word of the Goliad massacre made the blood of men and boys alike run hot with desire for vengeance. Yet revenge would have to wait. Houston retreated continuously from the advancing Mexican Army, often drawing the ire of his own men. The Texans clamored for a fight. Capt. Robert Coleman, who had fought at Concepcion and the siege of Bexar, bitterly criticized the general's actions. "Thirteen hundred Americans retreating before a division of 800 Mexicans!" Coleman recalled in an 1837 pamphlet that did not bear his name. "Can Houston's strong partisans presume to excuse such dastardly cowardice under the pretence of laudable prudence?"[18]

During the panic at Washington-on-the-Brazos, Josephus Sommerville Irvine entered the town with a company of fresh recruits from Sabine County, only to find the populace crossing to the east side of the Brazos River as fast as possible. Irvine bemoaned the situation when he walked into a tavern for dinner. Much to Irvine's dismay, the proprietor informed him that he had no time to prepare a meal. Everyone was too busy packing to leave. Irvine and his companions finally secured four eggs for what was then an exorbitant price: seventy-five cents. They then resumed their march to join the Texan army, which now was encamped on the Brazos. The army remained at that location before marching fifty-five miles to reach Harrisburg on April 18.[19] The Texan army would retreat no more.

Somewhere on the prairie, perhaps with Charles Travis by his side, Joe waited in suspense along with every man and woman left in Washington-on-the-Brazos. The fate of the army stirred in every mind. Finally, a rider appeared one afternoon on the horizon, approaching in a gallop. "The Mexicans have been whipped!" the rider announced as he passed. "The Mexicans have been whipped!" Bit by bit the story unfolded. A battle had taken place April 21 near Harrisburg at San Jacinto, a location familiar to Joe from his early days in Texas with Mansfield. More details followed: Houston wounded, 650 Mexicans slain, Cos killed, Almonte and more than 700 Mexicans taken prisoner. The battle had lasted only eighteen minutes, but the butchery continued much longer. Mexicans had pleaded with the frenzied Texan rebels by yelling, *"Me no Alamo! Me no Goliad!"* Coleman later recalled, "When quarter was demanded, the answer was 'Remember the Alamo!' and the victim was immediately dispatched.[20] Furious Texans killed until exhausted.

Some met details of the battle with skepticism. "I do not fully believe it, but others do," Gray penned in his diary. "It is likely there has been a battle and a victory, but the result is too much wholesale."[21] No one on the prairie knew what to believe. Then came the equally stunning news of Santa Anna's capture. If true, then the fate of the Texas Republic was secure. Joe's master and his men had traded their lives for Texas independence. But was it true?

Capt. James A. Sylvester would learn the truth on the morning of April 22 while patrolling for Mexican officers thought to be lurking in the timber a few miles from the Texan encampment. Riding alone, Sylvester spotted an object moving toward him near a ravine. Sylvester rode toward the object, only to have it vanish in the brush. He cautiously approached and soon encountered a man covered in a Mexican blanket. "I ordered him to get up, which he did, very reluctantly and immediately took hold of my hand and kissed it several times, and asked for General Houston," Sylvester recalled years later. Sylvester said the Mexican "seemed very solicitous to find out whether he [Houston] had been killed in the battle the day previous."[22]

Sylvester asked for the man's identity, but the man insisted he was only a "common soldier." Sylvester knew better from the fineness of the man's shirt, which the skittish man now tried to conceal. Finally, the man admitted he was an aide to Santa Anna. Unmoved, Sylvester escorted his prisoner to the Texan camp. "I left him with the camp guard," Sylvester recalled. "He was immediately recognized by his own soldiers who were prisoners in our camp, and was sent to General Houston's headquarters."[23] It was Santa Anna himself. Sylvester had captured the

self-proclaimed "Napoleon of the West," and news of the famous prisoner spread like wildfire from one refugee camp to the next.

Word of Santa Anna's capture likely conjured up unpleasant images
for Joe. Regardless, the tyrant was no longer free. Ironically, neither was
Joe. For all his loyalty to Travis, and for all his service to Texas, at the
end of the war Joe remained a prisoner to the institution of slavery. The
Alamo survivor would be returned to the Travis estate as human
chattel.

24

THE ESTATE

*This negro was in the Alamo with his master when it
was taken; and [he] was the only man from the
colonies who was not put to death.*
—*Travis executor John Rice Jones describing
Joe on May 21, 1837*

T he fruits of a victorious revolution did not belong to Joe. As the
first anniversary of his narrow escape at the Alamo neared,
Joe found himself working in a tavern and boardinghouse at
Washington-on-the-Brazos. The public house belonged to Henry Cartwell and Bernard W. Holtzclaw, the latter a former overseer for President Andrew Jackson at The Hermitage in Nashville.

A year earlier, Joe had held court at Washington-on-the-Brazos with
some of the most influential men in Texas. He had mesmerized them
with his vivid eyewitness account of the Alamo battle and the gallant
fall of his master and other defenders. Now Joe shoveled hay from the
tavern's horse stalls and performed menial chores. Holtzclaw and Cartwell leased Joe for two weeks from Travis estate executor John Rice Jones,
a friend of Travis and the new republic's first postmaster general.[1] The
two had begun their partnership in December 1836 with the purchase
of a corner-lot tavern overlooking the Brazos River. By March 1837

Holtzclaw and Cartwell were bickering often—a circumstance that would lead to the dissolution of their partnership by year's end and later a lawsuit.[2]

Holtzclaw always catered to his ambitions. As a young man, he had moved from his native Virginia to Tennessee and become politically active as a Democrat under the tutelage of Jackson in Nashville.[3] In 1832, Jackson hired Holtzclaw to oversee his farming operations at The Hermitage. Holtzclaw aggressively took charge. Fences and gates were repaired. The spinning jenny, wheels, and two looms were made to work again. Crops were in good order. Holtzclaw had a healthy 200 acres in cotton, 300 in corn, and 120 in oats planted during his first season. Only the hay fields were in poor shape. As for Jackson's slaves, Holtzclaw proudly reported them to be well clothed, especially the children, whose numbers had increased to fifty-eight. "Treat my Negroes with kindness," President Jackson admonished Holtzclaw. The president further instructed Holtzclaw to restrain Betty, his black cook, from "abusing the little Negroes that are under her about the kitchen. A small switch ought only to be used."[4]

Holtzclaw's tenure at The Hermitage ended in 1834, when Jackson replaced him as overseer. The decision might have had more to do with Andrew Jackson, Jr., than Holtzclaw. Jackson had left his son in charge of the finances at The Hermitage, and despite much coaching, Junior had run the farm into more debt.[5] The dismissal had spurred Holtzclaw and his family to Texas in 1835, and on March 4, 1836—two days before the final assault on the Alamo—Holtzclaw had experienced his own brush with death on a tributary of the Brazos River. More than one hundred Indians attacked him and nine fellow surveyors at daylight. Two of the surveyors died in the fight. Two others suffered wounds in making their escape, arriving at the nearest settlement naked and cut by briars. Holtzclaw escaped with a bullet hole through his pantaloons.[6]

The former overseer likely recounted the harrowing story more than once during Joe's short tenure at the tavern, which ended one year to the day after the fall of the Alamo. John Rice Jones arrived at the tavern on March 6, 1837, to take Joe back to his newly purchased plantation on Bailey's Prairie, located a short distance from the Gulf coast near the Brazos River. The farm sat seven miles from Columbia.[7]

The return trip spanned four days. Along the way, Joe probably learned firsthand of the fate of little Charles if he didn't already know. Jones had taken custody of Travis's son from Ayers in September, retrieving Travis's will and Shannon horse in the process. Two months later, William Cato, the boy's uncle, arrived in Texas from Alabama. Cato met Jones on November 10 to pay some of the debts against the Travis estate and to escort his nephew home to his grandparents in Alabama. Rosanna Cato, now planning a wedding with her fiancé, Samuel Cloud, didn't have custody of Susan and Charles. She moved on with her life, living and dying in Louisiana.[8] William Cato, meanwhile, died before departing Texas. Once again Charles found himself an orphan of sorts.[9]

Joe's fate also hung in the balance. By now he knew the routine all too well. He would be leased to various people to help pay off debts against the Travis estate. The work would vary, as would the kindness of those he served. Holtzclaw had been a tough man with an overseer's mentality. The next boss might be crueler, maybe even the kind of man who would flog a slave with a whip. John Travis, another of the late colonel's slaves, was also being leased. John was a field hand. He spent two weeks in January working for a Mr. Howell, and by the end of March would be contracted to Charles D. Sayre for one year at $300. Sayre was a sugar planter who also operated the Brazoria Insurance Company, a firm created to safeguard vessels, buildings, freight, and merchandise from fire or ocean damage.[10]

Joe surely figured it was only a matter of time before he too would be hired under a long-term agreement after arriving at Jones's plantation on March 10. In the meantime, Jones kept Joe busy. Joe worked alongside a familiar in John Travis for a short time before John's departure, as well as a prized female slave of Jones named Renah. She tended to her chores with her four-year-old son, Ben, and infant daughter, Caroline, in tow. Joe also worked with several Mexican parolees who had fought under Santa Anna at the Alamo and San Jacinto. All in all, life was probably not too severe for the slaves on Bailey's Prairie. Jones kept them well-clothed and fed, which was not always the case at other Texas plantations. Jones maintained a steady supply of potatoes, coffee, sugar, beef, and honey for his slaves, as well as necessary utensils such as knives and tin cups. Renah sold butter and eggs for cash, while John picked berries in the woods for extra change. Still, the slaves worked hard in the fields, and their lives were certainly not their own. Joe stayed busy throughout the remainder of March, planting corn in the prairie one day and assisting in the slaughter of a steer on another.[11]

By April, all focus at the Jones plantation shifted to an upcoming ball in the new town of Houston to commemorate the Battle of San Jacinto. The gala promised to be the social event of the year, if not a lifetime. Invitations arrived printed on white satin. Women from Brazoria, Columbia, San Felipe, Harrisburg, Lynchburg, Richmond, and Washington-on-the-Brazos, all important places of commerce on the Texas frontier, busied themselves with the design of new, elegant dresses, mulling carefully over choices of velvets, satins, and laces.[12]

Jones and his wife, Ruth, got caught up in the festive spirit of the day. Slaves groomed horses and polished saddles. The slaves were also dressed fashionably. Joe received a new pair of white cotton pantaloons eight days prior to the ball, perhaps the day he learned he would escort Jones and his wife to Houston. Meanwhile, Joe secretly planned his own way to celebrate the occasion. On the night of April 21, Jones and his wife arrived at the ball in style. Joe and a Mexican parolee named Domingo dropped the couple off in front of a large, unfinished, two-story frame building that would house the festivities. Joe would have heard the sound of violins and pianos, along with the buzz of conversation and laughter, carrying beyond the entryway. Yellow light glowed from every window. He also would have noticed an abundance of horses, mules, and shiny carriages lining the dirt street.[13]

Inside the big house, Sam Houston commanded great attention when he entered the ballroom. The band struck up "Hail to the Chief," and everyone politely applauded the San Jacinto hero and the republic's president-elect. Houston wore a striking ruffled shirt, a black silk velvet suit, and a scarlet cashmere waistcoat. He bypassed the traditional dancing slippers for a pair of boots to support his wounded ankle—boots accented by shiny, silver spurs.[14]

Joe also possessed a polished look on this night, decked out in a dark satin jacket and his new pantaloons. He played the role of refined servant well, a talent he and his brother William had developed years earlier in Missouri.[15] Yet Joe's mind was on escape.

In all likelihood, Joe figured no one would notice his absence until he had already safely slipped away. If so, he figured correctly. In Houston and throughout Texas, people energetically indulged themselves in song, drink, and dance to celebrate independence. The opportunity to run would never be better for a slave in Texas. As the moonlight shined brighter, and as folks settled in for a long evening of leisure, Joe made his move with Domingo by his side. The two men ran together, slipping away with the two horses that had carried them to the ball from Bailey's Prairie. Joe rode a heavily built bay horse with a Spanish-style, American-made saddle covered in blue cloth. The horse, suffering from a sore back, stood about fourteen hands high with a bushy mane and tail and had once belonged to Travis. Domingo rode a chestnut sorrel that stood sixteen hands tall.[16]

Jones discovered their disappearance late that night when leaving the ball. At daylight, Jones reluctantly gathered his rifle and supplies and took up their trail. He would hunt Joe and Domingo for nine days.[17] The fugitives' trail was elusive. Horse and mule tracks mixed along every road. Crisscrossing buggy and carriage wheel tracks added to the confusion. Still, Jones methodically checked every ferry crossing, public house, and frontier home for clues to their whereabouts. His efforts proved futile.

One month after their escape, Jones reverted to the usual practice of placing a runaway advertisement in a newspaper. He offered a reward in the *Telegraph and Texas Register* to anyone who could safely return Joe, Domingo, the two horses, and the saddles and bridles to his home on Bailey's Prairie. "This negro was in the Alamo with his master when it was taken; and [he] was the only man from the colonies who was not put to death," Jones noted in the ad. Jones clearly did not know—or perhaps care—how old Joe was, describing him as "about twenty-five years of age, five feet ten or eleven inches high, very black and good countenance." Jones offered forty dollars for Joe and his horse. For Domingo and his horse, the bounty was ten dollars. Jones concluded his ad with another standard offer: "If the runaways are taken more than one hundred miles from my residence, I will pay all reasonable traveling expenses, in addition to the above reward."[18] The ad would run numerous times.[19]

Joe's escape proved to be only one of many problems that would command Jones's attention in the coming months. On May 7, Mexican parolees Antonio, Aguelpeto, and Ruis also escaped his plantation, leaving one other comrade behind, a man named Garcia. Jones struck a deal with Garcia to have him work through August 1. At that time, Jones agreed to give Garcia fifteen dollar for traveling expenses to Mexico City.[20]

Days passed with no word about Joe or Domingo. Jones harbored little hope of recovering Domingo, whom he surmised had vanished into Mexico. Joe fit into a different category. He was an American-born slave who had had a chance to remain with the Mexican Army at the Alamo. Instead he had chosen to escape and reunite with the Texan colonists. Joe's whereabouts remained unknown through August, fostering much speculation.

By September, Jones had much more serious matters on his mind. His thirty-seven-year-old wife had become ill, and she died on September 5. Her passing left her husband "wretchedly miserable, distressed, and distracted"—with four sick children and a mountain of grief. In breaking the news to his older children in St. Louis, Jones wrote, "Never my dear children can I expect to enjoy that pure & entire happiness that it has been my lot to have shared."[21]

Jones dutifully carried on with life for the sake of his children. By October 8, he even returned to the business of overseeing the Travis estate. His first notation in his ledger that month referred to postage paid for a letter "from [Thomas] Gay concerning Joe." The content of the letter is unknown, but likely it regarded either the sighting or capture of Joe.[22]

Jones settled a $30 account with the *Telegraph and Texas Register* for the runaway ad on November 6, and soon afterward Joe's name again appeared in the ledger. No mention is made of his whereabouts the previous seven months, but he had clearly been captured. Now Joe was being leased to cotton farmer Elisha Maxey of Brazoria County for five days of hard labor. Maxey used Joe in December to help gin 2,766 pounds of cotton.[23]

The work was tedious and backbreaking, but Joe seems to have been merely biding his time until the arrival of warmer weather in the spring. If he remained with Jones, would he again suffer the terrifying indignity of being sold at a public auction? Joe weighed his options.

Only he knew what Travis had told him in the days and hours before his death at the Alamo. Joe had probably stood by his master's side when Travis scribbled his final note to David Ayers: "Take care of my little boy."[24] Did Travis express a similar message to Joe in that fateful hour? Regardless, Travis died bravely—a bravery Joe believed had spared his life at the Alamo. By now, Charles had rejoined the Travis clan in Alabama and was adjusting to his new home. Texas no longer offered anything in the way of a home for Joe. His family had been scattered to the wind by death, estate sales, and war. By now he too may have felt like an orphan. The survivor in him again told him to run. But to where? In the end, only one place prompted him to vanish from the Texas frontier without a trace.

25

Legendary Journey

My father, J. C. Travis, said this Negro gave the
people the most correct history of the massacre.
—Mark A. Travis, William Barret Travis's nephew

The freezing rains and bone-chilling Texas northers of early 1838 had disappeared with the coming of summer. Now in the twenty-third year of his life, Joe might have again pondered his greatest feat—cheating death at the Alamo. Memories of March 6, 1836, surely shadowed him wherever he went. In many respects, Joe had become the face of the Alamo, and he may have felt a responsibility to the Alamo defenders to tell of the bravery he had witnessed. He honored no one more than his late master William Barret Travis, whom he repeatedly depicted as a hero, which suggests that Travis had treated Joe decently. But no matter how much celebrity the title "Alamo survivor" may have conferred, it brought Joe little else.

No one knows what Travis had told people in Texas about his family. One influence on him must have been his uncle Alexander Travis, who would have supplied his nephew with a well of entertaining stories. The peace-loving Baptist preacher carried a mantle of leadership for not only the Travis clan but also for others who settled in southern Alabama.

Alexander had entered Conecuh County as one of its pioneer settlers in 1817 and hacked out a homestead amid the hardwoods and evergreens near a sprouting community called Sparta on the banks of Murder Creek. Alexander had not sought land and fortune, but rather the chance to save souls.[1]

Mark Travis, William's father, had trailed his God-fearing brother into the region from South Carolina in the late spring of 1818. Only eight years old when he made the journey with his family, the impressionable William, along with his family, then lived with Alexander for a while. The youngster even attended the Sparta Academy, where his uncle served as superintendent.[2] Alexander always acted as a spiritual light to others. During the day, he labored hard in the fields. By nightfall, he sat in the light of a roaring pine-knot fire and read the only book in his library—the Bible.[3] William may have years later spoken of those evenings to Joe.

Alexander's missionary work became legendary in southern Alabama, where he routinely traveled great distances to deliver a Sunday sermon and where he baptized slaves. He often left his farm with only a small wallet, his Bible, and a cotton cloth draped over his shoulder, trudging on foot through the woods. Some excursions carried him as far away as forty miles to some remote settlement. Nothing ever slowed Alexander. If the creeks or rivers swelled, he simply stripped, placed his bundle of clothes atop his head, and swam across with one arm. He dressed on the other bank and pressed onward.[4]

William might well also have mentioned to Joe his trusted younger brother Nicholas. Nicholas and William were close, separated by only a year. When William rode for Texas in 1831, Nicholas was one of six siblings he left behind. The others were Sarah (then eighteen), Emily (seventeen), Nancy (nine), Mark (three), and James (two). At the time of William's departure, Nicholas lived on a farm on the east side of the Conecuh River south of Sparta.[5]

In 1838 Joe appears to have wanted to seize control of his life. No longer would he endure the shame and humiliation of another estate sale. He would run, and this escape would be like none he had ever undertaken. He would head for Alabama, the only place he believed he might find sanctuary—with William Travis's family. If William would have wanted his brother Nicholas to know he had lived well, Joe may have wanted Nicholas to know that William had *died* well.

Joe planned a daring flight across parts of four slave states to find Nicholas Travis on the Conecuh River and there, he hoped, a safe haven. This would be a journey spurred equally by self-preservation and loyalty. The Travis family deserved the truth about what happened at the Alamo, and Joe likely believed that he deserved a chance for a more peaceful life. The next time he spoke about the Alamo, he wanted to be standing in front of the Travis family. Remaining in Texas would amount to nothing less than a death sentence for him, a lifetime of menial labor on some forgotten patch of ground. If the Alamo experience taught survivors anything, it was that a man or woman must be willing to risk death sometimes in order to live.

As a runaway slave Joe would again encounter hardships. He would have to avoid roads, travel at night, and cross countless creeks and rivers. He would have to live off the land, probably consuming a diet of wild honey, berries, nuts, bird eggs, fish, and plant roots. If he grew desperate, he might need to risk being shot or hanged for stealing food. At least Joe probably felt confident in his planned route. He was already familiar with the road that led eastward to the Mississippi River—the Opelousas Trail or La Bahia Road—which he and Mansfield followed from New Orleans. Joe probably planned to shadow the road and follow it to the Mississippi River, the great waterway he knew intimately from his days in St. Louis.

Once across the Mississippi, by far his greatest geographical barrier, the young slave probably hoped to parallel the river northward as far as Woodville, Mississippi. From there he would again turn eastward until he intersected the Second Creek Road, which cut across the Pine Woods of Mississippi and into the southern reaches of Alabama. The final leg of the journey would take him across the formidable Tombigbee and Alabama Rivers, and then to the farm of Nicholas Travis near Sparta.

The roads, frontier thoroughfares to all, would be easy to find. Joe may have also tapped into the information network of his fellow slaves for safe places to hide. No slaveholder could underestimate this sort of shared knowledge. Slaves commonly shared information about safe houses, trails, and sympathetic individuals.[6]

Once a slave named Jim made a similar journey from Mississippi to Texas. As the story goes, Jim had been ripped apart from his wife, Winnie, when her master moved to Texas. A heartbroken Jim escaped soon after and walked more than four hundred miles through the wilderness, avoiding public roads and traveling at night. He even swam the Mississippi River. Jim eventually straggled into Texas and managed to find his wife's cabin. He reaped ample reward for his courage. Winnie's master discovered what Jim had done in the name of love, and arranged to purchase him.[7]

Now Joe faced an equally daunting task. Where roads existed, one might also find roving bands of slave patrollers, bandits, murderers, snitches, and other shady characters. Staying out of sight would be crucial.

Joe vanished from Bailey's Prairie as quietly as he had arrived a year earlier, but this time on foot.[8] He embraced the unknown, knowing that the Texas frontier offered an abundance of dangers. Travelers openly shared their fears of encountering a bear or panther or pack of wolves.[9] Nighttime passage would have raised the stakes. Every cluster of trees brought the possibility of a startled animal. Near the trail—trampled by cattle and carved with wagon ruts—Joe would have heard noises he had often heard while traveling with Travis or as a child in the woods around Marthasville. Coyotes howled, owls hooted, and at times he might have even heard the chilling scream of a panther. Whether Joe carried a rifle or pistol is unknown.

Runaway slaves were keenly aware that they might have to duck into the brush at the first sign of an oncoming rider, just as Joe had done on the prairie route to Gonzales from Bexar. One stroke of bad luck or misstep could cost a slave his life, and perhaps nothing was more precarious than a river crossing. The Brazos presented the fleeing servant with his first major obstacle. The river flowed through a four-mile-wide swath of sycamore, ash, hickory, oak, cherry, cottonwood, and pecan. Joe weaved his way through the woods before arriving at a riverbank that stood variously between twenty and forty feet in height. The river stretched as wide as 150 yards at some popular crossings. Joe's options were few. He may have stolen a skiff, lashed together a makeshift raft from loose timber, paddled across while clinging to a large piece of wood,

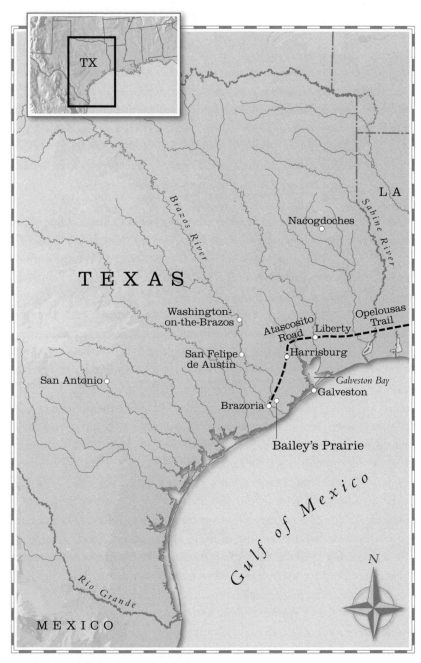

Eastern Texas as it looked in 1838 when Joe fled from the Travis estate at Bailey's Prairie for the last time. Decades later the Travis family would tell of Joe's unexpected appearance in Alabama and his mesmerizing account of the March 6, 1836, Alamo battle. Map by Carol Zuber-Mallison.

or swum. However Joe succeeded in crossing, he scrambled up the damp black soil on the eastern bank and trudged onward.[10]

Countless creeks, bayous, and full-fledged rivers remained in his path. As his journey continued, Joe reached the sprawling, murky waters of Pine Island Bayou. Alligators lay hidden everywhere. Traversing the bayou would have been daunting at night, especially with the occasional sound of an alligator plopping into the water. One traveler said he had often heard the alligators only a few yards away "drop like heavy logs into the water."[11]

On the banks of the Sabine River travelers beheld clusters of bald cypress, the trunks of which reached into the water like giant, bony fingers. Spanish explorers had marveled at the same scene hundreds of years earlier when they named it Rio de Sabinas—the river of cypress. For Joe, the Sabine would have served as the gateway into the United States. The landscape again changed dramatically farther east, opening into a vast expanse known as the Calcasieu Prairie. Largely treeless, the mostly flat region was broken only by tree-lined stream banks known as gallery forests. Normally the prairie offered a plush carpet of tall green grass, but 1838 brought a memorable drought, leaving the prairie brown and dry as Joe trudged through. Every once in a while the prairie swelled with undulating terrain from which a traveler at times could see for great distances. These swells likely served Joe well on clear, moonlit nights as he kept a constant vigil for houses and people.

Cotton plantations came into view more frequently the closer Joe drew to the Mississippi River, as did the slaves who supported these small empires. At dusk he might have seen hundreds of fellow slaves laboring in the fields.[12] Whether any of those slaves assisted Joe in his journey is unknown, but the likes of an escaped slave was nothing new in those parts. Fugitive slave camps were scattered all along the river, used as sanctuary from brutal overseers or the demands of backbreaking work, and by slaves running away and using the river as an avenue to freedom.

One former slave recalled, "[The] Mississippi River attracted me like a magnet, for as soon as I was free to move in my own selected direction I made straight for the river." The river meant the continual passage of riverboats and the potential for a fugitive slave to stow away on a vessel plying northward, or sometimes even deeper south. Riverside

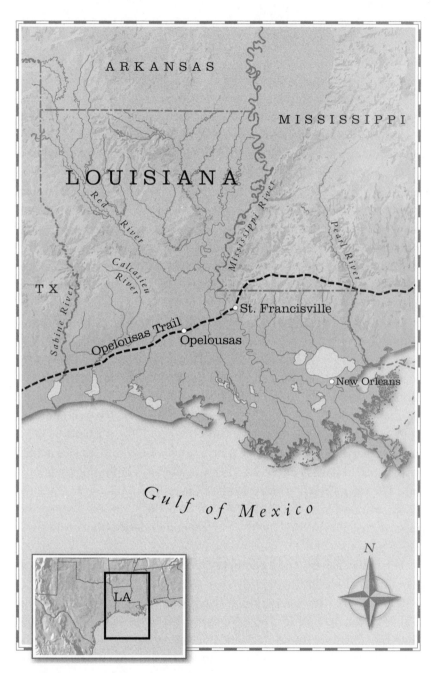

Louisiana, circa 1838, featured heavily-traveled trails. Joe would have been familiar with this part of the country after traveling from New Orleans to Texas with Isaac Mansfield in 1832. Map by Carol Zuber-Mallison.

authorities and steamboat captains worked diligently to corral any suspicious-looking person of color who milled around the levee. Captains, likewise, carefully examined papers of any person of color who boarded their steamboats.[13]

Runaway advertisements plastered docks, taverns, and boarding-houses along the river. Roving bands of citizen slave patrols combed the riverbanks, where a fugitive might sometimes obtain help from a free black farmer or a lumberman cutting wood for steamboats.[14] The men most feared by the fugitive were the slave catchers, who hunted runaway slaves for a bounty. These were generally rough men who would ruthlessly track a slave many miles, motivated by nothing more than pay. Some of the most notorious slave catchers operated out of Vidalia, Louisiana, across the river from Natchez. They roamed relentlessly up and down the river with great success.[15]

If Joe did not possess firsthand knowledge of the dangers and opportunities in the region, he would have learned them from his brother William, an experienced steamboat hand. This factor alone raised Joe's odds for a safe passage. Had Joe shadowed the Opelousas Trail to the Mississippi, he would have found himself standing on its banks, across from St. Francisville, Louisiana. The river was familiar to Joe, who had become acquainted with its dangers and learned daily of its lore at Mansfield's riverfront tin shop. Drowning stories were commonplace, which gave pause to slaves who needed to cross it before continuing their journey. The river stretched an awesome 2,320 miles from its source at Lake Itasca, Minnesota, to the Gulf of Mexico. At some points the river spread more than a mile in width, with a current and undertow that could swallow a person.

Ferrymen, fishers, and steamboat captains told stories of monster catfish lurking beneath the muddy river's surface. Catfish said to six feet long and more than 250 pounds—fish powerful enough to knock over a skiff or canoe. Nothing, however, spooked a free man or slave more than the alligators found in abundance along the lower reaches of the river. During the day, travelers could spot giant mudslides along the banks, places near where an alligator had constructed a mounded nest of mud and vegetation. At night, when the moon shined brightly, folks could sometimes catch the reflections of alligator eyes drifting along the river's edge. Rumors of human attacks were common, and reports of alligator sizes were always a matter of great conversation. Some claimed to have seen alligators up to nineteen feet long in the river. Most folks accepted these stories as fact. Nevertheless, slaves routinely risked their lives by plunging into the Mississippi in the quest for freedom. They often crossed at night to better elude capture. In doing so, they increased the danger, but such was their desperation.

By the time Joe reached the banks of the big river, he had endured many hardships. He had surely passed nights in wet, ragged clothes. He would have had blisters on his feet, as well as scratches and scabs on his body from pushing through briars and thickets. He must have known mental anguish from sleep deprivation and the fear of capture. All surely had taken a toll. Now Joe stared out at the rapid current of the mighty river, perhaps lit by the moon, and resigned himself to the fact that he would swim across.

Joe waded in until the water reached his waist and then began to swim furiously. Every muscle strained, and water went down his throat as he gasped for air. Like others who had attempted the swim he fought to keep his head up, and the powerful current carried him like driftwood. If he drowned, he would become another nameless casualty of slavery. His body might eventually be discovered miles from where he entered the river, perhaps snared on a protruding tree branch or washed atop a sandbar. Just as likely, his body might disappear forever in the murky water. He never stopped kicking or thrashing his arms and finally reached the distant bank nearly unconscious with exhaustion. Joe's secret to survival seems always to have been his will to live, and that instinct had not failed him. Once again Joe had cheated death. But how many more lives did he possess?[16]

The next leg of Joe's journey would have carried him northward, along the crude tracks of the West Feliciana Railroad Company. A line from St. Francisville, Louisiana to Woodville, Mississippi, was started in 1828 with mules hauling cars. Slave laborers had been building the road, wooden rails set five feet apart and capped by strips of iron fastened to the rails by iron spikes that with use would need to be hammered back into place daily.[17] Construction of the twenty-nine-mile line had been interrupted by the Panic of 1837, but the unfinished road still provided a path of cleared timber through the forest.[18]

At some point Joe likely skirted Woodville through the woods to the east until reaching the Lower Creek Road, which connected southern Mississippi with the southern Alabama and Georgia. The road began north of Woodville on the Mississippi River at Natchez and was probably intercepted at various points by smaller trails. Joe may have found one such route or simply cut his way through the woods.

Whether Joe visited Natchez is unknown, but he knew of its notorious reputation from his brother William and others in the St. Louis slave community. The home of the Forks on the Road slave market, the largest of its kind outside of New Orleans, Natchez played a significant role in the migration of slaves into the cotton plantations of the Deep South. One visitor described the market as "a cluster of rough wooden buildings . . . in front of which several saddle-horses, either tied or held by servants, indicated a place of popular resort." Slaves came to the market from throughout the South. Annual slave caravans were even brought from as far away as Virginia, creating what was said to be a festive atmosphere for the seller and buyer.[19]

Naturally, slaves wanted nothing to do with Natchez or even the smaller slave markets at Woodville. The mere thought of Natchez would have made Joe sick, perhaps arousing old feelings of his sister, Elizabeth. Slave patrols were thick near Woodville, but the trail grew quieter the farther one traveled east. By 1838, nearly half of Mississippi's population consisted of slaves. As might be expected, the majority of the slaves could be found concentrated around the cotton-producing plantations of the Natchez region and later the Yazoo Delta.[20]

Once Joe crossed the Pearl River, his path consisted mainly of virgin woods of magnificent longleaf pines.[21] Joe would have scaled the high, rolling hills that dominated the region, perhaps stopping during the day to scavenge for food before finding a safe spot in a secluded thicket to sleep. He also would have maintained a constant vigil for the citizen patrols that combed the roads, mainly after sunset, in search of traveling slaves.[22]

Night travel offered other obstacles. Changes in elevations of one hundred feet or more were not uncommon between the hilltops and stream bottoms, making his journey arduous given the darkness. Joe likely pressed on across the sandy clay. His dirty and worn clothing, stained red by the soil, would bear witness to his struggle through the pine woods.[23]

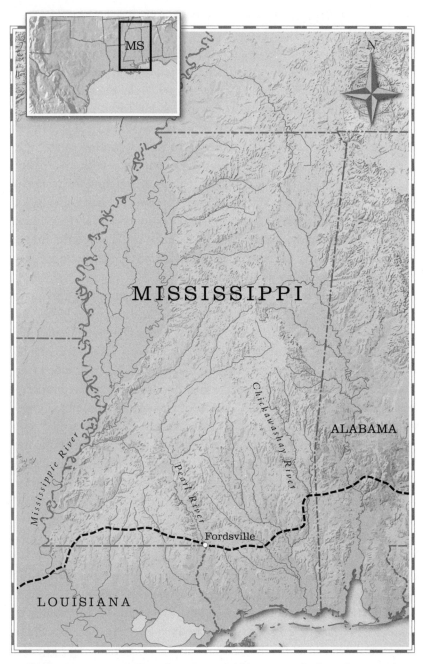

Mississippi, circa 1838, is where Joe would have rested after a harrowing swim across the Mississippi River en route to Alabama. Despite being unfamiliar with the terrain, Joe likely would have shadowed well-known trails eastward. Map by Carol Zuber-Mallison.

By the time Joe finally crossed into Alabama, he had been on the run for more than a month. Joe faithfully counted the days of his journey.[24] One mistake might be his last. Four- and six-man teams of slave patrols searched the roads in Alabama just as they did in Texas, Louisiana, and Mississippi. The patrols consisted of white, slave-owning males between the ages of eighteen and sixty—men eager to squelch a slave revolt or to apprehend any slave moving through the countryside without a pass.[25] The dangers were great, and so were the odds of reaching the Nicholas Travis farm unmolested. The Tombigbee River would have offered Joe the first clue that he was close to his final destination. The river's wide expanse and canebrakes gave away its identity and marked the first of two formidable rivers Joe had to cross in Alabama before reaching Conecuh County and ultimately the Travis family.

Thick fog clung to the Tombigbee each night and morning. Clear days were rare. Dense canebrakes extended as far as the eye could see, the roots of which easily ran another ten or twelve feet below the water. Big bucks and other creatures could easily disappear in the thick vegetation, and so might Joe. Steamboats regularly plied the river, albeit cautiously. Driftwood and fog slowed travel, and the rattle of tree branches smashing into the side of their vessels often startled passengers.[26] Occasionally crews from these steamboats had to jump ashore armed with axes and chop down a mammoth pine for fuel. The crashing of the timber shook the thickets in the forest for hundreds of yards. Crewmen would then feverishly chop up the felled tree with their axes, often to the banter and enjoyment of the passengers.[27]

Once at the river's edge, Joe might have looked for the faint lights of gallery lanterns in the distance—an approaching steamboat. The fog provided him with ample cover to cross, although the uncertainty of what drifted in front of him might have compelled him to cross during the light of day. Once across the Tombigbee, Joe journeyed eastward in search of his next major milestone: the Alabama River and the steep bluffs of Claiborne. The main road carried him to the foot of the Alabama, where he would have stared for the first time at the overwhelming sight of a bluff rising more than three hundred feet from the river's edge.[28]

Joe likely found himself in an uncomfortable position for a fugitive slave as he entered the unfamiliar surroundings of Conecuh County.

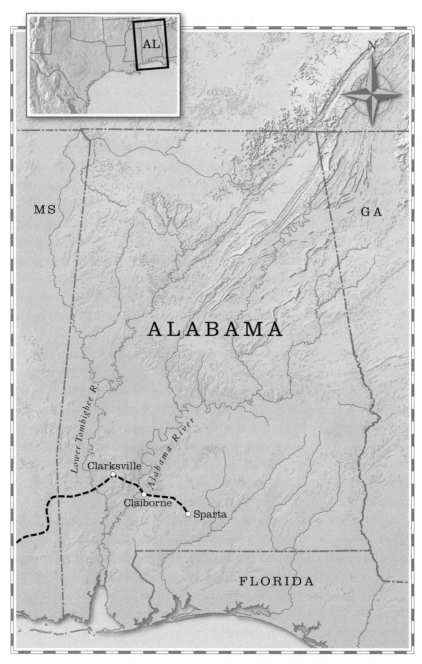

Alabama, circa 1838. Joe would have traversed through thickly wooded terrain during his 1838 journey to find the Travis family. He ultimately would have had to trust a stranger to find the home of Nicholas Travis, his former master's brother. Map by Carol Zuber-Mallison.

Suddenly, against all experience, the time had come to trust strangers. At some point, perhaps in the presence of a black freighter or field hand, Joe bravely approached and asked the question: Where could he find the Nicholas Travis farm?[29] In all likelihood someone pointed the way.

Huge pines towered above Joe on the final mile of his journey along a gently rolling terrain. A sandy, red, wagon-rutted road led him on, snaking into an open clearing where a few of the Travis slaves might have been seen working in the cotton fields, tending to hogs, or tilling a garden. Cattle grazed in an open pasture. The appearance of a strange black man likely drew the attention of everyone on the farm, from the servants to William Barret's eight-year-old niece, Martha Jane. A small crowd may have even gathered to behold the stranger. Soon Joe stood face to face with Nicholas Travis. Nicholas resembled his former master. By Travis's side might have stood his pregnant wife, Mary. The no-nonsense Travis, in turn, likely scanned Joe from head to toe.[30]

Joe looked pitiful. Scratches covered his arms and face from weeks of crawling through thickets and brush and crossing countless creeks and rivers. A cinnamon film from the red, sandy soil covered his skin and hair. Torn clothes hung on his now-gaunt body. Still, Nicholas beheld a resolute young man on a mission. Joe introduced himself as William Travis's body servant—the man who had stood by William's side at the Alamo and in his final moments on Earth. The words sent shivers through Nicholas, as well as doubts. Two years had passed since William had died at the Alamo. The family had learned of his death just as most of the families of Alamo defenders did. They read about it in regional newspaper, probably carried for hundreds of miles by steamboat, stagecoach, and horseback. The Travis family might have also received a letter, perhaps from William's close friend and Charlie's caretaker, David Ayers. However Nicholas received the news of his brother's death, it probably wasn't enough to satisfy his thirst for information. So many questions remained unanswered.

Now, without warning, an unknown slave stood before him who claimed to have been by his brother's side in that fateful hour at the Alamo. Nicholas stood shocked and in disbelief.[31] Then he fired questions at Joe in rapid succession. The slave's quick answers left no doubt about his legitimacy. The gravity of the moment may have hit Nicholas like

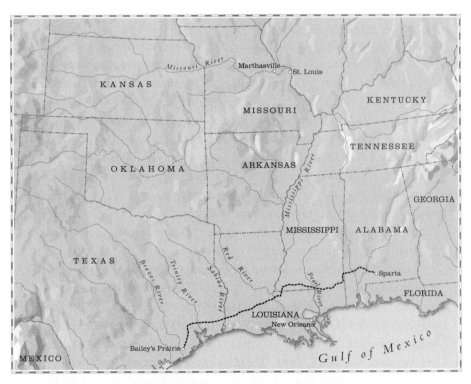

The Southern United States showing Joe's probable flight from Bailey's Prairie, Texas, to Sparta, Alabama, in 1838, two years after his survival at the Alamo. Travis family oral tradition states Joe gave them the first eyewitness account of William Barret Travis's death at the Alamo. Map by Carol Zuber-Mallison.

the kick of a mule. Through Joe, he now could experience the world as William saw it on the fateful morning of March 6, 1836.

Nicholas listened intently to Joe's sorrowful story. Joe told Nicholas what he felt he needed to hear the most: that William died a hero. Roused by the attacking enemy, his brother had boldly exposed himself to the enemy atop a rampart with a shotgun in one hand and a torch in the other. He had lit the fuse that fired a cannon, and he simultaneously had been sent cascading down the earthen rampart from a shot in the head. Stunned but not dead, William had then mustered all his strength to thrust a sword through the body of an onrushing Mexican officer. The two soldiers, Joe concluded eloquently, had died together on the spot.[32]

Eventually, Nicholas's curiosity turned to Joe himself, who admitted that he was lucky to have survived the battle. He too had fought in defense of the Alamo. The mulatto told Nicholas that he had initially been spared because he had been mistaken as a Mexican in the darkness. He had later been taken prisoner but escaped his Mexican guard and returned to the Texans.[33] Joe also spoke of his journey from Texas. He recounted the entire route and told of the many hardships he had endured along the way. Joe said the trip had taken him forty days, meaning that he traveled an average of fifteen miles a day.[34]

Nicholas surely milked Joe for more details. The inquiries must have continued into the night and for weeks and months to come as Joe relived his travels with William. Time after time Joe retold how William bravely met death at the Alamo and how he himself had risked his life to bring news of his master's death to his family in Alabama. Joe's epic journey, like William's heroic death, eventually became intertwined in the legend that would be cherished by generations of Travis kin. Few would tell the story of William Barret Travis without also relating the legendary journey from Texas to Alabama by his faithful servant. In time, Joe's loyal actions elevated him too to the status of hero—a noted sidekick augmenting the memory of his immortal master. In southern Alabama slave circles, Joe would become far more than a footnote to history. He would emerge as a bona fide black hero who had survived the Alamo battle, an epic journey from Texas, and—ultimately—the institution of slavery.[35] Joe would become a living legend.

26

SHADOWS AND GHOSTS

*The genuine Texas veteran is something to be
inordinately admired by everybody. He is entitled
to all the honor that can be crowded on him, and
ought to receive a much larger pension than he
is in the habit of drawing.*
—*Editorial*, Galveston Daily News,
April 16, 1880

James Calloway Travis grew up on Alamo stories. He had no choice.
He was the youngest brother of Alamo commander and hero William Barret Travis, and he was damn proud. William's legacy loomed
large in the Travis family, where God, country, and honor were sacred.
So was the memory of William. James idolized his older brother as he
grew up amid the piney woods of Conecuh County, Alabama, although
he had only been only one year old when William rode for Texas in 1831.
By the time William sacrificed his life for Texas independence at the Alamo, James was still five months shy of his seventh birthday. Regardless, William became the symbol to him of everything good and honorable about the Travis bloodline. And the Alamo became a family shrine.

James would spend his entire life in Conecuh County. He would serve
his community faithfully, first as a county surveyor and then as a tax

commissioner. All along the way he proudly fostered his brother's legacy—and longed to visit the sacred ruins of the Alamo. Now, in the twilight of his life, his dream would finally come true. In a pilgrimage to San Antonio he would gaze upon the unforgettable façade of the Alamo chapel for the first time. He would stand where his brother's blood had once flowed for freedom.

James C. Travis stood over six feet tall and walked with a long, gangly, limping gait, as well as the assuredness of a Travis. A neatly combed crop of silver hair sat atop his head, and his bulging cheekbones and wiry, silver beard gave way in appearance only to his piercing eyes.[1] He presented the portrait of a dignitary. Yet on this memorable day, the brother of the immortal William Barret Travis proudly walked in the presence of another venerable elder of greater historical note. He walked stride by stride with Joe, William's aged manservant and the most famous Alamo survivor next to Susanna Dickinson. This time Joe was returning to the Alamo as a freedman.[2]

Joe, fondly known to the Travis family as "Old Ben," escorted James to the Alamo at the turn of the century to recount the events of March 6, 1836, and to show him the exact spot where his famous brother had perished. In doing so, Joe evoked a lifetime of pride that had welled within James, as well as the ghosts of his own past.[3] Despite being decades removed from that tragic event, Joe likely remained leery of those ghosts. Joe must have approached with caution and great emotion.

Joe had remained an elusive figure in the years following the Alamo battle, although probably not entirely by design. As an Alamo survivor, he often fulfilled his duty to relate his eyewitness account time and again for eager listeners.[4] As with most Texas veterans of his era, Joe disappeared from the public arena and faded into the obscurity of daily life. He remained in Alabama after his epic, forty-day journey from Texas, and, according to James, lived with the Travis family "for many years."[5] By 1840, Joe may have been caring for William's children, Charlie and Susan Isabella. The two orphans then lived with their grandparents—the hard-working and well-to-do Catos—in neighboring Monroe County, Alabama. An 1840 U.S. Census showed one male slave in the Cato household between the ages of ten to twenty-four—an age range that does not exclude Joe's presence. He would have turned twenty-five that year.[6]

Naturally, it is entirely plausible that Joe remained permanently with Nicholas Travis after arriving in Alabama. Court records show that the Nicholas Travis family paid $650 to William's estate, a tantalizing sum that might have matched Joe's value on the open slave market.[7] If so, this might explain Joe's name change to Ben. Nicholas's second wife, Elizabeth, gave birth to Joseph Mark Travis on November 19, 1850. Two Josephs on the Travis farm would have been one too many, and just as his older brother William experienced years earlier in Marthasville, Joe might have been forced to change his given name to make room for the white relative of his master.[8] Ben, coincidentally, was the name of one of Joe's older brothers who had died when the family left Kentucky for the Missouri Territory.[9]

Another hint regarding Joe's whereabouts cropped up in 1877. An editor with the *Statesman* newspaper in Austin wrote the following tidbit in his daily column: "There are several old soldiers of the Texas Revolution in Austin and in adjacent towns and counties, and these should meet on the twenty-first instant—San Jacinto Day. Two years ago the old colored body servant of Gen. Travis was in this city and his home was not far away. Why not have him brought to the capital? The only white survivor of the Alamo is here, and we do not see why the veterans should not be *feted* by the city government or by the citizens of the capital."[10]

The "old colored body servant" mentioned by the editor might have very well been Joe, who may have drifted back into Texas in the late 1840s with a married Susan Isabella (Grissett) or a grown Charles Travis, who served as a Texas Ranger in the early 1850s. The man mentioned is more likely William's aged body servant, John, who was over forty when his master died at the Alamo and who was last reported living on Caney Creek in Washington County in June 1840. His home was located on a thousand-acre parcel belonging to the Travis estate. In all probability he was the John Hannig whom the *Statesman* reported on in 1883, noting that the freedman was born in 1777 and was once "the property of Mrs. Hannig (formerly Susanna Dickinson) of Alamo fame." The *Galveston Daily News* labeled John Hannig "the last survivor of the massacre of the Alamo," perhaps an assumption made by the reporter or the story being peddled by John. Either way, the *Statesman* editor could have fallen prey to the same assumption or claim in 1877.[11] Or did the Austin editor indeed encounter Joe?

Susanna Dickinson appears to have also crossed paths with Joe during this period. In an 1878 interview with the *San Antonio Express News*, Susanna refers to Joe by his new name—Ben. Eighteen months earlier, Susanna told the Texas State Adjutant General's Office in an affidavit that "Jo [*sic*] was the only negro in the Fort." It is highly doubtful that Susanna would have forgotten Joe's name in eighteen months while retaining other vivid details of her survival at the Alamo. In all likelihood, she met Joe in the time between those two interviews.

Another tantalizing clue appeared in an 1883 article that stated that Alamo survivor "Ben Travis" had last been seen visiting Austin in 1877. Although the article failed to mention where the freedman was living at the time, his 1877 appearance in Austin would have fallen between Susanna's two interviews—a time when she probably reunited with her fellow survivor.[12] Wherever life carried Joe, scars of slavery and his narrow escape from death at the Alamo would have shadowed him. Both experiences probably brought him great pride and great pain. And no place would have stirred his memories more than San Antonio. If he had demons, some surely dwelt at the Alamo. There, briefly, he had stood at a crossroads where yesterday's nightmares clashed with his dreams for tomorrow. Longing for freedom and clinging to the hope of someday being reunited with his family, the Alamo is where a youthful Joe stared down eternity in the wild eyes of an enemy horde. Now, with his former master's younger brother by his side, he would dare to revisit the past.

The last time Joe had likely seen San Antonio, he was running for his life from a Mexican guard, disappearing into the vast prairie beyond the ragged outline of a remote frontier outpost. As Joe entered Alamo Plaza with James, his eyes probably fixed on the Alamo chapel, where he would have noticed the unfamiliar hump and roof. The wooden palisade once defended by the eccentric David Crockett and his Tennesseans was gone, as was the north wall where Travis met his death. To the north of the chapel Joe also would have seen the unrecognizable outline of the two-story low barracks, now hidden by a commercial venture that resembled something like a wooden castle.

Still, Joe may have seen the ghosts of 1836 as clear as ever. "Come on, boys!" he remembered Travis crying. "The Mexicans are upon us, and we'll give them Hell!"[13] Did Joe scan the plaza and see it all happening again? Or did he blink and see nothing? The sights and sounds of metropolitan San Antonio would have confused the senses of any old Texas veteran. Horse-drawn trolleys, carriages, and wagons circled the plaza, a veritable carnival where food and wares were being sold. Old Mexican women cooked chili in large black kettles. The aroma of freshly baked tortillas and fresh meat mingled with the stench of livestock. Noise emanated from saloons on the plaza, including one next door to the Alamo chapel, which was now being used as a warehouse.

Joe would have also noticed the 1859-vintage Menger Hotel, an elegant symbol of luxury and progress across the street from the Alamo. Joe probably stood amazed, as if awaking from a long slumber. The old Texas veteran in him may have lamented the scene or felt a pang of sorrow. He had fought side by side with those patriots and stepped in their blood. Had the world forgotten who had died there and why? Such feelings were nothing new for the old veterans of his era, but it must have been even worse for Joe, who had risked his life in defense of the Alamo. Many of the surviving veterans now drew pensions for their service and sacrifices, but Joe never would qualify for a military pension. The state of Texas saw Joe as nothing more than a former slave, albeit a noteworthy one in the pages of its history. Though black, he carried the mantel of an Alamo survivor—rare from the start and now one of the last. No one had to tell Joe this fact.

Death and slavery had stolen his family from him: Elizabeth, his beloved mother; his sister Elizabeth; and his brothers William, Leander, Solomon, Benjamin, and Millford. Unknown to Joe, William had gone on to become the noted author and lecturer William Wells Brown, a tireless crusader on the front lines of the abolitionist movement. He became the first African American novelist in 1853 with the publication of *Clotel; or, The President's Daughter*. Joe never had the privilege of knowing the name of William's youngest child. William named her Josephine.[14] William died November 6, 1884, in Massachusetts, but as far as Joe was concerned, his big brother had died in 1832, when he was moved to Texas. If any of his siblings were still living, it is likely they had disappeared among the living dead of slavery.

Perhaps Joe harkened back to Marthasville and St. Louis, places where his family shared some of their last good times. If so, he would have remembered the laughter, the tears, and most of all the love. He might have even thought of the mystic Dinkie, the venerable Uncle Ned, and the powerful Randall—all long gone by now.

Joe had also outlived most of the Travis family. Charles Travis, the little boy remembered so fondly, died young like his famous father. Throughout his life he even seemed to sense his pending fate, and once confided to a friend on the eve of the Civil War, "I know there is soon to be a great war, but I may not live to see it. I have often thought I would fall as my father did, and on that account I have never married, or tried to do so. A soldier is better off who does not marry, as there are none who will be dependent on others in case he dies in battle."[15]

The young man's emotional scars were evident. Yet he never allowed darkness to shadow his life. He possessed many of his father's great qualities as a soldier and person. One contemporary remembered Charles as "cheerful, temperate and modest, and taking all his duties and details with much good will and charming everyone with his kindly voice and actions. There seemed to be nothing harsh in his disposition, and it is naturally followed that he was beloved by his soldiers. He rarely manifested anything approaching anger, but his bravery was beyond all question."[16]

Charles even shared his father's good fortunes with women. At six feet tall, he provided a striking pose as a bachelor with his "cheery face, curly brown hair and frank blue eyes." Still, his life always revolved around his lofty expectations for himself. Prior to his death in 1860, Charles spent his inheritance chasing his father's legacy. He bankrolled a frontier Ranger company, served as a member of the Texas Legislature (1853–54), and received the first law degree from Baylor University. In the end, it was consumption and not a bullet or sword that took his life—one that sadly mirrored his father's in one other respect: his was a promising life unfulfilled. He left no heirs.[17] Susan Isabella died ten years after her brother. She left behind one daughter.

Back in Alabama, where by now Joe had fathered children (according to a 1929 *Dallas Morning News* article), Nicholas Travis met a violent death in 1863. One account left by neighbor and Confederate veteran J. L. Mayo claimed that Travis was an "intense secessionist" who got waylaid for his overbearing views. Another story tells of Travis being murdered by a neighbor he caught stealing his hogs.[18] On the day Nicholas was killed, his horse returned to the homestead with an empty saddle. His wife immediately dispatched a servant to search for him. The servant—perhaps Joe—soon returned and reported his master's body had been found on a roadside near the Conecuh River. Nicholas Travis had been shot dead.[19]

Every corner of Joe's mind was crowded by the sadness of loss, yet his life still gave him much reason to rejoice. He could dwell on thoughts of his own children in Alabama and all that he had survived—the whippings, chains, slave auctions, escapes, battles, and killing. Along the way he had endured with dignity. Soon, like the wild Texas prairie, he would be gone. The wind would blow over an unmarked grave, leaving no trace of the life he had lived or the man he had become.[20] Still, on this day, in the shadow of the Alamo, his heart pounded with pride even as he felt sorrow. Briefly oblivious to the throng of the plaza surely jolted his senses, perhaps he could hear Santa Anna snapping orders. Perhaps he felt the point of the bayonet prodding him to identify the lifeless bodies of Crockett, Bowie, and his master. His stomach might have heaved from the recollection of the funeral pyres, the ashes of the defenders buried not far from where he now stood. His nostrils might have flared, the putrid smell of burning flesh having never left his memory. He had not forgotten the supreme sacrifice of the Alamo defenders, and today he would honor them with his remembrance. He stood among their ranks once again, tall and proud. No other defender remained to tell the story. Amid the Alamo's ruins, armed only with memories, in the presence of the brother of Alamo commander William Barret Travis, Joe was now the last soul standing.

AFTERWORD

R abbit holes. This is how Lee and I playfully referred to investigative leads in our eleven-year quest to piece together Joe's life. Most of those rabbit holes led to dead ends but a cherished few resulted in pay dirt.

At least one rabbit hole continues to fascinate us to this day: the story of Ben Riley. The first time we heard the name was in November 2000. Newspaper columnist Lydia Grimes ran an article that month in the *Brewton (Ala.) Standard*, telling readers about our search for Joe (or Ben, as Alabamans and the Travis family later identified him). The column referred to the Travis family story of Joe's flight to Alabama in 1838, and it issued an open invitation to anyone with information that might shed light on his final years.

The telephone rang at my Oklahoma home the morning Lydia's column ran.

"Ron," my wife Jeannia said excitedly, cupping the phone. "There's a man calling from Alabama who says he knew Joe!"

"What?" I replied. The man on the other end was Raymond Lynn, a fifty-year-old Brewton native and businessman.

"Mr. Jackson," Lynn said, "I know this will sound hard to believe, but I actually knew Ben when I was a little boy, and I distinctly remember hearing him tell stories about how he survived the battle of the Alamo. I heard these stories in the 1950s."[1]

Instantly, I realized that the numbers didn't add up. Joe was almost assuredly born in 1815. If he had lived into the 1950s, he would have been a somewhat biblical 135 years plus.

"His name was Ben Riley," Lynn continued. "He lived in a little shack in our family's backyard in Brewton. All I know is he was well over one hundred years old when he died."[2] Local legend stated that "Uncle" Ben Riley had survived the Alamo battle and then walked from Texas to Alabama "along the railroad."

In the days that followed, Lee and I flushed out the real Ben Riley to the best of our abilities. What we discovered left us intrigued by this elderly black man and the origins of his seemingly tall tale. Interviews with other Alabamans who grew up in Lynn's neighborhood revealed noteworthy tidbits about Riley. They painted a composite sketch of an elderly man who was prone to drinking too much alcohol, yet who was beloved by the neighborhood children. "Uncle" Ben loved to sit under the shade of a big pecan tree and tell his spellbound audience of his days at the Alamo with Lt. Col. William Barret Travis. Eyewitnesses claimed to have heard Riley's Alamo story as far back as the 1920s—long before the creation of television and Disney's Davy Crockett craze of the 1950s.

Ben Riley's story appeared to have local roots. His death certificate unveiled other tantalizing possibilities. Riley died October 30, 1956, in Brewton, Alabama, at age 107, after tripping over a box in his house. The certificate noted that he had once labored as a porter (probably the reason for the "railroad" reference in his story) and that he had been born into slavery February 22, 1849, in Rillisville, Monroe County, Alabama.[3] Monroe County is where Charles and Susan Travis were raised by their grandparents after the death of their father at the Alamo in 1836. In an 1840 census, the two children appear to be living under the roof of their grandfather, William Cato. One male slave between the ages of ten and twenty-four is also shown at that residence—a slave that could have been Joe. He would have turned twenty-five in 1840.[4] Regardless, we know that Joe appeared in neighboring Escambia County in 1838, when he arrived unannounced at the farm of William Barret Travis's brother Nicholas. The Travis clan eventually referred to Joe as Ben Travis.

Ben Riley, meanwhile, may have belonged to a white slaveholder named Enoch Riley. Enoch Riley lived in Monroe County. His son,

Benjamin F. Riley, Sr., was born in Pineville, Monroe County, Alabama, on July 16, 1849—five months before the birth of "Uncle" Ben Riley. Did Ben Riley hear of Joe's harrowing escape at the Alamo and daring flight to Alabama firsthand as a child in Monroe County? Did he embellish the story years later with himself as the main character to garner the attention of the neighborhood children? Could his story simply be attributed to the jumbled recollections of an elderly man?

Or could it be that Ben Riley was Joe's son or other relative? Joe answered to the name of Ben later in life. We may never know. Yet what shouldn't be lost in the fog of the mystery is the fact that a freedman from rural Alabama found it relevant to tell a story where a black man survives the Alamo battle.

And there was still another Ben. In 1916, Indiana historian J. Wesley Whicker wrote of a brawny African American named Ben Moore who claimed he had survived the Alamo battle as a child. The story is documented in Whicker's *Historical Sketches of the Wabash Valley*—a story found by Lee while scouring over thousands of published and unpublished slave narratives.[5] Moore, the story goes, journeyed to Texas as a child with David Crockett. Moore survived the carnage at the Alamo and later escaped from the Mexican Army and made his way back to Tennessee and then Kentucky. Prior to the outbreak of the Civil War, Moore gathered his family and fled north to Canada. The fugitives reached a black community in the woods north of the Bethel Church in Fountain County, Indiana, and decided to run no further. At the time, more than one hundred black fugitives were living in the refuge of those woods near Davis Township.

Whicker described Moore as "one of the most perfect specimens of physical manhood who has ever lived in this country. He was 6 feet 4 inches tall, weighed 316 pounds, and was raw-boned; without an ounce of surplus flesh." Once, Whicker wrote, Moore became boisterous and unruly in the town of Attica, Indiana. Reuben Beamer, the town marshal, enlisted "four or five deputies" to arrest Moore, and a hellacious fight ensued. Beamer later proclaimed that Moore was the strongest man to ever walk the streets of Attica. Whicker also noted that Moore had four powerful sons. Two of those sons had died of consumption in the community north of Bethel Church. Another son proved to be a good laborer, while the youngest and strongest of the boys eventually ended up as an inmate at a prison in Jeffersonville, Indiana.[6]

The historical evidence leaves more questions than answers. Ben Moore and Attica marshal Reuben Beamer both appear in the 1880 census at Fountain County, Indiana. This alone proves both men existed, as Whicker claimed. What doesn't add up is Moore's age. He is listed as a forty-year-old farmer who was born in 1840 in Kentucky.[7] That means Ben Moore was clearly not at the Alamo siege and battle in 1836. But is that the end of the story? Or is there, as is often the case with oral traditions, a thread of truth somewhere to be found? Could Ben Moore have been relating the story of a father who was an Alamo survivor? Or a relative or neighbor?

As for David Crockett, he was a slaveholder at the time he left for Texas, but there is no known documentation that he had a servant accompany him from Tennessee. The lack of documentation would have been nothing new where a slave is concerned. After all, William Travis made no mention of Joe in his known letters. Another possible scenario is that someone in Crockett's party took a servant to Texas, and the story became distorted in the retelling over the years. Black servants lived in a shadow world. Historical documentation doesn't always record their presence, yet they lived and roamed everywhere the slaveholder lived and roamed.

Just as there is more than one Ben, there is another Joe. Texan Joe E. Leonard, Sr., first came to our attention in 1999 after we presented a talk about blacks at the Alamo to a historical association in San Antonio. Dorothy Black, an employee at the Alamo shrine for the Daughters of the Republic of Texas, approached us afterward and kindly passed along Leonard's name and address. She told us that Leonard occasionally visited the Alamo with his wife and signed the guest register as a direct descendant of Joe. Naturally, Lee and I were excited to hear Black's tip. At the time we knew nothing of Joe's life prior to 1834 with Isaac Mansfield in Texas.

On March 6, 1999, while Lee honored the Alamo defenders inside the Alamo shrine, I knocked on Leonard's door. A tall, stately black man answered. I told him I was an author and reporter from Oklahoma, and I had been doing research with a close friend for the past year and a half for a book about Joe, a slave who survived the 1836 Battle of the Alamo. "Do you know of this man?" I asked.

Leonard smiled broadly. "Joe was my great-great-grandfather," he said proudly.

Overcome with emotion, and instantly sensing Leonard's desire to talk, we embraced as old friends. We then settled into his living room for the next three hours to discuss his family history. I scribbled notes as the then-sixty-five-year-old Leonard spoke. The following is a summary of the story he related.

One day as a child, in perhaps 1943 or 1944, Joe Leonard arrived at the Grapeland, Texas, home of his grandfather, Charles Leonard. The young Leonard had just spent the afternoon with classmates at a local fair in the nearby town of Crockett, where the patriotic fervor of the day had been abundantly on display. Stories of independence and freedom were repeated during the field trip. Leonard heard thrilling stories of legendary Texas figures like David Crockett, James Bowie, and Sam Houston. The boy eagerly ran home to tell his grandfather about his exciting day. Upon his arrival, Leonard found his grandfather relaxing on his rocking chair on the front porch. The elderly Leonard was a tall man who stood six foot four and had dark black skin. His reputation was that of a no-nonsense gentleman, a Baptist minister who interpreted the Bible literally. He was fond of saying, "Trust no one."

Young Leonard proudly handed his grandfather a paper he had received at the fair, which detailed the exploits of David Crockett and his heroic death at the Alamo. Charles Leonard peered over his glasses as he read the paper. "Uh-huh," the old man finally replied. "Is that right? And did they mention a black man named Joe who fought at the Alamo?"

"No," the boy replied.

The elder Leonard eased back in his rocking chair and said, "Let me tell you a story. Joe is your great-great-grandfather. You're named after him."

Joe, the story went, had been born in present-day Panama as José Leonardo. At the age of either seventeen or eighteen, he had arrived in New Orleans as a sailor aboard a Colombian merchant ship. On the eve of his ship's scheduled departure, Leonardo wandered into the red-light district to find a prostitute for the night. The next day he awoke to discover his ship had left port without him. Homeless and without work, Leonardo wandered New Orleans in search of a job. One day a well-dressed white gentleman with a wagon asked Leonardo if he would be interested in helping him haul supplies. Leonardo jumped at the chance to earn some money. Soon, he was traveling along a dirt road away from New Orleans. But the teamster had tricked Leonardo: he chained him and sold him into slavery. Leonardo, however, escaped and fled to the Mexican province of Texas, where he assumed he would be legally free.

Charles Leonard described Leonardo as a large, rugged man with coal-black skin who stood about six feet tall and weighed two hundred pounds. Leonardo spoke Spanish but could also speak English and some Indian languages. He eventually found work in Texas as a valet for William Barret Travis, who would become his close friend.

At the time, Gen. Sam Houston was recruiting men for the Texas army, enticing them with promises of land. Leonardo volunteered to fight, ending up with Travis inside the Alamo. There he narrowly escaped with his life. After the battle, Mexican general Santa Anna asked Leonardo if would fight in his army. Leonardo agreed as long as he would be permitted to escort fellow Alamo survivor Susanna Dickinson back to her ranch in Gonzales. Santa Anna agreed.

Upon reaching Gonzales, Dickinson gave Leonardo a letter she had written for Houston, who was then camped in East Texas at Groce's Plantation. Leonardo spurred his horse, and Susanna yelled, "Ride, Joe! Ride!"—and Leonardo soon rejoined Houston at Groce's Plantation.

Sometime prior to the Battle of San Jacinto, Houston sought Leonardo's services in helping to devise a plan to take Santa Anna and his troops by surprise. Leonardo told Houston the Mexicans had held a big fiesta prior to their attack on the Alamo, and at some point he expected them to hold a fiesta again. That would be a good time to strike, Leonardo advised.

The next day Houston and his troops descended upon stunned Mexican troops, who were still staggering drunk from their fiesta. Leonardo became a hero. For all his efforts, though, Leonardo was placed into the Travis estate as a slave, and he again escaped, likely with Houston's help. Leonardo ended up in the secret frontier community of Freewill in present-day Houston County and began going by the name "Joe Leonard." Freewill, founded by an outlaw named Freedman Willy, consisted of fugitive blacks and outlaw Indians and whites. Leonardo, now Joe Leonard, married Willy's daughter, Minnie, a petite black woman. Together they had a son and named him Levy. Leonardo is said to have picked the name because it reminded him of playing along the levees in his native Panama as a child.

Joe and Minnie eventually moved to the community of Cedar Branch (north of Grapeland), where he labored as a farmer and evetually died and was buried in an unmarked grave. His son Levy fathered a son named Charles, who in turn fathered a son named David. The Leonard line then extended to David's son, Joe Edd Leonard, Sr., who was born May 18, 1933.[8]

Joe E. Leonard, Sr., said that the family oral tradition was all he had to support his claim. No other living relative was aware of the story. The longtime Texas school administrator even confessed he couldn't trace his family tree beyond Levy Leonard and an 1880 census where Levy is listed as a Houston County resident.

The story sounded like a strange mix of bad Texas history and bad fiction, yet Lee and I were open-minded enough to consider its substance despite troubling inaccuracies. Susanna, for instance, never wrote Houston a letter. She was illiterate. And there would have been no reason for Joe to ride anywhere to find Houston. Houston was camped at Gonzales when the Alamo survivors arrived. Nor would José Leonardo, or anyone else for that matter, have negotiated terms of service with Santa Anna. The Mexican dictator would have executed anyone trying—on the spot, with no questions asked.

Mostly, we were bothered by the major facts we did know at the time:

- Joe was a slave. We had documents showing where Travis purchased Joe from friend John Cummings, who in turn had purchased Joe at the estate sale of Isaac Mansfield in San Felipe de Austin. Joe clearly was not a free man when he entered the Alamo.
- General Houston never mentioned a José Leonardo in any of his letters prior to or after the San Jacinto battle.
- There was no record of a José Leonardo or Joe Leonard ever serving in the Texian army during the revolution.

One other fact caused us to pause. Leonard freely admitted to trying to sell his story for a movie, confessing that he had "embellished it slightly" in inquiry letters to directors Spike Lee and Robert Redford.

Neither had responded. In all fairness, peddling a story for a movie doesn't render it invalid. We were simply suspicious as we diligently worked to either prove or disprove the story. We started by documenting the oral tradition. But what part of the story did Leonard embellish? He never made that clear.

The mystery deepened nine months later, when Lee and I traced Mansfield back to St. Louis and then discovered the existence of Joe's brother, William Wells Brown. Suddenly, we could trace Joe through ironclad documentation from the Travis estate to his birth in Kentucky and childhood in Marthasville, Missouri Territory. We learned at that moment that the Joe who cheated death at the Alamo was unequivocally not José Leonardo.

So what is the real story behind Joe E. Leonard, Sr., and his family oral tradition?

"I know what I was told," Leonard insisted in 1999, prior to our discovery of Brown. "And I don't give a damn about what someone else thinks."[9]

The most fascinating aspect of his story is the fact Leonard steadfastly believes he is a direct descendant of Joe. Leonard has passed that belief onto his son, Joe E. Leonard, Jr., who told us in 1999 that he was planning to write a book about his family story and therefore didn't desire to collaborate on research. We wished him the best and parted paths.[10]

Did José Leonardo ever exist? The answer may forever remain elusive. Perhaps the most important facet of the Leonard story is the retelling of a black man's survival at the Alamo. The theme has persisted in eastern Texas, rural Indiana, and rural Alabama—a member of the black community notes the importance of a black man surviving the legendary Alamo battle. A black hero emerges as the story is told with great luster and pride.[11] This may be Joe's greatest legacy.

NOTES

Preface

1. Davis, *Travis Diary*, 127, 138, 139, 146.

2. Isaac Mansfield probate, Austin County Court Clerk's Office, file no. 30, box 2, Bellville, Texas.

3. Ibid.

4. Ibid.

5. Receipt for one "large iron elbow" to Isaac Mansfield, dated April 25, 1825, P. Chouteau Maffitt Collection, Missouri Historical Society, Columbia; Mansfield character certificate, Texas General Land Office, Austin, Texas.

6. Early, *Ain't But a Place*, 9.

7. *Montgomery Advertiser*, February 4, 1905.

8. *New Castle* (Penn.) *News*, June 25, 1915; *Dotham* (Ala.) *Morning News*, August 30, 1914.

9. *Dallas Morning News*, September 8, 1929.

10. Fannie McGuire Papers, Alabama Department of Archives and History, Montgomery, Alabama.

Chapter 1

1. William Barret Travis letter to Jesse Grimes, March 3, 1836, *Telegraph and Texas Register*, March 24, 1836.

2. Sowell, *Early Settlers and Indian Fighters of Southwest Texas*, 836; Travis letter to Grimes, March 3, 1836.

3. Travis letter to Grimes, March 3, 1836.

4. Isaac Mansfield probate, Austin County Court Clerk's Office, file no. 30, box 2, Bellville, Texas.

5. "Extract of a Letter from a Friend to the Editor," *New Orleans Commercial Bulletin*, April 11, 1836; *Portland* (Maine) *Advertiser*, May 3, 1836; Travis letter to Grimes, March 3, 1836.

6. Ibid.

7. Juan Nepomuceno Almonte, "Journal of the Mexican Campaign," *New York Herald*, June 21–30, 1836; *Frankfort* (Ky.) *Commonwealth*, May 25, 1836.

8. William Barret Travis letter to the "People of Texas & All Americans in the World," February 24, 1836, Texas State Archives, Austin. In the letter, Travis notes that the garrison has "20 to 30 head of Beeves" within its walls.

9. Brown, *Narrative of William Wells Brown* (hereafter *Narrative*), 13–14, 16, 20, 31. This work is the primary source for the first twenty years of Brown's life. He was Joe's older brother (William called his younger brother Joseph), and it is through his memoirs that we are allowed a window into their childhood home. At least eight editions of Brown's *Narrative* are known to exist, but only the fourth edition will be cited unless otherwise noted. The first three editions of the book—eight thousand copies in all—were sold out eighteen months after the first printing.

10. Mansfield probate; *Telegraph and Texas Register*, May 26, 1837. John Rice Jones, a friend of Travis, placed a runaway advertisement in the *Telegraph and Texas Register* with the only known description of Joe.

11. *Frankfort* (Ky.) *Commonwealth*, May 25, 1836.

Chapter 2

1. Brown, *Narrative*, 14.

2. Brown, *Memoir of William Wells Brown: An American Bondman* (hereafter *Memoir*), 4. See also Josephine Brown, *Biography of an American Bondman by His Daughter*, 6. Caution: while Josephine undoubtedly heard many fascinating stories of her father's life firsthand, her text is nonetheless chalked with inaccuracies.

3. Mansfield probate; Brown, *Narrative*, 13.

4. Brown, *Narrative*, 13.

5. Brown, *The Black Man*, 12.

6. Twelvetree, ed., *The Story of the Life of John Anderson*, 6–7.

7. Trexler, *Slavery in Missouri*, 92–93.

8. Geyer, *A Digest of the Laws of Missouri Territory*, 374; Brown, *Narrative*, 35.

9. Duden, *Europa und Deutschland von Nordamerika*, 1:369–70.

10. John Young undoubtedly needed numerous horses and mules to carry on his large farming and milling industries. He once sold four of Marthasville's

lots to Benjamin Sharp "in consideration of one stud horse called Black Prince." Gregory, *A History of Early Marthasville*, 1.

11. Duden, *Europa*, 282–83.

12. Brown, *The Black Man*, 11. Brown writes of his mother's mixed blood, "Her father, it was said, was the noted Daniel Boone, and her mother a negress."

13. Bryan, *Pioneer Families of Missouri*, 103–104.

14. Breckenridge, *Journal of a Voyage up the River Missouri*, 19.

15. Brown's *Narrative* makes it quite plain that the "land of liberty" or "land of freedom" was something he and his family talked about routinely in private.

16. *Missouri Republican*, March 20, 1822.

17. Ibid., July 16, 1823. For more information on the life and legend of Mike Fink, see Blair and Meine, *Half Horse, Half Alligator*.

18. Bryan, *Pioneer Families of Missouri*, 225–26.

19. *Kentucky Gazette*, March 22, 1806.

20. Boyd and Boyd, *A History of Mt. Sterling, Kentucky, 1792–1918*, 16.

21. Quisenberry, *Kentucky in the War of 1812*, 186. The Kentucky Historical Society originally published this book serially between 1912 and 1915.

22. Bryan, *Pioneer Families of Missouri*, 226.

23. Boyd and Boyd, *A History of Mt. Sterling, Kentucky*, 202.

24. Ibid.

25. Carter, ed., *Territorial Papers of the United States*, 15:326–28.

26. Gregory, *A History of Early Marthasville*, 1. Ralph Gregory was an amateur historian who moved to Marthasville in 1978. Gregory said he knew of at least five extant log structures in Marthasville. No one knows when these were built. Marthasville's original plat was destroyed, but a copy has survived and can be found in the 1877 *Atlas of Warren County, Mo.*, on page 31. Young had a copy made for Harvey Griswold, and on November 17, 1826, Young testified in St. Louis County that it was a "true representation of said Town with all the lots, streets, lanes and allies in."

27. Ibid.

28. *Missouri Gazette*, June 21, 1817.

29. Bryan, *Pioneer Families of Missouri*, 226. In a copy of the Young-Hitt family Bible, printed in 1791 by Isaac Collins of Trenton, New Jersey, Aaron Young's birth date is listed as April 30, 1780. Leonard and Mary Young's other children and their birth dates: Ann (June 17, 1766); Elizabeth (November 4, 1767); William (May 17, 1770); James (November 20, 1773); Francis (November 20, 1773); Jane (July 12, 1775); Richard (May 30, 1777); John (February 25, 1779); Henry (October 20, 1782); Mary (December 15, 1783); Catron (July 12, 1786); and Benjamin (June 8, 1789). See also Brown, *Narrative*, 80, concerning a slave transaction that involved Aaron Young.

30. Brown, *My Southern Home*, 56. *My Southern Home* is Brown's last book. The work is a satirical account of Brown's childhood home in which he refers to

Dr. John Young as "Dr. John Gaines," his wife Sarah Young as "Sarah Scott (Pepper) Young," and himself in the third person as "Billy." He also dubs his home plantation "Poplar Farms." Nonetheless, *My Southern Home* is a nonintrusive, historical look into William and Joseph's childhood home—a place where real people come to life through Brown's humorous and candid recollections. Of all Brown's historical works, *My Southern Home* might be his most sincere, for it exposes raw human nature regardless of skin color or station in life.

31. Duden, *Europa*, 439–40.

32. Trexler, *Slavery in Missouri*, 92–93.

33. *Journal of the House of Representatives* (St. Louis, 1821), 1.

34. Brown, *Narrative*, 17.

35. Ibid., 18.

36. Ibid.

37. Ibid., 19.

38. Ibid.

39. Ibid., 1.

40. Brown, *Biography of an American Bondman by His Daughter*, 10; Brown, *Narrative*, 14.

41. Brown, *Narrative*, 14.

42. Brown, *My Southern Home*, 11, 73–74.

43. Ibid., 70.

44. Ibid., 37–38, 41; Brown, *The Black Man*, 15–16.

45. Brown, *My Southern Home*, 18–19.

46. Ibid., 12, 42–45, 49.

47. Ibid., 66.

48. Brown notes in his 1848 *Narrative* that Dr. Young owned "about forty slaves, twenty-five of whom were field hands" (13). In his *Memoir*, written eleven years later, Brown estimates that his master had between "forty-five and fifty slaves" (4). Brown lists ten of these slaves by name in his *Narrative*: his mother, Elizabeth; his sister Elizabeth; his brothers Benjamin, Solomon, Joseph, Leander, and Millford; Randall; Hannah; and himself. In *My Southern Home*, Brown counts among Dr. Young's slaves Ike, Cato, Sam, Dinkie, Uncle Ned, Aunt Nancy, Melinda, Sally, Susan, Nancy, Lola, Hannah, Jim, Peter, Dolly, and Isabella. Dr. Young's estate papers state that he owned slaves by the name of Jim, Charlotte, Peter, Martha, Anne, Robert, Eliza, Jane, Edward, Thomas, Henry, and Leander (Joseph's brother) at the time of his death. There are two slaves by the name of Dolly. (John Young's will is dated December 1, 1832, Land Records Book S, 450–453, Recorder of Deeds Archives, St. Louis.) These three sources account for thirty-four slaves. It could be that some of those named are Joseph's blood relations, although William never specifies any outside of his immediate family.

49. Trexler, *Slavery in Missouri*, 92–93.

50. Brown, *The Black Man*, 12.

51. Ibid.

52. Ibid. William was eventually put to work in Young's doctor's office (*Memoir*, 4).

53. Brown, *Narrative*, 96–98.

54. Ibid., 15.

55. Ibid.

56. Elizabeth may have been whipped sometime in 1824, since William states he was reportedly "about 10" when the brutal act took place (Brown, *Biography of an American Bondman by His Daughter*, 7). In 1852, William told British journalist William Farmer that as far as he understood, he had been born in the autumn of 1814 "about corn-cutting time" (Brown, *Three Years in Europe*, ix–x). This date was corroborated two years later by Enoch Price of St. Louis, William's third and last owner. Price signed a deed of emancipation for William on April 25, 1854, noting that the fugitive slave was in his fortieth year (Brown's deed of emancipation, Circuit Court of the City of St. Louis, Missouri, Permanent Record Book Number 24, 150). However, Josephine gives March 15, 1815, as her father's birth date in her biographical work—a date that, given her poor record with facts, may well not be accurate. Historians have differed on the date, but they have not previously been privy to one other valuable source when gauging William's true birth year: Joseph. The earliest known court record of Joseph cites his age as "about nineteen" on December 22, 1834, which would likely place his birth sometime in the year 1815 (Mansfield probate). For further treatment of William's birth date, see Farrison's *William Wells Brown*, 8–9.

57. Brown, *Narrative*, 15–16.

Chapter 3

1. Young-Hitt family Bible.

2. Brown, *Biography of an American Bondman by His Daughter*, 17. Josephine attributes Young's financial troubles to "speculation and mismanagement."

3. John Young's will.

4. "Aspects of Slavery in Missouri, 1821," 508.

5. Babcock, ed., *Forty Years of Pioneer Life*, 146.

6. Darby, *Personal Recollections of Many Prominent People*, 2.

7. Ibid., 2–4.

8. Brown, *Memoir*, 4; Brown, *Narrative*, 31. William never mentions his two deceased brothers by name, but they are clearly Solomon and Benjamin. Joseph, Millford, and Leander were still alive at this time.

9. Brown, *My Southern Home*, 70–78.

10. Ibid., 8–11.

11. Brown, *The Black Man*, 22.

12. Brown, *My Southern Home*, 37–39.

13. Lewis Hayden, quoted in Stowe, *A Key to Uncle Tom's Cabin*, 154–55. Also quoted in Johnson, *Soul by Soul*, 22. For a vivid glimpse inside the slave market,

read Johnson's *Soul by Soul*. Johnson is both meticulous in his research and humanistic in his extraordinary presentation.

14. As for Cook, he eventually shifted to another line of work. He left the St. Louis area in 1840, leading a party of thirty families from Independence, Missouri, toward California. (William D. Stewart letter to Perth Shire, July 16, 1841, William Stewart Collection, Missouri Historical Society, Columbia.)

15. Brown, *Narrative*, 20.

16. Ibid.

17. Ibid.

18. Ibid., 20–21.

19. Ibid., 21.

20. Ibid., 21–22.

21. *St. Louis Beacon*, November 4, 1829. William noted in his *Narrative* that the steamboat *Missouri* traveled "between St. Louis and Galena" (22). An advertisement that appeared in the November 4, 1829, *Beacon* reveals an even larger travel route. The ad states that Culver planned to depart with "freight and passage" the next morning to New Orleans. William might have been on board that day.

22. Brown, *Narrative*, 22.

23. Ibid., 23.

24. Ibid.

25. Ibid., 24.

26. Ibid., 31. William wrote, "My mother, my brothers Joseph and Millford, and my sister Elizabeth, belonged to Mr. Isaac Mansfield, formerly from one of the free states, (Massachusetts, I believe.)" Although William was mistaken on Mansfield's native state—he was born in Connecticut—he amply summed up his pain by stating that the sale "caused me great unhappiness" (*Narrative*, 25).

27. Brown, *Narrative*, 31; *St. Louis Beacon*, July 4, 1829; Mansfield character certificate, September 12, 1832, Texas General Land Office, Austin; *St. Louis Beacon*, June 10, 1830; and O. D. Filley letter to Marcus Filley, July 11, 1830, Filley Papers, Missouri Historical Society, Columbia.

Chapter 4

1. Slaves being transported by steamboats were routinely tied or chained to prevent escape during frequent shoreline stops to gather wood. See Brown, *Narrative*, 39.

2. Brown, *Narrative*, 38. Brown refers to the term "soul driver" when recalling the time he was hired in St. Louis to a slave trader named Walker.

3. *Missouri Republican*, September 30, 1828; *St. Louis Beacon*, September 23, 1829; *St. Louis Beacon*, October 31, 1829; and *St. Louis Beacon*, November 4, 1829.

4. White, "Early Days in St. Louis," 6. White first moved to St. Louis in 1819 with his father, remaining for the next thirty-two years and earning notoriety

as a gifted architect. In those early days of St. Louis, he even became acquainted with the legendary keelboater Mike Fink. White moved to California in 1849. He died October 17, 1882, in Suisun City, California, while writing his recollections. An excerpt from White's "Early Days in St. Louis" and biographical information can also be found in Blair and Meine, *Half Horse, Half Alligator*, 275–77.

5. "Missouri History Not Found in the Textbooks," 440–42. Quoted from a January 17, 1831, letter written by Archy Kasson of St. Louis to Isaiah and John Townsend of Albany [New York?].

6. Darby, *Personal Recollections*, 9; Reps, *Saint Louis Illustrated*, 14–15.

7. William's *Narrative* gives a few clues as to the year Joseph, his mother, and siblings were sold to Isaac Mansfield. Shortly after the family's removal to John Young's new farm on Grand Prairie in 1827, probably sometime during the spring, William was hired out to Major Freeland. William remained with Freeland for at least six months before the latter "failed in business" (21–22). The majority of slaves were generally hired on twelve-month contracts. Based on these odds, Freeland probably returned William to Young at the end of their contract, perhaps sometime in early 1828. Young then hired out William to William B. Culver aboard the steamboat *Missouri*, where William remained "during the sailing season" (22). William's work likely began in the spring and ended sometime before the arrival of winter in 1828. Finally, William was hired to the tyrannical John Colburn at the Missouri Hotel—again, probably for one year. William stated that it was while "living at the Missouri hotel" that Young sold his mother and siblings to Isaac Mansfield (25). Based on that timeline, Joseph and his family were probably purchased by Mansfield in late 1828 or sometime during 1829.

8. In an 1821 St. Louis directory, "several Hacks or pleasure Carriages, and a considerable number of 57 Drays and Carts" were already counted citywide. Paxton, *The St. Louis Directory and Register*, 262. Those numbers most likely increased drastically by the latter part of the decade.

9. *St. Louis Beacon*, April 15, 1830. Nearly every newspaper edition printed at this time is packed with advertisements for steamboats departing for and arriving from ports such as Pittsburgh, New Orleans, Louisville, and Galena.

10. "[James Cartwright Essex] Autobiography," circa 1866, in Caleb Green Papers, Missouri Historical Society, Columbia.

11. Ibid.

12. Ibid.; Brown, *Narrative*, 55. William told how he tricked a fellow slave into delivering a note to the jailer for him. The note directed the jailer to give him twenty lashes with the whip for insubordination. The slave agreed to deliver the note and soon found himself on the receiving end of the whip. When the tearful slave emerged from the jail, William claimed ignorance about the note's contents—an act he forever regretted—and gave the poor fellow fifty cents of his own money for his troubles. This story of desperation, in itself a brutal

statement about slavery, is merely another example of how slaves were some-times able to save money they earned through tips and labor.

13. "More about St. Louis," 32.

14. Laws in Missouri that permitted free blacks to carry firearms date back to the state's territorial days, when it was said that "every free negro or mulatto, being a housekeeper may be permitted to keep one gun, powder and shot" (Geyer, *A Digest of the Laws of Missouri Territory*, 374).

15. "Aspects of Slavery in Missouri, 1821," 523. John Mason Peck, an agent for the American Bible Society, sold slaveholders on the idea, first incorporat-ing blacks into his Sunday school and later into his regular school classes. In 1825 he wrote optimistically, "I am happy to find among the slaveholders in Mis-souri a growing disposition to have the blacks educated, and to patronise Sunday-schools for the purpose. I doubt not but by prudent efforts this may be effected extensively."

16. *St. Louis Republican*, September 30, 1828; *St. Louis Beacon*, October 24, 1829; *Missouri Republican*, July 7, 1829.

17. "More about St. Louis," 32–33.

18. *St. Louis Beacon*, July 4, 1829.

19. Darby, *Personal Recollections*, 10. Today Main Street is called Leonor K. Sul-livan Boulevard. Originally the street was called Grand Rue, so named by the city's early French pioneers.

20. "[James Cartwright Essex] Autobiography," in Caleb Green Papers, Mis-souri Historical Society, Columbia.

21. Ibid.

22. Darby, *Personal Recollections*, 10–11; see also "[James Cartwright Essex] Au-tobiography" for description of Chouteau's magnificent abode.

23. Flint, *Recollections of the Last Ten Years*, 81.

24. Christian Schultz, *Travels on an Inland Voyage, Performed in the Years 1807 and 1808, including a Tour of Nearly 6,000 Miles*, quoted in Stevens, *The Building of St. Louis*, 11–12.

25. Edwards and Hopewell, *Edward's Great West*, 340.

26. Mansfield character certificate, Texas General Land Office; *St. Louis Bea-con*, July 4, 1829.

27. Receipt for one "large iron elbow" to Isaac Mansfield, dated April 25, 1825, P. Chouteau Maffitt Collection, Missouri Historical Society, Columbia.

28. Filley letter to Filley, July 11, 1830.

29. "Missouri History Not Found in the Textbooks," 440–42.

30. Filley letter to Filley, July 11, 1830.

31. *Missouri Republican*, October 6, 1829.

32. U.S. Census of 1830, St. Louis County, St. Louis, Missouri.

33. Ibid. The daughter Elizabeth shows up on a legal document four years later as a five-year-old "mulatto" (Mansfield probate).

34. Ibid.

35. Trexler, *Slavery in Missouri,* 94–95.

36. *St. Louis Beacon,* January 27 and February 3, 1830.

37. Brown, *Narrative,* 82.

38. Ibid., 82–83.

39. Luke 12:47.

40. Brown, *Narrative,* 36. Young placed a high priority on God's sacred word after he found religion. William Brown recalled how Young and his wife entertained more traveling preachers than anyone in their part of the country, and how they devoutly attended services whenever at home. Sundays were thus reserved for God and little else. Young did his spiritual part by holding family worship twice each Sunday, once in the morning and again in the evening. The doctor also extended his hand of Christianity to his servants, but that hand only stretched so far, according to William. Slaves were permitted to attend evening prayer sessions only because Young required them to work as long as the sun shined—on God's time or not.

41. Ibid., 127.

42. Ibid.

43. For further reading on the natural and human-made caves beneath St. Louis, see Rother and Rother, *Lost Caves of St. Louis,* and the *Preliminary Research Report on the Soulard Neighborhood Historic District,* a copy of which can be found at the Missouri Historical Society. One of the more fascinating stories to emerge from the Soulard district, a southwest neighborhood of St. Louis, involved the slaveholding families of Creeley and Beauvois during the Civil War. Local legends told of how weapons and ammunition were smuggled to the Confederacy through a tunnel entrance at the Beauvois home that led to the river caves. From there, the supplies were loaded on barges and shipped south. In later years, local breweries used underground caves in the neighborhood to store beer.

44. Fugitive slave Lucy A. Delaney told how her mother, Polly Crockett, once used caves in her flight for freedom from St. Louis. Delaney wrote, "In the day time, she hid in caves and the surrounding woods, and in the night time, guided by the wondrous North Star, that blessed lodestone of a slave people, my mother finally reached Chicago, where she was arrested by the Negro-catchers." Delaney, *From Darkness Cometh the Light,* 22–23.

45. "[James Cartwright Essex] Autobiography." See also Darby, *Personal Recollections,* 2–3.

46. Trexler, *Slavery in Missouri,* 177.

47. Ibid., 182–83.

48. Joseph and his family certainly weren't unique in this regard. Former St. Louis slave Lucy Delaney wrote in her memoir, "I was beginning to plan for freedom, and was forever on the alert for a chance to escape and join my sister. I was then twelve years old, and often talked the matter over with mother and

canvassed the probabilities of both of us getting away. No schemes were too wild for us to consider!" Delaney, *From Darkness Cometh the Light*, 19–20.

49. "[James Cartwright Essex] Autobiography."

Chapter 5

1. Brown, *Narrative*, 32.

2. Drew, *The Refugee*, 177–78.

3. *St. Louis Beacon*, June 17, 1830.

4. Ibid., December 9, 1830.

5. Ibid., September 23, 1829.

6. Ibid.

7. Brown, *Narrative*, 30–32.

8. Ibid., 70.

9. Filley letter to Filley, July 11, 1830.

10. John Young's will, Lawrence County Court Clerk's Office, Moulton, Alabama.

11. Brown, *Narrative*, 30–32.

12. Filley letter to Filley, July 11, 1830; *St. Louis Beacon*, June 10, 1830; *St. Louis Beacon*, July 22, 1830.

13. Filley letter to Filley, July 11, 1830.

14. *Isaac Mansfield v. Charles Collins*, St. Louis County civil case, July 2, 1831, miscellaneous files of the Missouri Historical Society, Columbia.

15. Filley letter to Filley, July 11, 1830.

16. Ibid.; *St. Louis Beacon*, July 22, 1830.

17. *St. Louis Beacon*, June 10, 1830.

18. *St. Louis Beacon*, September 9, 1829.

19. *St. Louis Beacon*, December 9, 1830.

20. *St. Louis Beacon*, July 4, 1829.

21. Filley letter to Filley, July 11, 1830.

22. Darby, *Personal Recollections*, 430–31.

23. Brown, *Narrative*, 64–65.

24. Ibid.

25. Ibid., 65–66.

26. Ibid., 70.

27. Ibid., 62–64.

28. Ibid., 66–75.

29. *Isaac Mansfield v. John Shade*, St. Louis County civil case, April 20, 1833, miscellaneous files of the Missouri Historical Society, Columbia.

30. Ibid.

31. Brown, *Narrative*, 75–76.

32. Ibid., 77–78.

33. Ibid.

34. Ibid.

35. Ibid., 79.

36. Ibid., 92–93.

37. Ibid.

38. "The Reminiscences of Mrs. Dilue Harris," 88; Mansfield character certificate.

39. The dread of being sold "downriver" was widespread among slaves in Missouri, Tennessee, and Kentucky. Fugitive slave Lucy A. Delaney stated in her memoir that she continually faced the threat of being sold. Once Delaney's mother had irritated her mistress, Mary Cox, of St. Louis. Cox angrily declared, "I am just tired out with the 'white airs' you put on, and if you don't behave differently, I will make Mr. [H. S.] Cox sell you down the river at once." "Although mother turned grey with fear," Delaney wrote, "she presented a bold front." Delaney's mother was sold the next day for her sassy behavior (*From the Darkness Cometh the Light*, 21).

Former slave Lewis Clarke once explained the slave's fear of the South: "Why do slaves dread so bad to go to the south—to Mississippi or Louisiana? Because they know slaves are driven very hard there, and worked to death in a few years." Clarke, *Narrative of the Sufferings of Lewis Clarke*, 84. For further treatment of this subject, see Johnson, *Soul by Soul*, 20–24.

Chapter 6

1. Holley, *Texas*, 127.

2. Ibid., 31.

3. Ibid.

4. Gray, *From Virginia to Texas*, 113, 226. For further elaboration on the subject, see Sibley, *Travelers in Texas, 1761–1860*, 127–28.

5. *Missouri Republican*, December 15, 1829.

6. Morrell, *Flowers and Fruits*, 37.

7. Jackson, *Alamo Legacy*, 41–42. The source of this family legend is a September 16, 1975, letter written by Mabel Hitt to a Ms. Hansell. Hitt tells how William Wells, Sr., reportedly became "despondent over his wife's death" before leaving Georgia. Hitt's husband, Rabon, is William's great-great-grandson. A copy of this letter is at the Daughters of the Republic of Texas Library, San Antonio.

8. Jackson, *Alamo Legacy*, 88–90, based on testimony from a 1995 interview with Kevin R. Wornell, who has collected family stories for decades. The account of Henry Warnell's journey into Texas comes from an interview he conducted in the late 1970s with a distant cousin, Eydith Wornell Roach. At the time of their conversation, Roach was ninety-three years old.

9. Dick, *The Dixie Frontier*, 13–14.

10. Brown, *Narrative*, 64–65, 74.

11. Ibid., 39.

12. Mansfield probate.

13. For the most definitive work on slavery in Texas, see Campbell, *An Empire for Slavery*.

14. Barker, ed., *The Austin Papers*, 2:469–70.

15. Ibid., Stephen F. Austin letter to Mary Austin Holley, July 19, 1831, *Austin Papers*, 2:676.

16. Howren, "Causes and Origin," 415–16.

17. Mexico Minister of Relations Manuel Gómez Pedraza to General Manuel de Mier y Terán, September 12, 1827, transcripts from the *Archivo de Guerra y Marina, Operaciones Militares, Fraccion 1*, Austin Papers, Center for American History, University of Texas, Austin.

18. Ibid., in an unsigned letter dated June 30, 1828.

19. Gammel, comp., *The Laws of Texas*, 1:424.

20. *Alcance Al Num. 25, del Noticioso del Puerto de Matamoros*, March 23, 1831; Gammel, comp., *Laws of Texas*, 1:188–89, 202.

21. Barker, ed., *The Austin Papers*, 1:1716–20.

22. "Minutes of the Ayuntamiento of San Felipe de Austin, 1828–1832," 311.

23. Ibid.

24. *Laws and Decrees of Coahuila and Texas*, 103.

25. Bugbee, "Slavery in Early Texas," 409–10.

26. Dublan and Lozano, *Legislacion Mexicana*, 2:163; Bugbee, "Slavery in Early Texas," 648–49.

27. *Texas Gazette*, January 23, 1830.

28. Ibid., January 30, 1830. The full translation of the December 2, 1829, decree reads:

> Most Excellent Sire, his Excellency the President having been informed of the note your Excellency, No. 126, of the 14th of last month, manifesting, conformably with the exposition of the Chief of Texas, which you forwarded, the serious inconveniences apprehended by the execution of the Decree of 15th September last, on the subject of the abolition of slavery in that Department, and the fatal results to be expected, prejudicial to the tranquility and even to the political existence of the State; and having considered how necessary it is to protect, in an efficacious manner, the colonization of these immense lands of the Republic, has been pleased to accede to the solicitation of your Excellency and DECLARE THE DEPARTMENT OF TEXAS EXCEPTED from the general disposition, comprehended in said Decree. Therefore his Excellency declares that no change must be made as respects Slaves that legally exist in that part of your State governed by your Excellency, expecting from your patriotism and philanthropy, that you will cause the most vigorous vigilance to be used, in order that the general laws and those of the

State which prohibits the introduction of new slaves and establishes the liberty of the progeny that are born in your territory, be complied with, so that by this means the time may not be long before the melancholy and repugnant spectacle, may disappear from the Mexican soil, which is presented to the eyes of philosophy, in the slavery of part of the human species, born with equal rights of liberty, with the rest, and which could only have been so abused and vilified, but by rights of force, which is without dispute the most barbarous of any known.

I have the honor to communicate to your Excellency in reply to your before mentioned communication, offering to you my considerations and respect. God and Liberty. Mexico, 2 Dec. 1829 To his Excellency the Governor of the State of Coahuila and Texas.

29. McCormick, *Scotch-Irish in Ireland and in America*, 133–35.

30. Gammel, comp., *Laws of Texas*, 1:303.

31. Kendall, "Shadow over the City," 151.

32. Filley letter to Filley, July 11, 1830.

33. Gammel, comp., *Laws of Texas*, 1:303; Bugbee, "Slavery in Early Texas," 411–12.

34. Barker, "The Influence of Slavery," 18.

35. McCormick, *Scotch-Irish in Ireland and in America*, 134–35.

36. Ship records from this time period for the port of New Orleans don't show Isaac Mansfield's name. One can surmise with a high degree of certainty that Mansfield journeyed to Texas by land, thus avoiding the risk of fines or loss of property by transporting his slaves by sea.

37. Mansfield character certificate.

Chapter 7

1. "The Destiny of Buffalo Bayou," 96. Local legend insists the water was so clear that settlers could see the buffalo fish below, accounting for the stream's name.

2. "The Pioneer Harrises of Harris County," 365–67; "The Reminiscences of Mrs. Dilue Harris," 89–90; "Life of German Pioneers in Early Texas," 227.

3. "The Pioneer Harrises of Harris County," 365–73; Muir, ed., *Texas in 1837*, 24–25.

4. "The Destiny of Buffalo Bayou," 97.

5. "J. C. Clopper's Journal," 52.

6. "Life of German Pioneers in Early Texas," 227; "The Reminiscences of Mrs. Dilue Harris," 89.

7. "Reminiscences of Mrs. Dilue Harris," 88–89.

8. "Causes and Origins of the Decree of April 6, 1830," 393. Some fifteen years later, traveler Edward Smith described a similar environment where

slaves lived in the eastern region of Texas: "With few exceptions they are kindly treated, are not over-worked, and have an abundance of food, clothing, and efficient medical attention." Smith, *Account of a Journey through North-Eastern Texas*, 82, 84.

9. Muir, *Texas in 1837*, 24.

10. "Reminiscences of Mrs. Dilue Harris," 87. Slaves routinely worked alongside their masters in early Texas. One such example can be found in Canton family oral tradition in which slaves Henry Smith and John Scurlock were remembered for working side-by-side with their owner, Mial Scurlock, to build a log cabin in the Sabine district. Mial and his slaves cut timber from the nearby forest and hauled the logs on their backs. By late 1834, the bachelor Mial and his slaves moved into the new cabin (Soporhia Canton interview). Soporhia Canton is the great-great-granddaughter of Easter Scurlock, who journeyed to Texas from Mississippi in 1834 with her four-year-old son, Denis, Henry Smith, and John Scurlock. Mial's older brother, William Scurlock, owned Easter and her son. (The 1835 census of San Augustine, Texas, in "The Translation of Statistical Census Reports of Texas 1782–1836 and Sources Documenting the Black in Texas 1603–1803," 199.)

For more on the Scurlock slaves, see Martin, "Some Scurlock History," and her self-published book *The Scurlocks*, 67.

11. "Reminiscences of Mrs. Dilue Harris," 87.

12. "Minutes of the Ayuntamiento of San Felipe de Austin, 1828–1832," 162. See also Kemp, *The Signers of the Texas Declaration of Independence*, 224–31.

13. "Reminiscences of Mrs. Dilue Harris," 88; [Travis], petition, May 11, 1831, 72–73; Jonathan H. Kuykendall, *Sketches of Early Texians*, Kuykendall family papers, University of Texas, Austin; Davis, ed., *The William Barret Travis Diary* (hereafter *Travis Diary*), April 7, 1834, 152.

14. Kuykendall, *Sketches of Early Texians*.

15. "Harris County, 1822–1845," 202–203.

16. "The Pioneer Harrises of Harris County, Texas," 365–67; Beazley, "Harris, John Richardson."

17. *Texas Gazette*, October 3, 1829.

18. *Constitutional Advocate and Texas Public Advertiser*, September 5, 1832.

19. Ibid.

20. *Alcance Al Num. 25, Del Noticioso Del Puerto De Matamoros*, March 23, 1831.

21. *Constitutional Advocate and Texas Public Advertiser* (Brazoria), September 5, 1832.

22. Jacquelyn Waites, *Journey of the Heart*, 81–82.

23. Abraham Gallatin to Sarah Young, April 26, 1828, Grantees Book (A–Z, 1804–1854), Office of the Recorder of Deeds, St. Louis County, St. Louis.

24. Filley letter to Filley, July 11, 1830.

25. Albert R. Gallatin, telephone interview with Ron Jackson, January 24, 2002. Gallatin was born September 19, 1931. His father, Eugene E. Gallatin, was born

in 1888—ten years prior to the death of his great-grandfather, the Texas pioneer Albert Gallatin, born on August 1, 1809, in Kentucky.

Another family legend gives an additional clue as to the Gallatins' mode of travel into Texas in 1832. One night ten-year-old Eugene sat with his grandfather by the window. The elder Gallatin gazed out the window and asked, "See the golden wagons?" The boy looked out the window and saw only a creek in the distance. "Don't you see them?" the old man asked again. "And look up in the sky. My name is written in gold letters in the sky." The words baffled the boy. "At the time my father wondered if he was listening to the hallucinations of an old man," Albert R. Gallatin said later about the story of his great-grandfather and namesake. "But as the years passed, we often wondered if he was trying to tell a young boy something. Maybe he was trying to say that's how he and his family came to Texas—by wagon—and that's how he was going to heaven. The next day [February 17, 1896] Albert died." The pioneer Albert Gallatin is buried in Cottonwood Cemetery near Bryan, Texas.

26. *Isaac Mansfield vs. John Shade.*

27. Last will and testament of John Young, December 1, 1832, Lawrence County, Alabama. Recorded in St. Louis County, Missouri, April 30, 1833 (Probate Records, Book S, 450–453, Archives, Recorder of Deeds, City of St. Louis); Bryan and Rose, *Pioneer Families of Missouri,* 226.

28. John Young will.

29. Ibid.

30. Ibid.

31. Mansfield probate.

32. "Reminiscences of Mrs. Dilue Harris," 90–91.

Chapter 8

1. Davis, *Travis Diary,* 127; Brown, *Narrative,* 31.

2. "Minutes of the Ayuntamiento of San Felipe de Austin, 1828–1832," 303–304.

3. Davis, *Travis Diary,* 138.

4. Ibid., 139, March 8, 1834.

5. Brown, *Narrative,* 73–75.

6. "Minutes of the Ayuntamiento of San Felipe de Austin, 1828–1832," 305.

7. Smithwick, *Evolution of a State,* 81.

8. Davis, *Travis Diary,* 139.

9. Ibid.

10. Ibid.

11. Texas Land Office, Box 17, Folder 19, Austin.

12. *Austin's Register of Families,* Book 1:107–108.

13. Ibid., 146.

14. Brown, *Narrative*, 67–71.

15. Ibid., 78.

16. William Barret Travis letter to David G. Burnet, February 6, 1835, copy in the Travis File at the Daughters of the Republic of Texas Library, San Antonio; Mansfield probate. Together the documents clearly show how Joseph served Travis for most of 1834, while remaining Isaac Mansfield's property. Mansfield and Travis likely finalized the rental agreement after Joseph's release from the San Felipe jailer.

17. Brown, *Narrative*, 92–94.

18. Ibid., vii–viii.

19. Ibid., 75, 83.

20. Ibid., viii.

21. Ibid., 92–95.

22. Brown, *Memoir*, 23.

23. Ibid.

24. Brown, *Narrative*, 94–95.

25. Ibid., 98–99.

26. Ibid., 99.

27. Ibid., 100.

28. Ibid., 100–102.

29. Ibid., 102; Brown, *Memoir*, 25.

30. Brown, *Narrative*, 102, 104.

31. Ibid., 103.

32. Ibid., 104.

33. Brown, *Narrative*, 107–108.

34. Robert Gould Shaw letter to Amos A. Lawrence, March 25, 1863, Lawrence Papers, Massachusetts Historical Society, Boston.

35. William once wrote in 1859: "The last tidings that I had of my brothers was, that they had been bought by a planter, and sent to his farm on the Yazoo River. If still living, they are lingering out a miserable existence on a cotton, sugar, or rice plantation, in a part of the country where the life of the slave has no parallel in deeds of atrocity" (Brown, *Memoir*, 10). William had obviously been given false information. At the time of William's escape in January 1834, Joseph and Millford were living in Texas, and he was surely aware that Leander still resided in St. Louis. William never wrote about his mother's two youngest children, William and Elizabeth. Did he know of their existence? If so, why did he remain mum about them?

Chapter 9

1. Filley letter to Filley, July 11, 1830.

2. Mansfield probate.

3. Isaac Mansfield pledge to James Routh, July 31, 1834, miscellaneous documents, Austin County Clerk's Office, Bellville, Texas; Guardian, "David Levi

Kokernot." Kokernot first entered Texas in 1830 after his ship wrecked while reconnoitering smugglers near the Sabine estuary as a commissioned warrant officer for the U.S. Revenue Cutter Service. He moved his family to Anahuac in 1832 and engaged in farming. He also traded goods aboard several boats that plied along the coast and nearby bayous.

4. Mansfield pledge to Routh, July 31, 1834.

5. Mansfield probate.

6. For a superb treatment of slave pens and public auctions, see Johnson, *Soul by Soul*, 162–88.

7. Brown, *Narrative*, 38–61.

8. Ibid., 94–95.

9. Guardian, "David Levi Kokernot"; Mansfield probate.

10. Brown, *The Black Man*, 11–12; John Young's will.

11. Mansfield probate.

12. Ibid.

13. Ibid.

14. Ibid.; Davis, *Travis Diary*, 17.

15. Davis, *Travis Diary*, 100.

16. Ibid., 7.

17. Ibid., 139–140.

18. Mansfield probate.

19. Ibid.

20. John W. Moore bond to detain Elizabeth and her two children, May 28, 1835, miscellaneous documents, Austin County Court Clerk's Office, Bellville, Texas; *Alcance Al Num. 25, Del Noticioso Del Puerto De Matamoras*, March 23, 1831.

21. Howren, "Causes and Origins of the Decree of April 6, 1830," 415–16.

22. Harris, "Almonte's Inspection of Texas in 1834," 196–211. The letter from Mexico's secretary of foreign relations to Juan N. Almonte, dated January 17, 1834, is reportedly housed at the Mexican National Archives in Mexico City.

23. Ibid., 199. The instructions clearly refer to the legalities of a slave who is brought into Texas either under an indentured servitude contract or none whatsoever. On both accounts the decree of April 6, 1830, applies specifically to Joseph and his relatives who entered Texas in June 1832 with Mansfield.

24. Slave concubines were common among white men of early Texas, although recalled with great delicacy by all parties in the years after the Civil War. Many family legends on the subject have been embraced only in recent decades. One tells how Texas pioneer William Scurlock lived with his slave Easter as a concubine. The two are said to have had children together (Soporhia Canton interview). Another such relationship came to public light in 1840, when Adam Smith parted company with Margaret, a black woman whom he had lived with as his wife since 1836. Smith had purchased Margaret as a slave but did not regard her as his property. At the time the two separated, Smith even gave Margaret a paper that read: "The bearer, Margaret, a Negro woman, about thirty years of age, is free and at liberty to go and do the best she can to make an honest

livelihood in the world. Given under my hand this 19th day of March, 1840. Adam Smith." But the manumission was illegal because Smith never received the consent of the Republic of Texas Congress, and Margaret never left the country. Thus, at the time of Smith's death, his administrator claimed Margaret as part of his estate and the matter ended up before the Texas Supreme Court. The high court ruled that since Smith did not consider himself as her master at the time the constitution was adopted, Margaret was to be regarded as a free woman. Harold Schoen, "The Free Negro in the Republic of Texas," 98–99.

25. Howren, "Causes and Origins of the Decree of April 6, 1830," 397–98.

26. Inventory of assets belonging to William Barret Travis estate, William Barret Travis probate, Brazoria County Court Clerk's Office, Angleton, Texas. The document is dated March 30, 1840, and reads: "A Bill of Sale from John Cummings to WB Travis for a Negro man named Joe." No sale price is listed.

27. Mansfield probate; Davis, *Travis Diary*, 17.

28. William Barret Travis letter to David G. Burnet, February 3, 1835, Hassel Family Papers, Center for American History, University of Texas, Austin. Also reproduced in] Jenkins, comp., *The Papers of the Texas Revolution, 1835–1836,* 1:17–18.

29. Ibid.

Chapter 10

1. Gray, *From Virginia to Texas,* 136–37; John Young will; Brown, *The Black Man,* 12.

2. Brown, *The Black Man,* 11.

3. *Telegraph and Texas Register,* May 26, 1837.

4. Ibid. John Rice Jones placed the ad; Mansfield probate.

5. Brown, *Narrative,* cover.

6. Faragher, *Daniel Boone,* 30–31.

7. Gray, *From Virginia to Texas,* 136–37; "The Reminiscences of Mrs. Dilue Harris," 88; *Daily Democratic Statesman* (Austin, Tex.), April 7, 1877.

8. Mixon, "Travis," 83.

9. *Constitutional Advocate & Texas Public Advertiser* (Brazoria, Tex.), July 15, 1832.

10. Davis, *Travis Diary,* 45.

11. Ibid., 53.

12. Travis letter to Burnet, February 6, 1835.

13. On November 15, 1834, Travis hired a slave woman named Malinda to Ira R. Lewis for ten dollar a month on behalf of the Charles Baird estate (Thomas W. Streeter Collection, Beinecke Rare Book and Manuscript Collection, Yale University Library, New Haven, Connecticut); Randall Jones slave sale to Seaborn D. Jones, December 30, 1835, Deed Book A, Fort Bend County Court Clerk's Office, Richmond, Texas.

14. Travis letter to Burnet, February 6, 1835.

15. Davis, *Travis Diary*, 107–109, 125, 138.

16. Ibid., 106.

17. Bill of sale from William Barret Travis to John Rice Jones, May 29, 1835, copy in the Travis File at the Daughters of the Republic of Texas Library, San Antonio.

18. Mixon, "Travis," 60.

19. Davis, *Travis Diary*, 172.

20. Ibid., 169, 171, 174.

21. Ibid., 125.

22. Bill of sale from Eli Holley estate to William Barret Travis, April 16, 1834, copy in the Travis File at the Daughters of the Republic of Texas Library at the Alamo, San Antonio, Texas. Holley died September 9, 1833 (Davis, *Travis Diary*, 21). Davis, *Travis Diary*, 155.

23. Davis, *Travis Diary*, 106, 167; Eli Holley estate bill of sale.

24. The *Travis Diary* is littered with references to Travis's purchases of clothing and material.

25. Kuykendall, *Sketches of Early Texians*, Kuykendall Family Papers, University of Texas, Austin, Texas.

26. B. J. Fletcher letter to Mrs. I. C. Main, May 15, 1907, quoted in Davis, *Travis Diary*, 24. The letter was written as a remembrance of a family story told about their grandfather, Ephraim Roddy.

27. Ibid.; Davis, *Travis Diary* 71.

28. Travis letter to Burnet, February 6, 1835.

29. Davis, *Travis Diary*, 7, 92, 180.

30. Ibid., 182.

31. Ruby Mixon astutely notes this in her 1930 master's thesis "William Barret Travis," 94, 95.

32. Davis, *Travis Diary*, 171.

33. Ibid., 86–88.

34. Celia died October 10, 1841 in San Felipe. An inventory of her estate reveals a sizable amount of property for a Texan of that time period, including two feather beds, a quarter town lot, a dozen plates, one worn trunk, one bay horse, one gray Spanish filly, seven head of cattle, one sow, and five pigs. The property was willed to her minor children, Dollie Ann, Henry, George, Robin (commonly called Bob), and Yarboro (commonly called Sam). The children had inherited the surname of Allen after their mother's former master (Davis, *Travis Diary*, 95–96).

35. Owen, *History of Alabama and Dictionary of Alabama Biography*, 4:1680–81.

36. Davis, *Travis Diary*, 106.

37. Travis family Bible, Texas State Archives, Austin.

38. Clyde Glosson taped interview with Lee Spencer White, March 27, 1999, San Antonio, Texas. Glosson is the great-grandson of Elsie Boone, Dr. Scull's one-time concubine and servant. Elsie was said to have been part Indian and originally from South Carolina before ending up in Alabama with Scull. She

gave birth to Scull's first two children, Emma and Abby, prior to his marriage. Scull gave Elsie four hundred acres at the conclusion of the Civil War—land she later sold to buy a city block in San Antonio. She eventually married and began a new family with man named Richardson. She is is said to have died in either 1915 or 1916 at the age of 107, which would have made her about twenty-three when she traveled to Texas in 1831 with Scull and Travis.

Glosson remembered being around nine years old when he first saw his great-grandmother. His father told him she was dying and that she desired to see her grandchildren before her death. His first reaction upon seeing her was to run, but his father cut off his escape. The elderly woman frightened the young Glosson, who had never seen anyone so old and wrinkled. He noticed that her features were not typically African as she sat in a rocking chair with an apron over her dress, her hair braided on two sides, and smoking a corncob pipe.

Elsie is buried in an unmarked grave in a cemetery on San Antonio's east side.

39. Kuykendall, *Sketches of Early Texians*, Kuykendall Family Papers, Center for American History, University of Texas, Austin.

40. Rosanna E. Travis letter to James Dellett, September 6, 1834, from Natchez, Mississippi, James Dellett Family Papers, Alabama Department of Archives and History, Montgomery.

41. Ibid.

42. Davis, *Three Roads to the Alamo*, 203–204.

43. Last will and testament of William Barret Travis, May 25, 1835, Texas State Archives, Austin. The will is written in the handwriting of Travis's first executor, John Rice Jones, who reportedly made a copy of the original.

44. William Cato probate, Dallas County Court Clerk's office, Selma, Alabama.

45. Passenger and immigration lists from the port of New Orleans for March 16, 1835, aboard the ship *Elizabeth Jane*. National Archives microfilm series No. M259; Kuykendall, *Sketches of Early Texians*, Kuykendall Family Papers, Center for American History, University of Texas, Austin.

46. Kuykendall, *Sketches of Early Texians*, Kuykendall Family Papers, Center for American History, University of Texas, Austin.

Chapter 11

1. Kegans, "Memoirs."
2. Davis, *Travis Diary*, 33; Kegans, "Memoirs."
3. Kegans, "Memoirs."
4. Ibid.
5. Ibid.; Willits, "Almonte's Inspection of Texas in 1834," 199.
6. Ibid.
7. Davis, *Travis Diary*, 8. Travis attended the Holley funeral two days later on September 8, 1833.

8. Kegans, "Memoirs."

9. Davis, *Travis Diary*, 8, 49.

10. "The Reminiscences of Mrs. Dilue Harris," 85–127.

11. Davis, *Travis Diary*, 93, 137, 180.

12. John Henry Brown, *Indian Wars and Pioneers of Texas*, 137.

13. John Henry Brown, *The Encyclopedia of the New West*, 436, 437; Bowie, "Early Life in the Southwest," 378–83.

14. Brown, *Indian Wars and Pioneers of Texas*, 137.

15. Bowie, "Early Life in the Southwest," 379–80.

16. "Memoirs," John S. Ford Papers, ca. 1880s, Center for American History, University of Texas, Austin.

17. Brown, *Indian Wars and Pioneers of Texas*, 137.

18. Bowie, "Early Life in the Southwest," 379–80.

19. Davis, *Three Roads to the Alamo*, 209–18. Davis presents by far the best overall account of the sandbar melee based on primary sources of any historian to date. His account is also framed by the context of the petty feuds that had developed between various participants preceding the incident—a fascinating subject but one too far afield for this work.

Chapter 12

1. Davis, *Travis Diary*, 7, 106; Mary Austin Holley, notes, Austin Papers, University of Texas, Austin.

2. Robert Wilson letter to William Barret Travis, May 13, 1835, Franklin Papers, University of Texas, Austin.

3. Davis, *Three Roads to the Alamo*, 448.

4. Ibid.

5. Robert Wilson letter to William Barret Travis, June 9, 1835, Franklin Papers, Center for American History, University of Texas, Austin.

6. William Barret Travis letter to Henry Smith, July 6, 1835 in John Henry Brown, *Life and Times of Henry Smith*, 60–61.

7. *Texas Republican* (Brazoria), July 18, 1835.

8. William Barret Travis letter to James Bowie, July 30, 1835, copy in the Travis File at Daughters of Republic of Texas Library, San Antonio; Yoakum, *History of Texas*, 1:343.

9. Robert M. Williamson's address at San Felipe, June 22, 1835, in Jenkins, *The Papers of the Texas Revolution*, 1:194.

10. Travis letter to Smith, August 24, 1835; John Henry Brown, *Life and Times of Henry Smith*, 72–73.

11. Stephen F. Austin letter to Mary Austin Holley, August 21, 1835, Austin Papers, Center for American History, University of Texas, Austin.

12. *Texas Republican* (Brazoria), September 19, 1835.

13. Ibid.

14. *Texas Republican* (Brazoria), September 26, 1835.

15. Ibid.

16. William Barret Travis letter to Stephen F. Austin, September 22, 1835, Austin Papers, Center for American History, University of Texas, Austin.

17. "De Witt's Colony," 150–56.

Chapter 13

1. William Barret Travis to Henry Smith, January 28, 1836, Army Papers, Archives Division, Texas State Library, Austin.

2. Ibid., January 29, 1836.

3. Ibid. Travis told Smith, "I am now convinced that none but defensive measures can be pursued at this inclement season." Rodriguez, *Rodriguez Memoirs of Early Texas*, 8. Travis, like others, did not think Mexican president Santa Anna could organize his army and march into Texas so soon after the fall of Bexar in December.

4. Ruby Mixon Papers, Center for American History, University of Texas, Austin; William Brookfield file, Army Military Claims, Texas State Library, Austin; Jesse Burnham [*sic*] claim, Records of the General Council, Box 2–9/18, Texas State Archives, Austin.

5. Lee, "Some Recollections of Two Texas Pioneer Women," 209.

6. Thomas Chadoin file, Army Military Claims, Texas State Library, Austin.

7. "DeWitt's Colony," 150.

8. Muir, *Texas in 1837*, 94.

9. Binkley, ed., *Official Correspondence of the Texas Revolution, 1835–1836*, 1:328.

10. Ibid.

11. Binkley, *Official Correspondence of the Texas Revolution, 1835–1836*, 2:349–51.

12. De Zavala, *History and Legends of the Alamo and Other Missions in and around San Antonio*, 23–25.

13. Ibid.

14. Binkley, *Official Correspondence of the Texas Revolution, 1835–1836*, 2:381–83.

15. Ibid., 2:423–24.

16. "Testimony of Mrs. Hannig touching on the Alamo massacre, Sept. 23, 1876," Adjutant General's Letters Concerning the Alamo, Archives Division, Texas State Library, Austin (hereafter: Susanna Hannig interview, September 23, 1876, Texas State Archives, Austin). In this account, Alamo survivor Susanna (Dickinson) Hannig estimates the wounded to be between "50 and 60" men.

17. Muir, *Texas in 1837*, 98.

Chapter 14

1. Helen Chapman letter to Emily Blair, May 1, 1834, William W. Chapman Papers, Center for American History, University of Texas, Austin.

2. Menchaca, *Memoirs*, 22.

3. *Albany* (New York) *Journal*, December 11, 1835.

4. *Galveston Daily News*, January 27, 1895.

5. *Sunday Morning News* (New York), May 1, 1836.

6. Folmsbee, "Davy Crockett and West Tennessee," 20.

7. *Niles' Weekly Register*, May 3, 1834.

8. Shackford, *David Crockett*, 210–11.

9. Ibid., 212. There is no way of telling when Crockett first uttered these words; there are numerous sources for its usage.

10. *The* (New York) *Sun*, January 29, 1836.

11. *Arkansas Gazette* (Little Rock), May 10, 1836; *The* (New York) *Sun*, May 10, 1836; *Sunday Morning News* (New York), March 27, 1836.

12. David Crockett letter to Wiley and Margaret Flowers, January 9, 1836, copy in Samuel Asbury Papers, Center for American History, University of Texas, Austin.

13. *Telegraph and Texas Register*, April 28, 1838; John Forbes letter to Robinson, January 12, 1836, in Lamar, *The Papers of Mirabeau Buonaparte Lamar*, 1:296.

14. Crockett letter to Wiley and Margaret Flowers, January 9, 1836.

15. Lindley, *Alamo Traces*, 49. Lindley is the first historian to explore Crockett's role as a scout, methodically piecing together documents that together paint a new and exciting portrait of Crockett's experience at the Alamo. See chapter 16 of this book.

16. Swisher, *The Swisher Memoirs*, 18–19.

17. Calvin Jones letter to Edmund D. Jarvis, December 2, 1835, Calvin Jones Papers, Southern Historical Collection, University of North Carolina, Chapel Hill.

18. Menchaca, *Memoirs*, 22.

19. Ibid.

20. Sutherland, *The Fall of the Alamo*, 11–12.

21. Menchaca, *Memoirs*, 22–23.

22. Ibid.

23. Green B. Jameson letter to Henry Smith, February 11, 1836, in Binkley, *Official Correspondence of the Texas Revolution, 1835–1836*, 2:409–10.

24. William Barret Travis letter to Henry Smith, February 12, 1836, in Binkley, *Official Correspondence of the Texas Revolution*, 2:416–417.

25. Ibid.

26. Ibid.

27. James J. Baugh letter to Henry Smith, February 13, 1836, in Binkley, *Correspondence of the Texas Revolution*, 2:421–423.

28. Ibid.

29. William Barret Travis letter to Henry Smith, February 13, 1836, Binkley, *Correspondence of the Texas Revolution*, 2:419–420.

30. William Barret Travis and James Bowie letter to Henry Smith, February 14, 1836, in Binkley, *Correspondence of the Texas Revolution*, 2:425.

31. David P. Cummings letter to father, February 1, 1836, in Jenkins, *The Papers of the Texas Revolution*, 4:333–335.

32. Matovina, *The Alamo Remembered*, 114.

33. Ibid.

34. Lindley, *Alamo Traces*, 140–41. Harmon identifies two of the soldiers that day as Payton Bland and George Evans.

35. Antonio Saez, Texas Rebublic claims file, Texas State Archives, Austin.

36. *San Antonio Express*, April 28, 1881.

37. *Frankfort* (Ky.) *Commonwealth*, May 25, 1836. Joe stated that there were "several Negroes" in the Alamo. Based on the social order of the day, it is only realistic to conclude that Joe likely would have kept company with them whenever relieved of his services by Travis.

38. Hansen, *The Alamo Reader*, 698. For this book, Reuben M. Potter's work will be cited from Hansen's *The Alamo Reader*. Potter's historical narrative, "The Fall of the Alamo," originally appeared in the *Magazine of American History* (January 1878).

39. *New York Herald*, June 21–30, 1836.

Chapter 15

1. Brown, *Narrative*, 14.

2. John Sutherland's "The Alamo," John S. Ford Papers, Center for American History, University of Texas, Austin, 27.

3. Ibid., 25–26.

4. Phillip Dimmit letter to James Kerr, February 28, 1836, in Jenkins, *The Papers of the Texas Revolution*, 4:453.

5. Sutherland's "The Alamo," 27.

6. Ibid., 28–33.

7. Hansen, *The Alamo Reader*, 698.

8. *San Antonio Daily Express*, April 28, 1881.

9. *San Antonio Express*, November 22, 1902.

10. Ibid.

11. Hansen, *The Alamo Reader*, 698.

12. William Barret Travis letter to Andrew Ponton, February 23, 1836, *Telegraph and Texas Register*, February 27, 1836.

13. Foote, *Texas and the Texans*, 2:224.

14. Prior to coming to Texas, Nat Lewis once worked as a whaling man near Nantucket, Massachusetts (*San Antonio Daily Express*, October 23, 1872).

15. *San Antonio Light*, September 1, 1907.

16. The gun salute recalled by Enrique Esparza was likely the same heard by Pablo Diaz, who witnessed the Mexican Army's arrival. In a July 1, 1906, interview with the *San Antonio Express*, Diaz said, "The arrival of Santa Anna was announced by the firing of a gun from in front of the *alcalde's* [mayor's] house."

Chapter 16

1. *San Antonio Express*, July 1, 1906; Jenkins, *The Papers of the Texas Revolution*, 4:414.

2. William Barret Travis letter to Sam Houston, February 25, 1836, *Arkansas Gazette*, April 19, 1836; Bowie letter to commander of the [Mexican] Army of Texas, February 23, 1836, copy in Texas State Archives, Austin, Texas.

3. William B. Travis letter to Andrew Ponton, February 23, 1836, copy in Travis File of the Daughters of Republic of Texas Library, San Antonio; Susanna Hannig interview, Setepmber 23, 1876, Texas State Archives, Austin; Bowie letter to Commander of the [Mexican] Army of Texas, February 23, 1836.

4. *New York Herald*, June 21–30, 1836.

5. Jose Batres letter to James Bowie, February 23, 1836, in Jenkins, *The Papers of the Texas Revolution*, 4:415.

6. *New York Herald*, June 21–30, 1836.

7. Travis letter to the "People of Texas and all Americans in the world," February 24, 1836, copy in the Texas State Archives, Austin, Texas.

8. Ibid.

9. William Barret Travis letter to Samuel Houston, February 25, 1836, copy in Travis File of the Daughters of Republic of Texas Library, San Antonio.

10. *New York Herald*, June 21–30, 1836.

11. Ibid.

12. Travis letter to Houston, February 25, 1836.

13. Roller, "Capt. John Sowers Brooks," 178–80; John Sutherland statement, November 28, 1836, William Brookfield file, Audited Military Claims Collection, Texas State Archives, Austin; Lindley, *Alamo Traces*, 109.

14. James W. Fannin letter to J. W. Robinson, February 25, 1836, in Lamar, *The Papers of Mirabeau Buonaparte Lamar*, 3:338–39.

15. Roller, "Capt. John Sowers Brooks," 178–80.

16. Ibid.

Chapter 17

1. *New York Herald*, June 21–30, 1836.

2. J. C. Neill letter to the Provisional Government, January 28, 1836, in Jenkins, *The Papers of the Texas Revolution*, 4:174–75; Mixon, "William Barret Travis," appendix, 5–6. Both sources show where Travis purchased coffee and sugar for his men.

3. *New York Herald*, June 21–30, 1836.

4. Morphis, *History of Texas*, 174–77.

5. James M. Rose, Court of Claims File C-7115, Archives and Records Division, Texas General Land Office, Austin, deposition of Susanna Belles, formerly Susanna Dickinson, July 16, 1857.

6. Morphis, *History of Texas*, 174–77.

7. Micajah Autry letter to his wife, January 13, 1836, copy in Autry File of the Daughters of the Republic of Texas Library, San Antonio.

8. Micajah Autry letter to his wife, December 7, 1835, copy in Autry File of the Daughters of the Republic of Texas Library, San Antonio.

9. *Malone v. Moran*, case number 3644, Parker County District Court, Weatherford, Texas.

10. Daniel W. Cloud letter to John B. Cloud, December 26, 1835, copy in Cloud File at the Daughters of the Republic of Texas Library, San Antonio. John B. Cloud was Daniel's brother.

11. Ibid.

12. William P. Zuber, "Sketch of Tapley Holland: A Heroe of the Alamo, March 6, 1836," unpublished manuscript, 1910, copy in Tapley Holland File at the Daughters of the Republic of Texas Library in San Antonio. Zuber's sketch begins with a note: "Many of the facts herein stated were known to me at or near the times of their occurrence. For the rest, I am mainly indebted to Mr. Holland's sister, Mrs. Nancy Berryman, who stated them to me in conversation."

13. Brown, *Narrative*, 25–26.

Chapter 18

1. Linda (Halliburton) Tart, telephone interview with Ron Jackson, Luling, Texas, June 26, 1994. Tart used to hear Alamo stories as a child from her great-great-grandmother, Rhoda Elizabeth Kimble Hurt, a granddaughter of George C. Kimble. Tart is Kimble's great-great-great-granddaughter; *Alamo Legacy*, 118–20.

2. Jackson, *Alamo Legacy*, 7.

3. Ibid., 27.

4. Juan Seguín letter to William Winston Fontaine, June 7, 1890, William Winston Fontaine Collection, Center for American History, University of Texas, Austin.

5. Fannin letter to Robinson, February 25, 1836, in Lamar, *The Papers of Mirabeau Buonaparte Lamar*, 3:338–339.

6. James W. Fannin letter to J. W. Robinson, February 27, 1836, in Foote, *Texas and the Texans*, 2:225.

7. Ibid.

8. Gray, *From Virginia to Texas*, 120.

9. Asa Walker letter to John Grant, November 28, 1835, in Lord, *A Time To Stand*, 82–83.

10. *San Antonio Express*, November 22, 1902; *San Antonio Daily Express*, May 12, 1907.

11. *San Antonio Express*, November 22, 1902.

12. In of his book *Duel of Eagles* (225–26), author Jeff Long suggests that Wolfe was "an English Jew who had migrated from London (bound for

'Texsis,' according to synagogue records) and settled in Nacogdoches in 1835. His departure for the New World, with his young sons, Benjamin and Michael, had followed the death of his wife, Sarah." Long leaves no footnote for his source. Since Long's book, however, new information has emerged regarding the likely origins of Wolfe. He reportedly settled in the Louisiana-Texas territory prior to 1818 and worked as an Indian scout and interpreter. On October 6, 1822, Wolfe traveled to Nacogdoches, Texas, where he was introduced by James Dill to Governor Jose Felix Trespalacios. Dill described Wolfe as having been "born a Spanish subject." One month later Wolfe joined Jose Antonio Mexia to treat with the Cherokee nation. See Groneman, "Anthony Wolfe: Tracing an Alamo Defender"; Erickson, comp., *Citizens and Foreigners of the Nacogdoches District*; and Foreman, *Indians and Pioneers*.

13. DeShields, ed., *Tall Men with Long Rifles*, 152–67.

14. Morphis, *History of Texas*, 174–77; Amelia Williams, "A critical study of the siege of the Alamo and of the personnel of its defenders," *Southwestern Historical Quarterly* 37 (July 1932–April 1933): 271.

15. Samuel Bastian account in John Henry Brown, *Indian Wars and Pioneers of Texas*, 138.

Chapter 19

1. "Col. Jas. Butler Bonham," John Henry Brown Papers, Center for American History, University of Texas, Austin. The date and author of this document is unknown, although it was likely written by Milledge Luke Bonham, James's brother. Milledge did correspond with historian John Henry Brown, a historian; "Toasts & Editorials," "by Col. Augustus Maverick, in the Pendleton Messenger," undated, Brown Papers, Center for American History, University of Texas, Austin.

2. "Toasts & Editorials," Brown Papers; Sowell, *Early Settlers and Indian Fighters of Southwest Texas*, 9–10. Sowell's book relates an interview with Alamo courier Benjamin Highsmith. Sowell writes, "Mr. Highsmith sat on his horse on Powderhouse Hill and took in the situation. The Mexican flag was waving from the Church of Bexar across the river, and the flag of Travis from the Alamo. The country was open and nearly all prairie in the valley around San Antonio, and objects could be seen some distance from the elevated points. There was a great stir and perceptible activity in the town, and the forms of some of the doomed men at the Alamo could be plainly seen as from the walls of the fort they watched the Mexican cavalry."

3. "Toasts & Editorials," Brown Papers.

4. James Butler Bonham letter to Samuel Houston, December 31, 1835, Texas State Archives, Austin.

5. Milledge Luke Bonham letter to John Henry Brown, April 1889, Brown Papers, Center for American History, University of Texas, Austin.

6. "Toasts & Editorials," Brown Papers.

7. Ibid.

8. Ibid.

9. R. M. Williamson letter to William Barret Travis, March 1, 1836, Gonzales, *El Nacional* (Mexico City) *Suplemento al Numero 79*, copy in Travis File at the Daughters of the Republic of Texas in San Antonio, Texas.

10. Ibid.

11. Ibid.

12. Susanna Hannig interview, Setepmber 23, 1876, Texas State Archives, Austin; Lindley, *Alamo Traces*, 141–42, 164. Lindley builds a strong case for Crockett's departure, basing the foundation of his case on the Taylor affidavits—James Taylor and Edward Taylor affidavit (copy), March 3, 1836, Cibolo Creek, and J. C. Taylor affidavit (copy), September 6, 1890, Deed Records, 10:203, Montgomery County Court Records, Conroe, Texas; George Taylor affidavit, February 2, 1836, and J. C. Taylor affidavit, August 7, 1890, Deed Records E, Summerville County Court Records, Granbury, Texas; James Taylor, Edward Taylor, and William Taylor affidavit (copy), August 7, 1890, Deed Records, 19:596, Liberty County Court Records, Liberty, Texas.

"The Taylor documents place Crockett on the Cibolo Creek on the night of March 3, 1836," Lindley wrote. "The affidavits claim that Crockett was so sick at the time he could not execute his signature on the document. Thus he signed with an 'X.' Crockett did suffer from malaria. A sudden attack of the illness can be brought by extreme stress, which Crockett would have been under while he was on the Cibolo. If that was the case, he could have experienced shaking chills that would have prevented him from writing his name."

The Taylor affidavits, coupled with Susanna (Hannig) Dickinson's statement to the Adjutant General in 1876 that "Col. Crockett was one of 3 men who came into the Fort during the siege & before the assault," make a compelling case for Crockett's departure and return to the Alamo. The mission also seems in keeping with Crockett's proactive personality. In Crockett's own words, he didn't like being "hemmed up." Susanna Hannig interview, September 23, 1876, Texas State Archives, Austin.

13. Travis letter to Grimes, March 3, 1836; Travis letter to "the president of the convention" (Richard Ellis), March 3, 1836, *Telegraph and Texas Register*, March 12, 1836.

14. Travis letter to Grimes, March 3, 1836.

15. Defender Isaac Millsaps might have produced one of those letters. The Gonzales volunteer had left his wife and children at home, and as he watched the Mexican reinforcements stream into Bexar, he supposedly reflected on his family with the following missive:

My dear dear ones,
We are in the fortress of the Alamo a ruined Church that has most fell down. The Mexicans are here in large numbers they have kept

up a constant fire since we got here. All of our boys are well &
Capt. Martin is in good spirits. Early this morning I watched the
mexcans drilling just out of range they was marching up and
down with such order. they have bright red & blue uniforms and
many canons. Some here at this place believe that the main army
has not come up yet. I think they is all here even Santana. Col.
Bowie is down sick and had to be to bed I saw him yesterday & he
is still ready to fight. He didn't know me from last spring but did
remember Wash. He tells all that help will be here soon & it makes
us feel good. We have beef & corn to eat but no coffee, bag I had
fell off on the way here so it was all spilt. I have not see. Travis but
2 times since here he told us all this morning Fanning was going
to be here early with many men and there would be a good fight.
He stays on the wall some but mostly to his room I hope help
comes soon cause we can't fight them all. Some says he is going to
talk tonight & group us better for defense. If we fail here get to the
river with the children all Texas will be before the enemy we get
so little news here we know nothing. There is no discontent in our
boys some are tired from loss of sleep and rest. The Mexicans are
shooting every few minutes but most of the shots fall inside & do
no harm I don't know what else to say they is call for all letters,
kiss the dear children for me and believe as I do that all will be
well & God protects us all.
Isaac.
If any men come through there tell them to hurry with powder
for it is short I hope you get this & know—I love you all.

The Millsaps letter is dated March 3, 1836, and is presently housed in the
Special Collections of the University of Houston Libraries in Houston, Texas.
The letter has raised serious questions as to whether it was the work of a
forger because it had no known provenance prior to the 1960s. The question of
its authenticity is a valid one. However, the letter does include a number of
details that fit with known events within the Alamo at that time. Regarding
the line that there was a "call for all letters" on March 3, 1836, Travis sent out
three letters that day—to Richard Ellis, Jesse Grimes, and his friend David
Ayers, who was taking care of his son, Charles. In addition, Alamo defender
Willis A. Moore of Raymond, Mississippi, appears to have sent a letter on that
date. His heirs submitted a "Statement of Evidence" to the State of Texas on
September 22, 1856, as proof of Moore's service at the Alamo. Their list of evidence includes a "Letter from W. A. Moore dated San Antonio de Bexar March
3, 1836." (Willis A. Moore, September 22, 1856, Court of Claims File C-5893,
Texas General Land Office, Austin, Texas.) For further reading on this controversy, see Curtis, "Highly Suspect," 109, and Curtis, "Forgery, Texas Style,"
105–108, 178–85.

16. In "Memoirs," John S. Ford Papers, Center for American History, University of Texas, Austin. Ford relates an interview with Alamo survivor Juana Alsbury and writes, "Colonel Bowie was very sick with typhoid fever. For that reason he thought it prudent to be removed from that part of the buildings occupied by Mrs. Alsbury. A couple of soldiers carried him away. On leaving he said: 'Sister, do not be afraid. I leave you with Colonel Travis, Colonel Crockett, and other friends. They are gentlemen and will treat you kindly.' He had himself brought back two or three times to see and talk with her. Their last interview took place three or four days before the fall of the Alamo. She never saw him again, either alive or dead."

Alamo survivor Enrique Espazra recalled in his 1907 interviews with the *San Antonio Express* how "Bowie, although ill and suffering from fever, fought until he was so severely wounded that he had to be carried to his cot, which was placed in one of the smaller rooms on the north side of the church." Bowie was clearly confined to his cot at this time, and forced to rely on others to move him around.

17. *San Antonio Daily Express*, April 28, 1881.

18. Excerpts of testimony for heirs of M. B. Clarke, John Blair, and Marcus Sewell, "Proceedings of the Board of Land Comissioners," Nacogdoches County Clerk's Office, Nacogdoches, Texas. In the testimony, "Lewis Rose" states that he knew Clarke, Blair, and Sewell, and left each man "in the Alamo 3 March 1836." Another supporting document for Rose's escape comes from Susanna Dickinson, who testified for the adjutant general sometime in September of 1877. Dickinson, then Mrs. Hannig, states: "On the evening previous to the massacre, Col. Travis asked the command that if any desired to escape, now was the time, to let it be Known, & to step out of the ranks. But one stepped out. His name to the best of my recollection was Ross. The next morning he was missing." Dickinson may have been referring to Rose. Her statement that this man was "missing" the next morning probably means that Travis's ultimatum to his men was issued on the night of March 5 ("the evening previous to the massacre"). The probability that Dickinson would have known whether this man was present March 6 is highly unlikely given the chaos and carnage of the final battle. Still, her recollection of the Travis speech and of one man stepping from the ranks is consistent with the Rose story.

A recently discovered interview with Dickinson's grandson Almeron Griffith, conducted by Amelia Williams in the 1930s, sheds new light on the Rose story. Griffth remembered as an eight-year-old hearing many war stories about the Texas Revolution from his uncle, H. A. Griffith, and Capt. Frank Dupree. On one ocassion, Dupree told the young Almeron that he had spoken with Rose about his escape from the Alamo. Rose told Dupree that when Travis gave him the chance to leave, he "took it." Rose crawled "400 or 500 yards" outside the Alamo walls in order to slip by the Mexican lines. Dupree, in response, called Rose a "damn, dirty coward." Dupree remembered how the community scorned

Rose for his decision, and how there was talk of "mobbing him"—an atmosphere that caused Rose to "skip out" and leave Texas.

Based on Almeron's testimony, he heard Dupree's Rose story in 1857. This date is important because it predates William P. Zuber's long-debated 1873 article, "An Escape from the Alamo" in the *Texas Almanac*. In the article, Zuber recounts how Rose appeared at his family's house in 1836 with the story of his daring escape from the Alamo. Historians have debated the credibility of the story ever since. In retrospect, as new accounts have surfaced, one should now conclude that the Rose story is indeed true. (Amelia Williams Papers, Center for American History, University of Texas, Austin).

19. *San Antonio Daily Express*, May 12, 1907.

20. William Barret Travis letter to David Ayers, March 3, 1836, copy in Travis File at Daughters of the Republic of Texas Library, San Antonio.

Chapter 20

1. *Arkansas Gazette*, April 12, 1836; Morphis, *History of Texas*, 174–77; Susanna Hannig interview, Setepmber 23, 1876, Texas State Archives, Austin; Borroel, *The Itineraries of the Zapadores and San Luis Battalions*, 15, 18–22. The *Arkansas Gazette* reported: "Col. Crockett, with about 50 resolute volunteers, had cut their way into the garrison, through the Mexican troops only a few days before the fall of San Antonio."

2. *New York Herald*, June 21–30, 1836.

3. Ibid.; *San Antonio Daily Express*, May 12, 1907.

4. *New York Herald*, June 21–30, 1836.

5. *Frankfort* (Ky.) *Commonwealth*, May 25, 1836.

6. *Fort Worth Star-Telegram*, February 28, 1932.

7. *San Francisco Call*, March 4, 1900.

8. "Col. Jas. Butler Bonham," Brown Papers.

9. T. H. McGregor letter to Ed Kilman, January 21, 1942, Louis Wiltz Kemp Papers, Center for American History, University of Texas, Austin.

10. The Yturri house site is at the northeast corner of Commerce and Main Streets in downtown San Antonio.

11. Newell, *History of the Revolution in Texas*, 87–89. Biographical details on Ben Harris can also be gleaned from "Documents of the Texas Revolution," *Alamo Journal* 142 (September 2006).

Chapter 21

1. Peña, *With Santa Anna in Texas*, 46, 47. The authenticity of the Peña "diary" has been debated since its publication in 1975, primarily based on one paragraph that describes Crockett's death as an execution. We believe that the Peña account

is authentic, although it was clearly pieced together over several years before reaching its final form. Were sections of the "diary" added later by those seeking to profit from the manuscript's sale? Perhaps. To think this type of thing doesn't occur in the market of rare documents would be naïve. So the account should be critically analyzed. In the end, it's up to each historian to determine what is a reliable source.

2. Santos, *Santa Anna's Campaign against Texas*, 36.

3. *El Mosquito Mexicano*, April 5, 1836. Letter dated March 7, 1836, from an anonymous Mexican soldier to "Dear brothers of my heart"; Peña, *With Santa Anna in Texas*, 48.

4. Stiff, *The Texan Emigrant*, 313–15.

5. Hansen, ed., *Alamo Reader*, 92.

6. Peña, *With Santa Anna in Texas*, 47.

7. *Frankfort* (Ky.) *Commonwealth*, May 25, 1836. This newspaper article is the most detailed of those published at the time that relate Joe's account. The source of the article is likely William Fairfax Gray, heard the Alamo saga for the first time from Joe at Washington-on-the-Brazos.

8. Peña, *With Santa Anna in Texas*, 423.

9. Hansen, ed., *Alamo Reader*, 392.

10. Ibid., 392; *San Antonio Express*, April 12, 1896.

11. *Frankfort* (Ky.) *Commonwealth*, May 25, 1836.

12. Ibid.

13. Francisco Becerra's 1875 interview can be found in the John S. Ford Papers, Center for American History, Austin, Texas. Becerra's account is another that should be examined with a critical eye. Most of Becerra's remembrances seem genuine and carry a ring of truth, although there are clearly some concerns that can't be ignored. His recollections of Travis and Crockett being executed at the same time are as disturbing as they are false, yet there are other elements of his story that appear to be those of an eyewitness to the Alamo battle. Becerra's account is also delivered with some humility. Unlike most storytellers, he doesn't place himself in a heroic role. We have studied Becerra's account carefully and sifted through what we think is valid and what is not.

14. Peña, *With Santa Anna in Texas*, 49; Hansen, *Alamo Reader*, 439.

15. *San Antonio Daily Express*, June 30, 1889.

16. Francisco Becerra interview, John S. Ford Papers, Center for American History, University of Texas, Austin.

17. Peña, *With Santa Anna in Texas*, 51.

18. DeShields, *Tall Men with Long Rifles*, 152–67. As with the Peña "diary" and Becerra account, the reliability of the Soldana account has been debated. Soldana's recollections of battle are clear and authentic, while other parts of his account seem colored by an active imagination or the active imagination of his chronicler. Some historians like Lindley discarded *Tall Men with Long Rifles* completely, while others like Stephen L. Hardin have cited the book. Hardin used

the book when writing *Texian Illiad: A Military History of the Texas Revolution, 1835–1836* (Austin: University of Texas Press, 1994), which remains a solid overview of the Texas Revolution. Every source should be scrutinized, and most sources are problematic somehow. But if one discards every prospective source with issues, then what is left? This is the challenge each historian faces. We have therefore sifted through the Soldana account and used what we believe to be the most genuine passages of his account.

19. Francisco Becerra interview, John S. Ford Papers, Center for American History, University of Texas, Austin.

20. Ibid.

21. "Mrs. Alsbury's Recollections of the Alamo," ca. 1880s, John S. Ford Papers, Center for American History, University of Texas, Austin.

22. Ibid.; Juana Alsbury oral tradition related by her son, Alejo Perez, Jr. (Folder 3, Descendants of Gregorio Esparza, Adina Emilia de Zavala Papers, Center for American History, University of Texas, Austin).

23. *San Antonio Daily Express*, April 28, 1881.

24. Morphis, *History of Texas*, 174–77; John E. Elgin, "Reminiscences of the Story of the Alamo," September 23, 1936, typed manuscript in Adina Emilia de Zavala Papers, Center for American History, University of Texas, Austin.

25. *San Antonio Express News*, February 24, 1929.

26. *San Antonio Daily Express*, April 28, 1881; *Port Gibson* (Miss.) *Correspondence*, April 23, 1836. Copy in the Samuel Asbury papers at the Center for American History, University of Texas, Austin.

27. Morphis, *History of Texas*, 174–77; *Frankfort* (Ky.) *Commonwealth*, May 25, 1836.

28. *El Mosquito Mexicano*, April 5, 1836. A July 19, 1838, article in the *Pennsylvanian* reported that Almonte told him Bowie was "sick and helpless, and was butchered in bed." Mexican captain José Juan Sanchez-Navarro noted in his journal that "Buy [Bowie], the braggart son-in-law of Beramendi [died] like a coward." (Jose Sanchez-Navarro Papers, Center for American History, University of Texas, Austin.)

29. Hansen, *The Alamo Reader*, 703. In Hansen, Reuben Potter refers to the Texian as "Lieutenant Dickenson," which might be true. If so, the child was not Dickinson's. Angelina Dickinson, then an infant, survived the battle with her mother, Susanna. Potter received his information from Mexican sergeant Francisco Becerra, who claimed to have witnessed the valiant act. But Becerra never identifies the Texian by name. Susanna might have identified the Texian when she recounted, "During the final engagement one Milton [Eliel Melton], jumped over the ramparts & was killed" (Susanna Hannig interview, September 23, 1876, Texas State Archives, Austin). As for the identity of the child, that may never be known.

30. Ibid. Potter concluded that the powder was probably stored in one of the vaulted rooms on the north side of the chapel.

31. Deposition, July 30, 1858, Court of Claims Filed, Texas Land Office, Voucher No. 8490. This document claims Warnell made his escape to Port La Vaca, where he died of his wounds "less than three months" after the March 6, 1836, battle. Court of Claims Voucher No. 1579, File (S-Z) states that Warnell was sent from the Alamo with a message, succeeded in carrying his message to Houston, and died a few weeks later from his wounds. Warnell had participated in the storming of Bexar and remained in the Alamo as part of Capt. William Carey's artillery company.

32. *San Antonio Daily Express*, May 12, 1907.

33. *San Antonio Express*, November 22, 1902.

34. *San Antonio Daily Express*, May 12, 1907.

35. Ibid.; Pension Claim no. 996, November 2, 1874, Texas State Archives, Austin. Other combatants purportedly survived the Alamo battle. An article that appeared in the March 29, 1836 *Arkansas Gazette* also offers another intriguing possibility. The article states:

> LATER—*San Antonio re-taken, and the Garrison Massacred*—Just as our paper was ready for press, a gentleman who arrived this morning, from Red River, informs us that, on Thursday night last, he spent the night, on the Little Missouri, with a man and his family, who had fled from the vicinity of San Antonio, after that post was besieged by the Mexicans. This man, he says, informed him, that, on his arrival to Nacogdoches, he was overtaken by two men (one of them badly wounded), who informed him that San Antonio was re-taken by the Mexicans, and the garrison put to the sword—that, if any others escaped the general massacre, besides themselves, they were not aware of it.
>
> We give the above report, precisely as it was communicated to us by our informant, who was recently a citizen of this country, and is a man of veracity. We hope it may be unfounded—but fear that our next accounts from that quarter will confirm it.

The strangest survival account comes from Mexican sergeant Francisco Becerra, who relates a story told to him by ex-Brownsville mayor William Neale sometime prior to 1878. Neale reportedly told Becerra about a Texian who had hid "among some saddles and rubbish" and was overlooked by the Mexican troops. The man slipped out of the Alamo undetected and made his escape. Neale described the man as a German by birth and claimed he lived in Matamoros for years and gave lessons in fencing. The man was known as an "expert swordsman," a skill he apparently didn't put to good use if he were indeed part of the Alamo garrison. (Francisco Becerra interview, John S. Ford Papers, Center for American History, University of Texas, Austin.)

36. Francisco Becerra interview, John S. Ford Papers, Center for American History, University of Texas, Austin. William Neale (see note 35) told Becerra the account of Charlie and Bettie. Neale noted that Bettie had left with the

Mexican troops after the fall of the Alamo, presenting herself as Bowie's cook. She later took a job with Neale and remained in his service for the next "year or two." During that time she often recounted tales of the Alamo battle. When war vessels were spotted cruising near the mouth of the Rio Grande, Neale said Bettie became frightened that she would be carried back to Texas and fled to Monterrey where he lost contact with her. Bettie, however, might have returned to San Antonio. Was she the "old negro woman" whom one American soldier encountered in San Antonio in 1846? "The old Negro woman is the only being now living who can tell a true tale of the Alamo," the soldier writes. "She can hardly ever be prevailed upon to tell it, and when she does she weeps and trembles like a child" (*Green Bay (Wisconsin) Advocate*, November 12, 1846).

37. Morphis, *History of Texas*, 174–77.

38. *Galveston Daily News*, June 4, 1911.

39. Ibid.; Sutherland, *The Fall of the Alamo*, 138–58; Asbury papers.

40. *Frankfort* (Ky.) *Commonwealth*, May 25, 1836.

41. Ibid.; Gray, *From Virginia to Texas*, 136–42.

42. *Frankfort* (Ky.) *Commonwealth*, May 25, 1836.

43. Peña, *With Santa Anna in Texas*, 116; Gray, *From Virginia to Texas*, 136–42; Sutherland, *The Fall of the Alamo*, 138–58; Asbury papers.

44. Sutherland, *The Fall of the Alamo*, 138–58.

45. For the time of the battle, see Dubravsky "Alamo Timetable." Dubravsky convincingly argues that sunrise on March 6, 1836 would have been at 6:09 A.M., some forty-five minutes earlier than a present-day sunrise in San Antonio. Since several eyewitnesses stated that the battle commenced sometime between 5:00 and 5:30 A.M. and took over an hour, it's highly probably that plenty of fighting took place in the morning light.

46. *San Antonio Daily Express*, May 12, 1836.

47. *Frankfort* (Ky.) *Commonwealth*, May 25, 1836. The dead woman Joe saw may have been with Alamo defender Patrick Henry Herndon, a thirty-four-year-old Virginian who was being sued in 1831 by Ezekiel Hays of New Orleans. Hays claimed Herndon ran off to Texas with his female slave, Sarah. There were, in fact, several slaves within the Alamo compound at the time of the siege and battle. Joe stated so himself. This fact should not be surprising. A number of slaveowners died at the Alamo, including William Barret Travis, James Bowie, David Crockett, Micajah Autry, William Carey, Mial Scurlock, and Thomas R. Miller, among others.

Travis (Joe) and Bowie (Bettie) brought slaves with them into the Alamo. But any of the other slaveowners were also capable of being accompanied by a servant, as was the custom of the times. Carey likely did. Moses Carey, William's father, petitioned the Republic of Texas in 1839 on behalf of his son's estate. The elder Carey filed a claim for one "private servant," requesting the compensation of $64 in losses. Was this servant the brawny Charlie? Or some other unknown slave?

Bowie may have had more than one servant at the Alamo. Writer Andrew Jackson Sowell noted a Bowie slave named Jim in his 1900 book *Early Settlers and Indian Fighters of the Southwest*. Sowell reported that "this negro lived for many years after the death of Colonel Bowie at the Alamo, and went by the name of 'Black Jim Bowie.'" Was "Black Jim Bowie" an occupant of the Alamo garrison? Or had he been he left behind with Bowie's relatives (the Veramendis) in Bexar?

48. Sutherland, *The Fall of the Alamo*, 138–58.

49. *The Frankfort* (Ky.) *Commonwealth*, May 25, 1836; Gray, *From Virginia to Texas*, 136–42; *Niles' Weekly Register*, June 25, 1836.

50. *Niles' Weekly Register*, June 25, 1836.

51. Sutherland, *The Fall of the Alamo*, 138–58.

52. Ibid.; Gray, *From Virginia to Texas*, 136–42.

53. *Galveston Daily News*, June 4, 1911; *Galveston Daily News*, January 21, 1905; Morphis. *History of Texas*, 174–77. Crockett's death has stirred more controversy than any other aspect of the Alamo battle over the years. The long-standing debate centers on whether Crockett died fighting to the end or surrendered before being executed. As Todd Hansen so aptly stated in his analysis of Crockett's death in *The Alamo Reader*, "The sources themselves are more divergent on this topic than most and can support any of these versions." There is also a thin line between "surrender" and "capture." If Crockett were indeed one of the last defenders standing when taken prisoner, did those present— Crockett and his Mexican captors—see the futility of another death? If so, was Crockett captured or did he surrender? Regardless, some people have attached shame to this scenario, suggesting Crockett was somehow a coward for not fighting to the death. Crockett's actions prior to the final battle were those of a bona fide hero. In his February 25, 1836, letter, Travis states that Crockett "was seen at all points, animating the men to do their duty" during an attack by the Mexican soldiers. There is also evidence from more than one source that Crockett "slashed" his way back into the Alamo days before the final assault with reinforcements. These are certainly not the actions of a coward. We will probably never know with certainty how Crockett died. This debate will therefore rage for as long as people discuss the Alamo. For further reading on this subject, see Kilgore, *How Did Davy Die?*; Groneman *Defense of a Legend*; and Crisp, *Sleuthing the Alamo*.

54. Labadie, ed., "Urissa's Account."

Chapter 22

1. *San Antonio Express*, July 1, 1906; *San Antonio Express*, April 19, 1914; *San Antonio Express*, March 26, 1911. Tejano Juan Antonio Chavez, a boy at the time of the battle, recalled how his father removed his family from Bexar at the time of the siege. The family returned months later. "When we returned the bodies of those that had perished in the Alamo were still burning on two immense

pyres on the old Alameda," Chavez recalled in a 1914 interview with the *San Antonio Express*. "I went to look at them and the sight indelibly impressed itself upon my memory. One pyre occupied a position on the site of where the new Halff building is. The other was diagonally across the street on what is now known as the lawn of the Ludlow House and the recently built house adjoining it on the east. The bodies burned for several days and wood and tallow fuel used for consuming them was frequently replenished. I made several trips to the scene, which so fascinated me I could not stay away until all the bodies had been consumed. They were all reduced to ashes except a few charred heads, arms, and legs that were scattered about. These were all gathered up and placed in a shallow grave where the Ludlow House lawn now is." A historical marker erected by the Alamo Defenders' Descendants Association marks the location of the two funeral pyres today on Commerce Street.

2. *San Antonio Express*, July 1, 1906.

3. Morphis, *History of Texas*, 174–77; *San Antonio Light*, November 10, 1901; *San Antonio Express*, November 22, 1902. Known noncombatant survivors include Susanna Dickinson and her infant daughter, Angelina; Anna Esparza and her children Maria de Jesus Castro (ten), Enrique Esparza (eight), Manuel Esparza (five), and Francisco Esparza (three); Juana Alsbury, her sister Gertrudis Navarro, and her infant son, Alejo Perez, Jr.; Concepcion Losoya and her son, Juan; Juana (Losoya) Melton; Victoriana de Salinas and her three daughters; Trinidad Sauceda; Petra Gonzales; Bettie (Bowie's slave); and Charlie (a slave). Andrea Castanon de Villanueva may have also been a survivor, although her claim has often been thought false. (*San Antonio Light*, November 22, 1901; *San Antonio Daily Express*, May 12, 1907.) As for Villanueva's claim, perhaps Juana Alsbury summed it up best when she said, "There were people in the Alamo I did not see" ("Mrs. Alsbury's Recollections of the Alamo," John S. Ford Papers, Center for American History, University of Texas, Austin).

4. *Frankfort* (Ky.) *Commonwealth*, May 25, 1836; Gray, *From Virginia to Texas*, 136–142.

5. Ibid. One unidentified Mexican soldier later wrote, "The Most Excellent Sr. President made a beautiful speech to the entire division inside the Alamo, in sight of the enemy dead, and he has been pleased with everyone's performance" (*El Mosquito Mexicano*, April 5, 1836).

6. *Frankfort* (Ky.) *Commonwealth*, May 25, 1836.

7. *San Francisco Call*, March 4, 1900.

8. Ibid.

9. Ibid.

10. *San Antonio Express*, May 19, 1907.

11. Ibid., February 24, 1929; *Huron Reflector* (Norwalk, Ohio), May 3, 1836.

12. *San Antonio Daily Express*, May 19, 1907.

13. Susanna Hannig interview, September 23, 1876, Texas State Archives, Austin.

14. *San Antonio Express*, March 26, 1911.

15. *San Antonio Express News*, February 24, 1929; Kemp Papers, Center for American History, University of Texas, Austin.

16. *San Antonio Daily Express*, April 28, 1881. This is where Joe would be when Susanna Dickinson met him. The account states, "After leaving on the horse, she [Susanna] proceeded a short distance beyond the Salado, when she met with Travis' servant, who had escaped from the guard and was lurking in the brush."

17. *Galveston Daily News*, April 21, 1894.

18. *San Antonio Express*, February 24, 1929.

19. Ibid.; *San Antonio Daily Express*, April 28, 1881.

20. Jenkins, ed., *Recollections of Early Texas*, 37.

21. Texas State Archives, Austin.

22. Samuel Houston letter to James Fannin, March 11, 1836, A. J. Houston Collection, Texas State Archives, Austin.

23. Carrington, ed., *Women in Early Texas*, 75. The story of Susanna's arrival at the home of Sarah Nash is based on oral tradition, and, according to the story, Susanna arrived at home of "Sarah and John Bruno." Historians have been unable to find land documents with the Bruno name on the old Gonzales-Bexar Road, and for good reason. They don't exist. As with most oral traditions, facts sometimes become altered as the story is handed down from one generation to the next. Here are the facts: The home Susanna and Joe stopped at that night belonged to Prudence and George Kimble. Prudence married George after losing her first husband, Ira Nash, who was killed by Indians (Caldwell County Clerk's Office, Lockhart, Texas, Ira Nash Probate, Deed Book B). Nash left behind his fifteen-year-old daughter, Sarah. On June 30, 1836, Sarah Nash married Littleton Tumlinson, brother of Alamo defender George Tumlinson (Washington County Court Clerk's Office, Brenham, Texas, Marriage Records). She later married George C. Bruner—not "Bruno"—February 5, 1837, and it's from this line that the oral tradition likely survived (Gonzales County Records, Texas State Archives, Austin).

24. *San Antonio Daily Express*, April 28, 1881.

25. Connell O'Donnell Kelly letters concerning his service in the Texas Revolution. Reprinted in the *San Francisco Examiner*, date unknown, copy in author's collection.

26. *San Antonio Express*, February 24, 1929.

27. *New York Daily Tribune*, November 24, 1842.

28. Jenkins, *Recollections of Early Texas*, 37.

29. Foote, *Texas and the Texans*, 2:268.

30. DeShields, *Tall Men with Long Rifles*, 129–30.

Chapter 23

1. Gray, *From Virginia to Texas*, 135.

2. Ibid., 108, 135–36.

3. Ibid., 136.

4. Ibid., 136–37.

5. Sutherland, "The Alamo."

6. Gray, *From Virginia to Texas*, 137.

7. Ibid. Unlike Crockett, many Alamo defenders died in anonymity. The case of John Jones is probably more common than not. Jone's relatives traced his travels through his letters after he left home in 1835. Then the letters stopped. The family eventually traced John into Texas where the trail turned cold. Decades passed and the family mystery lingered. Finally, in 1896, Albert Jones—John's nephew—was reading a newspaper article about the new Alamo monument. He stopped reading when he saw the name "John Jones" listed among the Alamo's heroes. He promptly wrote a letter to the State of Texas, inquiring about the John Jones listed on the monument and discovered that this was indeed his uncle (*The News* (Frederick, Md.), July 10, 1896).

8. Gray, *From Virginia to Texas*, 137.

9. Taylor, *The Cavalcade of Jackson County*, 80.

10. Gormanous, *The Milsaps Family*, 12. Story is repeated in Jackson, *Alamo Legacy*, 133; Millsaps letter to "My dear dear ones," March 3, 1836, University of Houston Libraries, Special Collection, Houston, Texas.

11. Sam Houston letter to James Collinsworth, March 15, 1836, in *The Writings of Sam Houston, 1813–1863*, 1:373–75.

12. Ibid.

13. Helm, *Scraps of Early Texas History*, 56.

14. *Telegraph and Texas Register*, March 24, 1836.

15. Sam Houston letter to Thomas J. Rusk, March 23, 1836, in Jenkins, *The Papers of the Texas Revolution*, 5:168–69.

16. *New York Evening Star*, circa 1836, newspaper clipping in author's collection.

17. Ibid.

18. [Coleman], *Houston Displayed*, 13.

19. Josephus Sommerville Irvine letter to the editor, 1876, Kemp Papers, Center for American History, University of Texas, Austin.

20. [Coleman], *Houston Displayed*, 28.

21. Gray, *From Virginia to Texas*, 170.

22. Taylor, *The Calvalcade of Jackson County*.

23. Ibid.

Chapter 24

1. John Rice Jones ledger, Daughters of the Republic of Texas Library, San Antonio; John Rice Jones letters, Texas State Archives, Austin. Joe's services cost Holtzclaw and Cartwell fourteen dollars.

2. *B. W. Holtzclaw v. Henry R. Cartwell*, civil lawsuit, Washington County Court Clerk's Office, Brenham, Texas.

3. McLean, ed., *Papers concerning Robertson's Colony in Texas*, 444.

4. James, *The Life of Andrew Jackson*, 628.

5. Ibid., 677; McLean, ed., *Papers concerning Robertson's Colony in Texas*, 443.

6. McLean, ed., *Papers concerning Robertson's Colony in Texas*, 200.

7. Jones ledger.

8. Ibid.

9. William Cato probate, Brazoria County Court Clerk's Office, Angleton, Texas. Cato's inventory consisted of a note from Henry Austin for $4,466.66, one gold watch ($150), and two accounts paid against Travis's debts totaling nearly $1,900.

10. Jones ledger; Roell, "Sayre, Charles D."

11. Jones ledger.

12. Newspaper clipping, Sam Houston File, the Daughters of Republic of Texas Library, San Antonio.

13. Jones ledger.

14. Newspaper clipping, Sam Houston File, the Daughters of Republic of Texas Library, San Antonio.

15. *Telegraph and Texas Register*, May 26, 1837; Jones ledger.

16. Ibid.

17. Jones ledger.

18. *Telegraph and Texas Register*, May 26, 1837.

19. Jones ledger.

20. Ibid.

21. Jones letter to "My Dearly Loved Children," September 23, 1837, Jones letters.

22. Jones ledger.

23. Ibid.

24. Travis letter to Ayers, March 3, 1836.

Chapter 25

1. Riley, *Makers and Romance of Alabama History*, 96.

2. William Letford, *The Story of William B. Travis as Told by Phillip Alexander Travis*, in William Barret Travis, Surname File, Alabama Department of Archives and History, Montgomery.

3. Riley, *Makers and Romance of Alabama History*, 97.

4. Ibid.

5. Waters, *History of Escambia County, Alabama*, 203; "Descendants of Barret Travis," genealogy, private collection of W. B. Travis, Jr., Brewton, Alabama, a great-grandson of Nicholas Travis.

6. For more information on this subject, see Franklin and Schweninger's masterful *Runaway Slaves: Rebels on the Plantation*.

7. Official State Historical Marker, Shankleville, Texas. The story is that of Jim and Winnie Shankle.

8. "William Barret Travis," unpublished manuscript by Fannie McGuire, Alabama Department of Archives and History, Montgomery. McGuire compiled her manuscript in 1926 and revised it in 1936. In doing her research, she corresponded with William's nephew, Mark A. Travis, who related several Travis family stories.

9. Muir, *Texas in 1837*, 125–26.

10. Ibid., 65.

11. Muir, *Texas in 1837*, 13.

12. Crete, *Daily Life in Louisiana, 1815–1830*, 274. By early April, they would have sown cottonseeds, and within two weeks those young plants would have sprouted from the black clay soil. Flowering occurred in June, and by August the capsules would burst open, revealing the fluffy white tufts that were the focal point of every plantation owner. Slaves were kept busy during the entire process.

13. Buchanan, *Black Life on the Mississippi*, 102, 106–107. Those words were spoken by former slave John P. Parker.

14. Ibid., 105.

15. Franklin and Schweninger, *Runaway Slaves*, 157.

16. Daisy M. Burnett letter to Edward Leigh McMillan, undated 1936, McMillan Archives, Brewton, Alabama. Burnett related tidbits about Joe she had heard from James Travis, William's youngest brother and a man who knew Joe personally. Burnett wrote of Joe's journey: "This Negro claimed to have . . . had to swim the Mississippi River."

17. For more information on early Mississippi and Louisiana railroads, see "Railroad History of Lines Located in Mississippi."

18. McLemore, ed., *A History of Mississippi, Volume 1*, 269.

19. Libby, *Slavery and Frontier Mississippi, 1720–1835*, 65.

20. McLemore, ed., *A History of Mississippi*, 326.

21. Ibid., 9.

22. Ibid., 330.

23. Ibid., 9.

24. McGuire, "William Barret Travis," Alabama Department of Archives and History, Montgomery.

25. Denson, *Slavery Laws in Alabama*, 12.

26. Posey, ed., "Alabama in the 1830s as Recorded by British Travelers," 22, 26.

27. Sub Rosa, *Scenes and Settlers of Alabama*, 17.

28. Harvey H. Jackson, *Rivers of History*, 66.

29. Waters, *History of Escambia County, Alabama*, 203. Waters first learned of Joe's arrival at the Nicholas Travis farm in interviews with Nicholas Travis descendant Herman Jordan and Nellie Travis, wife of Walter B. Travis, Sr. (a grandson of Nicholas). Walter was the son of John Dixon Travis, Nicholas's ninth and last child. Nellie Travis, fondly called "Granny Travis," frequently told stories about the Travis family history.

30. Ibid. "Descendants of Barret Travis," copy in author's collection. Mary Travis would give birth to Sarah Stallworth August 11, 1838. At the time, Nicholas and Mary had two children: Martha Jane (eight) and Mary Ann (two). A third child, Nancy Elizabeth, appears to have died at childbirth, August 22, 1832.

31. Burnett letter to McMillan. Burnett wrote, "After the Alamo incident a negro showed up around here, claiming to have been in the Alamo." Burnett heard Joe's story from James Travis, William's youngest brother. James was about nine years old at the time of Joe's arrival in Conecuh County.

32. *Montogomery Advertiser*, February 4, 1905; *Dothan (Ala.) Morning News*, August 30, 1914; *Dallas Morning News*, September 8, 1929.

33. *Dothan* (Ala.) *Morning News*, August 30, 1914.

34. Burnett letter to McMillan; McGuire, "William Barret Travis," Alabama Department of Archives and History, Montgomery.

35. See afterword.

Chapter 26

1. Burnett letter to McMillan.

2. *Montgomery Advertiser*, February 4, 1905.

3. Ibid.; *Dothan* (Ala.) *Morning News*, August 30, 1914; Waters, *History of Escambia County Alabama*; Burnett letter to McMillan.

4. *New York Sun*, December 5, 1883. A man who identified himself only as "E. N. H" and "a child of Mission Refugio" claimed to have "often talked" with Alamo survivors Susanna Dickinson, her daughter Angelina, and Joe about the Alamo battle.

5. *New Castle* (Pa.) *News*, June 25, 1915.

6. United States Census of 1840, Monroe County, Alabama.

7. Orphan Court Orders, Book I (1833–1854), Court Clerk's Office, Monroe County, Alabama.

8. "Descendants of Barret Travis," copy in author's collection; Brown, *Narrative*, 96–97.

9. Ibid., 31; Brown, *Memoir*, 4.

10. *Statesman* (Austin, Tex.), April 7, 1877.

11. Mixon Papers, Center for American History, University of Texas, Austin; *Galveston Daily News*, November 4, 1883. The Galveston newspaper wrote the following:

> The Austin Statesman not only keeps alive the race of intelligent old colored men who knew George Washington, but improves on them. It finds that the last survivor of the massacre of the Alamo is also a relic of the American Revolution, and a prodigy in the matter of memory. That paper says:

Austin undoubtedly has the oldest negro in the State, and we doubt if there are any older than he in the United States. He was born in 1777, and is therefore 106 years old. He goes by the name of John Hannig, and was the property of Mrs. Hannig, of Alamo fame. He has a clear recollection of General Washington, and can give a clear account of his re-election to the presidency of the United States. He can faintly call to mind the stirring struggle for independence, and the superb patriotism of the revolutionary fathers, one of whom was then his master. He remembers with more distinctness the surrender of the British forces.

This took place in 1781, and shows not only a retentive memory, but a good deal of intelligence in a four-year-old darky to know so much. Four-year-old white boys of the present day are not so smart.

12. *Cleveland Plain Dealer*, Septmber 23, 1883.

13. *Frankfort* (Ky.) *Commonwealth*, May 25, 1836.

14. See Brown, *Narrative*; Farrison, *William Wells Brown*; and Ripley, ed., *The Black Abolitionist Papers*. William's oldest daughter was named Clarissa. Josephine and Clarissa were both last known to be living in Europe.

15. *San Antonio Daily Express*, Janurary 19, 1888.

16. Ibid.

17. Ibid.

18. Mixon Papers, Center for American History, University of Texas, Austin; *Dallas Morning News*, September 8, 1929; Waters, *History of Escambia County, Alabama*, 203. A tantalizingly brief mention of Joe having children living in Alabama is mentioned in the 1929 *Dallas Morning News* article. We have little doubt that Joe fathered children or that they were still living in the Brewton, Alabama area well into the twentieth century. Odds are that his descendants still reside in the region today, although they may not know their family history or think anyone outside the family would care. We have made attempts to locate Joe's descendants with searches of census records, probates, death certificates, funeral home records, old newspapers, and even with the placement of a notice in a local newspaper.

19. Waters, *History of Escambia County, Alabama*, 203.

20. McGuire, "William Barret Travis," Alabama Department of Archives and History, Montgomery. McGuire writes that Mark Travis, James Calloway Travis's son, told her in a letter that Joe was buried six miles south of Evergreen, Alabama. The old Travis homestead—Jay Villa—and Travis family cemetery are located six miles south of Evergreen. A search for Joe's grave yielded no results, but there are many unmarked graves. Slaves and whites alike are buried in the cemetery.

Afterword

1. Raymond Lynn telephone interview with Ron Jackson, November 3, 2000. Lynn said he was a child when he heard Ben Riley tell Alamo stories to neighborhood children.

2. Ibid.

3. Ben Riley certificate of death, Escambia County Health Department, Brewton, Alabama.

4. United States Census of 1840, Monroe County, Alabama.

5. Whicker, *Historical Sketches of the Wabash Valley.* Originally Whicker's stories were published in the *Attica (Ind.) Ledger.*

6. Ibid.

7. United States Census of 1880, Fountain County, Indiana. Moore is shown with wife, Julia (thirty-six), and children Ben (thirteen), Nancy (seven), Shannon (six), Anna (four), Bob (two), and George (four months). Only Ben is shown as being born in Kentucky (1867).

8. Joe E. Leonard, Sr., interview with Ron Jackson, Austin, Texas, March 6, 1999.

9. Joe E. Leonard, Sr., telephone interview with Ron Jackson, March 10, 1999.

10. Joe E. Leonard, Jr. telephone interview with Ron Jackson, March 10, 1999.

11. In the July 20, 1924, issue of the *San Antonio Express* a small headline proclaims, "Sole Male Survivor of Alamo a Fugitive." A researcher had discovered the long-forgotten May 21, 1837, runaway ad about Joe and presented a copy to the Texas State Library.

BIBLIOGRAPHY

Primary Sources

Archival Collections

Alabama Department of Archives and History, Montgomery, Alabama
 Dellett Family. Papers.
 McGuire, Fannie. Papers.
 Travis, William Barret. Surname File.
Beinecke Rare Books and Manuscript Collection, Yale University Library, New Haven,
 Connecticut
 Streeter, Thomas W. Papers.
Center for American History, University of Texas, Austin
 Asbury, Samuel. Papers.
 Austin, Stephen F. Papers.
 Barker, Eugene C. Papers.
 Bexar Archives.
 Brooks, John Sowers. Letters.
 Brown, John Henry. Papers.
 Bryan, Moses A. Papers.
 Chapman, William W. Papers.
 De Zavala, Adina. Papers.
 Fontaine, William Winston. Papers.
 Ford, John S. Papers.
 Franklin, Benjamin C. Papers.
 Hassel Family. Papers.
 Holley, Mary Austin. Papers.

Jenkins, John H. Reminiscences.
Kemp, Louis Wiltz. Papers.
Kuykendall Family. Papers.
Mixon, Ruby. Papers.
Rusk, Thomas Jefferson. Papers.
Sanchez-Navarro, José. Papers.
Starr, James Harper. Papers.
Zuber, William P. Papers.

Daughters of the Republic of Texas Library, San Antonio, Texas
Alamo Defenders. Vertical Files.
Cloud, Daniel W. Letter.
Hitt, Mabel. Letter.
Jones, John Rice. Ledger.
Rabia, Santiago. Papers.
Travis, William Barret. Vertical File.

Haley Memorial Library and History Center, Midland, Texas
Kegans, Clarinda Pevehouse. Memoirs.

Massachusetts Historical Society, Boston
Lawrence, Amos A. Papers.

McMillan Archives, Brewton, Alabama
McMillan, Edward Leigh. Letter from Daisy M. Burnett.

Missouri Historical Society, Columbia
Filley Family. Papers.
Green, Caleb. Papers.
Maffitt, P. Chouteau. Papers.
St. Louis County Civil Cases. Miscellaneous Files.
Stewart, William. Papers.

National Archives, Washington, D.C.
Port of New Orleans Passenger and Immigration Lists.

Southern Historical Collection, University of North Carolina, Chapel Hill
Jones, Calvin. Papers.

Texas General Land Office
Bounty and Donation Land Grant Records
Court of Claims Records
Character Certificate Records

Texas State Archives
Adjutant General Strays.
Adjutant General Correspondence.
Army Papers.
Audited Military Claims Collection.
Gonzales County Records.
Houston, A. J. Papers.
Jones, John Rice. Letters.

Republic of Texas Claims.
Republic of Texas Pension Claims.
Travis, William Barret. Letter.
Travis, William Barret. Papers.
University of Houston Libraries, Special Collection, Houston, Texas
Millsaps, Isaac. Letter.

Court Records

Austin County Court Clerk's Office, Bellville, Texas
Isaac Mansfield Probate.
Miscellaneous documents.
Brazoria Court Clerk's Office, Angleton, Texas
William Cato Probate.
William Barret Travis Probate.
Caldwell County Clerk's Office, Lockhart, Texas
Deed Book B.
Circuit Court of the City of St. Louis, Missouri
William Wells Brown. Deed of Emancipation. Permanent Record Book Number 24.
Dallas County Court Clerk's Office, Selma, Alabama
William Cato Probate.
Escambia County Health Department, Brewton, Alabama
Riley, Ben. Certificate of Death.
Fort Bend County Court Clerk's Office, Richmond, Texas
Deed Book A.
Lawrence County Court Clerk's Office, Moulton, Alabama
John Young Will. Probate Records.
Liberty County Court Clerk's Office, Liberty, Texas
Deed Records, 19.
Monroe County Court Clerk's Office, Monroeville, Alabama
Orphan Court Orders, Book I (1833–1854).
Montgomery County Court Clerk's Office, Conroe, Texas
Deed Records, 10.
Nacogdoches County Clerk's Office, Nacogdoches, Texas
Testimony for heirs of M. B. Clarke, John Blair, and Marcus Sewell.
Parker County District Court, Weatherford, Texas.
Malone v. Moran.
St. Louis County Clerk's Office, St. Louis, Missouri
Office of the Recorder of Deeds. Grantees Book (A–Z, 1804–1854)
St. Louis County Court Clerk's Office, St. Louis, Missouri
John Young Will. Probate Records.

Summerville County Court Clerk's Office, Granbury, Texas
  Deed Records E.
Washington County Court Clerk's Office, Brenham, Texas
  B. W. Holtzclaw v. Henry R. Cartwell. Civil lawsuit.
  Marriage Records.

Interviews

Canton, Soporhia. Telephone interview with Ron Jackson, May 13, 1997.
Gallatin, Albert R. Telephone interview with Ron Jackson, January 24, 2002.
Glosson, Clyde. Interview with Lee Spencer White, March 27, 1999, San Antonio, Texas.
Leonard, Joe E., Jr. Telephone interview with Ron Jackson, March 10, 1999.
Leonard, Joe E., Sr. Interview with Ron Jackson, Austin, Texas, March 6, 1999, and telephone interview, March 10, 1999.
Lynn, Raymond. Telephone interview with Ron Jackson, November 3, 2000.
Tart, Linda (Halliburton). Telephone interview with Ron Jackson, Luling, Texas, June 26, 1994.
Wornell, Kevin R. Interview with Ron Jackson, 1995.

Secondary Sources

Books, Articles, Pamphlets

Alcance al Num. 25. del Noticioso del Puerto de Matamoros. 1831. http://brbl-dl.library.yale.edu/vufind/Record/3518935.
Asbury, Samuel E., ed. "The Private Journal of Juan Nepomuceno Almonte, February 1–April 16, 1836." *Southwestern Historical Quarterly* 48 (July 1944).
"Aspects of Slavery in Missouri, 1821." *Missouri Historical Review,* Sesquicentennial Issue (1821–1971).
Atlas of Warren County, Missouri. Philadelphia: Edward Brothers, 1877.
Babcock, Rufus, ed. *Forty Years of Pioneer Life: Memoir of John Mason Peck.* Illinois: D. D. Carbondale, 1965.
Barker, Eugene C., ed. *The Austin Papers.* 4 vols. Washington, D.C.: Government Printing Office, 1924, 1928; Austin: University of Texas Press, 1926.
———. "The Influence of Slavery in the Colonization of Texas." *Southwestern Historical Quarterly* 28 (July 1924).
Barr, Alwyn. *Black Texans: A History of Negroes in Texas, 1528–1971.* Austin: Jenkins, 1973.
Baugh, Virgil E. *Rendezvous at the Alamo: Highlights in the Lives of Bowie, Crockett, and Travis.* New York: Pageant Press, 1960.
Beazley, Julia. "Harris, John Richardson." *Handbook of Texas Online.* www.tshaonline.org/handbook/online/articles/fha85.

Beck, Lewis Caleb. *A Gazetteer of the States of Illinois and Missouri*. 1823. Reprint, Manchester, N.H.: Ayers, 1975.

Benavides, Adan, ed. *The Bexar Archives (1717–1836): A Name Guide*. Austin: University of Texas Press, 1989.

Binkley, William C., ed. *Official Correspondence of the Texas Revolution, 1835–1836*. 2 vols. New York: D. Appleton-Century, 1938.

Blair, Walter, and Franklin J. Meine, ed. *Half Horse, Half Alligator*. Chicago: University of Chicago Press, 1956.

Borroel, Roger. *The Itineraries of the Zapadores and San Luis Battalions during the Texas War of 1836*. East Chicago, Ind.: La Villita Publications, 1999.

Bowie, John J. "Early Life in the Southwest—The Bowies." *DeBow's Review* 13 (October 1852).

Boyd, Carl B., Jr., and Hazel Mason Boyd. *A History of Mt. Sterling, Kentucky, 1792–1918*. [Mt. Sterling, Ky.], 1984.

Breckenridge, Henri Marie. *Journal of a Voyage up the River Missouri Performed in 1811*. Baltimore: Coale and Maxwell, 1816.

Brown, John Henry. *The Encyclopedia of the New West*. Marshall, Tex.: Hodge and Jennings Bros., 1881.

———. *History of Texas from 1685 to 1892*. 2 vols. St. Louis: L. E. Daniell, 1892–1893.

———. *Life and Times of Henry Smith*. Dallas: 1887.

———. *Indian Wars and Pioneers of Texas*. Austin: L. E. Daniell, 1896.

Brown, Josephine. *Biography of an American Bondman by His Daughter*. Boston: 1856.

Brown, William Wells. *The Black Man: His Antecedents, His Genius, and His Achievements*. New York: Thomas Hamilton, 1863.

———. *My Southern Home; or, The South and Its People*. Boston: A.G. Brown, 1880.

———. *Memoir of William Wells Brown: An American Bondman*. Boston: George C. Rand & Avery, 1859.

———. *Narrative of William Wells Brown: A Fugitive Slave*. London: Charles Gilpin, 1849.

———. *Three Years in Europe; or, Places I Have Seen and People I Have Met*. London: 1852.

Bryan, William S. *Pioneer Families of Missouri*. St. Louis: Bryan, Brand, 1876.

Buchanan, Thomas C. *Black Life on the Mississippi*. Chapel Hill: University of North Carolina Press, 2004.

Bugbee, Lester G. "Slavery in Early Texas." *Political Science Quarterly* 13 (September 1898).

Campbell, Randolph B. *An Empire for Slavery: The Peculiar Institution in Texas, 1821–1865*. Baton Rouge: Louisiana State University Press, 1989.

———. *Sam Houston and the American Southwest*. New York: HarperCollins College Publishers, 1993.

Carrington, Evelyn M., ed. *Women in Early Texas*. Austin, Tex.: Jenkins, 1975.

Carter, Clarence Edwin, ed. *Territorial Papers of the United States*. Washington: United States Government Printing Office, 1951.

Castaneda, Carlos, trans. *The Mexican Side of the Texan Revolution, 1836*. Washington, D.C.: Documentary Publications, 1971.

Chariton, Wallace O. *Exploring the Alamo Legends*. Plano, Tex.: Wordware, 1990.

———. *100 Days in Texas: The Alamo Letters*. 1968. Reprint, Plano, Tex.: Wordware/Republic of Texas Press, 1990.

Clarke, Lewis. *Narrative of the Sufferings of Lewis Clarke during a Captivity of More than Twenty-Five Years amongst the Algerines of Kentucky*. Boston, 1845.

[Coleman, Robert M.] *Houston Displayed; or, Who Won the Battle of San Jacinto? By a Farmer in the Army, Reproduced from the Original*. Introduction by John H. Jenkins. 1837. Reprint, Austin, Tex.: Brick Row Book Shop, 1964.

Crete, Liliane. *Daily Life in Louisiana, 1815–1830*. Baton Rouge: Louisiana State University Press, 1978.

Crisp, James E. *Sleuthing the Alamo: Davy Crockett's Last Stand and Other Mysteries of the Texas Revolution*. New York: Oxford University Press, 2005.

Curtis, Gregory. "Forgery, Texas Style," *Texas Monthly*, March 1989.

———. "Highly Suspect," *Texas Monthly*, March 1989.

Darby, John F. *Personal Recollections of Many Prominent People Whom I Have Known, and of Events—Especially of Those Relating to the History of St. Louis—During the First Half of the Present Century*. St. Louis: G. I. Jones, 1880.

Davis, Robert E., ed. *The William Barret Travis Diary: August 30, 1833–June 26, 1834*. Waco, Tex.: Texian Press, 1966.

Davis, William C. *Three Roads to the Alamo*. New York: HarperCollins, 1998.

Delaney, Lucy A. *From Darkness Cometh the Light*. St. Louis: J. T. Smith, 1891.

Denson, John V. *Slavery Laws in Alabama*. Auburn, Ala.: Alabama Polytechnic Institute Historical Studies, 1908.

DeShields, James T., ed. *Tall Men with Long Rifles: The Glamorous Story of the Texas Revolution, as Told by Captain Creed Taylor, Who Fought in That Heroic Struggle from Gonzales to San Jacinto*. San Antonio: Naylor, 1935.

"The Destiny of Buffalo Bayou." *Southwestern Historical Quarterly* 47 (July 1943–April 1944).

"De Witt's Colony." *Quarterly of the Texas State Historical Association* 8 (October 1904).

De Zavala, Adina. *History and Legends of the Alamo and Other Missions in and around San Antonio*. San Antonio: A. De Zavala, 1917.

Dick, Everett. *The Dixie Frontier: A Social History of the Southern Frontier*. New York: Capricorn Books, 1964.

"Documents of the Texas Revolution," *Alamo Journal* 142 (September 2006).

Donovan, James. *The Blood of Heroes: The 13-Day Struggle for the Alamo and the Sacrifice that Forged A Nation*. New York: Little, Brown, 2012.

Drew, Benjamin, ed. *The Refugee; or, The Narratives of Fugitive Slaves in Canada.* Boston: John P. Jewitt, 1856.

Drossaerts, Arthur J. *The Truth about the Burial of the Remains of the Alamo Heroes.* San Antonio, 1938.

Dubravsky, Ed. "Alamo Timetable." *Alamo Journal* (September 1992).

Duden, Gottfried. *Europa und Deutschland von Nordamerika aus betrachtet, order: Die Europäische Entwickelung im 19ten Jahrhundret in Bezug auf die Lage der Deutschen, nach einer Prüfung im innern Nordamerika.* 2 vols. Bonn: E. Weber, 1835.

Duden, Gottfried. Translated by William G. Bek. "Gottfried Duden's Report, 1824–1827." *Missouri Historical Review* 24 (October 1929–July 1930).

Edmonson, J.R. *The Alamo Story.* Plano, Tex.: Republic of Texas Press, 2000.

————. *Mr. Bowie with a Knife: A History of the Sandbar Fight.* Haltom City, Tex.: Watkins Printing Services, 1998.

Edwards, Richard, and M. Hopewell. *Edward's Great West and the Commercial Metropolis, Embracing a General View of the West, and a Complete History of St. Louis, from the Landing of Ligueste, in 1764, to the Present Time.* St. Louis: Edward's Monthly, 1860.

Ellis, Edward S. *The Life of Colonel David Crockett.* Philadelphia: Porter and Coates, 1884.

Erickson, Carolyn Reeves, comp. *Citizens and Foreigners of the Nacogdoches District, 1809–1836.* 2 vols. Nacogdoches, Tex.: Erickson, 1981.

Faragher, John Mack. *Daniel Boone.* New York: Henry Holt, 1992.

Farrison, William Edward. *William Wells Brown: Author and Reformer.* Chicago: University of Chicago Press, 1969.

Fehrenbach, T. R. *Lone Star: A History of Texas and the Texans.* New York: Macmillan, 1968.

————. *Seven Keys to Texas.* El Paso: Texas Western Press, 1983.

Filisola, Don Vincente. *Memoirs for the History of the War in Texas.* Translated by Wallace Woolsey. 2 vols. Austin, Tex.: Eakin Press, 1985.

Flint, Timothy. *Recollections of the Last Ten Years in the Valley of the Mississippi.* Carbondale: Southern Illinois University Press, 1968.

Folmsbee, Stanley J. "Davy Crockett and West Tennessee." *West Tennessee Historical Society Papers* 28 (1974).

Foote, Henry Stuart. *Texas and the Texans; or, Advance of the Anglo-Americans to the Southwest including a History of Leading Events in Mexico, from the Conquest of Fernando Cortes to the Termination of the Texas Revolution.* 2 vols. Philadelphia: Thomas, Cowperthwait, 1841.

Foreman, Grant. *Indians and Pioneers.* Norman: University of Oklahoma Press, 1936.

Franklin, John Hope, and Loren Schweninger. *Runaway Slaves: Rebels on the Plantation.* New York: Oxford University Press, 1999.

Gammel, H. P. N., comp. *The Laws of Texas, 1822–1897.* 10 vols. Austin, Tex.: 1898–1902.

Geyer, Henry S. *A Digest of the Laws of Missouri Territory.* St. Louis: Joseph Charles, 1818.

Gormanous, Nettie Milsaps. *The Milsaps Family: Patriotic, Hard Working, God Loving Americans.* Self-published: 1990.

Gray, William Fairfax. *From Virginia to Texas, 1835: Diary of Col. Wm. F. Gray, Giving Details of His Journey to Texas and Return in 1835–1836 and Second Journey to Texas in 1837.* 1909. Reprint, Houston: Fletcher Young, 1965.

Green, Rena Maverick, ed. *Memoirs of Mary A. Maverick.* San Antonio: Alamo Printing, 1921.

———. *Samuel Maverick, Texan: 1803–1870.* San Antonio, 1952.

Gregory, Ralph. *A History of Early Marthasville, Missouri.* Marthasville: Three Pines, 1980.

Groneman, Bill. *Alamo Defenders: A Genealogy—The People and Their Words.* Austin, Tex.: Eakin Press, 1990.

———. "Anthony Wolfe: Tracing an Alamo Defender." *Journal of South Texas* 3 (Spring 1990), 24–35.

———. *Defense of a Legend: Crockett and the de la Peña Diary.* Plano, Tex.: Republic of Texas Press, 1994.

———. *Eyewitness to the Alamo.* Revised ed. Plano, Tex.: Republic of Texas Press, 2001.

Guardian, Kent. "Kokernot, David Levi." *Handbook of Texas Online.* www.tsha online.org/handbook/online/articles/fko02.

Hansen, Todd. *The Alamo Reader: A Study in History.* Mechanicsburg, Penn.: Stackpole Press, 2003.

Hardin, Stephen L. *Texian Iliad: A Military History of the Texas Revolution, 1835–1836.* Austin: University of Texas Press, 1994.

Harris, Helen Willits. "Almonte's Inspection of Texas in 1834." *Southwestern Historical Quarterly* 41 (January 1938).

"Harris County, 1822–1845." *Southwestern Historical Quarterly* 18 (July 1914–April 1915).

Helm, Mary S. *Scraps of Early Texas History.* Austin: B. R. Warner, 1884.

Holley, Mary Austin. *Texas: Observations, Historical, Geographical and Descriptive, in a Series of Letters.* Baltimore: Armstrong & Plaskitt, 1833.

Houston, Sam. *The Writings of Sam Houston, 1813–1863.* 8 vols. Austin: University of Texas Press, 1938–1943.

Howren, Alleine. "Causes and Origins of the Decree of April 6, 1830." *Southwestern Historical Quarterly* 16 (1913).

Huffines, Alan C. *Blood of Noble Men: The Alamo Siege and Battle.* Austin, Tex.: Eakin Press, 1999.

———. *The Texas War of Independence 1835–1836: From Outbreak to the Alamo to San Jacinto.* Oxford: Osprey, 2005.

Huneycutt, C. D., ed. *At the Alamo: The Memoirs of Capt. Navarro*. New London, Conn.: Gold Star Press, 1988.

Hunter, Robert Hancock. *Narrative of Robert Hancock Hunter, 1813–1902*. Mesquite, Tex.: Ide House, 1982.

"J. C. Clopper's Journal and Book of Memoranda for 1828." *Quarterly of the Texas State Historical Association* 13 (July 1909).

Jackson, Harvey H., III. *Rivers of History: Life on the Coosa, Tallapoosa, Cahaba, and Alabama*. Tuscaloosa: University of Alabama Press, 1995.

Jackson, Ron. *Alamo Legacy: Alamo Descendants Remember the Alamo*. Austin, Tex.: Eakin Press, 1997.

———. "In the Alamo's Shadow." *True West*, February 1998.

Jackson, Ron J., Jr., and Lee White, comp. *Alamo Survivors*. Waco, Tex.: Nortex Press, 2010.

James, Marquis. *The Life of Andrew Jackson*. New York: Bobbs-Merrill, 1938.

Jenkins, John H., comp. *The Papers of the Texas Revolution, 1835–1836*. Austin, Tex.: Presidial Press, 1973.

———, ed. *Recollections of Early Texas: The Memoirs of John Holland Jenkins*. 1958. Reprint, Austin: University of Texas Press, 1987.

Jenkins, John H., III, and Kenneth Kesselus. *Edward Burleson: Texas Frontier Leader*. Austin, Tex.: Jenkins, 1990.

Johnson, Walter. *Soul by Soul: Life inside the Antebellum Slave Market*. Massachusetts: Harvard University Press, 1999.

Journal of the House of Representatives. St. Louis, Missouri, 1821.

Kemp, Louis Wiltz. *The Signers of the Texas Declaration of Independence*. Salado, Tex.: Anson Jones, 1959.

Kendall, John S. "Shadow over the City." *Louisiana Historical Society* 22 (January–October 1939).

Kilgore, Dan. *How Did Davy Die?* College Station: Texas A&M University Press, 1978.

King, Richard C. *Susanna Dickinson: Messenger of the Alamo*. Austin, Tex.: Shoal Creek, 1976.

Labadie, N. D., ed. "Urissa's account of the Alamo Massacre." *Texas Almanac* (1859), 61–62.

Lamar, Mirabeau B. *The Papers of Mirabeau B. Lamar: Edited from the Original Papers in the Texas State Library*. Edited by Charles Adam Gulick, Jr. 6 vols. Austin, Tex.: A. C. Baldwin, 1920–1927.

Lee, Mrs. A. J. "Some Recollections of Two Texas Pioneer Women." *Texas Methodist Historical Quarterly* 1 (January 1910).

"Letters of William Carr Lane." *Glimpses of the Past* 7, no. 7–9 (July–September 1940).

Libby, David J. *Slavery and Frontier Mississippi, 1720–1835*. Jackson: University Press of Mississippi, 2004.

"Life of German Pioneers in Early Texas." *Quarterly of the Texas State Historical Association* 2 (July 1898–April 1899).

Lindley, Thomas R. *Alamo Traces: New Evidence and New Conclusions.* Lanham, Md.: Republic of Texas Press, 2003.

Long, Jeff. *Duel of Eagles.* New York: William Morrow, 1990.

Lord, Walter. *A Time to Stand: The Epic of the Alamo.* New York: Harper and Row, 1961.

Martin, Essie Walton. *The Scurlocks: Seekers of Freedom.* E. W. Martin, 1985.

———. "Some Scurlock History." *Texas State Genealogical Society Quarterly* 33, no. 2 (June 1993).

Matovina, Timothy M., comp. *The Alamo Remembered: Tejano Accounts and Perspectives.* Austin: University of Texas Press, 1995.

McCormick, Andrew Phelps. *Scotch-Irish in Ireland and in America as Shown in Sketches of . . . Pioneer Scotch-Irish Families . . . in North Carolina, Kentucky, Missouri, and Texas.* New Orleans: 1897.

McDonald, Archie P. *Travis.* Austin, Tex.: Pemberton Press, 1976.

McLean, Malcolm D., ed. *Papers concerning Robertson's Colony in Texas.* Arlington: University of Texas at Arlington Press, 1988.

McLemore, Richard Aubrey, ed. *A History of Mississippi*, vol. 1. Hattiesburg: University of College Press of Mississippi, 1973.

Menchaca, Antonio. *Memoirs.* San Antonio: Yanaguana Society Publications, 1937.

"Minutes of the Ayuntamiento of San Felipe de Austin, 1828–1832." *Southwestern Historical Quarterly* 21 (July 1919–April 1920).

"Missouri History Not Found in the Textbooks." *Missouri Historical Review* 45 (October 1950–July 1951).

Mixon, Ruby. "William Barret Travis: His Life and Letters." Master's thesis, University of Texas, 1930.

"More about St. Louis: Views of a British Nobleman—1832." *Glimpses of the Past* 1 (1933–1934): 31–33.

Morphis, James M. *History of Texas from Its Discovery and Settlement.* New York: United States Publishing, 1874.

Morrell, Zachariah Nehemiah. *Flowers and Fruits in the Wilderness.* St. Louis: Commercial Printing, 1882.

Muir, Andrew Forest, ed. *Texas in 1837.* Austin: University of Texas Press, 1986.

Newell, Chester. *History of the Revolution in Texas, Particularly of the War of 1835 and 1836.* New York: Wiley & Putnam, 1838.

Owen, Thomas M. *History of Alabama and Dictionary of Alabama Biography.* 4 vols. Chicago: 1921.

Paxton, John A. *The St. Louis Directory and Register Containing the Names, Professions, and Residence of all Heads of Families and Persons in Business.* St. Louis, 1821.

Peña, Jose Enrique de la. *With Santa Anna in Texas: A Personal Narrative of the Revolution.* Edited by Carmen Perry. 1975. College Station: Texas A&M University Press, 1992.

"The Pioneer Harrises of Harris County, Texas." *Quarterly of the Texas State Historical Association* 22 (July 1918–April 1919).

Posey, Walter Brownlow, ed. "Alabama in the 1830s as Recorded by British Travelers." *Birmingham-Southern College Bulletin* 31, no. 4 (December 1938).

Potter, Reuben M. "The Fall of the Alamo." *Magazine of American History*, January 1878.

"Railroad History of Lines Located in Mississippi, with Some Information on Lines in Kentucky, Tennessee, Alabama, and Louisiana," Mississippi Railroad Information, http://www.icrr.net/rrhist.htm.

Quisenberry, Anderson Chenault. *Kentucky in the War of 1812.* Baltimore: Genealogical Publishing Company, 1969. Originally published by the Kentucky Historical Society serially between 1912 and 1915.

"The Reminiscences of Mrs. Dilue Harris." *Southwestern Historical Quarterly* (1901).

Reps, John W. *Saint Louis Illustrated: Nineteenth-Century Engravings and Lithographs of a Mississippi River Metropolis.* Columbia: University of Missouri Press, 1989.

Riley, B. F. *Makers and Romance of Alabama History.* N.p.: 1915.

Ripley, C. Peter, ed. *The Black Abolitionist Papers.* 5 vols. Chapel Hill: University of North Carolina, 1985–1992.

Rodriguez, Jose Maria. *Rodriguez Memoirs of Early Texas.* San Antonio: Passing Show, 1913.

Roell, Craig H. "Sayre, Charles D." *The Handbook of Texas Online.* http://www .tshaonline.org/handbook/online/articles/fsa43.

Roller, John E. "Capt. John Sowers Brooks." *Quarterly of the Texas State Historical Association* 9 (July 1905–April 1906).

Rother, Hubert, and Charlotte Rother. *Lost Caves of St. Louis.* St. Louis: Virginia, 1996.

Santos, Richard G. *Santa Anna's Campaign against Texas, 1835–1836.* Waco, Tex.: Texian Press, 1968.

Schoen, Harold. "The Free Negro in the Republic of Texas." *Southwestern Historical Quarterly* 40 (October 1936).

Seale, William. *Texas Riverman: The Life and Times of Captain Andrew Smyth.* Austin: University of Texas Press, 1966.

Shackford, James A. *David Crockett: The Man and the Legend.* Edited by John B. Shackford. 1956. Reprint, Chapel Hill: University of North Carolina Press, 1986.

Sibley, Marilyn McAdams. *Travelers in Texas, 1761–1860.* Austin: University of Texas Press, 1967.

Smith, Edward. *Account of a Journey through North-Eastern Texas.* London: Hamilton, Adams, 1849.

Smithwick, Noah. *Evolution of a State; or, Recollections of Old Texas Days.* Austin, Tex.: Gammel, 1900.

Sowell, A. J. *Early Settlers and Indian Fighters of Southwest Texas*. Austin, Tex.: Ben C. Jones, 1900.

Stevens, Walter. *The Building of St. Louis, from Many Points of View*. St. Louis: Lesan-Gould, 1908.

Stiff, Edward. *The Texan Emigrant*. Cincinnati: George Conclin, 1840.

Stowe, Harriet Beecher. *A Key to "Uncle Tom's Cabin," Presenting the Original Facts and Documents upon Which the Story Is Founded*. Boston: 1853.

Sub Rosa, *Scenes and Settlers of Alabama*. Mobile, 1885.

Sutherland, John. *The Fall of the Alamo*. San Antonio: Naylor, 1936.

Swisher, John M. *The Swisher Memoirs*. San Antonio, 1932.

Taylor, I. T. *The Cavalcade of Jackson County*. San Antonio: Naylor, 1938.

Thorp, Raymond W. *Bowie Knife*. 1948. Williamstown, New Jersey: Phillips Publications, 1991.

Tinkle, Lon. *13 Days to Glory: The Siege of the Alamo*. New York: McGraw-Hill, 1958.

Todish, Tim J., and Terry S. Todish. *Alamo Sourcebook 1836: A Comprehensive Guide to the Alamo and the Texas Revolution*. Austin, Tex.: Eakin Press, 1998.

[Travis, William B.] "Petition, May 11, 1831." *Frontier America Rare & Unusual Americana Catalog*, no. 37 (1996).

Trexler, Harrison Anthony. *Slavery in Missouri, 1804–1865*. Baltimore: Johns Hopkins Press, 1914.

Twelvetree, Harper, ed. *The Story of the Life of John Anderson, the Fugitive Slave*. London: William Tweedie, 1863.

United States Census. Fountain County, Indiana, 1880.

United States Census. Monroe County, Alabama, 1840.

United States Census. St. Louis County, St. Louis, Missouri, 1830.

Waites, Jacquelyn. *Journey of the Heart: The Story of Letticia (Bradley) Hall Gates Bullock, 1809–1861*. J. Waites, n.d.

Walraven, Bill, and Marjorie K. Walraven. *The Magnificent Barbarians: Little Told Tales of the Texas Revolution*. Austin, Tex.: Eakin Press, 1993.

Waters, Annie C. *History of Escambia County, Alabama*. Spartanburg, S.C.: Reprint Company, 1993.

Whicker, J. Wesley. *Historical Sketches of the Wabash Valley*. 1916. Reprint, Attica, Ind.: Attica Potawatomi Festival Committee, 1976.

White, James Haley. "Early Days in St. Louis." *Glimpses of the Past* 6 (January–March 1939).

Williams, Amelia. "A Critical Study of the Siege of the Alamo and the Personnel of Its Defenders," Master's thesis, University of Texas, 1931.

———. "A Critical Study of the Siege of the Alamo and of the Personnel of Its Defenders." *Southwestern Historical Quarterly* 37, no. 3 (January 1934): 157–84.

Winders, Bruce. *Sacrifice at the Alamo: Tragedy and Triumph in the Texas Revolution*. Buffalo Gap, Tex.: State House Press/McWhiney Foundation, 2004.

Yoakum, Henderson King. *History of Texas from Its First Settlement in 1685 to Its Annexation to the United States in 1846*. 2 vols. New York: Redfield, 1856.
Zaboly, Gary S. *An Altar for Their Sons: The Alamo and the Texas Revolution in Contemporary Newspaper Accounts*. Buffalo Gap, Tex.: State House Press, 2011.
Zuber, William P. "An Escape from the Alamo." *Texas Almanac* (1873), 80–84.

Newspapers

Albany (N.Y.) *Journal*
Arkansas Gazette
Constitutional Advocate and Texas Public Advertiser (Brazoria)
Daily Democratic Statesman (Austin, Tex.)
Dallas Morning News
Dothan (Ala.) *Morning News*
Fort Worth Star-Telegram
Frankfort (Ky.) *Commonwealth*
Galveston Daily News
Kentucky Gazette
Missouri Gazette
Missouri Republican
Montogomery Advertiser
El Mosquito Mexicana
El Nacional Suplemento al Numero (Mexico City)
New Orleans Commercial Bulletin
New York Daily News
New York Daily Tribune
New York Herald
New York Sun
Niles' Weekly Register
Port Gibson (Miss.) *Correspondence*
Portland (Me.) *Advertiser*
San Antonio Daily Express
San Antonio Express
San Antonio Express News
San Antonio Light
San Francisco Chronicle
Saint Louis Beacon
Statesman (Austin, Tex.)
Sunday Morning News (New York)
Telegraph and Texas Register
Texas Gazette
Texas Republican (Brazoria)

INDEX

Page numbers in *italics* indicate illustrations.

314 INDEX

Antonio (Mexican parolee), 220–21
Ashley, William H., 11
Ashley fur-trapping expedition, 10–11
Austin, Henry, 294n9
Austin, John, 75
Austin, Moses, 74
Austin, Stephen F., 63, 132; arrest for incitement of insurrection, 108, 125–26; on emancipation of slaves, 66; as emissary to Mexican government, 107–108; on indentured servitude, 65; political activities, 111–12; on slavery issue, 62; in St. Louis, 126; on Texas independence, 130–31; William Travis on leadership of, 131–32
Austin & Savage auction house, 43–44
Austin's Colony, 71
Autry, James, 166
Autry, Martha, 166
Autry, Mary, 166
Autry, Micajah, 166
Ayers, David, 136, 212, 218, 222, 236, 282n15
Ayuntamientos officials, 64–65, 108, 112

Badgett, Jesse B., 175
Bailey, Peter J., 167
Bailey's Prairie plantation, 217–19
Baird, Charles, 272n13
Barnett, Thomas, 87–89
Barragan, Miguel, 197
Bastian, Sam, 177
Batres, Jose, 160
Battle of Concepción, 168
Baugh, John J., 189
Beamer, Reuben, 249–50
Beauvois family, 263n43
Becerra, Francisco, 193, 286n13, 287n29, 288n35
Belinda (free black), 100

Ben (Jones slave), 218
Benavides, Placido, 147–48
Benjamin (Joe's brother), 7, 26
Berry, John, 146
Bettie (Bowie slave), 196, 288n36, 291n3
Betty (Jackson slave), 217
Bexar: civilian preparations for attack on, 155–57; lay out of, 140–41; strategic value of, 149; Texan seizure of, 132. *See also Alamo entries*
Bexar dances, 147–48, 152
Bexar garrison: requests for reinforcements, 151, 156, 160–61, 174; split command of, 149–50. *See also Alamo entries*
Black, Dorothy, 250
Black Jim Bowie, 289n47
Blair, Samuel, 162
Blanchard, Alfred, 111
Blanchard, Carey, 111
Blanchet, Pierre, 97
Bonham, James Butler, 107, 178–80, 186
Bonham, Milledge Luke, 281n1
Boone, Daniel, 9–10, 12, 95, 134, 257n12
Boone, Elsie, 273n38
Boone, Jesse B., 15
Borgara, Anselmo, 205
Bowie, James, 129, 132, 139, 144; in Alamo defense, 159, 182, 284n16; as Bexar garrison commander, 149–50; character, 109–10; death of, 194–95, 197, 287n28; physical appearance, 109; in sandbar fight, 110–11; on threat to Alamo, 140
Bowie, John J., 110
Brazoria Insurance Company, 218
Brazos River, 226, 228
Breedlove, James W., 66
Brewton (Ala.) Standard, 247

Bridger, Jim, 11
Briscoe, Andrew, 127
Brookfield, William, 136
Brooks, John Sowers, 163
Brown, Clarissa, 297n14
Brown, Josephine, 243, 297n14
Brown, Robert, 162
Brown, Wells, 84–85
Brown, William Wells (Joe's brother),
    7, 12, 23, *113, 114,* 169, 254; as
    assistant to slave trader, 89; birth
    date, 259n56; *Clotel,* 85; death of,
    243; on Dinkie's beating, 28;
    emancipation of, 259n56; escape
    attempts by, 53–56, 82–85, *115,* 170;
    as free man, 85–86, 170, 243; hiring
    out of, 33–35; on John Young, 33; on
    mother's beating, 22; *My Southern
    Home,* 257n30; name change, 21, 85;
    *Narrative of William W. Brown: An
    American Slave,* 95, 256n9;
    parentage, 20, 95; selection as
    playmate, 20–21; separation from
    family, 35, 53, 56–57, 86, 270n35; on
    slave auctions, 43–44; on slave
    overseers, 32; on slave trade, 31–32;
    as steamboat crewman, 34, 48–49
Bruner, George C., 292n23
Buffalo Bayou flood, 77–78
Buffalo Bayou topography, 70–71
Burgin, Abner, 144
Burnam, Jesse, 136
Burnet, David G., 88, 90, 96
Burnett, Daisy M., 295n16
Bustamante, Anastacio, 63, 67, 92
Butler, James A., 104

Calcasieu Prairie, 228
Callaway Post, 9
Canada, 10, 49
Canton, Soporhia, 268n10
Carey, Moses, 289n47
Carey, William, 162, 166, 289n47

Caroline (Jones slave), 218
Cartwell, Henry, 216–17
Cato, Rosana E., 101–105, 218
Cato, William, 101–102, 104, 218, 248,
    294n9
Cato (Young slave), 19, 30–31
cave system, St. Louis, 44, 263n43
Celia (free black), 100, 273n34
Chadoin, Thomas, 137
Chapman, John G., 143–44
character certificates, 72–73
Charette settlement, Missouri
    Territory, 9–10, 37
Charlie (Alamo slave), 196, 288n35,
    291n3
Chavez, Juan Antonio, 290n1
Chester (steamboat), 82
Choate, Moses L., 72, 75, 147
Chouteau, Auguste, 40
Chouteau, Henry, 77–78
Christy, William, 35
Claiborne (escaped slave), 47
Clark, William, 10, 40
Clarke, Lewis, 265n39
Clotel (Brown), 85, 243
Cloud, Daniel, 167–68
Cloud, Samuel G., 104, 218
Cochran, James, 90
Colburn, John, 34–35, 47, 261n7
Coleman, Robert, 213
Collinsworth, James, 211
Comanche tribe, 137
Connell's boardinghouse, 97–98
Constitution of the State of Coahuila
    and Texas, 64–65, 76, 92
Convention of 1833, 107
Cook, Grove, 6–7, 260n14; in beating
    of Joe's mother, 21–22; in Randall's
    beating, 15–17; showdown with
    Dinkie, 27–29
coon hunt, 30–31
Cos, Martín Perfecto de, 131–32, 189,
    214

Willy, Freedman, 252
Wilson, Robert, 87, 88, 127
Winn, Theodosia, 13–14
Winnie (Jim's wife), 226
Wolfe, Anthony, 176, 181, 182, 194,
    280n12
Wolfe, Benjamin, 280n12
Wolfe, Michael, 280n12
Wornell, Kevin R, 265n8
Wright, Norris, 111
W. Walter & Company, 41

Yorba, Eulalia, 200–201
Young, Aaron, 13–14, 257n29
Young, Benjamin, 13
Young, John, 6, 19, 30, 126, 134, 169,
    256n10; authority as master, 23–24;

on Dinkie's status, 27; early career,
11–12; financial difficulties, 24, 31–33;
in Marthasville founding, 12, 257n26;
political activities, 15; probate of
estate of, 77–78; religious practice
of, 263n40; relocation to St. Louis,
24–25; sale of William and, 54;
siblings of, 257n29; slave beatings
and, 15, 17, 28, 33, 43; slave birth
recordation by, 7; slave escape and,
55; slaves owned by, 258n48
Young, Leonard, 11
Young, Mary, 11
Young, Sarah, 20, 76, 257n30
Young, William M. L., 78

Zuber, William P., 284n18